POSIX Programmer's Guide

POSIX Programmer's Guide

Writing Portable UNIX Programs
with the POSIX.1 Standard

Donald A. Lewine
Data General Corporation

O'Reilly & Associates, Inc.

103 Morris Street, Suite A
Sebastopol, CA 95472

POSIX Programmer's Guide
by Donald A. Lewine

Editor: Dale Dougherty

Printing History

April 1991:	First edition
December 1991:	Minor corrections. Appendix G added.
July 1992:	Minor corrections.
November 1992:	Minor corrections.
March 1994:	Minor corrections and updates.

Please address comments and questions in care of the publisher:

O'Reilly & Associates, Inc.   INTERNET: letters@ora.com
103 Morris Street, Suite A
Sebastopol, CA 95472
(800) 998-9938

[8/98]   ISBN: 0-937175-73-0

To all my students

❦

To my wife, Susan,
who convinced me to do this
book and who put up with
all the time this effort took

Acknowledgments

I would like to thank all of my students who put up with all of the beta test quality revisions. They provided many useful suggestions.

I would like to thank some people who provided very complete technical reviews and provided useful comments: Hal Jespersen (Posix Software Group), Chuck Karish (Mindcraft, Inc.), Thomas Mitas (HBO & Company), Neil Todd (European UNIX Systems User Group), Andy Huber (Data General Corporation), Richard Eckhouse (University of Massachusetts), Andy Silverman (88open Consortium), Henry Spencer (University of Toronto), Jeffrey S. Haemer (Interactive Systems Corporation), Paul Rabin, Dave Kirschen, and Michael Meissner (Open Software Foundation), and John S. Quarterman (Texas Internet Consulting).

Thanks go to the following readers of previous printings who pointed out errors and typos: Eric Boweles, Eric Hanchrow, Milt Ratcliff, Stephen J. Friedl, Ed Myer, Chesley Reyburn. Derek M. Jones, Todd Stevenson, Bob Burchfield, Anthony Scian, and Wayne Pallock

Thanks to Allen Gray for his help with the reference material. Thanks to Mike Sierra and Ellie Cutler of O'Reilly & Associates for doing the production work and for writing the index.

Special thanks to Dale Dougherty for a great job of editing. His many useful suggestions were worth the months they took to implement.

Thanks to the POSIX standards committees for making this book possible.

Table of Contents

CHAPTER 4 *Files and Directories*   **63**

CHAPTER 6   *Working with Processes*   **101**

CHAPTER 10   *Porting to Far-off Lands*   **193**

Library Functions   **209**

Preface

In 1988, IEEE Std 1003.1-1988, commonly known as *POSIX* or the *IEEE Portable Operating System Interface for Computing Environments*, was published as an American National Standard. In 1990, IEEE Std 1003.1-1990 was published as an International Standard. POSIX defines a standard way for an application program to obtain basic services from the operating system. More specifically, POSIX describes a set of functions derived from a combination of AT&T UNIX System V and Berkeley Standard Distribution UNIX. All POSIX-conforming systems must implement these functions, and programs that follow the POSIX standard use only these functions to obtain services from the operating system and the underlying hardware. When applications follow POSIX rules, it is easier to move programs from one POSIX-conforming operating system to another.

Most programmers, and the companies that employ them, understand the benefits of developing programs that are highly portable across a variety of computer architectures and operating systems. To write portable programs you want to make use of only those features on a particular system that are also found on other systems. Writing POSIX-compliant programs does, in fact, result in more portable programs. However, writing these programs is not so easy if you rely solely upon the manufacturer's documentation.

A programming reference manual typically combines POSIX-compliant functions with non-compliant functions. A function might comply with the POSIX requirements but also add several new features peculiar to that computer system or operating system variant. A manufacturer may not always point out what features represent added value and are supported only on that make or model. Even though the computer system you use might conform to the POSIX standard, you can still write non-conforming applications by making use of the system-specific features added by the manufacturer.

This book is a guide to the operating system interface as guaranteed by the POSIX standard. You can write complete, conforming applications by using the information in this book. The POSIX library of functions is complete enough to write many useful and sophisticated applications. However, there are many areas that the POSIX standard does not yet address. Thus, programmers must implement strategies that isolate non-portable code from portable-code, such that even hardware-dependent features are easily identified. The object of this book is to help the programmers resolve portability issues at the design stage of development, and not after the program has been fully implemented on a particular system.

The POSIX Standard Documents

Not many people actually read a standard, nor are they expected to. It is more like reading an insurance policy. When a standards organization such as ANSI or IEEE publishes a standards document, they view it as a formal document in which the primary aim is to be unambiguous.

The language is very technical and precise. The statements "Applications should not set O_XYZ" and "Applications shall not set O_XYZ" mean very different (almost opposite) things. "Should" means that something is recommended but is not required. "Shall" signifies a requirement.

The primary aim of this book is to interpret the POSIX standard for the application programmer and explain it in language that he or she can understand. You can read this book without remembering the technical meaning of words like *may, should,* or *shall.*

The POSIX standard contains a lot of information that was written by and for system implementers. The standard describes how to write an operating system that conforms to the POSIX standard. A typical passage is:

> All of the described members shall appear in the stat structure. The structure members *st_mode, st_ino, st_dev, st_uid, st_gid, st_atime, st_ctime,* and *st_mtime* shall have meaningful values for all file types defined in this part of ISO/IEC9945.[*]

If you are an application programmer, you don't want to know how to construct an operating system. You need to know how to write programs using the POSIX library to obtain the services that an operating system provides. What this passage means to an application programmer is:

> The file size returned by the *stat ( )* function is only valid for regular files. It may not contain meaningful information for special files, such as */dev/tty.*

Finally, the POSIX standard is difficult to use; that is, it is not organized for a programmer who wants to consult it while writing programs. It follows the conventions of a standards document. This book is organized for use as a programmer's guide to POSIX and a reference guide to POSIX. The organization of this book is described in more detail in the next section.

In the POSIX standard, there are functions that are defined in relation to the ANSI C standard. Given the additional requirements placed on C standard functions by POSIX, the programmer has the chore of reading both the C standard and the POSIX standard to get complete information. In this book, standard C functions are described in full in one place.

---

[*] IEEE Std 1003.1-1990 Section 5.6.1.

This book is a clearly written, complete guide to writing POSIX-compliant programs. In fact, you may not need to own a copy of the POSIX standard. Or, if you do have it, we believe that you will come to rely on the information in this book and find that it is more accessible.

Guide to POSIX for Programmers

There are two separate guides that make up this book. The first is a programmer's guide to writing POSIX-compliant programs. It begins with an overview of what the POSIX standard actually defines. Then it covers the basic ingredients of a POSIX-compliant program. There are a set of chapters devoted to explaining the functional areas addressed by the standard. Each chapter covers a group of related functions. For example, all of the information on terminal I/O is in Chapter 8. In this part of the book, we discuss in more detail the relation between POSIX and Standard C, a set of issues regarding internationalization and portability, and finally, how to design programs that isolate system dependencies from POSIX-compliant code.

The second is a reference guide for everyday use. The library functions are listed in alphabetic order and there are sections covering error message codes, data structures and the standard header files.

Here is an outline of the book:

Programming Guide

Chapter 1, *Introduction to POSIX and Portability*, answers a number of questions anyone might have concerning POSIX. It addresses such basic questions as: Why is the POSIX standard important? What does the POSIX standard cover? What is the relationship between POSIX and UNIX?

Chapter 2, *Developing POSIX Applications*, covers the basics of writing a POSIX-compliant program. It describes how to make sure your program accesses the POSIX libraries and looks at the required elements of a conforming program. It also presents a complete sample program that uses many POSIX features. After reading this chapter you can read the following chapters in any order. If your main interest is POSIX terminal I/O, you can skip right to Chapter 8.

Chapter 3, *Standard File and Terminal I/O*, covers the Input/Output facilities of the Standard C library. These are highly portable functions that perform general-purpose file operations.

Chapter 4, *Files and Directories*, deals with the file system as defined by POSIX. It covers directory structures, filenaming conventions and the library functions to manipulate files and directories.

Chapter 5, *Advanced File Operations*, addresses the basic operations of the POSIX Input/Output system as well as some advanced concepts like pipes and FIFOs.

Chapter 6, *Working with Processes*, covers working with processes. It covers creating and terminating processes and signals.

Chapter 7, *Obtaining Information at Run–time*, describes how to obtain information about the environment, such as the user's name or the current time.

Chapter 8, *Terminal I/O*, covers Input/Output to terminals.

Chapter 9, *POSIX and Standard C*, covers POSIX and Standard C. This covers some portability pitfalls and other features of the Standard C language.

Chapter 10, *Porting to Far-off Lands*, is dedicated to internationalization. That is issues having to do with porting a program from one culture to another.

Reference Guide and Appendixes

Library Functions is, by far, is the largest chapter in the book. It is a complete list of library functions in alphabetic order. Every function is defined in its correct place. For example, the `isspace()` function is not listed under `ctype` as it is in traditional UNIX manuals. This makes this information much easier to find.

Appendix A, *Header Files*, lists the standard headers and the information that they define.

Appendix B, *Data Structures*, is a complete list of data structures and their members.

Appendix C, *Error Codes*, covers all of the error codes.

Appendix D, *Porting from BSD and System V*, provides information on porting applications from BSD and AT&T System V systems to POSIX.

Appendix E, *Changes and Additions in Standard C*, describes the changes and additions to the C language made by Standard (ANSI) C.

Appendix F, *Federal Information Processing Standard 151-1*, describes the Federal Information Processing Standard used by the U.S. Government to purchase systems with POSIX-like interfaces.

Related Publications lists related publications.

Assumptions

In this book, I assume that you understand the C language and have some experience programming in C for the UNIX operating system. I also assume knowledge of ANSI C syntax. By and large, I assume you are an intermediate to expert programmer who is interested in the substance of POSIX but has little or no interest in reading the standards document to find it out.

Conventions

Italic is used for:

- New terms where they are defined.
- Titles of publications.

`Typewriter Font` is used for:

- Anything that would be typed verbatim into code, such as examples of source code and text on the screen.
- POSIX functions and headers.
- UNIX pathnames, filenames, program names, user command names, and options for user commands.

Sample Programs Available on Internet

The examples in this book are available on `ftp.uu.net` in the directory `/published/oreilly/misc/posix_prguide`

CHAPTER 1

Introduction to POSIX and Portability

This chapter offers a basic introduction to the POSIX standard and the efforts that led to its development; it also explains the relationship between POSIX and UNIX and the ANSI C standard.

Early computers each had a unique program architecture and a unique operating system. When an application needed to be moved from one generation of hardware to the next, it had to be rewritten. In 1964, IBM introduced the System/360. This was the first family of compatible computers. They used one operating system, OS/360, and programs could easily be moved to more powerful models. A single vendor implementing a single hardware architecture across multiple machines was a first step in achieving portability.

In 1968, AT&T's Bell Labs began work on the UNIX operating system. It allowed a single operating system to run on multiple hardware platforms from multiple vendors. UNIX, however, developed along several different lines: AT&T System V, Berkeley Software Distributions, Xenix, and so on. None of the flavors works identically and the precise behavior of each flavor is not well defined. It can be difficult to move applications from one flavor to another.

Today there is a major battle of operating systems. Unix Systems Lab's System V, the Open Software Foundation's OSF/1, Digital Equipment's VAX/VMS, and Microsoft's OS/2 are all trying to set the standard. Yet, they all agree to support the POSIX standards.*

POSIX is an international standard with an exact definition and a set of assertions which can be used to verify compliance. A conforming POSIX application can move from system to system with a very high confidence of low maintenance and correct operation.

If you want software to run on the largest possible set of hardware and operating systems, POSIX is the way to go.

POSIX is based on UNIX System V and Berkeley UNIX, but it is not itself an operating system. POSIX describes the contract between the application and the operating system. POSIX does not say how to write applications programs or how to write the operating system. Instead, POSIX defines the interface between applications and their libraries. POSIX does not talk about "system calls" or make any distinction between the kernel and the user.

---

* AT&T Unix System V release 4.0 and OSF/1 release 1.0 are both POSIX-conforming. Digital Equipment Corporation and Microsoft have both publicly committed to making their operating systems POSIX conforming.

POSIX completes the generalization started by IBM with the System/360. POSIX is a standard independent of vendor, operating system, and architecture.

The formal name for the POSIX standard is *IEEE Standard 1003.1-1988 Portable Operating System Interface for Computer Environments.* We call it POSIX (pronounced *pahz-icks*, similar to *positive*). In fact, IEEE Std 1003.1-1988 is the first of a group of proposed standards collectively known as POSIX.

In 1990 POSIX became International Standard ISO/IEC 9945-1: 1990. The International Standard is slightly different from IEEE Std 1003.1-1988. The IEEE reaffirmed the standard as IEEE Std 1003.1-1990. The changes are mainly clarifications with no technical impact. We will point out the few significant differences as we go along.

Who is Backing POSIX?

The United States Government has adopted the POSIX standard as a Federal Information Processing Standard (FIPS 151) for use in computer systems procurement. The European Community is getting ready to do the same thing. This has inspired the following System vendors† to announce support for POSIX:

AEG Modcomp	Harris Computer Systems Division
Alliant Computer Corp.	Hewlett-Packard
Amdahl Corp.	Hitachi
Apple Computer	Intel
AT&T	Intergraph Corp.
Bull	International Business Machines
Charles River Data Systems	Kendall Square Research Corp.
Concurrent Computer	Motorola
Control Data Corporation	NeXT, Inc.
Convergent Technology	Stratus Computer
Cray Research Inc.	Sun Microsystems
Data General Corporation	Tandem Computer
Digital Equipment Corp	Texas Instruments
Fujitsu Limited	Unisys
Gould Computer Systems Division	Xerox
Grumman Data Systems	

Of course, a list of hardware vendors like that will get lots of software vendors signed up to help. Some of the major software vendors are The Open Software Foundation, AT&T Unix System Laboratories, and Microsoft.

Now, if all these players agree on something, it must be important!

---

* The name POSIX comes from Portable Operating System interface for unIX. The name was suggested by Richard Stallman.

† By the time you read this there will be even more!

The POSIX Family of Standards

POSIX, in time, will be a rich family of standards. The project names for the various POSIX projects was revised in 1993. The current list* of POSIX projects is:

1003.1 defines the interface between portable application programs and the operating system, based on historical UNIX system models. This consists of a library of functions that are frequently implemented as system calls. This project is now complete and is IEEE Std 1003.1-1990.

P1003.1a Miscellaneous interpretations, clarifications and extensions (including symbolic links) to the 1990 standard. Look for an expanded POSIX.1 standard by the end of 1994.

P1003.1b (formerly POSIX.4) Real-time extensions approved as IEE Std 1003.1b-1993 and covers:

- Binary Semaphores
- Process memory locking
- Memory-mapped files and shared memory
- Priority scheduling
- Real-time signal extensions
- Timers
- Interprocess communication
- Synchronized I/O
- Asynchronous I/O

P1003.1c (formerly POSIX.4a) add functions to support threads (light weight processes) to POSIX. This will allow multiple flows of control within a POSIX process, a requirement for tightly coupled real-time (as well as transaction processing) applications.

P1003.1d (formerly POSIX.4b) further real-time extensions

P1003.1e (formerly POSIX.6) is a set of security enhancements meeting the criteria published by the United States Department of Defense in *Trusted Computer System Evaluation Criteria* (TCSEC). This covers four areas:

- Access control lists on POSIX objects.

---

* This list was correct in February 1994. POSIX is very active and this information will be out of date by the time you read it. Late breaking information is posted to the USENET comp.std.unix newsgroup. The USENIX Association publishes a quarterly update of standards activities. Membership information is available from USENIX association, 2560 Ninth Street, Suite 215, Berkeley CA 94710 or *office@usenix.org*.

- Support for labeling of subjects and objects, and for mandatory access control rules to avoid leaking information.

- Defining auditable events for POSIX.1 interfaces, and standard audit trail record formats and functions.

- Defining interfaces for altering process privileges.

P1003.1e is currently balloting the required extension to P1003.1.

P1003.1f   (formerly POSIX.8) is working on Transparent File Access over a network. Transparent File Access is the ability to access remote files as if they were local.

P1003.1g   (formerly POSIX.12) covers Protocol Independent Interfaces to network services.

P1003,1h   (new) real-time distributed systems.

P1003.2   specifies a shell command language based on the System V shell with some features from the C Shell and the Korn Shell. It provides a few services to access shell services from applications. POSIX.2 provides over 70 utilities to be called from shell scripts or from applications directly.

POSIX.2 was originally intended to allow shell scripts to be portable. Later, it was decided to add a User Portability Extension (now called POSIX.2a) to allow users to move from one system to another without retraining. The POSIX.2a covers about 35 additional utilities like the `vi` editor, `more`, `man`, `mailx`, etc.

POSIX.2/.2a has passed all of the steps in the standardization process and is now approved as ISO/IEC 9945-2:1993 and IEE Std 1003.2-1992.

P1003.2b   miscellaneous extensions (including symbolic links) to the P1003.2 standard.

P1003.2c   security extensions. These are the command and utilities that go along with P1003.1e

P1003.2d   (formerly POSIX.15) batch queueing extensions

P1003.3   provides the detailed testing and verification requirements for the POSIX family. The standard (IEEE Std 1003.3-1991) consists of general requirements for how test suites should be written and administered.

The National Institute for Standards and Technology (NIST), part of the United States Government, produced the POSIX FIPS Conformance Test Suite (PCTS). The ability to test that an implementation meets the standard allows programmers and users to get the full portability that they expect. The specific tests for a POSIX component are numbered 2003 so the tests for IEEE Std 1003.1-1990 are called IEE Std 2003.1-1992.

P1003.5   is a set of ADA bindings to the basic system services defined in POSIX.1 (IEEE Std 1003.5-1992).

P1387   (formerly POSIX.7) is going to provide standard system administration. System administration is one of the least standard areas in UNIX. There are several subprojects:

P1387.1 Framework for system administration

P1387.2 Software management

P1387.3 User management

P1387.4 Printer management

P1003.9   is a set of FORTRAN-77 bindings to the basic system services defined in POSIX.1 (IEEE Std 1003.9-1992)

P1003.10   is a supercomputing Application Environment Profile (AEP). The idea is to specify the requirements that supercomputer users have for the other POSIX groups. For example, batch processing and checkpoint/restart facilities.

P1003.11   was the Transaction Processing AEP currently inactive.

P1003.13   is the Real-Time AEP. There is no POSIX.13 committee. The work is done by POSIX.4

P1003.14   is the Multiprocessor AEP.

P1003.16   is a set of C language bindings to the basic system services defined in POSIX.1 (inactive)

P1224.2   (formerly POSIX.17) covers programming interfaces to network directory services (IEEE Std 1224.2-1993).

POSIX.18   is the POSIX Platform Environment Profile. It will cover what options are required to support POSIX applications.

POSIX.19   is a set of Fortran 90 bindings to the basic system services defined in POSIX.1 (inactive)

POSIX.20   is a set of Ada bindings to the real time services defined in POSIX.4

POSIX.0   is a Guide to POSIX Open Systems Environment. This is not a standard in the same sense as POSIX.1 or POSIX.2. It is more of an introduction to the other standards.

Most of these projects have not yet produced a standard. 1003.1, .2, .3, .5, .9 and 1224.2 are official standards. The rest are in ballot or still in the hands of their respective committees.

The POSIX.1 Standard Document

The POSIX.1 Standard Document is dedicated to POSIX.1 which produced an IEEE standard in 1988 and an international standard in 1990. The full legal name is: IEEE Std. 1003.1-1990 *Standard for Information Technology—Portable Operating System Interface (POSIX)—PART 1: System Application Programming Interface (API) [C Language]*. The Publications section in the Reference Manual at the back of this book gives the ordering information for this and other standards.

For the rest of this book, we will use the word POSIX to mean POSIX.1.

POSIX covers the basic operating system interface. This includes:

1. The POSIX standard starts out with a set of definitions and general requirements. I have distributed this information throughout this book so that you are not hit with 89 definitions all at once.

2. POSIX next covers the *Process Primitives*. I cover this information in Chapter 6, *Working with Processes*.

3. Next comes *Process Environment*, which I cover in Chapter 7, *Obtaining Information at Run–time*.

4. The POSIX sections on *Files and Directories* and *Input and Output Primitives* are covered in Chapter 3, *Standard File and Terminal I/O*, Chapter 4, *Files and Directories* and Chapter 5, *Advanced File Operations*.

5. *Device- and Class-Specific Functions* are covered in Chapter 8, *Terminal I/O*. Terminals are the only device that POSIX standardizes.

6. The POSIX chapter *Language-specific Services for the C Programming Language* is covered in Chapter 9, *POSIX and Standard C*. The POSIX standard assumes that you have complete knowledge of *ANSI Std X3.159-1989—American National Standard for Information Systems—Programming Language—C*. I have brought the relevant information from that standard into Chapter 9 (as well as other places in this book).

7. The early drafts of POSIX had a chapter on *System Databases* covering the /etc/passwd and /etc/groups files. These files are no longer part of POSIX. The system database is accessed with library functions such as getpwnam(). The POSIX chapter remained *System Databases*. I cover the related functions in Chapter 7, *Obtaining Information at Run–time*.

8. The POSIX standard defines the tar and cpio -c file formats. I do not cover these because they do not affect application programs. What you do need to know is that you can write an archive on one POSIX system using tar or cpio -c and read it on another POSIX system.

POSIX provides the facilities you will need to write most ordinary character-based application programs. However, POSIX.1 does not address some significant areas such as networking and graphics. Networking is being addressed by POSIX.8. This is a large complex area and will require several standards that will take until the mid-90s to complete. Graphics, graphic user interfaces, and windowing systems standards are all under development.

POSIX also ignores system administration. How do you add users? How do you back up the file system? How do you install a package? These are not considered issues for portable applications.

The same force that made POSIX.1 a success is delaying these other areas: a large body of existing practice and a consensus on the best solution. Most of the features of POSIX and Standard C had been built and tested by several vendors before being included in an international standard. Is OSF/Motif the correct user interface? Should it be an international standard? It is too early to have a broad consensus.

The Design of POSIX

The committee that worked on POSIX had several "grand principles" to guide their work:

- POSIX is aimed at application portability across many systems. These include not only UNIX systems but non-UNIX systems such as VAX/VMS and OS/2. Unisys Corp. has developed a POSIX front end for the CTOS operating system.

- POSIX describes the contract between the application and the operating system. POSIX does not say how to write applications programs or how to write operating systems.

- The standard has been defined exclusively at the source code level. A strictly conforming source program can be compiled to execute on any conforming system. The standard does not guarantee that the object or binary code will execute under a different conforming implementation, even if the underlying hardware is identical. This applies even to two identical computers with the same operating system.

- The standard is written in terms of Standard C. The standard does not require that an implementation support Standard C. FORTRAN and ADA interfaces to POSIX are being developed.

- There was no intention to specify all aspects of an operating system. Only functions used by ordinary applications are included. There are no system administration functions.

- The standard is as small as possible.

- The POSIX interface is suitable for the broadest possible range of systems.

- While no known UNIX system was 100% POSIX compatible, the changes required to meet the standard were kept as small as possible.

- POSIX is designed to make less work for developers, not more. However, because no UNIX system prior to POSIX was POSIX conforming, some existing applications had to change to become strictly portable.

POSIX and UNIX

POSIX is based on UNIX System V and Berkeley UNIX, but it is not itself an operating system. Instead, POSIX defines the interface between applications and their libraries. POSIX does not talk about "system calls" or make any distinction between the kernel and the user.

Vendors can adapt any UNIX variant, or even another operating system, to provide POSIX interfaces. Applications can be moved from one system to another because they see only the POSIX interface and have no idea what system is under the interface.

An *implementation* consists of both a set of libraries and an operating system. The POSIX standard defines only the interface between the application and the library. Consider Figure 1-1.

FIGURE 1-1. Software layers

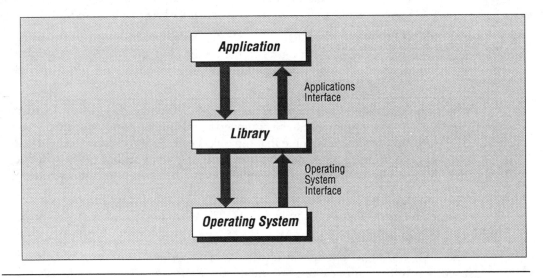

POSIX defines how the application talks to the library and how the library and underlying operating system behave in response. Each implementation can have its own way of dividing the work between the library and the operating system.

POSIX and Non-UNIX Operating Systems

Because the POSIX standard is the contract between the application and the library, POSIX allows applications to be ported between operating systems by using a different library to "glue" the application to the operating system.

For example, there is a function called `getcwd()` which returns the current working directory. Some systems may have an operating system trap that returns this information. Other systems may have a much larger chore of reading directories and computing the current working directory. The applications programmer does not care. All systems must provide a `getcwd()` which works exactly as described in this book.

POSIX, C, ANSI C, and Standard C

This book covers POSIX and Standard C. It is possible to write a book about POSIX without getting involved in programming languages. The standards committees are moving in that direction: one topic per standard.

However, programmers must program in a programming language. Divorcing the operating system interface from the way a programmer accesses that interface may be good for the standards lawyers, but it is bad for the programmer. We are going to talk about POSIX and Standard C together.

The IEEE POSIX.5 committee is defining the ADA interface to POSIX and the IEEE POSIX.9 committee is defining the FORTRAN interface to POSIX. In early 1991 those standards are in the first round of balloting. At some point, it will be possible to write POSIX programs in ADA or FORTRAN. At the moment, C is the only real choice.

The POSIX standard is written in terms of the C programming language. POSIX supports two programming environments. One is based on the traditional C language. The other is based on the Standard C language defined by *American National Standard for Information Systems—Programming Language—C*, X3.159-1989. Standard C defines the C language in a more precise way and allows for more portability than traditional C.

Since Standard C was developed by the American National Standards Institute (ANSI), some people call it ANSI C. The International Organization for Standards has adopted ANSI X3.158-1989 as ISO/IEC 9899: *Information Processing Systems—Programming Language—C*. I will use the term Standard C instead of ANSI C to reflect its status as an international standard.

Since POSIX was being developed in parallel with Standard C, the POSIX committee did not want to require its use. Today, there are many Standard C compilers on the market and most platforms support one or more of them. Writing a new application in traditional C exposes you to additional portability risks. Standard C also allows better compile-time checking. This makes your programs easier to debug. There is no need to use traditional C if Standard C is available.

Why Standard C?

We could look for a subset of C that works on all computers. Let's call that Least Common Denominator (LCD) C. The problem is that LCD C is hard to define. There are two major reasons for this:

1. Documentation prior to the publication of *American National Standard for Information Systems—Programming Language—C* was unclear at times.

2. Even where the books were clear, implementations got it wrong and there were no test suites to validate the implementation.

As a result, finding a common subset of C requires a large amount of trial and error. Several books have been written on C-compiler compatibility. Harbison and Steele's *C: A Reference Manual* does a good job of pointing out the fuzzy edge of C and how to avoid it. In the 1990s, avoiding the fuzzy edge is unnecessary. POSIX became a standard in 1988 and C in 1989. Systems that implement those standards are just coming to market in 1991. It is unlikely that you will find a system that conforms to the POSIX standard and does not also supply a Standard C compiler and libraries.

The Standard C libraries are important. POSIX supplies only one part of the programming toolkit. We need the libraries provided as part of Standard C in order to write interesting programs. It is not worth wasting brain cells remembering which tools are in the Standard C box and which are in the POSIX box. It is better to remember our tools by function. This is like sorting our tools into screwdrivers and wrenches instead of Craftsman tools and Stanley tools. In this book, I have attempted to integrate the two standards and present them as a complete toolkit.

Working Outside the Standards

Most programs have only a few areas which need to go outside of the standards. Keep those area isolated to a few modules. Keep most of the code POSIX conforming.

For example, I have an amateur radio application which I share with many friends. The program's structure is shown in Figure 1-2.

Modules in the Program Core do not have any knowledge of the user interface. If I need, for example, to get a decimal number from the user, I call `get_decimal_with_prompt()`. That is one of the routines I wrote in the user interface module. On a system with a graphic user interface, there is a dialog box. On an ordinary terminal there is a question and a pause for the user to type a number.

Most of the program remains unchanged over several operating systems and user interfaces. I can build a version for different operating systems and user interfaces by changing that module.

FIGURE 1-2. Example of a portable application

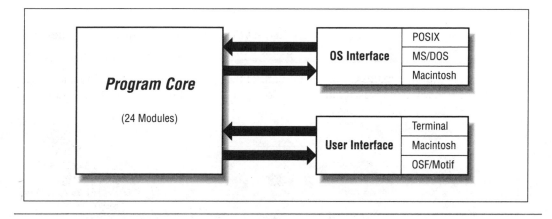

Finding The POSIX Libraries

The POSIX libraries are part of the standard system libraries. You can indicate that you want all vendor extensions hidden from you by defining the symbol _POSIX_SOURCE with the statement:

```
#define _POSIX_SOURCE 1
```

According to the rules of Standard C, only those symbols that are in the base standard or are enabled by a specific #define feature test are allowed to be visible. However, many vendors require a special command to get the Standard C behavior. They include their *added value* by default. By defining _POSIX_SOURCE you should protect yourself from this added value.

Every conforming POSIX system must provide a "conformance document" that describes its implementation. This document will tell you if there is any magic you need to perform to get standard behavior. We will talk more about the POSIX development environment in the next chapter.

Converting Existing Programs

Since POSIX is based on existing practice, this is often very easy. It does require checking the library functions that you use and verifying that you are using them as defined in the standard.

The Functions section in the Reference Manual in the back of this book lists every library function. For each function there is a section labeled CONVERSION. This is a description of the changes you have to make from the various releases of AT&T System V and Berkeley Software Distribution (BSD) to make your application POSIX-conforming.

One easy test is to add the statement:

```
#define _POSIX_SOURCE 1
```

to the front of each module, compile and test your application. While this will not verify complete POSIX conformance, it is a quick way to get close.

Several companies make C portability verifiers. A good one is Flex Lint available from Gimpel Software, 3207 Hogarth Lane, Collegeville, PA 19426. The phone number is (215)584-4261 and the FAX is (215)584-4266

CHAPTER 2

Developing POSIX Applications

In this chapter, we discuss how to access the C language bindings as well as the POSIX libraries. We look at what a system vendor must provide for a system to be POSIX-compliant. We demonstrate two different program development problems—porting an existing program to a POSIX-conforming system, and developing a program that is designed to be POSIX-compliant.

The POSIX Development Environment

POSIX provides portability at the source level. This means that you transport your source program to the target machine, compile it with the Standard C compiler using conforming headers, and link it with the standard libraries. The system vendor provides the compiler, the libraries, and headers. Strictly speaking, these are all black boxes and you do not need to know how they work. However, it is instructive to look into some of these black boxes, and we will do that in this chapter.

The Standard C Compiler

Each POSIX-conforming system must provide a POSIX-conformance document. This document describes the behavior of the system for all *implementation-defined* features identified in the standard. For maximum portability, applications should not depend upon any particular behavior that is implementation-specific. The conformance document is dull reading, but it is valuable because it contains information on how to access the standard C language bindings.

For AT&T UNIX System V Release 4, the Standard C language bindings are accessed by specifying –Xc on the cc command line. The command:

```
cc -Xc subs.c main.c -o prog
```

will compile subs.c and main.c and link them together to form prog.

The Open Software Foundation's OSF/1 operating system comes with the GNU C compiler.[*] The Standard C bindings are accessed by specifying -ansi on the cc command line. A command there looks like:

```
cc -ansi subs.c main.c -o prog
```

For other systems, you will have to buy (or at least look at) the conformance document, look for on-line manual pages, or ask someone.

On most systems, the default is not Standard C but a C compiler that is compatible with the historic behavior of that system. In many cases, your program will not notice the difference. The historic behavior probably includes defining symbols that are not part of Standard C and POSIX. It is easier to specify strict conformance and clean up small problems as you go than to deal with a large mess at the end of the project.

Strict ANSI conformance is a good answer to the question: "What can I do to make my programs more portable?"

POSIX and C Libraries

POSIX defines a library of functions for conforming programs to use. Many of these functions are also defined in the Standard C library.

Each function in the library requires you to include at least one header. This is done with a statement like:

```
#include <stdio.h>
```

The header provides a prototype for the function, plus any necessary types and additional macros to facilitate using the function.

The POSIX and C standards do not require headers to be source files. They may be some sort of magic command to the compiler. The standards specify only the net effect of including a header. On most systems (and all UNIX systems) the headers are files that live in the directory /usr/include.

Many systems support multiple development environments. How do you get the POSIX headers? You must define the symbol _POSIX_SOURCE before including any of the standard headers. The best way to do this is to place the statement:[†]

```
#define _POSIX_SOURCE 1
```

at the start of each file.

---

[*] The Open Software Foundation ships GNU C to resellers as part of the reference implementation. The reseller might ship a different compiler with his or her product.

[†] The standard merely requires that the symbol _POSIX_SOURCE be defined. There is no required value. I prefer to define symbols with values.

You could also place the option **-D_POSIX_SOURCE** on the **cc** command-line; however, this is error prone. It is better to put the **#define** into your source file along with the rest of your program. As a rule of thumb, restrict command-line macro definitions to things that change from one compile to the next. For example, **-DNDEBUG** turns off the debug test in **assert()**. Use **#define** statements for symbols that must always be defined, such as **_POSIX_SOURCE**.

On some systems the header files you include do not do much. They merely select one of several possible other headers based on the symbols that you have defined. This might look like:

```
#include <common/stdio.h>
#ifdef _SYSV_SOURCE
#include <sysV/stdio.h>
#endif
#ifdef _BSD_SOURCE
#include <BSD/stdio.h>
#endif
#ifdef _POSIX_SOURCE
#include <POSIX/stdio.h>
#endif
```

Under most circumstances, you do not need to know how the system defines the correct symbols. The Header Files section in this book details every POSIX and Standard C header file. If you follow the rules in this section, the standards guarantee the following:

1. Every symbol required by the standards will be defined with a meaningful value.

2. No symbol not permitted by the standards will be defined. This protects your application from namespace pollution.* Of course, if you include a header not specified by the standard, all bets are off.

Converting Existing Programs

Porting an existing application to run on a new system requires two major steps. These tasks can range from very easy to almost impossible. First, you have to transport the program to the target computer. Second, you have to modify the program to run in the new environment. The POSIX standard (and this book) can help you in both steps.

The POSIX standard defines the format of both the **cpio** and **tar** archives. You can create an archive with the command:

```
ls files | cpio -oc >archive
```

or:

```
tar -cf archive files
```

---

* For example, if the header <stdio.h> defined the symbol count, there could be a conflict with the symbol count in your program.

and load it onto the target with the command:

```
cpio -ic <archive
```

or:

```
tar -xvf archive
```

See your system documentation for the exact details. You will still need some form of compatible disk, tape, or network to move the archive file to the target.

Once the files are moved, you will have to convert system-specific function calls to calls defined by the POSIX standard. There are several aids in the reference guide in this book that are designed to make conversion easier. For every function defined by either POSIX or Standard C, there is a conversion entry in the Functions section. This entry points out the changes that may be required to convert the function from older UNIX systems to ones that conform to the POSIX standard. The Porting section covers functions in BSD and System V that are not in POSIX and suggests ways to build equivalent functions using POSIX calls.

A Porting Example

One day, the boss walks in the door and says, "Here is a program that needs to be ported from Berkeley UNIX to a Data General AViiON 310. Get it done quickly!"

Now, you could try to find the correct Data General manuals and port the program to the AViiON, but the next day the boss will want it ported to some other machine. Since you are clever, you decide to port the program to POSIX. It will then run on any POSIX system.

Let's look at the program:

```
#include <stdio.h>
#include <sys/time.h>

main(argc,argv)
int argc;
char **argv;
{
struct timeval tv;
struct timezone tz;

    gettimeofday(&tv,&tz);
    printf("The current time is:\n%s",
                    ctime(&tv.tv_sec));
if (tz.tz_dsttime)
    printf("Daylight savings time\n");
else
    printf("Standard time\n");
exit(0);
}
```

This program prints out the current time in the following format:

```
The current time is:
Sun Nov 11 18:44:00 1990
Standard time
```

Now, in the real world you would not be confronted by a program this tiny. It might be easier to throw the whole thing away and write a new program from scratch.* However, we will look at the process of porting this program.

As a first test, we can compile the program and see if it works. We may have a very portable program. At least, we will get a hint at what must be fixed.

This program will not compile because there is no <sys/time.h> header. This can be solved by deleting the #include statement. This will get us past that compiler error and point out any remaining compatibility problems.†

Next the compiler points out that there is no definition for struct timeval or struct timezone. These seem to be used by the gettimeofday() function. A quick check of the Functions section of this book reveals that there is no gettimeofday() function in POSIX. However, it looks like gettimeofday() returns something that can be used as an argument to ctime(). It also seems to return a daylight savings indication.

If we look up ctime() in the Functions section, it tells us:

1. The #include <sys/time.h> must be changed to #include <time.h>. (We already knew that there was no <sys/time.h>!)

2. ctime() is equivalent to asctime(localtime(timer)).

This gives a good indication of what must be done to convert the program. The description of localtime() in the Functions section states:

> The localtime() function converts a time_t pointed to by timer into year, month, day, hours, minutes, seconds, etc., and stores the information in a struct tm. A pointer to the struct tm is returned. The current time can be obtained with the time() function.

---

* The option of throwing the existing program away and starting from scratch should not be ignored even in much larger projects.

† In fact, many systems provide a BSD compatibility package. If we tried to run this program there is a good chance it would work correctly without any changes. For the purposes of illustration, we will ignore that possibility.

We can replace `gettimeofday()` with `localtime()`. A quick check of the `tm` structure in the Data Structures section reveals that it contains a flag, `tm_isdst`, to indicate daylight savings time. Our program now looks like:

```
#define _POSIX_SOURCE 1

#include <stdio.h>
#include <time.h>

main(argc,argv)
int argc;
char **argv;
{
struct tm *tmptr;
time_t timer;

    timer = time(NULL);
    tmptr = localtime(&timer);
    printf("The current time is:\n%s",
                        ctime(&timer));
if (tmptr -> tm_isdst)
    printf("Daylight savings time\n");
else
    printf("Standard time\n");
exit(0);
}
```

This program will work and can be considered "ported." There are a couple of things that we should do to make sure that the program is 100% standards-conforming. First, we should check that we have included all of the required headers. The `exit()` function requires that we include the `<stdlib.h>` header. While we are looking at `exit()` we should change the 0 to `EXIT_SUCCESS`. This change is not required for correct operation on POSIX systems. As an act of kindness to those who will look at the program after we are done with it, we will add some comments (ensuring portability from one programmer to another!).

The final maximally portable program is shown in Example 2-1:

EXAMPLE 2-1. daytime.c

```
/* Define _POSIX_SOURCE to indicate
 * that this is a POSIX program
 */
#define _POSIX_SOURCE 1

/* System Headers */
#include <stdlib.h>
#include <stdio.h>
#include <time.h>

main(argc,argv)
int argc;           /* Argument count -- unused */
char **argv;        /* Argument list -- unused */
{
```

```
struct tm *tmptr;   /* Pointer to date and time
                     * broken down by component.
                     * The only member used is
                     * tm_dst
                     */
time_t timer;       /* Number of seconds since
                     * January 1, 1970.
                     */

    timer = time(NULL);         /* Get current time */
    tmptr = localtime(&timer);  /* Break it down */
    printf("The current time is:\n%s",
                    ctime(&timer));
if (tmptr -> tm_isdst)          /* tm_isdst is non-zero
                                 * if daylight savings
                                 * is in effect
                                 */
    printf("Daylight savings time\n");
else
    printf("Standard time\n");
exit(EXIT_SUCCESS);             /* Return to system */
}
```

We can now tell the boss, "I ported the program to AViiON, and to ULTRIX, and to System V.4. I even ported it to VAX/VMS. About that raise..."

An Alternate Approach

The previous example ported a program from an old system to one that supports the POSIX and C standards. The new program is conforming but may no longer run on the old system. Of course, we still have the old version for that system. If we are going to continue to fix bugs and enhance the old version, we will have two source bases to deal with. We can try to get around that problem by using #ifdefs as in:

```
#ifdef BSD
struct timeval tv;
struct timezone tz;
#endif
#ifndef BSD
struct tm *tmptr;   /* Pointer to date and time
                     * broken down by component.
                     * The only member used is
                     * tm_dst
                     */
time_t timer;       /* Number of seconds since
                     * January 1, 1970.
                     */
#endif
```

After a few ports this gets very ugly and hard to read.

Another scheme is to build BSD compatible functions out of POSIX functions. For programs like this, the emulation does not have to be perfect or complete. You need to supply only the specific things required by the application you are porting.

Of course, after a while you may have a large set of compatibility functions to support. User frustration with the complexity of supporting a large number of ports was a major driving force behind POSIX.

Standard Header Files

To write a POSIX program you must specify in your source code that you want it to be POSIX-compliant (using #define _POSIX_SOURCE) and then use the library functions that are defined by POSIX. You can become familiar with them by reading the remaining chapters and using the reference section. The Header File section lists all of the standard headers and the symbols that they define. This list merely hits the highlights so that you will know what headers are available:

Header File	Function
<assert.h>	Defines the assert() macro. This is used to check for bugs.
<ctype.h>	Defines the character-testing functions such as isdigit() and isupper().
<dirent.h>	Defines the contents of directory entries and the functions that read them.
<errno.h>	Defines all of the error codes.
<fcntl.h>	Defines symbols used by the file control functions creat(), open(), and fcntl().
<float.h>	Defines a set of symbols used for floating-point processing.
<grp.h>	Defines the functions that read the group database.
<limits.h>	Defines a set of implementation limits. This includes both hardware limits like INT_MAX and software limits like NGROUPS_MAX.
<locale.h>	Defines symbols for use in multi-national applications.
<math.h>	Defines standard math functions such as sin() and sqrt().
<pwd.h>	Defines the functions that read the user database. This is called <pwd.h> because the user database file has historically been called /etc/passwd.
<setjmp.h>	Defines the C setjmp()/longjmp() macros. The POSIX extensions sigsetjmp() and siglongjmp() are also defined here.
<signal.h>	Defines the symbols and functions used by signals.
<stdarg.h>	Defines macros to support functions with a variable number of parameters.

Header File	Function
`<stddef.h>`	Defines NULL, `size_t`, and a few other popular symbols.
`<stdio.h>`	Defines the standard I/O library.
`<stdlib.h>`	Defines functions that historically did not require a header. These include `exit()`, `malloc()`, `free()`, and many others.
`<string.h>`	Defines the string functions `strcat()`, `strlen()`, `strspn()`, etc.
`<sys/stat.h>`	Defines the `stat` structure and file manipulation functions such as `chmod()`.
`<sys/times.h>`	Defines the `times()` function and the structure it uses.
`<sys/types.h>`	Defines the POSIX datatypes `dev_t`, `gid_t`, `ino_t`, etc.
`<sys/utsname.h>`	Defines the `uname()` function and the structure it uses.
`<sys/wait.h>`	Defines the `wait()` and `waitpid()` functions.
`<termios.h>`	Defines many symbols used to manipulate terminals.
`<time.h>`	Defines the time-of-day functions.
`<unistd.h>`	Defines a large number of POSIX symbols. This header also defines all of the UNIX functions which historically have not required a header. These include `chdir()`, `close()`, `fork()`, `pipe()`, and so on.
`<utime.h>`	Defines the `utime()` function and the structure it uses.

Section 4.1.2 of the C Standard states, "A header is not necessarily a source file, nor are the < and > delimited sequences in header names necessarily valid source file names." That is, the compiler is free to define the symbols using any method that it wants. A POSIX system may not have any headers that you can look at. Having said that, let's look at a typical header file. A sample `<utime.h>` is given in Example 2-2:

EXAMPLE 2-2. `utime.h` header file

```
#ifndef _UTIME_
#define _UTIME_

struct utimbuf
    {
    time_t actime;      /* access time */
    time_t modtime;     /* modification time */
    };

#ifdef __STDC__
    int utime(const char *path,
             const struct utimbuf *times);
```

```
#else
    extern int utime();
#endif /* __STDC__ */
#endif /* _UTIME_ */
```

This is a very simple header file but it still has many interesting points.

The header is wrapped with an #ifndef _UTIME_. This means that the header can be included any number of times without causing any errors. The symbol _UTIME_ is reserved for the people who write system header files. All symbols that begin with an underscore followed by either another underscore or an upper-case letter are for system headers. You should not use them in your code.

The header then declares struct utimebuf, which is the main job of the header.

Lastly, if the header is being used by a Standard C compiler, the utime() function is declared. If a compiler supports Standard C, the symbol __STDC__ is defined by the compiler to have the value 1. Some compilers define the symbol __STDC__ to have a value other than 1 to indicate "sort of standards-conforming."

Now let's look at <sys/types.h> which is slightly more complex:

EXAMPLE 2-3. sys/types.h header file

```
#ifndef _TYPES_
#define _TYPES_


#if (__STDC__ != 1) || defined(_IN_KERNEL)
/*
 * Machine specific system types
 */
typedef   struct{int r[1];}    *physadr;
typedef   unsigned short       iord_t;
typedef   int                  label_t[13];
typedef   unsigned short       pgadr_t;
typedef   char                 swck_t;
typedef   unsigned char        use_t;
#define   MAXSUSE              255


/*
 * Machine independent system parameters
 */
typedef   long                 daddr_t;
typedef   char                 *caddr_t;
typedef   unsigned char        uchar_t;
typedef   unsigned char        u_char;
typedef   unsigned short       u_short;
typedef   unsigned int         u_int;
typedef   unsigned long        u_long;
typedef   unsigned char        unchar;
typedef   unsigned int         uint;
typedef   unsigned short       ushort;
typedef   unsigned long        ulong;
typedef   ulong                ino_tl;
typedef   short                cnt_t;
typedef   long                 ubadr_t;
```

```
#endif   /* (__STDC__ != 1) || defined(_IN_KERNEL) */

#if (__STDC__ != 1) || defined(_POSIX_SOURCE)  || defined(_SYSV_SOURCE)
typedef  unsigned long        clock_t;
typedef  unsigned long        dev_t;
typedef  unsigned long        gid_t;
typedef  unsigned long        ino_t;
typedef  unsigned long        mode_t;
typedef  unsigned long        nlink_t;
typedef  long                 off_t;
typedef  long                 pid_t;
typedef  unsigned long        size_t;
typedef  long                 ssize_t;
typedef  unsigned long        uid_t;
#endif /* (__STDC__ != 1) || defined(_POSIX_SOURCE) */

#if (__STDC__ != 1) || defined(_SYSV_SOURCE)
typedef  unsigned char        uchar_t;
typedef  unsigned short       ushort_t;
typedef  unsigned int         uint_t;
typedef  unsigned long        ulong_t;

typedef  char *               addr_t;
typedef  char *               caddr_t;
typedef  long                 daddr_t;
typedef  short                cnt_t;
typedef  ulong_t              paddr_t;
typedef  short                sysid_t;
typedef  short                index_t;
typedef  short                lock_t;
typedef  long                 id_t;
typedef  short                o_dev_t;
typedef  unsigned short       o_gid_t;
typedef  unsigned short       o_ino_t;
typedef  unsigned short       o_mode_t;
typedef  short                o_nlink_t;
typedef  short                o_pid_t;
typedef  unsigned short       o_uid_t;
typedef  unsigned char        uchar_t;
typedef  unsigned char        u_char;
typedef  unsigned short       u_short;
typedef  unsigned int         u_int;
typedef  unsigned long        u_long;
typedef  unsigned char        unchar;
typedef  unsigned int         uint;
typedef  unsigned short       ushort;
typedef  unsigned long        ulong;
#endif   /* (__STDC__ != 1) || defined(_SYSV_SOURCE) */
#endif   /* _TYPES_ */
```

Here we see a header that uses three feature tests: _IN_KERNEL, _POSIX_SOURCE, and _SYSV_SOURCE. Unless the header is being compiled with Standard C, every name in the header is defined. Most of these are symbols that end in _t and are reserved anyway. Some of them are symbols that could conflict with our application: physadr, unchar, etc. Using Standard C, these symbols are hidden until we expose them with a feature-test macro.

Template for a POSIX Application

There are many ways to structure programs. Many are legal and will work, but some formats seem to work better. The programs are easier to write, have fewer bugs, and are easier to maintain. If you are developing new programs, you have the opportunity to establish a template that assists in producing code with consistent format. As we said earlier, a well-structured program is portable among the different programmers who may maintain it. Placing program elements in a consistent order makes finding things easier. We look at a template for writing POSIX programs.

Before we look at the template, we should say a few words about breaking a program into several files (or modules). Breaking a large program into several files has some good points and some bad points. First, the benefits:

1. Compile times can be reduced because only those modules that change need to be recompiled. This can make a big difference during debugging. The make utility makes this very easy.

2. Multiple people can work on the program at one time.

3. Well-designed modules can be reused in future projects, a major advantage.

Now the drawbacks:

1. Compile times are larger when everything has to be recompiled. Link times are also longer.

2. It is more difficult to keep track of a large number of files than a small number of files.

3. There can be more global variables.

As a rule-of-thumb, modules should contain between 300 and 1500 lines of codes. We should always try to design reusable modules. Even though you might not know how the module can be reused, you can design it in such a way that reuse is easier. We do not write the module with explicit knowledge of where it will be reused. Our template tries to make it easier to write and document modules that can be reused.

Let's look at the template and then discuss each part.

```
/* Feature test switches */
#define _POSIX_SOURCE 1

/* System headers */

/* Local headers */

/* Macros */

/* File scope variables */

/* External variables */
```

```
/* External functions */

/* Structures and unions */

/* Signal catching functions */

/* Functions */

/* Main */
```

You can place this template in a file, for example `empty.c`, and edit it each time you need to create a module. This file is also handy if your company uses disclaimers and copyright statements. They can all be placed into `empty.c` and used as a starter for new programs.

/* Feature test switches */

This section should define the `_POSIX_SOURCE` macro to enable the POSIX symbols and disable all unspecified symbols.

/* System headers */

Each Standard C or POSIX function has one or more headers that must be included to define the symbols used by that function. You should use an `#include` statement for each required header. I try to keep these headers in alphabetic order. It is then easy to check to see if a given header is included.

If you have an `empty.c` template file, you can put in an `#include` statement for every header. Then, after your module is written, you can delete the headers that are not needed. It is easier to delete things with a text editor than to add them.

/* Local headers */

Most projects have at least one project header. These define common data structures and symbols that are used in many files.

You may also have things that are part of your personal programming style. These are macros and functions that you seem to use all of the time. These may be placed in a personal header and included here.

/* Macros */

Define all of your macros here. Make sure there is a comment to describe any macros that are not obvious. It is handy to have all macros defined in one place.

/* File scope variables */

These are variable that are shared by several functions in the same file. Again, use comments to describe how the variables are used. Keeping the variables in one place near the front of the file makes them easy to find.

/* External variables */

This is the list of variables defined in other modules and used in this module.

/* External functions */

There should be a prototype for each user-written external function that you use. An alternative is to have a header with a prototype for every function in the project. I prefer to list explicitly the external functions that each module uses.

/* Structures and unions */

Define all of the structures that are used only in this file. Any structure that is used in multiple files should be in a local header file. In fact, any structure that may be used in multiple files should be in a header file. Placing definitions in header files makes it easier to expand and enhance your program.

/* Signal catching functions */

Place signal catching functions in one place. Signals are an unusual calling mechanism and often hard to debug. Unless you point it out clearly in your source code, it may not be obvious that something is a signal catching function.

/* Functions */

I like to define each function before it is used. That way I do not have to declare any of the functions that are local to this file. I also find it easier to read source files where the functions are defined before they are used. That is merely a matter of personal preference.

/* Main */

If there is a `main( )` function in this file, I put it last.

Sample Program

Let's look at a complete program that uses many POSIX facilities. At this point, it is not important that you understand the complete program. We will cover each function in detail in the following chapters.

One easy way to write a program is to start with a program that does one thing and modify it to do something else. The program that follows uses many POSIX features and can be used as a starting point for other programs.

The sample is a simple directory listing program. It lists all of the files in the current directory along with their size in bytes.

I have added a few special features. If the user's terminal is running at 2400 baud or higher, the program will pause every 24 lines to give the user a chance to read the screen. If the user interrupts the program with Control-C (or whatever key is assigned for interrupt), the program prints a partial total and exits.

The output from the program looks like this:

```
Directory /usr/don/POSIX/c:
Special .
Special ..
    175 addcr.c
   1406 comm.c
    855 dirhack.c
    463 i.c
    529 include.c
   1662 ldirs.c
   2162 lstuser.c
    172 malloc0.c
    247 malloc1.c
    342 malloc2.c
    449 malloc3.c
    179 panic.c
   1758 pathconf.c
   5344 sample.c
  17984 BSD.h
  18180 POSIX.h
     41 panic.h
Total of 51948 bytes in 19 files
```

If a Control-C is used to interrupt the program, the output would look like:

```
Directory /usr/bin:
Special .
Special ..
 118264 acctcom
 117672 admin
  29080 asa
    754 assist
    754 astgen
 148656 awk
  27912 banner
   1206 basename
  49432 bc
  39288 bdiff
  68264 berk_diff
    634 berk_diff3
  53320 bfs
  38520 cal
   1280 calendar
  70920 captoinfo
  34536 cat
  43912 cb
   2114 cflow
  78184 chgrp
  34632 chgtinfo
  29128 chmod
  88424 chown
Interrupted after 25 files and 1076886 bytes
```

At this point it is a useful exercise to stop reading and write a program that matches this specification. Do not concern yourself with portability. Just write the program so that it works on your system. How do you read the directory? How do you handle getting interrupted? How do you find out the speed of the terminal? What assumptions do you make about the operating system interface? Even if you don't write the program, stop and think about how you might go about it.

Welcome back. Let's look at how POSIX solves these problems. Basically, what POSIX defines is a standard interface between an application and the services it depends on from the operating system. The POSIX interfaces have several attributes that make them portable:

1. The interfaces are symbolic. They use symbols and the C compiler to map those symbols onto a given system. For example, the file mode word in BSD 4.2 is an `unsigned short`; in AT&T System V.3 it is an `int`. POSIX defines a new type, `mode_t`. The `<sys/types.h>` header defines `mode_t` for each specific system.

2. POSIX defines functions to mask system differences. The `readdir()` function is used to read a directory. The information is returned in a `struct dirent` where the actual format of the directory can be hidden from the application. Compare that to System V where programs "know" that filenames are 14 characters long and are preceded by a two-byte i-node number.

3. Multi-purpose functions like `ioctl()` have been replaced by a large number of special-purpose functions. These functions are easier to describe and easier to test.

4. POSIX also provides methods to test the interfaces and make sure that they work as described. This does not show up as anything you see while programming. However, it does help assure that the people who wrote the POSIX library got it right. That increases the chance that your program will be portable.

Now, what services will this sample program require from the system?

- We need to interact with the user's terminal. We will use the Standard C library described in Chapter 3, *Standard File and Terminal I/O*, to read and write formatted data. We will use `tcgetattr()` and `cfgetospeed()` to determine the terminal speed. These are described in Chapter 8, *Terminal I/O*.

- We will need to read directories and get information about files. The `opendir()`, `readdir()`, and `stat()` functions will do this for us. They are described in detail in Chapter 4, *Files and Directories*.

- We will use POSIX signals and the `sigaction()` function described in Chapter 6, *Working with Processes*, to intercept the Control-C.

- We also make good use of the Standard C library for much of our work. For example, the div() function is used to test to see if we have printed a multiple of 24 lines. These functions are not covered in the tutorial part of this book. However, they are all described in the Library Functions section in the reference part.

Using the interfaces defined by standards helps us achieve portability. What other portability concerns might we have? For this program, the maximum length of filenames and pathnames is the only remaining concern. I have written the program so that it will work correctly* even if the paths or filenames are huge.

As a last step before looking at the code, we should consider how we are going to structure the program. What are the major blocks? Figure 2-1 shows a flow chart that will do everything we need.

This will become the main() function. Now, some of those blocks are a bit complex. They will become functions. The block that says "Print the directory entry" will become the print_dir_entry() function. The flow for that function is shown in Figure 2-2.

The other routines are not very complex. The cwdname() routine returns a pointer to the name of the current working directory. The baud() routine returns the terminal output speed in baud. Both of these routines are fully described in the example.

The intr_key() routine is a signal catching function; it is called when the user types the interrupt key (usually Control-C). The intr_key() function is called by the system as if a function call were magically inserted between two statements. Because we don't know exactly what our program (or the library) might have been doing when the intr_key() function is called, the function is careful not to disturb any "work-in-progress." The only thing that intr_key() does is set the variable intr_flag to TRUE.

Here is the complete program. The program is divided into two files: dsksub.c and dskuse.c. The first file contains the major subroutines for this program. These functions are written with the hope that they will be useful in future projects. The second file contains the main function and subroutines that are not reusable.

If you wrote your own version of this program, compare what you wrote to this sample. What system-specific things did you do?

---

* The program might truncate the filename if it is longer than the terminal width.

FIGURE 2-1. Flowchart for `main()`

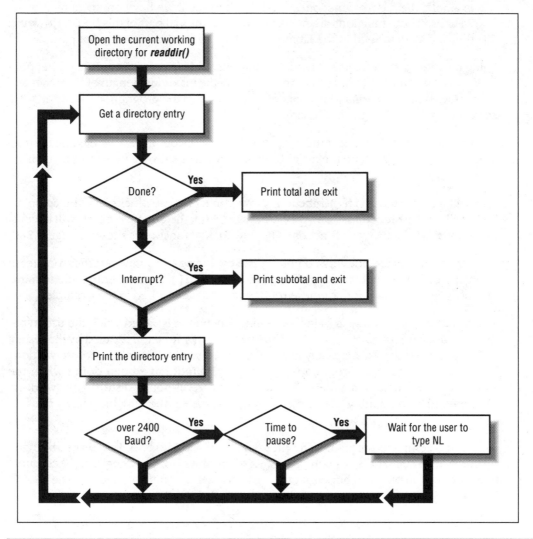

Here is the first file, `dsksub.c`:

EXAMPLE 2-4. dsksub.c

```
1 /*
2  * Functions for program to print file names and sizes
3  */
4 /* Feature test switches */
5 #define _POSIX_SOURCE 1
6
7 /* System Headers */
8 #include <assert.h>
9 #include <dirent.h>
```

FIGURE 2-2. Flowchart for `print_dir_entry()`

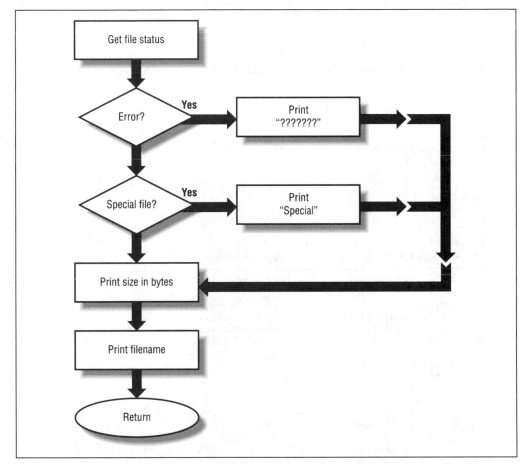

```
10 #include <errno.h>
11 #include <stdio.h>
12 #include <stdlib.h>
13 #include <sys/stat.h>
14 #include <sys/types.h>
15 #include <termios.h>
16 #include <unistd.h>
17
18 /* Local Headers */
19 #include "panic.h"   /* Defines the PANIC macro.
20                       * PANIC prints an error
21                       * message when a library
22                       * function fails
23                       */
24
25 /* Macros */
26 #define TRUE    1
27 #define FALSE   0
28 #define SIZE    256 /* Arbitrary size */
```

```
29 /* File scope variables */
30 long nbytes = 0;      /* Number of bytes */
31 long nfiles = 0;      /* Number of files */
32
33 /* External Variables */
34      /* NONE */
35
36 /* External Functions */
37      /* NONE */
38
39 /* Structures and Unions */
40      /* NONE */
41
42 /* Signal Catching Functions */
43      /* NONE */
44
45
46
47
48
49
50 /*
51  * Function to process one directory entry
52  */
53 void print_dir_entry(struct dirent *p)
54 {
55 /* Prints the file size in bytes followed by the
56  * file name.  If the stat() function fails,
57  * print question marks.  For special files, which
58  * may not have a valid size, print special.
59  */
60 struct stat statbuf;
61     if(stat(p->d_name,&statbuf) != 0)
62         (void)printf("??????? ");
63     else
64         {
65         if (S_ISREG(statbuf.st_mode))
66             {
67             (void)printf("%7ld ",(long)statbuf.st_size);
68             nbytes += statbuf.st_size;
69             }
70         else
71             (void)printf("Special ");
72         }
73     (void)printf("%s\n",p->d_name);
74     nfiles++;
75     return;
76 }
77 /*
78  * Function to return a pointer to the name
79  * of the current working directory
80  */
81 char *cwdname(void)
82 {
83 int     size = SIZE;
84 char    *ptr;
85     while(TRUE)
86     {
87     ptr = (char *)malloc(size);
```

```
 88      if (ptr == NULL) PANIC;        /* Give up if we run out
 89                                      * of memory
 90                                      */
 91      if (getcwd(ptr,size-1) != NULL) return(ptr);
 92      if (errno != ERANGE) PANIC;  /* Any error other than a
 93                                    * path name too long for the
 94                                    * buffer is bad news.
 95                                    */
 96      free(ptr);                    /* Return the storage */
 97      size += SIZE;                 /* Try again with a bigger buffer */
 98      }
 99 }
100
101
102 /*
103  * Function to return speed of terminal in baud
104  */
105 long baud(void)
106 {
107 struct termios t;
108 speed_t         baud_code;
109     if(tcgetattr(fileno(stdout),&t) == -1)
110         {
111         /* If standard output is not a terminal
112          * return 0.  Any other error is bad news
113          */
114         if (errno == ENOTTY) return(0);
115         PANIC;
116         }
117     baud_code = cfgetospeed(&t);
118
119 /*
120  * We must decode the baud rate by hand because the Bxxxx
121  * symbols might not be in order.
122  */
123     switch(baud_code)
124         {
125     case B0:
126         return(0);
127     case B50:
128         return(50);
129     case B75:
130         return(75);
131     case B110:
132         return(110);
133     case B134:
134         return(134);
135     case B150:
136         return(150);
137     case B200:
138         return(200);
139     case B300:
140         return(300);
141     case B600:
142         return(600);
143     case B1200:
144         return(1200);
145     case B1800:
146         return(1800);
147     case B2400:
148         return(2400);
```

```
149        case B4800:
150            return(4800);
151        case B9600:
152            return(9600);
153        case B19200:
154            return(19200);
155        case B38400:
156            return(38400);
157        default:
158            (void)fprintf(stderr,
159                    "WARNING: Unknown terminal speed\n");
160            return(0);
161            }
162 }
```

Notes for dsksub:

Line	Note

8 These headers are required by the various library functions. Each library function has one or more required header. The Functions Section lists the headers for each function.

19 The PANIC macro is defined in the sample program at the end of Chapter 3. It is used throughout the book.

53 The dirent structure has a member called d_name which is the name of a file in the directory.

62 The (void) before the call to print() tells the reader (and programs like lint) that we know that printf() returns a value and we are explicitly ignoring it.

62 If the stat() function fails for some reason, question marks are printed instead of the file size.

65 This tests for a regular file. On most UNIX systems, the stat() function will return a valid size for directories. The POSIX standard does not guarantee that this size is valid for directories so this program will print Special and ignore the size.

Also we are using the POSIX defined macro S_ISREG instead of looking at the system-defined bit pattern in st_mode.

67 The format of %7ld and the cast of (long) cause the file size to be printed correctly if st_size is a long or a short.

81 This function gets around a problem with the POSIX standard. There is no way for an application to determine the maximum path length it might encounter. The string returned by getcwd() may be huge. This function allocates space for the name of the current working directory in 256 byte increments. In almost all cases 256 bytes will be enough and the function will return after only one call to getcwd(). In rare cases where more space is required, the program will still work correctly. It is important to write programs that work in the rare cases as well as common cases.

If we were not trying to write portable code, we could know the longest path that a given system might return. This is another case where we have to go the extra mile for portability.

103   This is a case where portability has a cost, at least in development effort. For any specific system, the documentation would tell you how to determine the line speed. The test for a line over 2400 baud would be rather simple using a system specific `ioctl()`. Using `tcgetattr()` and making no assumptions about the values of the `Bxxxx` symbols makes this routine more complex.

It is possible to determine if the terminal is over 2400 baud with slightly less code than I use here to determine the actual baud rate. This routine seems more useful and should be no slower than a less general case.

107   This is a structure that can hold information about a terminal.

109   Get the terminal information for the file associated with **stdout** and store it into structure **t**.

117   The `cfgetospeed()` function extracts a code for the output speed of the terminal from structure **t**.

158   Normal output goes to **stdout**, errors and warnings go to **stderr**.

Here is the main function in **dskuse.c**. It calls the routines that we defined above.

EXAMPLE 2-5. dskuse.c

```
 1 /*
 2  * Main function
 3  */
 4
 5 /* Feature test switches */
 6 #define _POSIX_SOURCE 1
 7
 8 /* System Headers */
 9 #include <dirent.h>
10 #include <errno.h>
11 #include <signal.h>
12 #include <stdio.h>
13 #include <stdlib.h>
14 #include <unistd.h>
15
16 /* Local Headers */
17 #include "panic.h"          /* Defines the PANIC macro */
18
19 /* Macros */
20 #define TRUE    1
21 #define FALSE   0
22 #define SIZE    256
23 /* File scope variables */
24 volatile sig_atomic_t intr_flag = FALSE;
25                           /* Later, set to TRUE if user
26                            * types Control-C
27                            */
28
```

```
29 /* External variables */
30 extern long nbytes;          /* Number of bytes */
31 extern long nfiles;          /* Number of files */
32
33 /* External functions */
34 void print_dir_entry(struct dirent *p);
35 char *cwdname(void);          /* Get working directory name */
36 long baud(void);             /* Get terminal baud rate */
37
38
39 /*
40  * Signal catching functions
41  */
42
43 /* Interrupt key */
44 void intr_key(int signo)
45 {
46
47     intr_flag = TRUE;        /* Set flag for main loop */
48     return;
49 }
50
51
52
53 /*
54  * Main function
55  */
56
57 int main(int argc, char *argv[])
58 {
59 int      fast = FALSE;       /* Set to TRUE if terminal is
60                              * 2400 baud or faster
61                              */
62 struct sigaction sa;         /* Used to establish
63                              * signal handler for
64                              * interrupt key
65                              */
66 DIR      *dirptr;            /* for readdir() */
67 struct dirent *entry;        /* Returned by readdir() */
68 char     *dirname;           /* Current working directory */
69 char     junk[SIZE];         /* Used to read <NL>.  Extra size
70                              * allows user to type junk.
71                              */
72     dirname = cwdname();
73     (void)printf("\nDirectory %s:\n",dirname);
74     dirptr = opendir(dirname);
75     if (dirptr == NULL)
76         {
77         (void)fprintf(stderr,"Can not read directory\n");
78         perror("opendir error");
79         exit(EXIT_FAILURE);
80         }
81     free(dirname);               /* cwdname() allocated space */
82     if (baud() >= 2400) fast = TRUE;
83 /* Cause interrupt key to call intr_key() */
84     sa.sa_handler = intr_key;
85     if (sigemptyset(&sa.sa_mask) != 0) PANIC;
86     sa.sa_flags = 0;
87     if (sigaction(SIGINT,&sa,NULL) != 0) PANIC;
88
89
```

```
 90 /*
 91  * Here is the main loop
 92  */
 93     while((entry = readdir(dirptr)) != NULL)
 94         {
 95         print_dir_entry(entry);
 96         if (intr_flag)
 97             {
 98             (void)printf("\nInterrupted after %d files"
 99                          " and %d bytes\n",nfiles,nbytes);
100             exit(EXIT_SUCCESS);
101             }
102         if(fast && (div(nfiles,24).rem  == 0))
103             {
104             /* Terminal is over 2400 baud and we printed
105              * a multiple of 24 lines. Allow the user to
106              * read the screen
107              */
108             (void)fprintf(stderr,"Type <NL> to continue");
109             (void)fgets(junk,SIZE,stdin);
110             }
111         }
112 /* End of directory */
113     (void)printf("Total of %d bytes in %d files\n",
114                 nbytes, nfiles);
115     exit(EXIT_SUCCESS);
116 }
```

Notes for main:

Line	Note

24   The keyword volatile tells the compiler that this variable may change in ways that can not be predicted by the rules of C. In this case, intr_flag is changed by a signal catching function.

The type sig_atomic_t is defined by Standard C for a signal catching function. The variable intr_flag will all change at one time.

44   The intr_key function merely sets intr_flag to be TRUE. If it attempted to print the message and exit directly, it would be subject to many race conditions. Also, the printf() family of functions is not usable in a signal catching function.

It is best to do as little as possible in signal catching functions. Your programs will be much easier to debug.

81   In this program there would be no problems caused by not calling free(). In general, it is good practice to return storage allocated by malloc() as soon as it is no longer needed.

83   We are using the POSIX signal routines instead of system-specific signals. The POSIX signal mechanism solves a number of problems with the AT&T System V signal() function. The advantages include:

- Support for greater than 32 signals.

- Freedom from many race conditions.

- Enhanced portability. The format of **sa_mask** can change wildly from system to system but functions like **sigemptyset()** allow this program to keep working without change.

87   The third argument to **sigaction()** is a pointer to a place to store the previous action for this signal. In this case, I don't care.

102   The **div()** function returns a structure with 2 members. The notation **div().rem** selects the remainder element of that structure.

This tests to see if the remainder of **nfiles** divided by **24** is equal to zero.

109   This just reads the new line to cause the program to continue. It would be possible for **junk** to be only 2 bytes long (one for the new line and one for the null). Making it longer causes the program to eat anything that may have been types before the new line. If 400 spaces were typed before the new line, the program would not pause on the next call to **fgets()**. This is more of a user error than a program bug.

Portability Lab

To review the contents of this chapter, try to do the following exercises:

1. What information is in the POSIX conformance document? Why would you read one?

2. Why is it better to port an application to POSIX instead of to a specific system?

3. What is the difference between **exit(0)** and **exit(EXIT_SUCCESS)**? When would it make a difference?

4. What symbol must you define to tell the system that you want to use the POSIX symbols?

5. Can you include header files multiple times? Why would you want to?

6. What does it mean if the symbol **__STDC__** has a value other than 1?

7. What is an advantage of breaking a program into several files? What is a disadvantage?

8. Why should you write **(void)printf("Hello, world\n");** instead of **printf("Hello, world\n");**? What does the **(void)** do?

9. What is the maximum buffer size required for **getcwd()**? Is there a symbol you can use for this?

10. What types of messages should go to **stderr**?

11. What is the value of **div(17,3).rem**?

CHAPTER 3

Standard File and Terminal I/O

*The standard I/O library is one of the first things a programmer learns about.
In this chapter, we assume that you are familiar with* printf(), scanf(),
*and friends. We will concentrate on the portability aspects of these functions
and consider how common practices may have portability problems. We will
also look at functions and features that have been added by Standard C and
POSIX.*

Libraries and System Calls

Since we are concerned with source portability, it does not make much difference what
goes on "under the covers" when we call a library function such as printf(). On the
other hand, it is useful to have some understanding of what the system is doing.

Some library functions can do all of their work without ever calling the operating system.
In almost all systems, the math functions like sin() and exp() fall into this category.
Many functions do call the operating system. A single library function might make
several operating system calls. In other cases, you may call a library function many times
before it makes a system call. There are also library functions that map directly onto a
system call.

The point is that you, as an author of portable software, should not care how the library
does its work. On most systems, the malloc() function uses a much more primitive
system service and does most of the work in the library, while the open() function
maps directly to a system service. Your programs should not depend on this division of
labor.

Standard Files

Every program starts out with three open files with which you are probably familiar. The
files are:

stdout   is the standard output file. stdout is normally write-only.[*] It is most often
the user's terminal. Many simple programs can be written that send all of
their output to stdout.

---

[*] This statement is not strictly true. It may be possible to read stdout and stderr or write to stdin. For example,
the more program sends its output to stdout, but uses stderr for both the --MORE-- prompt and reading
commands. Most programs do not need to do this sort of thing.

---

stdin   is the standard input file. `stdin` is normally read-only. It is also often the user's terminal. Many UNIX commands take all of their input from `stdin` and send their output to `stdout`. This is useful for pipelines. The UNIX text processing programs, for example, use standard input and standard output to allow pipelines like:

```
pic file | tbl | eqn | troff | lp
```

stderr   is a file for messages and is normally write-only. In some cases, it is important to have error messages go to someplace different from `stdout`.

Each of the variables `stdin`, `stdout`, and `stderr` points to an object of type `FILE`. The information in this object is for use by the system. A portable application should never directly reference the members of the structures pointed to by these variables.

POSIX does not make any statements about the members of the `FILE` structure. Any program that makes assumptions about the internals of standard I/O is not portable.

Formatted Output

One of the most portable programs you can write is the famous example:

```
printf("hello, world\n");
```

Why? Because all it does is write to standard output, and `printf()` is part of the Standard C library.[*]

You still need to be careful using the `printf()` function. There are portability pitfalls related to the various conversion directives. The list of conversion directives defined by Standard C is:

Directive	Meaning
%c	Convert the `int` argument to `unsigned char` and write the resulting byte in the output file.
%d	Convert the `int` argument to a decimal string of the form `[-]ddddd`.
%e	Convert the double argument to scientific notation in the style `[-]d.ddd edd`.
%E	Convert the double argument to scientific notation in the style `[-]d.ddd Edd`.
%f	Convert the double argument to a string in the style `[-]ddd.dddd`.
%g or %G	Same as `%f` for small numbers and `%e` (or `%E`) for large numbers.
%i	Same as `%d`.

---

[*] There is one portability problem. What happens if the person using the program understands only French or Japanese? Chapter 10 will cover that issue in detail.

Directive	Meaning
%n	The argument is a pointer to an integer into which is written the number of characters output so far. Nothing is written to the output stream by the %n directive.
%o	Convert the `unsigned int` argument to octal.
%p	Convert the argument (assumed to be a pointer) to characters.
%s	Write the argument (assumed to be a pointer to a null-terminated character string) to the output stream.
%u	Convert the `unsigned int` argument to decimal.
%x or %X	Convert the `unsigned int` argument to hex. %x uses the letters `abcdef` while %X uses the letters `ABCDEF`.
%	Outputs a %.

You will notice that most of these directives are found even on non-conforming systems. The %c, %d, %o, %s, %u, and %x options work almost everywhere. The %f, %g, and %e directives work on all systems that support floating point. The %E, %F, and %G, directives are derived from System V and are not supported by BSD. The %i, %n, and %p directives were added by Standard C and are not found on older systems.

Even on systems that conform to the C Standard, some of the directives produce different results depending on whether an `int` is 16- or 32-bits.

The full details of the format conversion specifiers are described in the Functions section of the Reference Manual (see `printf()`).

Examples

Here are some examples of various formats. The first column is the format specification, the second column is the output. (The single quotation marks (') are included in the output column to make it clear where spaces are produced: they are not actually generated by the `printf()` function.)

For a value of zero:

```
%f              '0.000000'
%e              '0.000000e-001'
%E              '0.000000E-001'
%g              '0'
%-20e           '0.000000e-001
%025.20e        '0.00000000000000000000e-001'
```

For a value of Pi:

```
%f              '3.141593'
%e              '3.141593e+000'
%-15.2f         '3.14           '
%010.1f         '00000003.1'
%#010.1f        '00000003.1'
%+10g           '  +3.141593'
%+10e           '+3.141593e+000'
%-20e           '3.141593e+000       '
%025e           '0000000000003.141593e+000'
%025.20e        '3.14159265358979300000e+000'
```

For a value of ULONG_MAX on a machine where int is 16 bits:

```
%d              '-1'
%o              '177777'
%u              '65535'
%x              'ffff'
%X              'FFFF'
%lo             '37777777777'
%lu             '4294967295'
%lX             'FFFFFFFF'
%10d            '        -1'
%10X            '      FFFF'
%#x             '0xffff'
%3d             ' -1'
%3x             'ffff'
%10hX           '      FFFF'
```

For a value of ULONG_MAX on a machine where int is 32 bits:

```
%d              '-1'
%o              '37777777777'
%u              '4294967295'
%x              'ffffffff'
%X              'FFFFFFFF'
```

Pitfalls

When using printf( ), be aware of the following:

- The exact information printed is not tightly specified. Various implementations may produce slightly different results. For example, the %e format must have *at least* two digits of exponent, but may contain more.

- The %d, %i, %o, %u, %x, and %X specifiers assume that the value they are converting has the size of an int. This is machine-specific. If the argument is short, use %hd, %hi, %ho, %hx, or %hX; if the argument is long, use %ld, %li, %lo, %lx, or %lX.

- The implementation is free to do something reasonable for cases such as minus zero, not-a-number, and infinity. The results will vary from system to system.

- On some systems, printf( ) is limited to producing 509 characters on a single call. On other systems, the limit is much larger. In order to avoid hitting the limit, break up large blocks of output into several calls to printf( ).

- As far as the compiler is concerned, `printf` is an ordinary function with a variable number of parameters of indeterminate type. Most compilers will not flag errors such as:

```
double d;
printf("This answer is %s",d);
```

The run-time `printf` function may have no way of knowing it was given a `double` instead of the `char*` expected by the `%s` directive.

Some UNIX systems support a utility called `printfck`, which will check for exactly this type of error. If your development system supports the utility, consult the manual entry for `printfck`.

- Give `printf` only format strings that are safe to print. The correct way to print out a data string is:

```
printf("%s",string);
```

and not:

```
printf(string);
```

which would fail if `string` contained a `%`.[*]

The vfprintf( ), vprintf( ), and vsprintf( ) Functions

Suppose you wanted to write a function that worked just like `printf( )` except that it wrote to two files: How would you do it? This is an important problem. For example, if you want to write a message both to the user's terminal and to a log file, what do you do?

Before Standard C, there were several solutions that have various problems. None of the solutions is very good. Some of the possibilities are:

1. Avoid the problem. Use `sprintf( )` to format a string and pass the string to the function.

2. Pick some maximum number of parameters and write the function like this:

```
errmsg(fmt, a1, a2, a3, a4, a5)
char *fmt;
int a1, a2, a3, a4, a5;
{
        printf(fmt,a1,a2,a3,a4,a5);
        fprintf(log,fmt,a1,a2,a3,a4,a5);
        return;
}
```

If `errmsg( )` is called with fewer than five arguments, this will work and is fairly portable. It will not work if the caller needs to write more than five values.

---

[*] The command "!a%888888f" will crash many versions of csh when it tries to print out an error message.

We also have a problem with some modern compilers. They will optimize the generated code for the number of parameters expected. If we write:

```
errmsg("hello, world\n");
```

it might not work because **a1** to **a5** are missing.

3. We can look at the **FILE** structure and copy the data to another file. This is not portable. As an example of non-portable programming, look at this program fragment that runs under 4.2BSD on a VAX:

```
#include <stdio.h>
. . .
FILE    fake;
char    buffer[132];
. . .
     fake.flag = _IOWRT + _IOSTRG;
     fake.ptr = buffer;
     fake.cnt = 32767;
     _doprnt(format,&args,&fake);
```

This code knows the internals of the **printf()** function. It creates a **struct FILE** and fills it in. It also calls the documented, but highly non-portable, BSD **_doprnt()** function.

Standard C solves this problem with three new functions: the functions **vfprintf()**, **vprintf()**, and **vsprintf()** are identical to **fprintf()**, **printf()**, and **sprintf()** except that they use a pointer to an argument list. This is best seen with an example:

```
#include <stdarg.h>
#include <stdio.h>

/*
 * Write a message to stderr and to a log file
 */
void errmsg(char *fmt, ...)
{
va_list    ap;

    va_start(ap, fmt);          /* Set ap to point to
                                 * the argument list.
                                 */
    vfprintf(stderr, fmt, ap); /* Write the message to
                                 * stderr.
                                 */
    va_end(ap);                 /* Done */

    /* Now, do the same thing except write the message
     * to logfile.
     */
    va_start(ap, fmt);
    vfprintf(logfile, fmt, ap);
    va_end(ap);

    return;                     /* All done. */
}
```

This code declares a function called `errmsg()` with a variable number of arguments. The `vfprintf()` function works just like `printf()` except it writes its data to both `stderr` and `logfile` instead of `stdout`. The call to `va_start()` sets `ap` to point to all of the arguments that follow `fmt`. The `vfprintf()` function then takes `fmt` and the variable number of arguments that follow it and prints them.

This gives you a portable solution to a common problem. It lets you write functions that are called the same way `printf()` is called but do something extra.

Character Output Functions

In addition to the powerful `fprintf()` function, there are five lighter-duty character output functions.

The fputs() and puts() Functions

```
fputs(str,stream);
```

does exactly the same thing as:

```
fprintf(stream,"%s",str);
```

That is, writes the string pointed to by the pointer `str` into the output stream.

The function `puts(str)` writes `str` followed by a newline to the standard output stream and is the same as `fprintf(stdout, "%s\n", str)`.

These functions are extremely portable.

The fputc(), putc(), and putchar() Functions

The `fputc()` function writes a single character to a stream. The `putchar()` function writes a character to the standard output file. Thus, `putchar(ch)` is the same as `fputc(ch,stdout)`.

The function `putc()` is the same as `fputc()`. In some systems, `putc()` is a macro while `fputc()` is a real function. The macro may evaluate its arguments several times. This means that `putc(i,file++)` may not work as desired.

If you avoid cases like `putc(i,file++)`, these functions are also extremely portable.

Reading Lines of Input

Here `fscanf()` reads input from `stream` and analyzes it according to `format` using subsequent arguments as pointers to objects to receive the converted input. The `fscanf()` function is very similar to `fprintf()`, however, not nearly as widely used.

Like `printf()`, some directives are more portable than others. Here is the list defined by Standard C:

Directive	Meaning
%c	Reads a byte—argument should be `char *`.
%d	Reads a sequence of decimal digits—argument should be `int *`.
%e	Reads a floating point number—argument should be `float *`.
%f	Same as %e.
%g	Same as %e.
%i	Reads a sequence of decimal digits—argument should be `int *`.
%n	Store the number of characters read so far into the argument. The argument should be `int *`. This does not read anything from the input stream.
%o	Reads a sequence of octal digits — argument should be `unsigned int *`.
%p	Reads a pointer—argument should be `void *`.
%s	Reads a string of non-white-space characters—argument should be a `char *`.
%u	Reads a sequence of decimal digits — argument should be `unsigned int *`.
%x	Reads a sequence of hex digits—argument should be `unsigned int *`.
[	Reads a set of expected characters—argument should be `char *`.
%	Matches a single %.

The [, %c, %d, %o, %s, and %x, directives work everywhere. The %e and %f work on all systems that support floating point. The %g directive is not supported on BSD.

The %i, %n and %p directives are new to Standard C. They will work on all systems supporting the standard, but not on many older systems.

The full details for format directives are given in the Functions Section under `scanf()`.

Pitfalls

There are a few things to be careful about when you use `fscanf()`. The important ones are:

- A size should always be given on the `%s` specifier. If there is no size specified, bad input could overflow available storage and destroy data. The size should include the `NULL`, which is stored automatically.*

- The popular pattern of `"[A-Za-z]"` will match a string of letters on many systems but is not provided on all systems. Even on systems where it is supported, it may fail on strings like `"ÅLBË"`.

Additional Pitfall

- Remember that `scanf()` stores values into locations specified by *pointers*. To place a value into the variable `var`, use `&var` in the `scanf()` call. Forgetting the `&` is a common mistake that can be very difficult to find.

Other Character Input Functions

There are a few input functions which are less complex than `fscanf()`. In many cases, these functions give better control than `fscanf()`.

The fgetc(), getc() and getchar() Functions

The call `fgetc(stream)` returns the next character from `stream`. If `stream` is at end-of-file, `EOF` is returned.

The `getc()` function is the same as `fgetc()` except it may be implemented as a macro.

The `getchar()` function returns the next character from `stdin`. It requires no arguments.

These functions are very portable. There is only one pitfall: the data must be read into a variable of type `int` and not of type `char`. `EOF` is not a `char` value.

---

*Unchecked `fscanf()` and `gets()` calls have been exploited to break computer security. For details read: D. Seeley, "A Tour of the Worm," Proc. of the 1989 Winter USENIX Technical Conference, pp. 287-304 (January 1989).

The fgets() Function

The call:

```
char *fgets(char *s, int n, FILE *stream);
```

reads up to n-1 characters from stream into the array pointed to by s. A null character is written immediately after the last byte. Reading stops when a newline or end-of-file is encountered. If reading stops because a newline character is read, the newline is stored in the array.

This call is very portable.

The gets() Function

The call:

```
char *gets(char *s);
```

reads characters from stdin into the array pointed to by s.

Unlike fgets(), the gets() function does no limit checking. If the input line is too long for the buffer pointed to by s, the results may be disastrous and are certainly not portable. For this reason, do not use gets(). The scanf() function may be used instead, as in:

```
char  inbuf[82];
int   status;

    status = scanf("%82s",inbuf);
/* Check status for EOF */
/* If (strlen(inbuf) == 81) the input line may
 * have been truncated.
 */
```

☞ The POSIX.2 standard (Shell and Utilities) allows for lines of 2048 bytes. You should be aware that such long lines may exist.

The ungetc() Function

The call:

```
int ungetc(int c, FILE *stream);
```

pushes one character back onto stream. The pushed back characters will be returned by subsequent reads on that stream in the reverse order of their pushing.

Unfortunately, the maximum number of characters we can push back portably is one.

The ungetc() function returns c on success and EOF on failure.

Opening and Closing Files

We have been looking at using the files that the system already opened for us. Almost all interesting programs need to use other files. The `fopen()` function is used to connect a file with a stream:

```
FILE *fopen(const char *path, const char *mode);
```

The argument `path` points to the file we want to open. For example, "`/usr/don/book/ch3`" is the name of the file with this text in it. The next several chapters discuss portable pathnames and files in greater detail.

The argument `mode` points to a string beginning with one of the following:

r   Open file for reading.

w   Create new file for writing. If a file with this name already exists, its contents are lost.

a   Append to existing file or create file if it does not exist.

r+   Open file for update (reading and writing). All existing data is preserved.

w+   Open new file for update (reading and writing). If the file already exists, it is truncated to zero length.

a+   Open or create text file for update. If the file already exists, the first write will add new data after the current end-of-file.

Some systems make a distinction between text files and binary files. While there is no such distinction in POSIX, a `'b'` may be appended to the mode string to indicate binary. The b does not do anything but may be useful for compatibility with non-POSIX systems. If you are creating a binary file, include the b to make your program more portable. Most systems that do not support the b option will just ignore it.

Upon success, the `fopen()` function returns a pointer to a file descriptor. This pointer is used only as an argument to other functions. Do not attempt to manipulate the object it points at. If the open fails, `fopen()` returns a null pointer.

When you are finished with a file, you should close it. The call `fclose(stream)` will complete any pending processing, release system resources, and end access to the file. If there are no errors, `fclose()` returns zero. It returns `EOF` if any errors are detected.

If you fail to close a file, it will be closed automatically when your program completes. There are four reasons for closing the file explicitly:

1.   If there is other processing to be done, you will free up system resources and are less likely to hit some implementation limit.

2.   Buffers are written out in a timely fashion.

3. Closing the file yourself lets you check for errors. It is good practice to report any errors that take place.

4. If your program ends with a call to **_exit( )**, buffers may not be written out.

Direct Input/Output functions

The fwrite( ) and fread( ) Functions

Often, you do not need to format your data for human consumption; you need only to save some information in a file and get it back later. The **fwrite( )** function lets you dump data structures to a file, and the **fread( )** function lets you get them back.

The definition of **fwrite( )** is:

```
size_t fwrite(const void *ptr,
              size_t size,
              size_t nmemb,
              FILE *stream);
```

This is not as complex as it looks. The **fwrite( )** function writes, from the array pointed to by **ptr**, up to nmemb elements whose size is specified by **size**, to the stream pointed to by **stream**. It returns the number of elements written. This will equal nmemb unless a write error occurs.

For example:

```
fwrite(tbl,sizeof(int),(size_t)100,outfile);
```

will write 100 **int** elements from the array **tbl** into **outfile**.

To get the data back, we use the **fread( )** function. The arguments to **fread( )** are exactly the same as **fwrite( )**. The only difference is the direction of transfer.

☞ Programs that use **fwrite( )** and **fread( )** can be completely portable. The data that is written will not always be portable.

In some systems, **fread( )** and **fwrite( )** are very fast. On others, these functions result in repeated calls to **getc( )** and **putc( )**; in this case **printf( )** is faster that **fwrite( )**. In general, use **fread( )/fwrite( )** for binary files and **printf( )**, **fputs( )**, and **fgets( )** for text. This will give you maximum performance and program portability.

File Positioning Functions

So far, we have done all our reading and writing in order. Often, you need to select the place where you are going to read or write. There are several functions that let you select your position.

The fgetpos() and fsetpos() Functions

The call:

```
int fgetpos(FILE *stream, fpos_t *pos);
```

stores the current file position of `stream` in the variable pointed to by `pos`. The value stored is used only by `fsetpos()`. Your program should respect its privacy.

The `fsetpos()` function has the same arguments as `fgetpos()` and is used to restore the file position. This function was introduced by Standard C and is not available on older systems.

The ftell() and fseek() Function

The function `ftell(stream)` returns a `long int` which is the number of characters from the beginning of the file. In case of error, it returns `-1L`.

```
int fseek(FILE *stream, long off, int whence);
```

The previous example sets the position of the file `stream`. The new position is determined by adding `offset` to the position specified by `whence`. The values for `whence` are:

SEEK_SET   Indicates the beginning of the file. This can be used with the value returned by `ftell()` to restore a remembered position.

SEEK_END   Indicates the end of the file.

SEEK_CUR   Indicates the current position.

The `fseek()` function returns nonzero if a request cannot be satisfied.

At this point you may be wondering why we have both the `fgetpos/fsetpos` pair and the `ftell/fseek` pair. Can't we do everything we need with `ftell/fseek`?

The answer is yes; however, `fgetpos/fsetpos` have two potential advantages:

1. Possibility of higher performance on some systems.

2. Ability to support files that have more than LONG_MAX bytes.

If there is no need to do anything other than remember a saved file position, `fgetpos/fsetpos` are a good bet.

The rewind() Function

The function `rewind(stream)` is the same as:

```
(void)fseek(stream, 0L, SEEK_SET);
```

except the error indication for the stream is cleared and no errors are reported.

Managing Buffers

If each call to `fgetc()` were required to read a byte off the disk, programs would run very slowly. Disks are mechanical devices and may take 100,000 times longer to access than main memory. To avoid this penalty, data is transferred from disk to main memory in large hunks. These hunks of data are stored in areas of memory called buffers and functions like `fgetc()` and `fscanf()` get their data from the buffer, accessing the disk only when the buffer is empty.

Functions like `fputc()` and `fprintf()` perform an analogous operation on output.

While the system's defaults for buffering usually work well, the `setvbuf()` function is provided to give the programmer some control over buffering.

The call to `setvbuf()` must be made after the file is opened and before any other operation is performed. The definition of `setvbuf()` is:

```
int setvbuf(FILE *stream, char *buf, int mode,
            size_t size);
```

`stream`   Identifies the I/O stream.

`buf`   Is a pointer to an array to be used as a buffer. If `buf` is the null pointer, `setvbuf()` will allocate a buffer.

`mode`   Must be one of the following macros:

    `_IOFBF`   Causes input/output to be fully buffered. Data will be transmitted only when a buffer is full.

    `_IOLBF`   Causes input/output to be line-buffered. Data will be transferred when a newline character is encountered. This is useful for I/O to terminals.

    `_IONBF`   Causes input/output to be unbuffered. This is useful for terminal and other communications devices where we want something to happen on character sequences that are shorter than a full line.

`size`   Is the size of the buffer.

The `setvbuf()` function advises the system of your program's needs, but does not obligate the system.

The function `setbuf(FILE *stream, char *buf)` is equivalent to `(void)setvbuf(stream,buf,_IOFBF,BUFSIZ)`. The `setbuf()` call is new with Standard C. Of course, the most portable thing to do is to stick to the default buffering provided by the system.

The function `fflush(FILE *stream)` causes any buffered output data for `stream` to be written. The call `fflush(NULL)` causes this action for all open streams.

Sample Program

We will now write a complete example. While the example we have chosen might seem a bit simple-minded, the idea is to show off some of the input/output functions and the logistics of building an application without getting bogged down in complex computation. Here is a brief specification for our program:

1. Accept a filename for an output file from the user.

2. Accept two integers from the user: a lower limit and an upper limit.

3. For each integer between the lower limit and the upper limit, write the integer and its square root to the output file. The output should be nicely formatted text.

The first design question is: How am I going to split the program into reusable modules? One model that many programs can follow is three modules: one module accepts the input, another that does the work, and a third that creates the output.

The basic design becomes:

1. A module to ask the user for a filename as well as a starting and an ending value. These tasks can be performed in `main( )`.

2. A module, `compute_square_root,`* to calculate the square roots.

3. A module, `format_output`, to take the square roots and print them.

Now that we know what the program should do, we can consider how to make portability an element of its basic design. We begin by listing those tasks that require our program to depend upon services provided by the system libraries. Here's a sequential list of those tasks:†

1. Prompt the user for a filename.

2. Accept the filename from the user.

---

* I have a strong preference for descriptive function names. I find the name `compute_square_root` much nicer than say `csqrt` for instance. On some systems, longer names may produce a portability problem. The linker may support only six-character external names. Instead of making my code more obscure for all machines in order to support a brain-damaged linker, I use #define to work around the problem. In this case, I need an include file which contains:

```
#define compute_square_root   CS01
#define format_output         FO01
```

to map my names into something short and portable. This makes debugging harder, so I do my development on a more friendly system.

† Some of the services are provided by the Standard C library, some by the math library, some by the POSIX library, and some by the kernel of the operating system. From a programmer's point of view, there is no need to make a distinction among the various providers of a service. Application modules are written by the programmer and everything else is provided by the system. The C and POSIX standards call the part not provided by the programmer the implementation.

---

3. Create the output file.

4. Write to the output file.

5. Compute square roots.

6. Report and process errors.

7. Return control to the system.

If we use the POSIX-defined functions, we are assured that these functions are portable among POSIX-compliant systems.

What other portability issues might affect the design of this program?

- A target machine may have a 16-bit `int`. Since that would limit us to numbers less than 65,535, we use `long` for integer variables.

- We need to know the maximum length filename that a user might type. Unfortunately, POSIX does not give us this information. We can determine the maximum length of a filename that we are guaranteed to be able to create, but that is not what we need. We define the macro `MAX_NAME` to be the longest path name a user may type. In this example, we set the value to 255, which should cover most cases. An alternate technique is to define a huge limit (e.g., 5000). That change can be made by modifying a single line.

- The program needs to know the language the user understands. Our example assumes that the user understands English. Chapter 10, *Porting to Far-off Lands*, describes methods to allow an application to be portable from culture to culture.

We can now start to write some code. First, accept a filename from the user:

```
(void)printf("What is the name of the output file: ");
(void)fgets(filename,MAX_NAME+1,stdin);
filename[strlen(filename) - 1]= '\0';
outfile = fopen(filename,"w");
```

The `printf()` function prompts the user for a filename. The use of `(void)` in front of the call to `printf()` tells the reader that we are ignoring the value returned by the function. There is not much we can do if messages to the user's terminal fail. Casting the value to be `void` also prevents warnings from `lint`.

The `fgets()` function reads up to `MAX_NAME+1` characters into the array `filename` from the user's keyboard (`stdin`). The newline character is also stored in the array. The next statement discards the newline character. The `fopen()` function opens the file for output and sets `outfile` to the resulting file descriptor. Our program does not place any restrictions (other than total length) on the filename.

We need to prompt the user to supply starting and ending values. Because we do the same thing to get each value, a function can be defined to do this task. We can call the function with:

```
from = get_long("Starting value");
to = get_long("Ending value");
```

We define the get_long() function later.

Next, we write the values and the series of square roots into a file. Again, we will define a function and write the code for it later.

```
compute_square_root(outfile, from, to);
```

Last, we return to the operating system and report our success with:

```
return(EXIT_SUCCESS);
```

The (almost) complete main() program looks like:

```
main()
{
FILE    *outfile;           /* The output file */
char    filename[MAX_NAME];/* Name of the output file */
long    from,to;            /* The limits for the output table */

    (void)printf("What is the name of the output file: ");
    (void)fgets(filename,MAX_NAME,stdin);
    filename[strlen(filename) - 1]= '\0';
    outfile = fopen(filename,"w");

    from = get_long("Starting value");
    to = get_long("Ending value");

    compute_square_root(outfile, from, to);

    return(EXIT_SUCCESS);
}
```

Not bad; however, it would be a good idea to make sure that the fopen() worked correctly, and to report the error if it did not.

```
if (outfile == NULL)
    {
    perror("Cannot open output file");
    exit(EXIT_FAILURE);
    }
```

after the call to fopen(). We should also add:

```
if (fclose(outfile) != 0)
    perror("Error on close");
```

to close the output file and check for errors before returning to the operating system. The perror() function converts the error number stored in errno to an error message. The string given as the argument is written to stderr, followed by a colon and a space. Then, the error message is written followed by a newline. If the system has some non-standard error codes, perror() should correctly convert them to text. Using perror() is more portable than trying to decode the error number in our program.

We left three functions—get_long(), compute_square_root(), and format_output to be defined later. The get_long() function has an argument that is the prompt message. The prompt can be displayed as follows:

```
(void)printf("%s: ",prompt);
```

We can read in the number with a simple call to scanf():

```
scanf("%d",&value);
```

It would be nice , however, to do more error checking and keep asking the question until we get a valid response.

```
while (1)
    {
    (void)printf("%s: ",prompt);
    if (fgets(line, BUFF_MAX, stdin) == NULL)
            exit(EXIT_FAILURE);
    if (sscanf(line,"%d",&value) == 1) return(value);
    (void)printf("Please input an integer\n");
    }
```

The scanf() function scans characters from the user's terminal (stdin). The sscanf() function is very similar except it scans characters from a string; in this case, line. The return value of 1 tells us that exactly one specifier (%d) was matched. By using fgets() to read the data and sscanf() to parse it, we can tell the difference between I/O errors and format errors. The symbol BUFF_MAX is the maximum number of digits the user may type. We define BUFF_MAX after the #include statements at the start of the program.

After adding a few declarations, our function is complete:

```
long get_long(char *prompt)
{
long value;
char line[BUFF_MAX];

    while (1)
        {
        (void)printf("%s: ",prompt);
        if (fgets(line, BUFF_MAX, stdin) == NULL)
                exit(EXIT_FAILURE);
        if (sscanf(line,"%ld",&value) == 1) return(value);
        (void)printf("Please input an integer\n");
        }
}
```

The compute_square_root function must calculate a series of square roots using the sqrt() function in the math library. The sqrt() function returns the square root of its argument. It would be simple enough to write your own square root function. However, using a library function, we get maximum performance without knowing any of the details of the hardware. We construct a simple `for` loop to do the main work of the function:

```
void compute_square_root(FILE *fileid,long start,long stop)
{
long i;
double f;

    for (i=start; i <= stop; i++)
        {
        f = (float)i;
        fprintf(fileid, "%10.0f    %10.6f\n",
            f,sqrt(f));


        }
}
```

We should check for errors when writing to a file, so we revise the `for` loop as follows:

```
    for (i=start; i <= stop; i++)
        {
        f = (float)i;
        if (fprintf(fileid, "%10.0f    %10.6f\n",
            f,sqrt(f)) < 0)
            {
            perror("Error writing output file");
            exit(EXIT_FAILURE);
            }
        }
```

We can write a heading into the file with:

```
    fprintf(fileid,"     N           SQRT(N)\n");
```

We don't actually need the `format_output` function, after all. The `fprintf()` function is powerful enough to do the job. A separate function to format the output would not make the program any clearer or more reusable. We modify our initial idea about how to do the job and as the program takes shape.

It is a problem that we never check for errors when printing the header to the file. Instead of adding more `perror()` statements, we add a new macro, PANIC. The PANIC macro prints an error message and stops. The first `printf()` becomes:

```
    if (fprintf(fileid,"     N           SQRT(N)\n") < 0)
        PANIC;
```

We use the PANIC macro when an error is possible but very unlikely.

The PANIC macro deserves a few comments. It is defined to call an external `panic()` function with two arguments:

__FILE__ Defined by the C compiler as a character string literal containing the name of the program being compiled.

__LINE__ A decimal constant for the current source line number.

The panic() function is defined in panic.c:

```
#define _POSIX_SOURCE 1
#include <stdlib.h>
#include <stdio.h>

void panic(char *filename,int line)
{
        (void)fprintf(stderr,"\n?Panic in line %d of file %s\n"
                        ,line,filename);
        (void)perror("Unexpected library error");
        abort();
}
```

and a typical error message is:

```
?Panic in line 27 of file example.c
Unexpected library error: disk full
```

The message helps the programmer locate the place where the error was detected. It also may give the user some idea of how to get around the problem.

The abort() function causes abnormal program termination. On some systems it may generate information that is useful for debugging, such as a **core** file. POSIX does not specify any debugging facilities, but provides the hooks for vendors to add rich debug environments. The abort() function will stop the application on all POSIX systems.

The last step is to include the required headers. Each library function requires at least one header. The only way to know which headers to include is to look up each function in the Function section of the Reference Manual at the end of this book. After a while, you will learn which headers are required for each function. In this case, we need only two headers: <stdio.h> and <math.h>.

Example 3-1 is a strictly conforming C program and does not need the #define POSIX_SOURCE. I am in the habit of including the #define. If you want to have as many modules as possible depend only on standard C, it would be a good idea to use the #define POSIX_SOURCE statement only on modules that depend on POSIX calls. The Functions section in the Reference Manual tells you which functions are in all standard C implementations and which are only in POSIX systems.

Our complete source is shown in Example 3-1:

EXAMPLE 3-1. sqrt.c

```
#define _POSIX_SOURCE 1
#include <stdio.h>
#include <stdlib.h>
#include <math.h>

#define BUFF_MAX 10
#define MAX_NAME 255
```

```
#define PANIC (panic(__FILE__,__LINE__))
extern void panic();


void compute_square_root(FILE *fileid,long start,long stop)
{
long i;
double f;

    if (fprintf(fileid,"     N          SQRT(N)\n") < 0)
        PANIC;
    for (i=start; i <= stop; i++)
        {
        f = (float)i;
        if (fprintf(fileid, "%10.0f    %10.6f\n",
            f,sqrt(f)) < 0)
            {
            perror("Error writing output file");
            exit(EXIT_FAILURE);
            }
        }
}


long get_long(char *prompt)
{
long value;
char line[BUFF_MAX];

    while (1)
        {
        (void)printf("%s: ",prompt);
        if (fgets(line, BUFF_MAX, stdin) == NULL)
            exit(EXIT_FAILURE);
        if (sscanf(line,"%ld",&value) == 1) return(value);
        (void)printf("Please input an integer\n");
        }
}

main()
{
FILE    *outfile;           /* The output file */
char    filename[MAX_NAME+1];/* Name of the output file */
long    from,to;            /* The limits for the output table */

    (void)printf("What is the name of the output file: ");
    (void)fgets(filename,MAX_NAME+1,stdin);
    filename[strlen(filename) - 1]= '\0';
    outfile = fopen(filename,"w");
    if (outfile == NULL)
        {
        perror("Cannot open output file");
        exit(EXIT_FAILURE);
        }

    from = get_long("Starting value");
    to = get_long("Ending value");

    compute_square_root(outfile, from, to);

    if (fclose(outfile) != 0)
```

```
            perror("Error on close");
        return(EXIT_SUCCESS);
}
```

Portability Lab

To review the contents of this chapter, try to do the following exercises:

1. What will the following program fragment print?

    ```
    short      d=17;

    printf("%07d\n",d);
    printf("%7d\n",d);
    printf("%-7d\n",d);
    ```

    It is **not** considered cheating to try it!

2. When should one use a %hd format specifier? How about %ld? What are the portability problems, if any, with plain %d?

3. If we need to transfer some floating-point data from one machine to another and write it to an ASCII file using the %f format specifier, what are some of the machine-specific things that may show up?

4. What is the difference between fputs() and puts()? What about the difference between fputc() and putc()?

5. What does the fscanf() pattern "[A-Z]" do? Does it work on all computers?

6. What is one of the problems in using the %s specifier in fscanf()?

7. The function gets(buffer) is the same as fgets(buffer,INT_MAX, stdin) with one exception. What is that exception?

8. The gets() function has a weakness that was exploited to invade a major computer network. What is that weakness? When can gets() be safely used?

9. What is the difference between a stream opened with:

    ```
    fopen("foo","w");
    ```

    and one opened with:

    ```
    fopen("foo","wb");
    ```

10. Why is it a good idea to use the fclose() function?

11. What does:

    ```
    fwrite(array,2,100,outfile);
    ```

    do? Assume that array is an array of short int and outfile is a stream open for writing.

12. Improve the fwrite() function call in Exercise 11 to make it more portable.

13. What is a possible advantage of fsetpos() over fseek()?

14. What is the difference between:

    ```
    (void)printf("Help!");
    ```

    and:

    ```
    printf("Help!");
    ```

    Would you expect one to be faster than the other? Why or why not?

15. Modify the square root program given at the end of this chapter to make more use of the PANIC macro. What advantages and disadvantages does the new program have compared to the old one?

CHAPTER 4

Files and Directories

This chapter discusses the portable use of files and directories. We describe the POSIX file system, covering the many things that can be done portably as well as the traps and pitfalls that may be hidden in these operations. The functions described in this chapter perform the operating system services that deal with the creation and removal of files and directories and with the detection and modification of their characteristics. They allow applications to gain access to files for the I/O operations described in the next chapter.

The POSIX file system is based on existing UNIX systems. POSIX defines a common portable interface to files. Applications do not need to know if they are using an AT&T or a BSD file system.

The UNIX "less is better" philosophy imposed a few simple rules on files:

- All input and output is done using files. Disks, tapes, displays, and scientific instruments are all manipulated using the same function calls.

- A file is an ordered sequence of bytes. All meaning is provided by the program that reads or writes the data.

- One type of file is a list of other files; this type of file is called a directory.

While these rules may seem obvious, each one represents a breakthrough. Many systems before and after UNIX have required one set of calls to write to a user's terminal, another set to write to a disk, and yet another set to write to a printer. Other systems distinguish between various types of files and the system gets involved in the job of managing the contents of the file. There are systems with many formats of files and records. While more complex systems may provide "more services" for the programmer, UNIX has a powerful advantage: There is less to learn.

Portable Filenames

For a filename to be portable across systems, it must consist of only the following characters:

```
A B C D E F G H I J K L M N O P Q R S T U V W X Y Z
a b c d e f g h i j k l m n o p q r s t u v w x y z
0 1 2 3 4 5 6 7 8 9 0 . _ -
```

That is, uppercase and lowercase letters, numerals, period, underscore, and hyphen. The hyphen must not be used as the first character of a portable filename. Uppercase and lowercase letters retain their unique identities. For example, `makefile`,

`Makefile`, and `MAKEFILE` name three unique files. Fully portable filenames have 14 or fewer characters.

If the world were simple, all files would be named using portable filenames. In practice, UNIX filenames may contain any character except slash (/) and null. Users may have good reasons for using these characters. If an application is to handle any filename and yet be portable, here are a few guidelines:

- If a program accepts a filename from the user, assume that the filename may contain any combination of characters and may be hundreds of characters long.

- If a program has built-in filenames, use only portable filenames with 14 or fewer characters. Include the name of your program or some other unique text to avoid conflicts. For example, `dirlst.rc` or `scalc.save`.

- Use the `tmpnam()` or `tmpfile()` functions for temporary files.

- POSIX does not reserve any filenames. However, some filenames are used by various systems and should be avoided. These include: `a.out`, `core`, `.profile`, `.history`, and `.cshrc`. Do not read or write any file in the `/etc` directory.

Directory Tree

The file system starts with a master file directory called *root*. The root directory is simply a list of files, some of which may be directories. Each directory, in turn, is simply a list of files, some of which may be directories.

This structure is typically represented as a tree, as shown in Figure 4-1.

The root directory is called `/`. In this case, `/` contains the files `usr`, `lib`, `etc`, `bin`, and `test`. The directory `usr` in the root directory contains two other files, `don` and `sue`.

In order to locate a file, we can start at root and name all of the directories until we get to the target file. This is called the *absolute pathname* of the file. Given the tree above, `/usr/don/book/chapters/4` is the path to the file called 4 at the bottom of the tree. This contains the text for this chapter. The string `/usr/don/book/chapters/` is the *path prefix* and the string 4 is the *filename*. The `/` character is the delimiter used between filenames. The `/` character may not be used in a filename and no other character may be used in its place.

Current Working Directory

Most of the time, an application works with a small set of files that have a common path prefix. For example, it is convenient to be able to specify 4 as a filename rather than the pathname `/usr/don/book/chapters/4`. We can supply a default path prefix to apply whenever a pathname does not begin with a slash. This is called the *current working directory* or sometimes the *working directory*. A *relative pathname* specifies a file or directory in the current working directory.

FIGURE 4-1. Directory tree

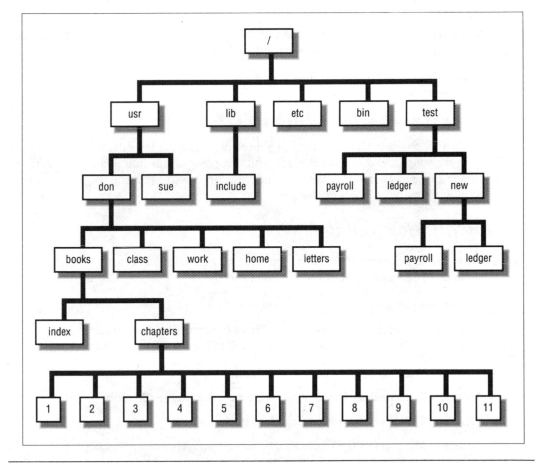

The pathname of the current working directory can be obtained with the `getcwd()` function. It is defined as:

```
char *getcwd(char *buf,size_t size);
```

The argument `buf` is the address of a character array in which to place the absolute pathname of the current working directory. The `size` argument is the maximum number of bytes to be stored in `buf`. If successful, the `buf` argument is returned. If an error occurs, `NULL` is returned.

There is one portability issue: `buf` may need to be huge. There is no way for an application to know how much storage to allocate. A declaration of:

```
char buf[256];
```

or even:

```
char buf[256000];
```

may not be enough. See the `cwdname()` function in Example 2-5 for a way to avoid this problem.

We can select a new working directory with the `chdir()` system service. This is defined by:

```
int chdir(const char *path);
```

where `path` points to the pathname of a directory. The named directory becomes the current working directory. Upon successful completion, this function returns zero. If the `chdir()` function fails, `-1` is returned; `errno` is set to indicate the error, and the current working directory is unchanged.

Making and Removing Directories

You can create a new directory using the `mkdir()` function or remove a directory with the `rmdir()` function. For example, if you specify:

```
int mkdir(const char *path, mode_t mode);
```

a directory with name `path` is created. The file permission bits for the new directory are set from `mode` with the bitwise inclusive OR of one or more of the following flags:

S_IRUSR   The directory owner has read permission.

S_IWUSR   The directory owner may create new files in the directory.

S_IXUSR   The directory may be searched by the owner.

S_IRGRP   Members of the directory owner's group have read permission.

S_IWGRP   Members of the directory owner's group may create new files in the directory.

S_IXGRP   Members of the owner's group may search the directory.

S_IROTH   The world has read permission.

S_IWOTH   Anyone can create new files in the directory.

S_IXOTH   Anyone can search the directory.

For example:

```
mkdir("test", S_IRUSR | S_IWUSR | S_IXUSR);
```

will create the directory `test`, allowing the owner read, write, and search access and granting no other permissions.

Do not set any other bits of the `mode` argument.

The rmdir() Function

You may delete a directory using the `rmdir()` function. It is defined as:

```
int rmdir(const char *path);
```

The directory must be empty and must not be either the current working directory of any process or the root directory.

Simulating the mkdir() and rmdir() Functions

The `mkdir()` and `rmdir()` functions are very portable across POSIX systems but are not available in System V.3. These functions can be simulated on those systems by using the `mkdir` and `rmdir` commands. For example:

```
int mkdir(char *dirname, mode_t mode)
{
int          status;
pid_t     pid;

    pid = fork();      /* Create a new process */
    if (pid < 0) return(-1);

    /* Now have the child execute the mkdir
     * command
     */
    if (pid == 0) execl("/bin/mkdir", dirname);

    wait(&status);     /* Wait for the child */
    if (status != 0) return(-1);
    return(chmod(dirname, mode));
}
```

Although this code may be much slower than the `mkdir()` function on POSIX systems, the speed of creating or removing a directory is generally not an issue.

Directory Structure

Before looking at additional directory operations, we need to understand more about how directories work.

Each file in the file system has a unique *file serial number.*[*] A directory maps character strings into file serial numbers. Many directory entries can point at the same file. This is shown in Figure 4-2.

There are three data files shown here. They have serial numbers 100, 101, and 102. File 100 has three links to it (`file.a`, `file.b`, and `file.c`). All three names refer to the same file and the same data. File 101 has two names (`data.1` and `data.2`). File 102 has only one name (`prog.c`), which is the most common case.

---

[*] "File serial number" is a POSIX term. UNIX systems use the term *i-node number.* The POSIX committee felt that file serial number is a more portable phrase because i-nodes do not need to be used in a conforming file system.

FIGURE 4-2. Directory structure

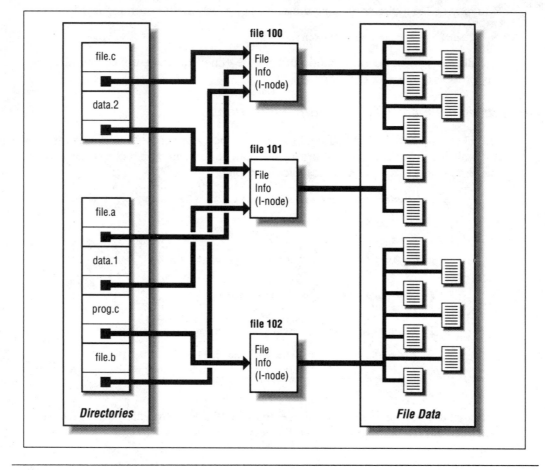

Manipulating Directories

When we create a file, for example with the `fopen()` function, a new file serial number is assigned and a directory entry is created.[*] The pointer from the directory to the i-node is called a link. In this case, there will be exactly one link to the i-node.

---

[*] The POSIX standard deals only with the application's view of the system. This is only one of many possible ways to implement the underlying system. For example, VAX/VMS does not have i-nodes. This does not have any consequences for a POSIX application.

Linking to a File

Additional links to a file may be created with the `link()` function. This function is defined as:

```
int link(const char *path1, const char *path2);
```

where `path1` points to a pathname naming an existing file and `path2` points to a pathname naming the new directory entry to be created. The `link()` function is very portable.

Removing a File

The `unlink()` function removes directory entries. It is defined as:

```
int unlink(const char *path);
```

where `path` points to a pathname to be deleted. When all links to the file have been removed, and no process has the file open, the file is deleted and is no longer accessible.

Standard C defines the `remove()` function to perform the same function as `unlink()`. The ANSI C Committee felt the name remove was less system-specific than unlink.

Renaming a File

A file's path may be changed with the `rename()` function. This is defined as:

```
int rename(const char *oldpath, const char *newpath);
```

The effect of `rename()` is to create a new link to an existing file and then delete the existing link. If both `oldpath` and `newpath` refer to the same file, `rename()` does not change the file system.

It is very safe and portable to rename a file. For example, `rename("Julie", "Jenny")` or `rename("/usr/don/old", "/usr/don/new")`. Renaming a directory is also portable: `rename("/usr/phred", "/usr/fred")`. However, renaming a file across directories is not.

The call `rename("/usr/don/file", "/usr/sue/file")` may not work under all conditions. You cannot rename a file from one file system to another. If your application must be able to move a file from one directory to another, it should be prepared to copy the file if the `rename()` function fails.

File Characteristics

The file system maintains useful information about each file. For example, it maintains the time and date the file was last written and the size of the file in bytes.

The system also maintains the file's file mode, as shown in Figure 4-3.

FIGURE 4-3. File mode

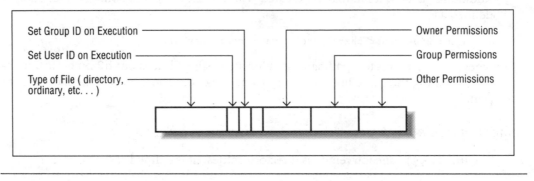

Each of the permission fields is a three-bit group that defines execute, read, and write permissions, as shown in Figure 4-4.

FIGURE 4-4. Read, write, and execute permission bits

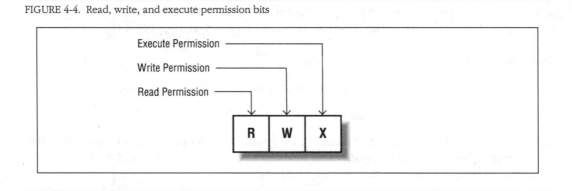

Of course, POSIX does not specify that the bits will be in this order. Instead, there are symbols defined for the bits and fields. These symbols are:

S_IRWXU   Read, Write, and Execute bits for the file owner.

S_IRWXG   Read, Write, and Execute bits for the file owner's group.

S_IRWXO   Read, Write, and Execute bits for others.

S_ISUID   Set user ID on execution. When this program is run, the effective user ID will be the same as the owner of the file.

S_ISGID   Set group ID on execution. When this program is run, the effective group ID will be the same as the owner of the file.

There are symbols for all nine of the permission bits. The symbols use this pattern:

$$\text{S\_I} \begin{bmatrix} R \\ W \\ X \end{bmatrix} \begin{bmatrix} U\ S\ R \\ G\ R\ P \\ O\ T\ H \end{bmatrix}$$

Therefore, the symbol for the Read permission for the group class would be `S_IRGRP` and the Execute permission for the owner is `S_IXUSR`.

POSIX does not define the file-type bits. Instead, it defines macros to test for a specific type of file. These macros are:

S_ISDIR(m)   Test for directory.

S_ISCHR(m)   Test for character-special file.

S_ISBLK(m)   Test for block-special file.

S_ISREG(m)   Test for a regular file.

S_ISFIFO(m)   Test for a FIFO.

The argument to the macro, *m*, is the file mode. The macro evaluates to non-zero if the test is true and to zero if the test is false. These macros are POSIX inventions. Traditional UNIX systems have defined the absolute octal values for the mode word. For example, System V.2 defines:

0170000	File type
0010000	FIFO
0020000	Character-special file
0040000	Directory
0060000	Block-special file
0100000	Ordinary file
0000000	Ordinary file

Your program will be most portable if you use the POSIX macros. If you need to, you can define them for older systems.

Retrieving a File's Characteristics

A file's characteristics may be retrieved using the stat() function. This function fills in a struct known as the stat structure. The stat structure contains the following members:

Member Name	Member Type	Description
st_mode	mod_t	File mode, as described above.
st_ino	ino_t	File serial number.
st_dev	dev_t	ID of device containing this file. The st_dev/st_ino pair uniquely identify a file.
st_nlink	nlink_t	Number of links.
st_uid	uid_t	User ID of file's owner.
st_gid	gid_t	Group ID of file's group.
st_size	off_t	File size in bytes. This is defined only for regular files.
st_atime	time_t	Time of last access.
st_ctime	time_t	Time of status last change, for example, changing the permission bits.
st_mtime	time_t	Time of last data modification of the file.

The stat structure is defined in the header file <sys/stat.h>.

The various data types (dev_t, ino_t, uid_t, etc.) are defined in the header file <sys/types.h>. These types are defined because the POSIX committee decided to provide maximum flexibility instead of selecting a common data type.* This means that the size of ino_t or uid_t changes from system to system. Do not assume that they are of a given size or that they are small. But you can assume they are arithmetic (including floating point).

The stat() function itself is defined as:

```
int stat(const char *path, struct stat *buf);
```

The first argument is a pointer to a pathname. The second argument is a pointer to a buffer in which to store the status information.

The stat() function is very portable. Most of the information returned is also portable. The st_dev and st_ino members should be used with care. It is portable to compare

---

* In fairness to the POSIX committee, they worked hard to increase consensus. The goal was not to make a selection by narrow majority but instead to build a broad coalition. These types are defined to increase portability and compatibility with existing programs.

these fields to see if two names refer to the same file. Do not make any other assumptions about these numbers.

Changing File Accessibility

It is possible to change a file's permission bits using the chmod() function. This is defined as:

```
int chmod(const char *path,mode_t mode);
```

The path argument points at the name of a file and the mode argument contains the new permission bits. Do not set bits other than the permission bits, S_ISGID or S_ISUID.* In some implementations, setting additional bits changes the entire meaning of the call.

The chmod() function is very portable. You can make your code portable to older UNIX systems by defining the permission bits you need with something like:

```
#include <sys/stat.h>
#ifndef  S_IRUSR
#define  S_IRUSR 0400
#endif
#ifndef  S_IWUSR
#define  S_IWUSR 0200
#endif
#ifndef  S_IXUSR
#define  S_IXUSR 0100
#endif
      . . .
     chmod(myfile,S_IRUSR|S_IWUSR|S_IXUSR);
```

The ifndefs will prevent you from changing any values defined in a POSIX header while providing portability to pre-POSIX systems.

Changing the Owner of a File

The owner of a file may be changed with the chown() function. This is defined as:

```
int chown(const char *path,uid_t owner,gid_t group);
```

where the path argument points at the pathname of an existing file. The user ID and group ID are set to the values in owner and group.

There is a historical problem with the chown() function. UNIX System V allows a user to give away files; that is, the owner of a file may change the user ID to anything. This presents a security problem in some environments. Berkeley UNIX restricts chown() to the superuser.

---

* Attempt to modify S_ISGID or S_ISUID only for ordinary files. In particular, never use chmod() in a way that would affect the S_ISGID bit on a directory.

The POSIX committee left the actual operation of chown() as an implementation option indicated by the symbolic constant _POSIX_CHOWN_RESTRICTED. If chown() is restricted for a particular file:

- The owner may be changed only by a privileged process (most likely not yours).

- The group may be changed, if and only if owner is equal to the file's user ID and group is equal to either the calling process's effective ID or one of its supplementary group IDs.

A program may determine if chown() is restricted by looking at the variable _POSIX_CHOWN_RESTRICTED in the header file <unistd.h>. It has three possible states:

- Defined to have the value −1. In this case, no files have chown() restricted.

- Defined to have a value other than −1. In this case, all files have chown() restricted.

- Not defined in <unistd.h>. In this case, the pathconf() or fpathconf() function must be used because chown() restrictions may depend on the directory. See Chapter 7, *Obtaining Information at Run–time*, for details.

Of course, you can ignore all of the rules about _POSIX_CHOWN_RESTRICTED and just try it. If if works, you can do it. If it fails with errno set to EPERM, you can't. For example:

```
if (chown("file",newuser,newgroup) != 0)
    {
    if (errno == EPERM)
        printf("Sorry, chown is restricted\n");
    else
        {
        perror("unexpected chown failure");
        exit(EXIT_FAILURE);
        }
    }
```

The only completely portable use for chown() is to change the group of a file to the effective group ID of the caller or to a member of its group set.

As a security precaution, the S_ISUID and S_ISGID bits of the file mode are cleared upon successful return from chown(). If this were not done, a user could give away a file and assume the identity of the new owner.

Setting File Access and Modification Times

The utime() function is used to update the access time and modification time of a file. This is defined as:

```
int utime(const char *path, const struct utimbuf *tm);
```

Here, `path` points to a pathname for an existing file. The `tm` argument is either `NULL` or a pointer to a `utimbuf` structure. If the `tm` argument is `NULL`, the access and modification times are set to the current time.

If the `tm` argument is not `NULL`, it is assumed to be a pointer to a `utimbuf` structure. This contains the following members:

`actime`   Access time

`modtime`   Modification time

Both members have type `time_t`.

System V did not provide a `<utime.h>`. Instead, it said that `utimbuf` must be defined as:

```
struct utimbuf
{
time_t actime;
time_t modtime;
};
```

You may have to supply a `<utime.h>` with that definition if you port your POSIX code to older System V systems.

Reading Directories

A traditional portability problem in UNIX has been knowledge of the format of directories. A program would open a directory and read the information directly. There is a great deal of UNIX software that "knows" that a directory contains a 2-byte i-node number followed by a 14-byte filename. While true for AT&T System V.2, it is far from universal.

To solve this problem, POSIX adapted from BSD several functions for performing operations on directories. These functions allow a program to obtain directory entries without defining the format of the directory file. In fact, the internal format of directories is completely unspecified.

The header file `<dirent.h>` defines a structure that is used to obtain filenames from a directory, the `struct dirent`, that includes one member `d_name`, an array of `char` that may be up to `NAME_MAX` bytes long. All other information in the `dirent` structure should be ignored for portability.

The opendir() Function

The opendir() function is defined as:

```
DIR *opendir(const char *dirname)
```

and returns a *directory stream* that has type DIR. The dirname argument is the name of the directory file to open and it must be a directory.

If the opendir() function fails, NULL is returned and errno is set to indicate the error.

The readdir() Function

The readdir() function is defined as:

```
struct dirent *readdir(DIR *dirp);
```

and returns a pointer to a dirent structure. The only argument is dirp, the pointer returned by opendir().

In case of an error, readdir() returns NULL and errno is set to indicate the error. When the end of the directory is encountered, readdir() also returns NULL; however, errno is unchanged.

The closedir() Function

The closedir() function is defined as:

```
int closedir(DIR *dirp)
```

and is used to indicate that we are done reading a directory. Upon successful completion, closedir() returns a value of zero. On error, a value of −1 is returned and errno is set to indicate the error.

The rewinddir() Function

The rewinddir() function is defined as:

```
void rewinddir(DIR *dirp);
```

and resets the position of the directory stream indicated by dirp to the beginning of the directory. No value is returned.

General Comments

Files may be added to or removed from a directory at any time. The readdir() function may or may not see changes to a directory made after the opendir() (or rewinddir()) function is called.

POSIX is also vague on the interaction between `opendir()` and `fork()`. For best results, do not perform a `fork()` while reading a directory.

Complete Example

To demonstrate the use of the functions for reading directories, let's write a program to print out a directory tree. Here is a brief specification for the program:

1. Prompt the user and accept the name of a starting directory.

2. Print the name of the starting directory.

3. Read the directory and ignore everything except directories.

4. Print the names of any directories encountered along with any directories that they contain.

5. Indent each level of directory two spaces. This will make it easy to see what is contained in each directory. The output should look something like this:

```
Starting directory: /etc
  log
  zoneinfo
    Australia
    Canada
    Mideast
    SystemV
    US
  yp
  master.d
  boot.d
  init.d
  startup.d
    fwdicp.d
  install.d
    boot.d
    init.d
    master.d
    startup.d
      fwdicp.d
  uninstall.d
  eschatology
  bind
    master
    tools
    doc
      BOG
```

Where `/etc` was given as the starting directory and `/etc/bind/doc/BOG` a nested subdirectory.

An obvious structure suggests itself: one routine to process one directory and another routine to call it for each directory encountered. The flowchart for the main program is shown in Figure 4-5.

FIGURE 4-5. Flowchart for main()

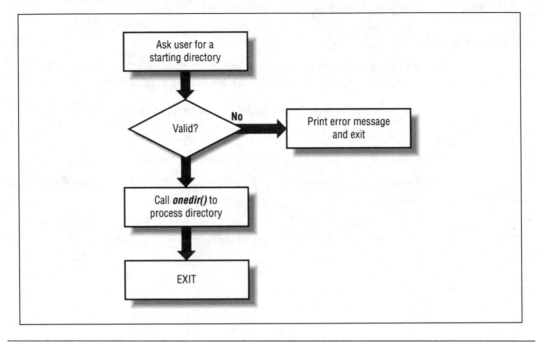

The onedir() function is recursive. Each time it encounters a directory, onedir() calls itself. The flowchart for the onedir() function is shown in Figure 4-6.

Let's start by writing the function to process a single directory, as shown in Example 4-1.

EXAMPLE 4-1. onedir()

```
 1 /*
 2  * This function will process 1 directory. It is called with
 3  * two arguments:
 4  *   indent -- The number of columns to indent this directory
 5  *   name -- The file name of the directory to process.  This
 6  *           is most often a relative directory
 7  *
 8  * The onedir function calls itself to process nested
 9  * directories
10  */
11 void onedir(short indent,char *name)
12 {
13 DIR     *current_directory;          /* pointer for readdir */
14 struct dirent *this_entry;           /* current directory entry */
15 struct stat status;                  /* for the stat() function */
16 char cwd[MAX_PATH+1];                 /* save current working
17                                       * directory
18                                       */
19 int i;                               /* temp */
20
```

FIGURE 4-6. Flowchart for onedir()

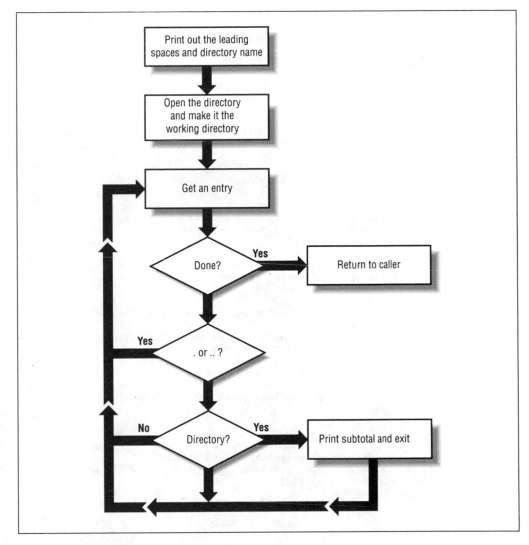

```
21      /*
22       * Print out the name of the current directory with
23       * leading spaces.
24       */
25      for (i=1; i <= indent; i++) (void)printf(" ");
26      (void)printf("%s\n",name);
27
28      /* Now open the directory for reading */
29      current_directory = opendir(name);
30      if (current_directory == NULL)
```

```
31                {
32                (void)perror("Can not open directory");
33                return;
34                }
35        /* Remember the current working directory and connect to
36         * new directory.  We will then be able to stat() the
37         * files without building a prefix.
38         */
39        if (getcwd(cwd,MAX_PATH+1) == NULL) PANIC;
40        if (chdir(name) != 0) PANIC;
41
42
43
44
45
46
47
48
49
50        /* Now, look at every entry in the directory */
51        while ((this_entry = readdir(current_directory))
52                      != NULL)
53             {
54             /* Ignore "." and ".." or we will get confused */
55             if ((strcmp(this_entry->d_name,".") != 0) &&
56                 (strcmp(this_entry->d_name,"..") != 0))
57                 {
58                 if (stat(this_entry->d_name,&status) != 0)
59                        PANIC;
60                 /* Ignore anything that is not a directory */
61                 if (S_ISDIR(status.st_mode))
62                     {
63                     /* If this is a nested directory,
64                      * process it */
65                     onedir(indent+2,this_entry->d_name);
66                     }
67                 }
68             }
69        /* All done.  Close the directory */
70        if (closedir(current_directory) != 0) PANIC;
71        /* change back to the "previous" directory */
72        if (chdir(cwd) != 0) PANIC;
73        return;
74 }
```

Notes for onedir:

Line   Note

51   This block will be executed for each file in the directory.

54   Programs must not assume that "." and ".." exist or are first. This example works
      correctly. A program that discards the first two directories returned by
      readdir() is not portable.

59   It would be nice to provide some error recovery here. We could print a message
      and continue.

65   This is the recursive call. Each level will indent by an additional two spaces.

There is only one strange thing here. We want to read a string from the user that may be up to MAX_PATH characters long. We cannot just write a call to scanf() using MAX_PATH. That is:

```
(void)scanf("%<MAX_PATH>s",root)
```

will not work. We have to build the correct string at run time. We could also use fgets(root,MAX_PATH,stdin) to read the filename, but then we would need to remove the newline from the end of the buffer.

The complete program with all the required headers is shown in Example 4-2.

EXAMPLE 4-2. direct.c

```
/*
 * Include all of the required headers
 */
#define _POSIX_SOURCE 1
#include <stdio.h>
#include <sys/types.h>
#include <dirent.h>
#include <sys/stat.h>
#include <limits.h>
#include <stdlib.h>
#include <string.h>
#include "panic.h"          /* Defines the PANIC macro */
                            /* See Page 58 for a description of PANIC */

#define MAX_PATH    256
/*
 * This function will process 1 directory. It is called with
 * two arguments:
 *   indent -- The number of columns to indent this directory
 *   name -- The file name of the directory to process.  This
 *           is most often a relative directory
 *
 * The onedir function calls itself to process nested
 * directories
 */
void onedir(short indent, char *name)
{
DIR     *current_directory;     /* pointer for readdir */
struct dirent *this_entry;      /* current directory entry */
struct stat status;             /* for the stat() function */
char cwd[MAX_PATH+1];           /* save current working
                                 * directory
                                 */
int i;                          /* temp */

    /*
     * Print out the name of the current directory with
     * leading spaces.
     */
    for (i=1; i <= indent; i++) (void)printf(" ");
    (void)printf("%s\n",name);

    /* Now open the directory for reading */
    current_directory = opendir(name);
    if (current_directory == NULL)
```

```
                  {
                  (void)perror("Can not open directory");
                  return;
                  }
          /* Remember the current working directory and connect to
           * new directory.  We will then be able to stat() the
           * files without building a prefix.
           */
          if (getcwd(cwd,MAX_PATH+1) == NULL) PANIC;
          if (chdir(name) != 0) PANIC;

          /* Now, look at every entry in the directory */
          while ((this_entry = readdir(current_directory))
                          != NULL)
              {
              /* Ignore "." and ".." or we will get confused */
              if ((strcmp(this_entry->d_name,".") != 0) &&
                  (strcmp(this_entry->d_name,"..") != 0))
                      {
                      if (stat(this_entry->d_name,&status) != 0)
                              PANIC;
                      /* Ignore anything that is not a directory */
                      if (S_ISDIR(status.st_mode))
                              {
                              /* If this is a nested directory,
                               * process it */
                              onedir(indent+2,this_entry->d_name);
                              }
                      }
              }
          /* All done.  Close the directory */
          if (closedir(current_directory) != 0) PANIC;
          /* change back to the "previous" directory */
          if (chdir(cwd) != 0) PANIC;
          return;
      }

  int main()
  {
  char root[MAX_PATH+1];           /* array to store the pathname of
                                    * the starting directory
                                    */
  char scanf_string[20];           /* used to hold a format string
                                    * for scanf
                                    */
  struct stat root_status;         /* stat structure for starting
                                    * directory
                                    */

      /* Build a format string for scanf that looks like
       * %<MAX_PATH>s.
       */
      (void)sprintf(scanf_string,"%%%ds",MAX_PATH);
      (void)printf("Starting directory: ");
      /* Read the name of the starting directory which
       * may be up to MAX_PATH bytes long
       */
      (void)scanf(scanf_string,root);
```

```
              /* Verify that it is an existing directory file */
              if (stat(root,&root_status) != 0)
                  {
                  (void)perror("Can not access starting directory");
                  (void)exit(EXIT_FAILURE);
                  }
              if (S_ISDIR(root_status.st_mode) == 0)
                  {
                  (void)fprintf(stderr,"%s is not a directory\n",root);
                  (void)exit(EXIT_FAILURE);
                  }

              /* If all is well, list the directory */
              onedir(0,root);
              return(0);
          }
```

Pitfall: Symbolic Links

There is a feature of some UNIX systems called *symbolic links*. A symbolic link is a special type of file that points to another file. For example, a link from `file` to `/usr/opt/lib/X11/realfile` links the name `file` to the file `/usr/opt/lib/X11/realfile`. When we open `file`, we will get `realfile` instead. That is what the user usually wants.

Although symbolic links originated in BSD, many vendors have now included them in AT&T ports. POSIX does not support symbolic links and you should not have to concern yourself with them. Unfortunately, symbolic links may confound your program.

There are several operations which can cause problems. For example, deleting `file` will delete the link but will leave `/usr/opt/lib/X11/realfile` unaffected, which may or may not be OK.

The real problem comes when the symbolic link is to a directory. If there is a symbolic link in the directory `/usr/don/test` of the form:

```
    loop -> /usr/don
```

the program in Example 4-2 will crash and burn.

Each time `readdir()` returns `loop`, the `onedir()` routine will try to process it. The loop will continue until some system limit is encountered.

There is no good way to defend against symbolic links. There is no portable way for a POSIX-conforming program to test for symbolic links. The POSIX.1 committee is adding symbolic links to a future version of the standard; these changes may be approved in 1992. About the only thing we can do in the mean time is to warn users of our software that if they use (abuse?) symbolic links, they may cause applications to fail.

Of course, the fact that no POSIX-conforming application will ever create a symbolic link does not help much.

Portability Lab

To review the contents of this chapter, try to do the following exercises:

1. Write a function to accept the name of a directory and to make it the current working directory. Print the full pathname of both the old and the new working directories.

2. Write a program that keeps creating directories called dir until some error occurs. The result should be /dir/dir/dir/dir/dir/dir/dir/dir... as far as your system will let you go.

   NOTE: Some systems may fail in unfortunate ways. Use caution when attempting this.

3. Write a program to delete the directories created in exercise 2.

4. Why would a program need to know a file's i-node number (ST_INO)?

5. Why would it be useful to have multiple directory entries (links) for the same file?

6. When does the unlink() function delete a file? Is there any portable way to know that the file is really gone?

7. Name one piece of information contained in a file's mode word.

8. What does the symbol S_IXUSR mean?

9. Why do you think that POSIX defined S_ISDIR as a macro instead of a value?

10. Is sizeof(ino_t) always less than or equal to sizeof(int)? Is sizeof(ino_t) always less than or equal to sizeof(long)?

11. How can chown() be used to break system security? What is the only completely portable use for the chown() function?

12. Why might a program use the utime() function?

13. Write a program to display a file without changing its access time. Is there any way to detect that the file has been read?

14. Does the dirent structure contain any members other than d_name? If so, what are they?

15. Modify the onedir() function given at the end of this chapter to print the file serial number of each directory.

16. The onedir() function ignores the files ".". and "..". Why does it do this? What would happen if that check were removed?

17. Modify the main() function in Example 4-2 to use fgets() instead of scanf(). Is this an improvement?

18. Invent a scheme to allow symbolic links to be transparent to strictly conforming POSIX 1003.1-1988 applications. Mail your solution to the author for a cash reward.

CHAPTER 5

Advanced File Operations

This chapter covers the basic POSIX systems calls such as read ( ), write ( ), open ( ), *and* close ( ). *You might think that since these calls are some of the most basic building blocks of the system, and since there is so much existing practice to look at, that there would be few portability issues. Surprise! These routines have many more pitfalls than the higher-level routines that use them.*

When the C programming language was invented, it was designed to work with the UNIX operating system. The original scheme had a C language library that made calls on the operating system using system calls. The scheme is represented in Figure 5-1.

FIGURE 5-1. Traditional UNIX software layers

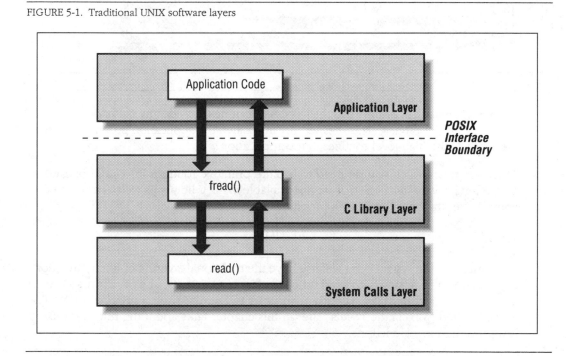

The "high-level" routines such as printf ( ) and fread ( ) would call more primitive "low-level" system calls.

In a traditional implementation, the system calls were more efficient than the library, so some programmers avoided using high-level calls. Today, there is no reason for this practice because many systems provide very high-performance libraries. For maximum portability, the high-level routines are your best bet.

The Standard C and POSIX interfaces do not require a layered implementation. It is quite possible to provide an alternate implementation, as shown in Figure 5-2.

FIGURE 5-2. Possible POSIX software layers

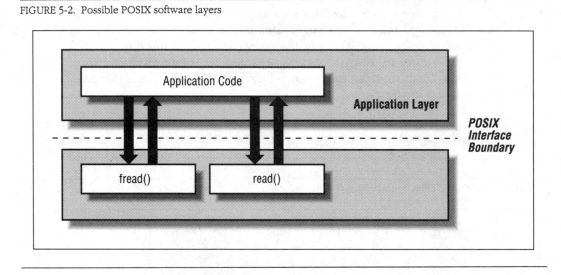

There is no reason to assume that the low-level routines provide any better performance than the high-level ones. This is especially true when the application programmer does the work of the high-level routines in the application.

There are times when you do need to use the primitive routines in your applications: they often provide functions that are not available in the C library as well as more precise control over the behavior of your program.

CAUTION

Since many of the systems you will use have the traditional layering of library functions and system calls, mixing high-level functions (`fprintf()`, `fgets()`, `fputs()`, etc.) and the low-level functions (`read()`, `write()`, `lseek()`, etc.) requires care. The section called "Mixing the Levels" later in this chapter talks about the rules for mixing low- and high-level functions.

Primitive File Operations

The primitive (or low-level) file operations can be thought of as the building blocks for more complex functions, such as `fprintf()` and `fscanf()`.

File Descriptors

The primitive file operations all operate on *file descriptors*. A file descriptor is a small, non-negative integer used to identify an open file. File descriptors are assigned in order (0, 1, 2, 3, ...) on a per-process basis. The number of open file descriptors is limited; however, the limit is 16 or larger. The exact number is given by the symbol OPEN_MAX in the header file <limits.h>.

Opening a file

The connection between a file descriptor and a file is established by the open() and creat() functions. The open() function is used to assign a file descriptor for a new or existing file. The function is defined as:

```
int open(const char *path, int oflag, ...);
```

The ... indicates an unspecified number of additional arguments. It allows for an optional third argument, a mode_t called mode that can be used to set the file permission bits when a file is created.

The path argument is a string that names the file to be opened. It can be either an absolute path (starting with a /) or a relative path.

The oflag argument is the bitwise inclusive OR of the values of symbolic constants. The programmer must specify exactly one of the following three symbols:

O_RDONLY	Open for reading only.
O_WRONLY	Open for writing only.
O_RDWR	Open for reading and writing.

Any combination of the following symbols can also be used:

O_APPEND	Set the file offset to the end-of-file prior to each write.
O_CREAT	If the file does not exist, allow it to be created. This flag indicates that the mode argument is present in the call to open().
O_EXCL	This flag may be used only if O_CREAT is also set. It causes the call to open() to fail if the file already exists.
O_NOCTTY	If path identifies a terminal, this flag prevents that terminal from becoming the controlling terminal for this process. It prevents an application from unintentionally acquiring a controlling terminal as a side-effect of open(). It is always safe to set this flag for data files. O_NOCTTY has no effect if the file being opened is not a terminal. See Chapter 8 for a description of terminal I/O.

O_NONBLOCK   Do not wait for the device or file to be ready or available. After the file is open, the `read()` and `write()` calls always return immediately. If the process would be delayed in the read or write operation, `-1` is returned and `errno` is set to `EAGAIN` instead of blocking the caller.

System V provides a flag called O_NDELAY that is similar to O_NONBLOCK. The O_NDELAY flag causes `read()` or `write()` to return zero instead of blocking. Since `read()` also returns zero on end-of-file, it is difficult to distinguish the two cases. BSD also has an O_NDELAY flag that causes the error EWOULDBLOCK to be returned if the process would block. POSIX resolved this incompatibility by inventing the O_NONBLOCK flag. Port with care!

O_TRUNC   This flag should be used only on ordinary files opened for writing. It causes the file to be truncated to zero length.

Traditional UNIX systems used the values 0, 1, and 2 for O_RDONLY, O_WRONLY, and O_RDWR. These values should be changed to macros. To allow your code to continue to work on old systems, include the following:

```
#ifndef O_RDONLY
#define O_RDONLY 0
#endif
#ifndef O_WRONLY
#define O_WRONLY 1
#endif
#ifndef O_RDWR
#define O_RDWR   2
#endif
```

The call:

```
creat(path,mode);
```

is equivalent to:

```
open(path, O_WRONLY | O_CREAT | O_TRUNC, mode);
```

and has the same portability issues.

Reading from a File

The only low-level function for reading from a file is the `read()` function. It is defined as:*

```
ssize_t read(int fildes, void *buf, size_t nbyte);
```

and reads `nbyte` bytes from the file open on `fildes` into buffer `buf`. The `read()` function returns the number of bytes placed in the buffer. This value will never be greater than `nbyte`. The value will be smaller than `nbyte` if the file has fewer bytes immediately available for reading. If there is an error, a value of `–1` is returned and `errno` is set.

That seems easy enough. What portability problems can it have? Here are a few:

- The standard does not specify exactly what happens on an error. It is almost impossible to do portable error recovery if `read()` returns `EIO`.

- Section 6.4.1.2 of POSIX states, "If a `read()` is interrupted by a signal after it has successfully read some data, either it shall return `–1` with `errno` set to `EINTR`, or it shall return the number of bytes read." Therefore, applications must treat `EINTR` as a fatal error because they cannot tell if any data were lost.

  The U.S. Government (in FIPS 151-1) requires that `read()` return the number of bytes read. Since the Federal Government is the world's largest buyer of POSIX systems, it is a good bet that most POSIX systems will return the number of bytes read.

- The `nbyte` argument has type `size_t` in IEEE Std 1003.1-1990, but has type `unsigned int` in the 1988 standard and in most UNIX systems. It was changed because the largest block that can be read in a single call is `UINT_MAX` bytes (65,535 on 16-bit systems). Programs that need to operate using both the 1988 and 1990 standard should limit reads to 65,535 or fewer bytes.

Writing to a File

The `write()` function writes to a file. This is defined as:

```
ssize_t write(int fildes, const void *buf, size_t nbyte);
```

and attempts to write `nbyte` bytes from the buffer pointed to by `buf` to the file open on `fildes`. The `write()` function returns the number of bytes written to the file. This may be less than `nbyte` if an error occurred during the write operation. If an error

---

* The definition of `read()` uses two POSIX types: `ssize_t` and `size_t`. There are `typdefs` for these in `<sys/types.h>`. A `size_t` is a type that can hold a number of bytes, for example, `unsigned long`. A `ssize_t` is a signed `size_t` and is used because `read()` returns `–1` if there is an error. Unfortunately, this is one of the conflicts between IEEE Std 1003.1-1990 and IEEE Std 1003.1-1988. The 1988 standard defines `read()` as:

```
int read(int fildes, char *buf, unsigned int nbyte);
```

condition prevented any bytes from being written, -1 is returned and errno is set to indicate the error.

The write() function has the same portability issues as read().

Fast File Copy Example

At this point, it is helpful to look at a simple example showing the use of read() and write(). The following simple file copy program asks for an input path and an output path and then copies the input to the output. We assume that both input and output files are ordinary files. To make our copy program fast, the file is read in one large hunk and then written out.

The program that fills the bill is shown in Example 5-1.

EXAMPLE 5-1. ffcopy.c

```
#define _POSIX_SOURCE 1

#include <unistd.h>
#include <stdio.h>
#include <limits.h>
#include <sys/types.h>
#include <stdlib.h>
#include <sys/stat.h>
#include <fcntl.h>
#include "panic.h"              /* Defines the PANIC macro */

#define HUNK_MAX INT_MAX
#define MAX_PATH 2048           /* It would be nice if POSIX
                                 * provided some way to determine
                                 * the longest path name a user
                                 * may need to type.  Since there
                                 * is no way to get that number,
                                 * I am picking something large.
                                 */

int main()
{
char ifpath[MAX_PATH+1];        /* name of input file */
char ofpath[MAX_PATH+1];        /* name of output file */
char scanf_string[10];          /* argument string for
                                    scanf() */

struct stat ifstat;             /* result of stat() call */
char *bigbuf;                   /* pointer to buffer */
int ifdes,ofdes;                /* input/output file
                                    descriptors */

size_t hunk;                    /* number of bytes to
                                    transfer in one piece */

size_t left;                    /* number of bytes left to
                                    transfer */

     /* Build the string "%2048s" */
     (void)sprintf(scanf_string,"%%%ds",MAX_PATH);
     /* Get the input path */
     (void)printf("Input file: ");
     if (scanf(scanf_string,ifpath) != 1) PANIC;
     /* See if the file exists and how big it is */
```

```
if (stat(ifpath,&ifstat) != 0)
    {
    (void)perror("? Can not stat file");
    exit(EXIT_FAILURE);
    }
left = hunk = ifstat.st_size; /* left is the amount left
                               * to copy.  Start it out
                               * with the size of the
                               * whole file.
                               */
if (hunk > HUNK_MAX) hunk = HUNK_MAX;
/* Get a buffer for the whole file (or 1 hunk if the file
 * is too big.
 */
if((bigbuf = (char *)malloc(hunk)) == NULL)
    {
    (void)fprintf(stderr,
        "? File is too big for fast copy\n");
    exit(EXIT_FAILURE);
    }
/* Open the input file */
if ((ifdes = open(ifpath,O_RDONLY)) == -1) PANIC;
/* Now that we have the input file open, ask for the
 * path for the output file
 */
(void)printf("Output file: ");
if (scanf(scanf_string,ofpath) != 1) PANIC;
/* Open the output file */
if ((ofdes = open(ofpath,O_WRONLY|O_CREAT|O_TRUNC,S_IRUSR|S_IWUSR))
        == -1) PANIC;
while (left > 0)
    {
    /* Read the file in one big bite */
    if (read(ifdes,bigbuf,hunk) != hunk)
        {
        (void)fprintf(stderr,
            "? Error reading file %s\n",ifpath);
        exit(EXIT_FAILURE);
        }
    /* Write out the copy */
    if(write(ofdes,bigbuf,hunk) != hunk)
        {
        (void)fprintf(stderr, " Error writing file %s\n",ofpath);
        exit(EXIT_FAILURE);
        }
    left -= hunk;
    if (left < hunk) hunk = left;
    }
/* Close the files */
if (close(ifdes) != 0) PANIC;
if (close(ofdes) != 0) PANIC;

/* Print out a status message */
(void)printf("%s copied to %s (%d bytes)\n",
    ifpath,ofpath,ifstat.st_size);
return(0);
}
```

There is an interesting portability sidelight here. On systems where an int is 32-bits, the file will be copied using a single call to read() and a single call to write(). It is possible that a system has a 16-bit int and a 32-bit st_size. The read() and write() functions use a size_t* for the number of bytes to transfer. It is possible that there are systems that cannot read a large file with a single read() call. On these systems, large files are broken up into multiple hunks.

Control Operations on a File

One of the reasons for using the low-level I/O functions is to get better control. The file control function fcntl() is a multi-purpose function that performs various operations on open file descriptors. The definition is:

```
int fcntl(int fildes, int cmd, ...);
```

The exact arguments depend on the command, cmd, given. The commands are:

cmd Value	Description
F_DUPFD	Duplicate a file descriptor.
F_GETFD	Get file descriptor flags.
F_GETLK	Get record locking information.
F_SETFD	Set file descriptor flags.
F_GETFL	Get file status flags.
F_SETFL	Set file status flags.
F_SETLK	Set record locking information.
F_SETLKW	Set record locking information; wait if blocked.

F_GETFD/F_SETFD

Every file descriptor has a close-on-exec flag. In the default case, the fork() and exec()† function calls allow one process to inherit the open files from the parent process that created it. That is how the shell passes stdin, stdout, and stderr to programs it runs.

Sometimes you do not want to pass an open file. If the file is not useful to the new program, it not only uses up valuable open file slots, but also allows the child to interfere with the parent. One way to prevent this is to set the close-on-exec flag for a file descriptor. The exec() function will close that descriptor prior to starting the new program.

---

* The 1990 revision of 1003.1 quietly changed the type of this argument from unsigned int to size_t.

† These are described in detail in the next chapter.

There may be `fcntl()` flags that are specific to a system but are not defined by POSIX. If we want our code to be portable, we need to preserve those implementation-defined bits. You set/unset only what you want and avoid the rest. The sequence:

```
flags = fcntl(fildes,F_GETFD);
fcntl(fildes,F_SETFD,flags | FD_CLOEXEC);
```

will set the close-on-exec bit. The sequence:

```
flags = fcntl(fildes,F_GETFD);
fcntl(fildes,F_SETFD,flags & ~FD_CLOEXEC);
```

will clear the close-on-exec bit. All other bits are preserved.

F_GETFL/F_SETFL

Two of the flags that can be set in the `open()` call may be modified by the `fcntl()` function. The `O_APPEND` and `O_NONBLOCK` flags may be changed while the file is open. The most portable way to modify them is first to read the flags with:

```
flags = fcntl(fildes,F_GETFD);
```

Then set any desired bits with a statement such as:

```
flags |= O_NONBLOCK;
```

Next, clear any flags no longer desired:

```
flags &= ~(O_APPEND);
```

Finally, reset the flags with:

```
fcntl(fildes,F_SETFD,flags);
```

This preserves any implementation-defined flags. The normal open flags, such as `O_CREAT`, are also preserved by this technique. The POSIX standard does not specify what happens if you attempt to modify these flags with `fcntl()`, and it is best not to try it.

You may wonder why POSIX defines both `F_SETFD` and `F_SETFL`. Can't we get away with only one? Well, `F_SETFD` applies only to a single file descriptor. `F_SETFL` applies to all file descriptors that share a common open file description, either by inheritance through `fork()` or as the result of an `F_DUPFD` operation with `fcntl()`; for example:

```
fd1 = open(path,oflags);
fd2 = dup(fd1);
fd3 = open(path,oflags);
```

An `F_SETFD` on `fd1` applies only to `fd1`. An `F_SETFL` on `fd1` applies to `fd1` and `fd2` but not to `fd3`.

F_SETLK/F_SETLKW/F_GETLK

POSIX supports a form of interprocess communication called "advisory record locking." This feature is found in POSIX and System V Release 3 and later, but not in BSD. Record locking lets one process indicate its intent to read or write part of a file. Other processes may observe these intents. This is called advisory locking because the system does not supervise programs that read or write locked files. The scheme depends on the good will and proper coding of each application program.

Record locking is controlled by the flock structure. The flock structure contains the following members:

Member Type	Member Name	Description
short	l_type	One of the symbolic constants: F_RDLCK: to indicate a read (shared) lock F_WRLCK: to indicate a write (exclusive) lock F_UNLCK: to remove a lock
short	l_whence	One of the symbolic constants: SEEK_SET, SEEK_CUR, or SEEK_END to indicate that l_start is measured from the start of the file, the current position, or the end of the file.
off_t	l_start	Relative offset in bytes.
off_t	l_len	The number of bytes to lock. This value should not be negative. If it is zero, it indicates "until EOF."
pid_t	l_pid	Process ID of the process holding the lock; used only by the F_GETLK function.

The F_SETLKW function sets and clears locks for a record. A call looks like:

```
fcntl(fildes,F_SETLKW,flock_ptr);
```

where fildes is the file to lock and flock_ptr points to a struct flock. This call can establish or remove shared or exclusive locks. If the lock is not available, the F_SETLKW call will wait for some other process to unlock the lock.

The F_SETLK call is identical to the F_SETLKW call except when the lock is not available. Instead of waiting, F_SETLK returns −1 and sets errno to EAGAIN.

The F_GETLK function is called with:

```
fcntl(fildes,F_GETLKW,flock_ptr);
```

and searches for a lock that would block the one in the struct flock pointed to by flock_ptr. If no lock is found that would prevent this lock from being created, the lock type is set to F_UNLCK. Otherwise, the structure is overwritten with lock information for an arbitrarily chosen lock.

You can build a simple semaphore system using advisory record locking. A file can be used as an array of locks. You do not need to read or write the file to use record locking.

F_DUPFD

The final use for `fcntl()` is to duplicate an open file descriptor. The call:

```
fcntl(fildes,F_DUPFD,minfd)
```

returns a new file descriptor which is associated with the same open file as `fildes` and is greater than or equal to `minfd`. If `minfd` is unused then that is the file descriptor that will be used. Otherwise, the lowest numbered unused file descriptor greater than `minfd` is returned.

The new file descriptor shares any locks with the original file. The close-on-exec flag for the new descriptor is clear.

Setting the File Position

I covered the `fseek()` function in Chapter 3, *Standard File and Terminal I/O*. The `lseek()` function does exactly the same thing (sets the position of the file), except that it operates on file descriptors instead of on streams. The function is defined as:

```
off_t lseek(int fildes, off_t offset, int whence);
```

The `whence` argument is either:

Argument	Meaning
SEEK_SET	To set the file position to `offset`.
SEEK_CUR	To set the file position to be the current position plus `offset`.
SEEK_EOF	To set the file position to be the end-of-file plus `offset`.

The file position may be set beyond the current end-of-file. If data is written at this point, the gap is filled with zeros.[*]

The `lseek()` function returns the resulting offset measured as the number of bytes from the beginning of the file. In case of error, it returns `((off_t)-1)` and sets `errno` to indicate the error.

Seeking is portable only for disk files. The effect of `lseek()` on pipes, FIFOs, terminals, and other non-disk devices is undefined. In System V and BSD, an `lseek()` on a device incapable of seeking has no effect. You should not count on all systems providing such benign results.

---

[*] The standard does not actually specify that zeros are written into the file, only that an attempt to read the gap shall return zeros. It is possible to implement a system with "sparse" files where no disk space is used for the holes.

In historical UNIX implementations, seek() used an offset of type int and lseek() (which was added later) used an offset of type long. Today, seek() is obsolete. POSIX defined the offset for lseek() as an off_t. All useful POSIX systems will define off_t as a long or larger. You can safely assume that lseek() will work on files of a billion bytes.

The dup() and dup2() Functions

The function dup(fildes) is equivalent to:

```
fcntl(fildes,F_DUPFD,0)
```

and saves some typing.

The function dup2(fildes,fildes2) is more or less equivalent to:

```
close(fildes2);
fcntl(fildes, F_DUPFD, fildes2);
```

but dup2() is considered outdated and should not be used in new programs. Use the close()/fcntl() combination instead because it does a better job of error reporting.

Closing a File

When you are done with a file, the close() function should be used to deallocate the file descriptor and clean up the file. When our program terminates, all of the open files are closed. There are still good reasons for explicitly calling close() for each file:

- Open files are a limited resource. It is a good idea to give them back as soon as possible.

- It is always a good idea to check for errors. If you let exit() close your open files, errors will be ignored.

The close() function is about as portable as you can get.

FIFOs and Pipes

One of the original ideas of the UNIX system was to build complex programs out of simple ones. A pipeline allows you to use the output of one program as the input to the next program.

A *pipe* is a type of file where one process writes to one end and another process reads from the other end. Pipes are created by the pipe() function, which is defined as:

```
int pipe(int fildes[2]);
```

It places an open file descriptor into `fildes[0]` and `fildes[1]`. The file descriptor in `fildes[0]` is the read end of the pipe and the file descriptor in `fildes[1]` is the write end of the pipe.

Pipes are quite portable. POSIX defines a number of properties for pipes. You can count on all POSIX systems supporting these features. Older UNIX systems may or may not support these properties and your program will be more portable if you do not depend on these properties.

- There is no file offset associated with a pipe. Each write appends to the end of the pipe.

- A write of fewer than `PIPE_BUF` bytes is atomic; the data will not be interleaved with data from other processes writing to the same pipe. A write of more than `PIPE_BUF` may have data interleaved in arbitrary ways.

  For example, if `PIPE_BUF` is 5120,[*] a write of 5000 bytes will be contiguous. A write of 6000 bytes may be broken into 60 100-byte chunks.

- If `O_NONBLOCK` is not set, a write will return after writing all the requested data.

- If `O_NONBLOCK` is set, a write of fewer than `PIPE_BUF` bytes will either write the entire buffer or write nothing. A write of more than `PIPE_BUF` bytes will write what it can.

You can also create a "named pipe" or FIFO using the `mkfifo()` function. This is defined as:

```
int mkfifo(const char *path, mode_t mode);
```

and creates a new FIFO special file named by the string pointed to by `path`. The file permission bits of the new FIFO are set from `mode`. Permission bits and the `mode` argument were described in Chapter 4, *Files and Directories*.

Because pipes are used for interprocess communication, I will leave the discussion for the next chapter.

File Creation Mask

There is one file operation that does not fit into any other category: set file creation mask. Each process has a file creation mask. The `open()`, `creat()`, `mkdir()`, and `mkfifo()` calls use the file creation mask to turn off permission bits when they create files. For example, setting the `S_IRWXO` bits in the mask would turn off read, write, and execute permission bits for the "other" class.

---

[*] The value of `PIPE_BUF` is usually 4096 or 5120. POSIX requires that it must be 512 or greater.

The umask() Function

The umask() function is defined as:

```
mode_t umask(mode_t cmask);
```

It sets the file creation mask to cmask and returns the previous value. No errors are detected.

The umask() function itself is very portable. Programs developed where the umask value of 000 (no protection) is used may not work in a high security environment where the umask value may be 077. It is a good idea to test your applications with a umask value of 077. You can avoid this problem by executing a umask(0) at the start of your program; however, that may not be what the end-user of your software wants.

Mixing the Levels

Sometimes you need to perform a low-level call on a file you are using at a high level. For example, you may want to set the close-on-exec flag for a stream. In other cases, you may need to convert a file descriptor to a stream; for example, to write a pipe using fprintf() calls. There are some handy functions to perform this mapping.

The fdopen() Function

The fdopen() function associates a stream with a file descriptor. The function is defined as:

```
FILE *fdopen(int fildes, const char *type);
```

The fildes argument is the file descriptor you want to convert. The type argument is exactly the same as described in Chapter 3, *Standard File and Terminal I/O*, for fopen() except the file is never truncated.

In general, the functions described in Chapter 3 are more portable than the ones described in this chapter. The fdopen() call is a handy way to avoid using the low-level routines when you are given a file descriptor.

The fileno() Function

The fileno() function returns the file descriptor associated with a stream. It is defined as:

```
int fileno(FILE *stream);
```

A return value of −1 indicates an error; however, fileno() is not required to detect an invalid argument and I am sure that some systems do not.

The file number returned by fileno() can be used by the functions described in this chapter. For example, fcntl() can be used to lock and unlock records.

Pitfalls

Accessing a single open file description using both streams and file descriptors can cause problems. Attempting to write a file using both `fprintf()` and `write()`, for example, can cause data to be written out of order and may work differently from system to system.

There are safe operations. For example, `fcntl()` can be used to perform record locking while `fread()` and `fwrite()` are used to update the file.

If all of the operations that could affect the file offset (for example `read()`, `write()`, `lseek()`, `scanf()`, `printf()`, and so on) are done exclusively through streams, everything will work correctly. If all of the operations that could affect the file offset are done exclusively through file descriptor calls, everything will work correctly.

If you have been exclusively using file descriptor functions (`read()`, `write()`, `lseek()`) to access the file, you can switch to using stream functions exclusively (`fgets()`, `fputs()`, etc.) at any point.

To switch from using stream functions exclusively to using file descriptor functions, special care must be used. If the stream is unbuffered and the `ungetc()` function has not been used, you can switch to using file descriptor functions.

In most other cases* the interaction is not defined and the functions should not be mixed.

Portability Lab

To review the contents of this chapter, try to do the following exercises:

1. If you were to write a routine to simulate the library function `printf()` and call the `write()` function directly from your code, would it be faster or slower than the library routine. Why?

2. What is the effect of setting the `O_CREAT` flag when opening an existing file?

3. The fast file copy example program in this chapter claims to be fast because it uses only one read and one write to copy the entire file. When might this be slower than using several reads and writes?

---

* There are a number of obscure cases which are still defined. For example, if a file is open for read and positioned at the end of the file, we can freely switch between `fread()` and `read()`.

If there is an overwhelming reason to mix stream-based and descriptor-based I/O, read section 8.2.3 of the POSIX standard several times.

---

4. Why is the sequence:

```
flags = fcntl(fildes,F_GETFD);
fcntl(fildes,F_SETFD,flags | O_NONBLOCK);
```

a better way to set the O_NONBLOCK flag for a file than the following?

```
fcntl(fildes,F_SETFD,O_NONBLOCK);
```

5. Assume an application opens a file and sets some exclusive record locks. While the file is open, you attempt to copy it using the fast file copy example program given in this chapter. What would happen? Why?

6. Why would one use `lseek()` instead of `fseek()`?

7. Why would an application call `umask()`? Why not just set the permission bits correctly in the call to `open()`?

8. What practical reason is there for the use of the `fileno()` function? What about `fdopen()`?

9. What problems might occur if `printf()` and `write()` are intermixed writing a file? How can these problems be eliminated?

CHAPTER 6

Working with Processes

This chapter covers process creation, process termination, and signals. Process creation involves the fork() and exec() calls, that are familiar to a UNIX programmer. Process termination involves the wait() and waitpid() calls. POSIX.1 adds some new ideas here: signals are different in POSIX. Although based on Berkeley signals, the POSIX library defines different functions that have somewhat different behavior than what you may be familiar with from using BSD.

Process Creation

The fork() and exec() functions are present in all UNIX systems, and POSIX documented the common existing practice. In this section, we look at the process creation features that POSIX guarantees to be portable.

The fork() Function

A process is created with the fork() system call. It takes no arguments and creates a new process called a *child*. If it fails, it returns –1.

The original process is called the *parent*; the child is an exact copy of the parent except for the following:

- The child process has a unique process ID.

- The child's parent process ID is set to the process ID of the process executing the fork().

- The child has its own copy of the parent's file descriptors. The child has access to all of the parent's open files.

- The child's run time is set to zero.

- Pending alarms are cleared for the child.

- The set of pending signals is set to the empty set.

- File locks are not inherited.

The child starts out life right after the fork() call that created it. The fork() call returns zero to the child and returns the process ID of the newly created child to the parent. A program that calls fork() typically tests the return value and does one thing in the parent and something different in the child.

The fork() call is very portable. BSD has a special flavor of fork() called vfork(). The vfork() call is a special case designed to speed up the fork()/exec() operation. You may replace a BSD vfork() operation with fork() to make your program more portable. You can also do the following:

```
#ifdef BSD
      pid = vfork();
#else
      pid = fork();
#endif
```

to retain the performance boost on BSD systems while being POSIX-conforming.[*]

The exec() Family of Function

A child process can run another program. For example, most commands cause the shell to fork a new process and then exec a program.

There is no function named exec(): instead, there is a family of similar calls, each of which have slightly different arguments. The family is:

```
int execl(const char *path, const char *arg, ...);
int execv(const char *path, char * const argv[]);
int execle(const char *path, const char *arg, ...);
int execve(const char *path, char * const argv[],
                    char * const *envp);
int execlp(const char *file, const char *arg, ...);
int execvp(const char *file, char * const argv[]);
```

The exec family of calls replaces the current process image with a new program. The new program is read from an ordinary executable file. There is no return from a successful exec; instead, the new program is started.

The main() function in the new program is called as:

```
int main(int argc, char *argv[]);
```

where argc is the argument count and argv is an array of character pointers to the arguments themselves. In addition, the variable:

```
extern char **environ;
```

is initialized as a pointer to an array of character pointers to the environment strings. The argv and environ arrays are each terminated by a NULL pointer. The NULL pointer terminating the argv array is not counted in argc.

The argument file should contain just the filename of the new program. The path prefix for this file is obtained by a search of the directories passed as the environment variable PATH. The call execlp("more","more",(char *)0); looks for more in each directory in the search path.

---

[*] The BSD vfork() function must be followed by an exec.

The argument `path` points to a pathname that identifies the file to be executed. No searching takes place on calls with a `path` argument.

The `const char *arg` and subsequent ellipses in the `execl()`, `execlp()`, and `execle()` functions can be thought of as a list of one or more pointers to null-terminated character strings that represent the argument list available to the new program. The first argument should point to a file containing the program to be started, and the last argument should be a `NULL` pointer. For the `execle()` function, the environment pointer follows the `NULL` pointer that terminates the argument list.

The argument `envp` to `execve()`, and the final argument to `execle()`, name an array of character pointers to null-terminated strings. These strings constitute the environment for the new process. The environment array is terminated by a `NULL` pointer. For `execl()`, `execv()`, `execlp()`, and `execvp()`, the environment for the new program is inherited from the caller.

When you terminate the list with `NULL`, make sure that you cast it to a pointer with `(char *)`. On some 80x86 or 680x0 systems, an `int` is 16 bits but a pointer is 32 bits. A naked zero will not work on those systems.

The POSIX standard does not say exactly what is a legal "executable file." This is intentional. Systems based on BSD allow shell scripts as executable files, while AT&T systems do not.[*] Some systems allow shell scripts for the `execlp()` and `execvp()` functions but for no others. If the file you are trying to execute is not executable, the call will return −1 with `errno` set to `ENOEXEC`.

The requirements for an application state that the value passed as the first argument must be a filename associated with the process being started. When you `exec()` a program, you should pass the filename (not the full path) as `argv[0]`. The most common usage of `argv[0]` is in printing error messages. The standard does not say that `argv[0]` must be the actual filename of the executable file. For example, the `login` utility may prefix the filename with a hyphen to indicate to the command interpreter being invoked that it is a "login shell."

Example: Piping Output Through more

The actions of `fork()` and `exec` can be made much clearer by using an example. Consider the sample program at the end of Chapter 3, *Standard File and Terminal I/O*. This program writes square roots to a file. Let's modify the program to display the square roots on the screen.

To allow the user to control the output, we will use the `more` program to display the results.

---

[*] This applies only to the `exec()` functions.

All we need to do is replace the `write_file` function with a new function to send the output to the display. Here is what that new function looks like:

```
void display(long start,long stop)
{
FILE *fileid;
int fildes[2];
long i;
double f;
int status;

/* The first thing we do is create a pipe.  The array fildes
 * contains a file descriptor for each end of the pipe,
 * where fildes[0] is the "read" side and fildes[1] is
 * the "write" side.
 */
    if (pipe(fildes) != 0) PANIC;

/* Next we attempt to create a child using the fork()
 * function.  This has three possible returns: failure,
 * normal return to child, and normal return to the parent.
 *
 * The switch statement covers the first two cases.  Failure
 * is detected and a PANIC message is issued.  Otherwise, we
 * get things set for the child.
 */
    switch (fork())
        {
        case -1:
            PANIC;
            break;
        case 0:
/*
 * This is the child.
 * The first step here is to change the child's
 * standard input to be the pipe we just created.
 * Doing this uses an old UNIX trick.  We close
 * the existing STDIN file and then call
 * dup() to create a new descriptor.  This
 * will use the lowest available file descriptor.
 * Since we just closed STDIN, dup() will reuse it
 * and standard input will be connected to the
 * pipe.
 *
 * It is now required to close the child's side of
 * both fildes[0] and fildes[1].  The child will
 * see EOF, when all writers of the pipe close
 * their side.  If we forgot to close the side
 * inherited from the parent, the program would
 * never terminate.
 */
                if (close(STDIN_FILENO) != 0) PANIC;
                if (dup(fildes[0]) != STDIN_FILENO) PANIC;
                /* Close left over file descriptors */
                if (close(fildes[0]) != 0) PANIC;
                if (close(fildes[1]) != 0) PANIC;
/* The final step for the child is to replace
 * itself with the more program.  The execlp()
 * function does that for us.
 */
```

```
                    execlp("more","more",(char *)0);
                    PANIC; /* Should never return */
            }
        /*
         * This is the parent
         */

    /* In the meantime, the parent will skip both cases of the
     * switch statement and hit the call to fdopen().  The
     * fdopen() function converts a file descriptor to a stream.
     * This allows the use of standard I/O functions, like
     * fprintf() to do our output.
     */
            fileid = fdopen(fildes[1],"w");
            if (close(fildes[0]) != 0) PANIC;
            if (fprintf(fileid,"        N             SQRT(N)\n") < 0)
                PANIC;
    /* Next, we do all our computing.  The output will flow
     * through the pipe to the more program which will display
     * it.
     */
            for (i=start; i <= stop; i++)
                {
                f = (float)i;
                if (fprintf(fileid, "%10.0f    %10.6f\n",
                    f,sqrt(f)) < 0)
                    {
                    perror("Error writing output file");
                    abort();
                    }
                }

    /* When we have computed all of our results, we close fileid.
     * This causes more to see EOF and exit.  Note: the fclose()
     * function will perform a close() on fildes[1] as part of
     * its work.  We do not have to (can't) close it again.
     */
            if (fclose(fileid) != 0) PANIC;

    /* The last step is the wait(). This waits for more to exit.*/
            (void)wait(&status);
    }
```

Portability Note

The first argument to `execlp()` is "more". This will cause the `execlp()` function to search the path specified by the PATH environment variable. This may not get us the system utility more. You may instead find some other program called more. This is a security hole (or at least a reliability hole).

Another choice is to build in the absolute pathname for the more utility. Something like /bin/more will work on many UNIX systems but is not guaranteed to work on all POSIX systems.

A third choice is to have some sort of installation procedure which asks for a path name for more and includes it as part of building this application. This is one of the more common techniques used today.

When POSIX.2 is an approved (and implemented) standard, it will specify functions to find the system utilities. Until then you will have to use one of the ideas given above.

Process Termination

You sometimes need to wait for children processes to complete their work. You also need to terminate the current program and other programs. Let's look at some of the ways of doing this.

The wait() and waitpid() Functions

In the previous example we used the `wait()` function to make sure that `more` was done. Let's now look at `wait()` in some more detail. The function is defined as:

```
pid_t wait(int *stat_loc);
```

and waits for status to become available for a child process. A call to `wait()` with an `int *` parameter is very portable and works on all UNIX systems.

The `wait()` function returns the process ID of a terminated child. If the argument `stat_loc` is not NULL, information is stored in the location pointed to by `stat_loc`. If the child returned a value of zero from `main()` or passed a value of zero to `exit()`, the value stored in the location pointed to by `stat_loc` will be zero. The status value can interpreted using the following macros:

WIFEXITED(`stat_value`)	Evaluates to a non-zero value if status was returned for a child that terminated normally.
WEXITSTATUS(`stat_value`)	Evaluates to the low-order eight bits of the `status` argument that the child passed to `exit()`, or the value the child process returned from `main()`. This macro can be used only if `WIFEXITED` returned a non-zero value.
WIFSIGNALED(`stat_value`)	Evaluates to a non-zero value if status was returned for a child that terminated due to a signal that was not caught.[*]
WTERMSIG(`stat_value`)	Evaluates to the number of the signal that caused the termination of the process. This macro can be used only if `WIFSIGNALED` returned a non-zero value.
WIFSTOPPED(`stat_value`)	Evaluates to a non-zero value if the status was returned for a child that is currently stopped. The `waitpid()` function with the `WUNTRACED` option is the only way this value can be returned.

---

[*] Signals are covered in detail later in this chapter.

WSTOPSIG(stat_value)   Evaluates to the number of the signal that caused the child process to stop. This macro can be used only if WIFSTOPPED returned a non-zero value.

Here is how you might use these macros:

```
pid = wait(&s);         /* s gets termination status
                         * of child
                         */
if (pid==-1) PANIC;
if ((WIFEXITED(s) != 0) && ((WEXITSTATUS(s) != 0))
    fprintf(stderr,"Child exited with code %d\n",
            WEXITSTATUS(s));
if (WIFSIGNALED(s))
    fprintf(stderr,"Child died with signal %d\n",
            WTERMSIG(s));
```

These macros are POSIX inventions so they will not work on older systems. The following definitions will work on most BSD and System V systems:

```
#define  LO(s)           ((int)((s)&0377))
#define  HI(s)           ((int)(((s)>>8)&0377))

#define  WIFEXITED(s)    (LO(s)==0)
#define  WEXITSTATUS(s)  HI(s)
#define  WIFSIGNALED(s)  ((LO(s)>0)&&(HI(s)==0))
#define  WTERMSIG(s)     (LO(s)&0177)
#define  WIFSTOPPED(s)   ((LO(s)==0177)&&(HI(s)!=0))
#define  WSTOPSIG(s)     HI(s)
```

Traditional UNIX systems provided only the wait() function. The POSIX working group felt the need for better control and added the waitpid() function. It is defined as:

```
pid_t waitpid(pid_t pid, int *stat_loc, int options);
```

The pid argument is one of the following:

-1   To wait for any child process. This is the same as wait().

positive   To wait for the specific child whose process ID is equal to pid.

zero   To wait for any child process whose process group ID is equal to that of the calling process.

less than -1   To wait for any child process whose process group ID is equal to the absolute value of pid.

Process groups are normally used only by shells supporting job control and not by ordinary applications. This book does not discuss process groups.

The options argument is constructed from the bitwise OR of zero or more of the following flags, defined in the header <sys/wait.h>:

WNOHANG   Causes the `waitpid()` function not to suspend execution of the calling process if status is not immediately available for any of the child processes specified by `pid`.

WUNTRACED   Causes the status of any child processes specified by `pid` that are stopped, and whose status has not yet been reported since they stopped, to be reported to the calling process. This is normally used only by the shell program to support job control.

                                 By the way, the name `WUNTRACED` comes from BSD. BSD supports several other functions that are not part of POSIX, so the name made sense in the BSD context.

The `wait()` and `waitpid()` functions release any resources that the child was using. If you do not care about the final status of the child, it is not good enough to simply omit the `wait()` or `waitpid()` call. A common way to produce a child that does not need to be waited for is to `fork()` a child and `wait()` on the child. The child performs another `fork()` to produce a grandchild. The child then exits and the parent's wait returns. The grandchild is thus disinherited by the grandparent. The spawned grandchild will release all its resources when it terminates because there is no process left to wait for it. This technique is much more portable than the alternative:

```
system("command &");
```

which depends on features that are outside the scope of POSIX.1.

Terminating the Current Process

There are four ways to terminate the current process:

- Returning from `main()`.
- Calling `exit()`.
- Calling `_exit()`.
- Calling `abort()`.

Let's look at them in detail.

Returning from main()

The normal way for a program to terminate is to execute a `return(EXIT_SUCCESS)` statement from the `main()` function. The action of returning a value from `main()` is exactly the same as calling `exit()` with that value.

Executing a `return` with no value is not portable.

Calling exit()

The `exit()` function causes normal program termination. The `EXIT_SUCCESS` macro can be used to indicate successful termination. Since the POSIX standard requires that `EXIT_SUCCESS` be defined as zero, it is safe to write `exit(0)`, keeping with historical practice. The call `exit(0)` is extremely portable.

The `exit()` function performs the following functions:

1. All functions registered by the Standard C `atexit()` function are called in the reverse order of registration. If any of these functions calls `exit()`, the results are not portable.

2. All open output streams are flushed (data written out) and the streams are closed.

3. All files created by `tmpfile()` are deleted.

4. The `_exit()` function is called.

Calling _exit()

The `_exit()` function performs operating system-specific program termination functions. These include:

1. All open file descriptors and directory streams are closed.

2. If the parent process is executing a `wait()` or `waitpid()`, the parent wakes up and status is made available.

3. If the parent is not executing a `wait()` or `waitpid()`, the status is saved for return to the parent on a subsequent `wait()` or `waitpid()`.

4. Children of the terminated process are assigned a new parent process ID. Note: the termination of a parent does not directly terminate its children.

5. If the implementation supports the `SIGCHLD` signal, a `SIGCHLD` is sent to the parent.

6. Several job control signals are sent.

7. All of the resources used by the process are returned.

Portable programs should use `exit()` instead of `_exit()`. The `_exit()` function exists mainly because of the structure of traditional implementations and also the structure of standards committees. The `exit()` function is defined by the C standard with some features that are beyond the scope of POSIX. The only reason for an application to call `_exit()` is to defeat the flushing of streams and the calling of functions registered by `atexit()`.

Calling abort()

The `abort()` function causes abnormal program termination. Exactly what that means is not well-defined.

Portable applications should avoid using `abort()` except in the case of fatal errors. On some systems, it may provide useful debugging information, such as a `core` file.

Terminating Another Process

The `kill()` function can be used to terminate another process. For example:

```
kill(pid,SIGKILL);
```

will kill the process identified by `pid`. It returns zero on success and –1 on failure.

In general, it is safe and legal to kill your children and their children. It may be legal to kill other processes in the system; however, ordinary applications should not kill any process that they did not create (or cause to be created).

The `kill()` function can be used for other functions unrelated to terminating a process. `kill()` is discussed in greater detail later in this chapter.

Signals

Signals inform a process of the occurrence of an event. There are two general types of events:

Errors	For example, division by zero, illegal instruction, or an invalid memory reference.
Asynchronous events	For example, termination of a child or parent process.

The general concept of signals is as old as UNIX. Early versions of UNIX had a number of design flaws in the signal mechanism. The BSD system fixed many of these problems, and the signals standardized by POSIX are very similar to BSD signals with a few improvements.

Each process has an action to be taken in response to each signal defined by the system. A signal is *delivered* to a process when the appropriate action is taken.

During the time between the generation of a signal and the delivery of that signal, the signal is *pending*. In most cases, this interval cannot be detected by an application. However, a signal can be *blocked*.

Each process has a *signal mask* that defines the set of signals currently blocked from delivery to it. The signal mask from a process is inherited from its parent. The `sigaction()`, `sigprocmask()`, and `sigsuspend()` functions control the manipulation of the signal mask.

One of several actions is taken when a signal is delivered:

- The process is terminated.
- The signal is ignored.
- The process is stopped.
- The process is continued.
- The signal is *caught* by a signal-handling function in the application.

There is a set of standard signals which a process can use. These signals are:

SIGABRT   Abnormal termination signal caused by the `abort()` function. A portable program should avoid catching `SIGABRT`.

SIGALRM   The timer set by the `alarm()` function has timed-out.

SIGFPE   Arithmetic exception, such as overflow or division by zero.

SIGHUP   Hangup detected on controlling terminal or death of a controlling process.

SIGILL   Illegal instruction indicating a program error. Applications may wish to catch this signal and attempt to recover from bugs. A portable program should not intentionally generate illegal instructions.[*]

        After a `SIGILL` is caught, the only portable thing to do is to `siglongjmp()` back to a known place in your program (or call `exit()`).

SIGINT   Interrupt special character typed on controlling keyboard.

SIGKILL   Termination signal. This signal cannot be caught or ignored.

SIGPIPE   Write to a pipe with no readers.

SIGQUIT   Quit special character typed on controlling keyboard.

SIGSEGV   Invalid memory reference. Like `SIGILL`, portable programs should not intentionally generate invalid memory references.

SIGTERM   Termination signal.

SIGUSR1   Application-defined signal 1.

SIGUSR2   Application-defined signal 2.

Unless the application changes the action, any of the above signals cause the abnormal termination of the process.

---

[*] Even non-portable programs should avoid intentionally generating illegal instructions. What happens if a new model defines the instruction to do something?

There is also a set of job control signals. They are:

SIGCHLD   Child process terminated or stopped. By default, this signal is ignored.

SIGCONT   Continue the process if it is currently stopped; otherwise, ignore the signal.

SIGSTOP   Stop signal. This signal cannot be caught or ignored.

SIGTSTP   Stop special character typed on the controlling keyboard.

SIGTTIN   Read from the controlling terminal attempted by a member of a background process group.

SIGTTOU   Write to controlling terminal attempted by a member of a background process group.

Most systems will have signals in addition to those listed here. The POSIX interface allows an application to manipulate the signals it knows about without disturbing the signals it does not know about.

Signal Actions

There are three types of actions that can be associated with a signal: SIG_DFL, SIG_IGN, or a *pointer to a function*. The actions for these values are:

SIG_DFL   Signal-specific default action.

SIG_IGN   Ignore the signal.

It is possible to ignore SIGFPE, SIGILL, and SIGSEGV; however, programs with illegal instructions, erroneous arithmetic operations, and invalid memory references are not portable.

The default for SIGCHLD is to ignore the signal. Applications that wish to ignore SIGCHLD should set the action to be SIG_DFL, not to SIG_IGN.[*]

Pointer to a function to catch signal

On delivery of the signal, the receiving process executes the signal-catching function. After returning from the signal-catching function, the process resumes execution.

Signal-Catching Functions

A signal-catching function receives control when a signal is delivered. A signal is somewhat like an unseen hand placing a call statement in the middle of our program—the signal-catching function gets control and is able to do things. When the signal catcher returns, the interrupted program continues without a trace.

---

[*] If a process sets the action for the SIGCHLD signal to SIG_IGN, the behavior is unspecified.

There are some cautions that a signal-catching function must observe:

- While a portable program can catch errors such as illegal instructions; it should not assume that it can continue from a SIGFPE, SIGILL, or SIGSEGV signal. Thus a portable program can establish signal catchers to be more robust, but it should not *depend* on illegal instructions or invalid memory references.

- The program may be in the middle of some function when the signal is delivered. It is not safe to call arbitrary functions from a signal-catching function. The following library functions are defined by the standard as safe:

_exit()	getegid()	rename()	tcdrain()
access()	geteuid()	rmdir()	tcflow()
alarm()	getgid()	setgid()	tcflush()
cfgetispeed()	getgroups()	setpgid()	tcgetattr()
cfgetospeed()	getpgrp()	setsid()	tcgetpgrp()
cfsetispeed()	getpid()	setuid()	tcsendbreak()
cfsetospeed()	getppid()	sigaction()	tcsetattr()
chdir()	getuid()	sigaddset()	tcsetpgrp()
chmod()	kill()	sigdelset()	time()
chown()	link()	sigemptyset()	times()
close()	lseek()	sigfillset()	umask()
creat()	mkdir()	sigismember()	uname()
dup2()	mkfifo()	sigpending()	unlink()
dup()	open()	sigprocmask()	ustat()
execle()	pathconf()	sigsuspend()	utime()
execve()	pause()	sleep()	wait()
fcntl()	pipe()	stat()	waitpid()
fork()	read()	sysconf()	write()
fstat()			

All other library functions (including printf() and friends) are *unsafe* and should not be called from signal-catching functions.

Examine and Change Signal Action

Both Standard C and the POSIX standard define a set of signal-handling functions. The Standard C functions are limited. They may be useful for programs that need to operate on non-POSIX systems, such as MS/DOS or System V.3.

Standard C Signals

First, the C Standard defines only a subset of the POSIX signals. These signals are:

SIGABRT   Abnormal termination signal. This is caused by the abort() function. Standard C suggests that other events may cause SIGABRT; however, it does not say what those events might be.

SIGFPE   Arithmetic exception, such as overflow or division by zero.

---

* IEEE Std 1003.1-1988 defines ustat() as safe to call from signal-catching function. The POSIX standard never defines ustat(), and it was deleted from the 1990 revision.

SIGILL   Illegal instruction.

SIGINT   Interrupt special character typed on controlling keyboard.

SIGSEGV   Invalid memory reference.

SIGTERM   Termination signal.

Standard C does not require that any of these signals be generated. An illegal memory reference may, or may not, generate a SIGSEGV.

The Standard C function used to specify signal handling is called signal() and is defined by:

```
void (*signal(int sig, void(*func)(int)))(int);
```

where sig is a signal number. The func argument is a pointer to a signal-catching function or to one of the following macros:

SIG_DFL   Set the signal to the default action.

SIG_IGN   Ignore the signal.

For example:

```
signal(SIGINT,SIG_IGN);
```

will cause the interrupt key (usually Control-C) to be ignored, and:

```
signal(SIGSEGV,oops);
```

will cause the function oops(SIGSEGV) to be called on illegal memory references.

Standard C also defines the raise() function as:

```
int raise(int sig);
```

to send signal sig to the executing program. The raise() function returns zero if successful and non-zero if unsuccessful. The raise() function should be used only in programs that need to meet the C standard and do not use any POSIX features. The raise() function is more portable than kill() for non-POSIX systems that conform to the C standard. The kill() function is much more portable to older UNIX systems.

POSIX Signals

The Standard C signal() function has several problems:

- There is no way to determine the current action for a signal. This means that a called function cannot use the signal() function without disturbing the caller. There is no way to save and restore signal state.

- When a signal occurs, there is no way to block other signals to keep the signal handler from being interrupted.

• There is no way for an implementation to cleanly extend the signal mechanism.

The POSIX-defined signal functions correct these problems.

The main function for manipulating signals is `sigaction()`. It is defined as:

```
int sigaction(int sig, const struct sigaction *act,
              struct sigaction *oact);
```

The `sigaction` structure is defined in the header `<signal.h>` to include the following members:

Member Type	Member Name	Description
`void(*)()`	`sa_handler`	`SIG_DFL` for the default action.
		or:
		`SIG_IGN` to ignore this signal.
		or:
		pointer to the signal-catching function.
`sigset_t`	`sa_mask`	Additional signals to be blocked during the execution of the signal-catching function. (`sigset_t` and blocked signals will be defined soon.)
`int`	`sa_flags`	This member is used only for the `SIGCHLD` signal. If the value `SA_NOCLDSTOP` is used, then `SIGCHLD` will not be generated when children stop.
		There may be other flags defined by a particular implementation. A portable program should not use them. It should not be disturbed by them either.

The `sigaction()` function sets the structure pointed to by `oact` to the old action for signal `sig` and then takes the action indicated by the structure pointed to by `act`.

There may be additional members in a given implementation's `struct sigaction`. Portable programs are guaranteed that these members will not affect them. To use implementation-defined members, implementation-defined flags must be set.

Example: Read with a timeout

Before getting too deeply into signals, it would be useful to go through a complete example.

The following program reads a line from the user. If the user does not type anything for 30 seconds, the `SIGALRM` signal will interrupt the read and the `gettext()` function will return zero. The caller of `gettext()` can then take some alternate action, such as, giving the user some help.

The program looks like this:

```
#define _POSIX_SOURCE 1

/* System Headers */
#include <stdio.h>
#include <signal.h>
#include <unistd.h>

/* Local Headers */
#include "panic.h"

/* Macros */
#define TIMEOUT 30
#define TRUE    1
#define FALSE   0

/* File scope variables */
volatile int flag;          /* The keyword volatile warns the
                             * compiler that the variable flag
                             * may change in a way that is not
                             * predictable by the compiler.
                             */

/* External variables */
    /* NONE */

/* External functions */
    /* NONE */

/* Structures and Unions */

/* Signal Catching Functions */

/*
 * The ding() function catches the SIGALRM signal and
 * merely sets flag to FALSE.
 */
void ding()
{
    flag = FALSE;
    return;
}

/*
 * The gettext function reads a line from the user's
 * console.  If the line is not typed within TIMEOUT
 * seconds, the gettext() function aborts the read and
```

```
 * returns zero.
 */
int gettext(char *buffer,int bufsize)
{
struct sigaction act,oact;
int             nchars;

    act.sa_handler = ding;   /* Call ding() when the
                              * alarm goes off
                              */
    sigemptyset(&act.sa_mask);
    act.sa_flags = 0;
    if (sigaction(SIGALRM,&act,&oact) != 0) PANIC;
    flag = TRUE;
    (void)alarm(TIMEOUT);
    nchars = read(STDIN_FILENO,buffer,bufsize);
    (void)alarm(0); /* Cancel outstanding SIGALRM (if any) */
    /* Restore previos signal handler for SIGALRM */
    if (sigaction(SIGALRM,&oact,NULL) != 0) PANIC;
    if (flag) return(nchars);
    return(0);
}
```

Signal Sets

The POSIX standard allows a great deal of flexibility for an implementation while still providing portable interfaces. This is evident in the type **sigset_t**, which holds some sets of signals. On some systems, it may be a simple **int** with one bit per signal. BSD uses a **long** for signal sets. On other systems, it may be a complex structure with version numbers, lists of signals, or other extensions.

Because an application program does not know the format of a signal set, several functions are provided to operate on signal sets. All of these functions are new to POSIX.

The sigemptyset() Function

The **sigemptyset()** function is defined by:

```
int sigemptyset(sigset_t *set);
```

and is used to initialize the signal set pointed to by **set**. All signals are excluded from the set.

The sigfillset() Function

This is the same as **sigemptyset()**, except all signals are included.

The sigaddset() Function

The **sigaddset()** function is defined by:

```
int sigaddset(sigset_t *set, const int signo);
```

and adds the signal specified by **signo** to the set pointed to by **set**.

This function will return zero if `signo` is valid. It will return -1 and set `errno` to `EINVAL` if the signal number is invalid.

The sigdelset() Function

This function is the same as `sigaddset()` except that the signal is removed from the set.

Using the sigset Functions

A programmer can then build a signal set which includes only the signals `SIGFPE`, `SIGILL`, and `SIGSEGV` with:

```
sigset_t set;

    . . .

sigemptyset(&set);
sigaddset(&set,SIGFPE);
sigaddset(&set,SIGILL);
sigaddset(&set,SIGSEGV);
```

It is also possible to build a set which includes all signals *except* SIGFPE, SIGILL, and SIGSEGV with:

```
sigset_t set;

    . . .

sigfillset(&set);
sigdelset(&set,SIGFPE);

sigdelset(&set,SIGILL);
sigdelset(&set,SIGSEGV);
```

The sigismember() Function

The `sigismember()` function is used for testing signal sets. It is defined by:

```
int sigismember(const sigset_t *set, const int signo);
```

and returns a value of 1 if `signo` is a member of the signal set pointed to by `set`, zero if `signo` is not a member and -1 if `signo` is invalid.

The sigprocmask() Function

Blocked signals are signals that are temporarily prevented from delivery. It can be useful to inhibit signals during execution of a critical section of code.

You have already seen one way to block signals. The `sa_mask` member of the `struct sigaction` indicates which signals to block during the execution of a signal-catching function. For example, `SIGALRM` can be blocked during the delivery of `SIGINT`.

The list of blocked signals can also be changed using the `sigprocmask()` function. This is defined as:

```
int sigprocmask(int how, const sigset_t *set,
                        sigset_t *oset);
```

The action of `sigprocmask()` depends on the how argument:

how	Description
SIG_BLOCK	The set of blocked signals is the union of the current set of blocked signals and the set pointed to by the argument **set**.
SIG_UNBLOCK	The set of signals pointed to by the argument **set** is removed from the current set of blocked signals. It is not an error to attempt to unblock signals that are not blocked.
SIG_SETMASK	The current set of blocked signals is set from the **sigset_t** pointed to by **set**.

In all cases, if the argument **oset** is not NULL, the previous mask is stored into the space pointed to by **oset**.

This function returns zero unless an invalid argument is used.

The sigpending() Function

If a condition that would cause a signal occurs while that signal is blocked, the signal is said to be *pending*. A pending signal will be delivered after it is unblocked.

A program can examine the set of pending signals using the `sigpending()` function. This is defined as:

```
int sigpending(sigset_t *set);
```

It stores the set of signals that are blocked and pending in the space pointed to by **set**.

Wait for a Signal

Sometimes, a program has nothing to do until a signal is delivered. The `pause()` function suspends the caller until a signal is delivered. There are no arguments to `pause()`. The `pause()` function is very portable but rarely used. Its main use is by the `sleep()` function.

The `sleep()` function is a `pause()` with a timeout. The `sleep()` function takes an argument of a `unsigned int` number of seconds to sleep. Any signals that are delivered cause `sleep()` to wake up returning the amount of time left to sleep. If no signals occur, `sleep()` returns zero.

The sleep() function may or may not be built using SIGALRM. A library that builds sleep() using SIGALRM will be careful to hide this from the caller. A program that uses both sleep() and SIGALRM at the same time is not advised.

The sigsuspend() function is a combination of sigprocmask() and pause(). It is defined by:

```
int sigsuspend(const sigset_t *mask);
```

and temporarily replaces the process signal mask with the one pointed to by mask. The process then suspends until a signal is delivered.

If the action is to terminate the process, the sigsuspend() function never returns.

Why would one ever use sigsuspend()? Consider a program that checks a condition and calls pause() if the condition is not true. If a signal occurs between the test and the call to pause(), the program may hang indefinitely. A flow diagram is shown in Figure 6-1.

FIGURE 6-1. Potential race condition

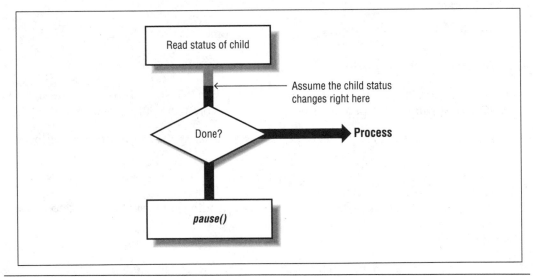

The signal is delivered right before the test for done. The test uses stale data and goes to the pause(). The signal-catching function could try to update the status. This makes signal catching very complex. A better way to avoid the problem is to:

1. Block the possible signals using sigprocmask().

2. Test the condition.

3. Use the sigsuspend() function to unblock the signal and pause.

Sending a Signal

You have already seen the use of `kill()` to terminate child processes. In fact, it is a general mechanism that allows delivery of arbitrary signals to arbitrary processes. The definition of `kill()` is:

```
int kill(pid_t pid, int sig);
```

The `sig` argument must be a valid signal. If the calling process has permission to send the signal, a signal will be delivered to the process (or group of processes) indicated by `pid`. For the caller to have permission to send a signal, the real or effective user ID of the sender must match the real of effective ID of the target.

The exact action depends of the value of `pid`:

pid	Description
Positive	Send the signal to the process whose process ID is equal to `pid`.
Zero	Send the signal to all processes in this process group. This is normally used only by the shell.
-1	Not defined by POSIX. In many systems, this sends a signal to every process in the system.
Less than -1	Send the signal to every process in the process group given by the absolute value of `pid`.

The `kill()` function will return zero if at least one signal was sent. Otherwise, -1 will be returned and `errno` will be set to indicate the error.

The `kill()` function can be used with `SIGUSR1` or `SIGUSR2` to send signals to a cooperating process. Remember, the default action for `SIGUSR1` and `SIGUSR2` is to terminate the process. Do not send them until the receiver has established a signal-catching function.

Portability Lab

To review the contents of this chapter, try to do the following exercises:

1. The `fork()` function starts a new process. Where does this new process start?

2. What is the return from a successful call to `exec()`?

3. The example function `display()` ends with the lines:

    ```
    if (fclose(fileid) != 0) PANIC;
    wait(&status);
    ```

    What would be the ill effects of leaving out the `fclose()`? What about the `wait()`?

4. Give one advantage of `waitpid()` over `wait()`.

5. What is the difference between the exit() function and the _exit() function? When is it a good idea to use _exit() instead of exit()?

6. What is a signal mask? How is the initial value for the signal mask determined?

7. Give an example of a portable action a signal catcher for the SIGSEGV signal might take.

8. What happens to a program that calls alarm() but fails to establish a signal-catching function for the resulting SIGALRM?

9. Can a portable program call printf() from a signal-catching function? Why or why not?

10. Give one advantage of the POSIX sigaction() function over the ANSI signal() function.

11. Write a program fragment to block all signals except SIGINT and SIGHUP.

12. Expand the program fragment from problem 11 to check to see if SIGALRM is pending.

13. What advantage does sigsuspend() have over pause()? When is this important?

14. Write a program to run another program and limit it to 60 seconds of elapsed time.

15. Write a program to compute and display prime numbers until the user types a return.

CHAPTER 7

Obtaining Information at Run–time

There is a great deal of system-specific information available for use by your programs. Much of this information is contained in header files like `<limits.h>` *and* `<sys/types.h>`, *and is built into your programs at compile-time. There is other information, such as the user name, that is known only at run-time. And still other information, like the maximum number of open files, may be available at either compile-time or run-time. This chapter deals with information that is typically available only at run-time.*

Process Identification

Each process in the system is uniquely identified during its lifetime by a positive integer called a process ID. A process ID has type `pid_t` defined in `<sys/types.h>`. Historically, process IDs have been `short`. As systems grew larger, many implementors made process IDs `long`. The `pid_t` type is used to allow programs to work with both sizes.

You can retrieve your own process ID using the `getpid()` function. This function takes no arguments and returns the process ID. You can retrieve the ID of the parent process using the `getppid()` function. It also takes no arguments and returns the process ID of the parent process.

User Identification

When you log in, you have a login name, a user ID, and a group ID. The user and group IDs are positive numbers which you can convert to the corresponding login names.

Let's write a program to generate a simple report. The report will look like:

```
Login name is 'don'
Terminal pathname is '/dev/tty'
Real UID is 13(don) and effective UID is 2(bin)
Real group ID is 13(don) and effective group ID is  25(demo)
The following supplementary groups are available:
        13(don)
        25(demo)
        101(group1)
        102(group2)
        103(group3)
```

Before we start to design the program, let's look at each item in the report:

- The *Login name* is the name the user used to gain access to the system. The `getlogin()` function takes no arguments and returns a pointer to a string giving a user name associated with the calling process.

  The `getlogin()` function returns `NULL` if the user's login name cannot be found. If `getlogin()` returns a non-`NULL` pointer, that pointer points to the name under which the user logged in, even if there are several login names with the same user ID.

- The *Terminal pathname* is a name our program can give to the `open()` or `fopen()` functions to access the controlling terminal. This string may not uniquely identify the terminal. The `ctermid()` function is used to obtain the terminal pathname and is defined as:

  ```
  char *ctermid(char *s);
  ```

  If `s` is not NULL, the terminal pathname is stored in `s` and `s` is returned. If `s` is NULL, `ctermid()` returns a pointer to a possibly static string. The header `<stdio.h>` defines the symbol `L_ctermid`, defined in `<stdio.h>`, and gives the maximum length of the string returned by `ctermid()`. A typical use is:

  ```
  char           termid[L_termid];
  . . .
  (void)ctermid(termid);
  ```

- The *Real UID* identifies the group of users who created the process; in most cases, this is the user ID associated with the login name. The `getuid()` function takes no arguments and returns the real user ID.

  When one of the `exec` functions runs a program with the SETUID bit set, the *effective ID* of the process is set to the owner of the program file. The effective user ID is used to check permissions. For example, the owner of a game program can make the program SETUID so that it can update scores. The `geteuid()` function takes no arguments and returns the effective user ID.

- A group ID is a non-negative integer used to identify a group of system users. Each system user is a member of at least one group. The *Real group ID* identifies the user who created the process. The `getgid()` function takes no arguments and returns the real group ID.

- When the `exec` function runs a program with the set-GID bit set, the *effective group ID* of the process is set to the group of the program file. The use of the set-GID is very similar to SETUID. The `getegid()` function takes no arguments and returns the effective group ID.

- A process has access to zero or more *supplementary group* IDs in addition to the effective group ID. A process can set its effective group ID to any one of the supplementary group IDs.

Now, let's consider the design of the sample program. There is some information that occurs multiple times, for example, `userID(user name)`. Formatting and printing user IDs and group IDs are good candidates for functions. Printing all the supplementary groups is complex enough to deserve a function. Everything else can go into `main()`.

The main purpose of this program is to demonstrate the use of functions that obtain information about our process. We mention the portability and design concerns as we go along.

User IDs

In order to convert a user ID to a user name, we use the `getpwuid()` function. On most systems, this function looks up the user in the file `/etc/passwd` and returns one entry. However, there is no requirement for the system to have a password file; `getpwuid()` might work some other way.

The `getpwuid()` function takes a single UID as an argument and returns a pointer to a `struct passwd`. This structure is defined in `<pwd.h>` and contains the following members:

Member Name	Member Type	Description
`pw_name`	`char *`	User's login name.
`pw_uid`	`uid_t`	User ID number.
`pw_gid`	`gid_t`	Group ID number.
`pw_dir`	`char *`	Initial working directory.
`pw_shell`	`char *`	Initial user program.

The structure may contain other members and the members may be in any order. The `getpwuid()` function returns a `NULL` pointer if the entry is not found.

There is another function called `getpwnam()`. This takes a single `char *` argument and looks up the user by name instead of number. The `getpwnam()` function also returns a pointer to a `struct passwd`.

The `getpwuid()` and `getpwnam()` functions are very portable. Some systems may have additional members in `struct passwd`. If you use these members, your program is less portable.

The `printuser()` function takes a single argument of type `uid_t` and prints the argument in decimal form followed by the corresponding user name. Nothing is returned:

```
/*
 * Print out the user ID in decimal followed by
 * (username)
 */
void printuser(uid_t userid)
{
unsigned long     lt;                 /* temp */
struct passwd *pwptr;                 /* pointer to user info */

    lt = (unsigned long)userid;       /* make the uid a long */
    (void)printf(" %lu(",lt);         /* print the number */
    pwptr = getpwuid(userid);         /* get the information */
    if (pwptr == NULL)                /* print question marks if
                                       * user ID is not known
                                       */

        {
        (void)printf("??????)");
        return;
        }
    (void)printf("%s)",pwptr->pw_name);
    return;
}
```

There is one complex step involved. On some POSIX systems, `uid_t` will be a `short`; on other systems, it will be a `long`. The `printf()` function requires that we explicitly specify the size of the value we are printing. To handle this in a portable fashion, we "promote" the user ID to a `long` and then tell `printf()` to print a `long`. On systems with 32-bit `int`s, the default promotion rules give the correct results. On a system with 16-bit `int`s, the defaults may not work. Explicitly converting to `long` works in all cases. If this function returned the UID instead of printing it, we could just return a value of type `uid_t`.

Group IDs

To print the group number and name, use the `getgrgid()` function, which is very similar to the `getpwuid()` function. It returns a pointer to `group` structure based on a group ID. This structure is defined in the header file `<grp.h>` and contains the following members:

Member Name	Member Type	Description
gr_name	char *	The name of the group.
gr_gid	gid_t	Group ID number.
gr_mem	char **	Pointer to a null-terminated array of `char *`. Each element of the array points to an individual member of the group.

As with `getpwuid()`, the members of the structure may be in any order and there may be additional members. A return value of `NULL` indicates that no entry was found.

There is also a `getgrnam()` function which is identical to `getgrgid()` except that it takes a `char *` group name as an argument instead of a group ID.

Our `printgroup()` function takes a single argument of type `gid_t` and prints it in decimal followed by the corresponding group name. No value is returned.

```
/*
 * Print out the group number in decimal followed by
 * (groupname)
 */
void printgroup(gid_t groupid)
{
unsigned long lt;                       /* temp */
struct group *grpptr;                   /* pointer to group info */

    lt = (unsigned long)groupid;   /* make the gid a long */
    (void)printf(" %lu(",lt);      /* print it */
    grpptr = getgrgid(groupid);    /* get group structure */
    if (grpptr == NULL)            /* print question marks if
                                    * group name is unknown
                                    */
        {
        (void)printf("??????)");
        return;
        }
    (void)printf("%s)",grpptr->gr_name);
    return;
}
```

Next, we turn our attention to a function to print a list of all groups of which the process is a member. We already have a function called `printgroup()` that prints out a single group ID. It is tempting to name the function that prints all the groups `printgroups()`. Long and bitter experience has taught that it is a bad idea to have many functions with very similar names. The functions `printgroup()` and `printgroups()` are too close together. The name `printallgroups()` is less likely to cause confusion. We have to live with `getgid()` and `getegid()` because they are library functions. Do not use them as an example of good software engineering practice.

The key to the `printallgroups()` function is the POSIX function `getgroups()`, which is defined as:

```
int getgroups(int gidsetsize,gid_t grouplist[]);
```

and fills in the array `grouplist` with up to `gidsetsize` supplementary group IDs. The actual number of groups in use is returned.

We could allocate an array with `NGROUPS_MAX` elements; however, on some systems that may be a large value. Instead, we call `getgroups()` with `gidsetsize` equal to zero and, because it returns the number of groups in use, we can use this number to allocate the array. A second call will then exactly fill the array.

There is one other complication. The system you are using may not support multiple groups.* This depends on the symbol NGROUPS_MAX being greater than 1. Future versions of POSIX may not require NGROUPS_MAX to be defined. We use #ifdefs in our function to be sure that NGROUPS_MAX is always defined.

So, the code ends up looking like this:

```
void printallgroups()
{
int         ngroups;        /* number of active groups */
gid_t     *grpptr;          /* pointer to the list of
                             * active groups
                             */

int         i;
gid_t     gid;

#ifndef NGROUPS_MAX         /* If NGROUPS_MAX is not defined */
#define NGROUPS_MAX 0       /* assume that it is zero */
#endif

#if NGROUPS_MAX < 1
/* This printf is compiled if NGROUPS_MAX is less than 1 */
     (void)printf("Supplementary group IDs are "
                           "not supported\n");
#else
/*
 * This is compiled if there is at least one
 * supplementary group.
 */
     ngroups = getgroups(0,(gid_t *)NULL);   /* get the number
                                              * of supplementary group
                                              * IDs in use
                                              */
     if (ngroups == -1)
        {
        (void)perror("getgroups() failed");
        return;
        }
     if (ngroups == 0)
        {
        (void)printf("No supplementary groups are "
                               "available\n");
        return;
        }
     grpptr = calloc(ngroups,sizeof(gid_t));
                                    /* Allocate an array with
                                     * ngroups members each big
                                     * enough for a gid_t.
                                     * grpptr points to the
                                     * array.
                                     */

     if (getgroups(ngroups,grpptr) == -1) /* Get group IDs */
```

---

* It is likely that the system will support multiple groups. The Federal Information Processing Standard (FIPS) version of POSIX requires that multiple groups be supported. This means than any vendor who would like to sell to the United States Government must support multiple groups. However, a fully portable program must tolerate any legal environment.

```
                    {
                    (void)perror("getgroups() failed");
                    return;
                    }
            (void)printf("The following supplementary groups are "
                                            " available:\n");
            for (i=1; i <= ngroups; i++)         /* Loop over all IDs */
                    {
                    gid = *grpptr++;             /* Load an ID into gid and
                                                  * update grpptr to point
                                                  * to the next ID.
                                                  */
                    (void)printf("\t");          /* Print a tab */
                    printgroup(gid);             /* Then the group ID */
                    (void)printf("\n");          /* Then a newline */
                    }
    #endif
        return;
    }
```

Now, let's write the `main()` function. The first thing we need is the login name; the `getlogin()` function returns a pointer to the name. To get the terminal pathname, we pass `ctermid()` a pointer to a character array and it fills in the pathname.

The user and group IDs are obtained with `getuid()`, `geteuid()`, `getgid()`, and `getegid()`. These functions are always successful and there is no return value to indicate an error. On very old UNIX systems, `uids` and `pids` were 8-bits. Most System V and BSD systems use 16 bits for IDs. POSIX allows 32-bit numbers as vendors expand their systems to 32-bits. A typical 1991 operating system defines a `pid_t` as a `long` and restricts the values to be less than 65535. This practice avoids breaking old applications. Your programs should assume that `pids` and `gids` may be 32 bits.

All that is left is to add the required `#includes` and `#defines` in the front and the complete program is shown in Example 7-1:

EXAMPLE 7-1. printinfo.c

```
    #define _POSIX_SOURCE 1

    #include <stdio.h>
    #include <limits.h>
    #include <unistd.h>
    #include <sys/types.h>
    #include <grp.h>
    #include <pwd.h>

    /*
     * Print out the group number in decimal followed by
     * (groupname)
     */
    void printgroup(gid_t groupid)
    {
    unsigned long    lt;                  /* temp */
    struct group *grpptr;                 /* pointer to group info */
```

```
        lt = (unsigned  long)groupid;  /* make the gid a long */
        (void)printf(" %lu(",lt);       /* print it */
        grpptr = getgrgid(groupid);     /* get group structure */
        if (grpptr == NULL)             /* print question marks if
                                         * group name is unknown
                                         */
            {
            (void)printf("??????)");
            return;
            }
        (void)printf("%s)",grpptr->gr_name);      /* print group name */
        return;
    }

/*
 * Print out the user ID in decimal followed by
 * (username)
 */
void printuser(uid_t userid)
{
unsigned long      lt;                 /* temp */
struct passwd *pwptr;                  /* pointer to user info */

        lt = (unsigned long)userid; /* make the uid a long */
        (void)printf(" %lu(",lt);   /* print the number */
        pwptr = getpwuid(userid);   /* get the information */
        if (pwptr == NULL)          /* print question marks if
                                     * user ID is not known
                                     */
            {
            (void)printf("??????)");
            return;
            }
        (void)printf("%s)",pwptr->pw_name);
        return;
    }


void printallgroups()
{
int         ngroups;                   /* number of active groups */
gid_t      *grpptr;                    /* pointer to the list of
                                        * active groups
                                        */

int         i;
gid_t      gid;

#ifndef NGROUPS_MAX
#define NGROUPS_MAX 0
#endif

#if NGROUPS_MAX < 1
        (void)printf("Supplementary group IDs are "
                          "not supported\n");
#else
        ngroups = getgroups(0,(gid_t *)NULL);     /* get the number
                                                   * of supplementary group
                                                   * IDs in use
                                                   */

        if (ngroups == -1)
```

```
            {
            (void)perror("getgroups() failed");
            return;
            }
        if (ngroups == 0)
            {
            (void)printf("No supplementary groups are "
                                      "available\n");
            return;
            }
        grpptr = (gid_t *)calloc(ngroups,sizeof(gid_t));
        if (getgroups(ngroups,grpptr) == -1)
            {
            (void)perror("getgroups() failed");
            return;
            }
        (void)printf("The following supplementary groups are "
                                      " available:\n");
        for (i=1; i <= ngroups; i++)
            {
            gid = *grpptr++;
            (void)printf("\t");
            printgroup(gid);
            (void)printf("\n");
            }
#endif
        return;
}

int main()
{
uid_t       uid;
gid_t       gid;
char        *login;
char        termid[L_ctermid];

        login = getlogin();
        if (login == NULL)
            {
            (void)printf("Login name is not known\n");
            }
        else
            {
            (void)printf("Login name is '%s'\n",login);
            }
        (void)ctermid(termid);
        (void)printf("Terminal pathname is '%s'\n",termid);
        uid = getuid();
        (void)printf("Real UID is");
        printuser(uid);
        uid = geteuid();
        (void)printf(" and effective UID is");
        printuser(uid);
        gid = getgid();
        (void)printf("\nReal group ID is");
        printgroup(gid);
        gid = getegid();
        (void)printf(" and effective group ID is ");
        printgroup(gid);
        (void)printf("\n");
```

```
        printallgroups();
        return(0);
}
```

System Identification

POSIX provides the uname() function to give us some minimal information about the system you are using. The function is defined as:

```
int uname(struct utsname *name);
```

and fills in the struct utsname passed by the caller. If uname() is successful, a non-negative value is returned. Upon failure, −1 is returned.

The struct utsname is defined in the header file <sys/utsname.h> as a set of null-terminated character arrays. The structure contains the following members:

Member Name	Description
sysname	Name of this operating system.
nodename	Name of this node within a network. Note: There is no guarantee that this name can be used for anything. The name returned in nodename may (or may not) be useful for network use.
release	Current release level of this implementation.
version	Current version level of this release.
	While POSIX provides the release level and version, it never defines them.
machine	Name of the hardware type the system is running on.

As with most POSIX structures, these members can be in any order and other members can be present.

A typical use is:

```
#include <sys/utsname.h>

struct utsname unamebuf;

    . . .
    if (uname(&unamebuf) == −1)
        (void)printf("The system name is unknown\n");
    else
        (void)printf("This system is called '%s'\n",
            unamebuf.sysname);
    . . .
```

The format of each member is implementation-defined. POSIX does not specify the format of any of the members. There is no way a fully-portable program can interpret the information.

Date and Time

One important part of the environment is the current date and time. Programs have lots of reasons to obtain and manipulate this information. The Standard C/POSIX environment provides a set of utilities for dealing with time.

The time() Function

The `time()` function returns the number of seconds since midnight January 1, 1970 Coordinated Universal Time.[*] The function is defined as:

```
time_t time(time_t *tloc);
```

It returns the time and stores it into `tloc`. The call `time(NULL)` merely returns the time and no value is stored.

The type `time_t` is defined in `<time.h>`. While it is typically an `unsigned long`, it can be a `double` or `long double`.

The localtime() and gmtime() Functions

The `time()` function is really all you need. Given the number of seconds since a known time, it is possible to compute any time component you need. However, to prevent every programmer from reinventing the wheel, some handy library functions are provided. Two functions, `gmtime()` and `localtime()`, convert a `time_t` to a `struct tm`. The `gmtime()` function returns UTC, while `localtime()` returns the local time. The `struct tm` contains the following members:

Type	Name	Range	Description
int	tm_sec	0 - 61[†]	Seconds after the minute.
int	tm_min	0 - 59	Minutes after the hour.
int	tm_hour	0 - 23	Hours after midnight.
int	tm_mday	1 - 31	Day of the month.
int	tm_mon	0 - 11	Months since January.
int	tm_year		Years since 1900.
int	tm_wday	0 - 6	Days since Sunday.
int	tm_yday	0 - 365	Days since January 1st.

---

[*] Coordinated Universal Time is the new name for Greenwich Mean Time. The standard abbreviation is UTC because if England was going to get "universal time" at least the name was going to be in French. Such are the politics of standards.

[†] The range for `tm_sec` allows for two leap seconds.

Type	Name	Range	Description
int	tm_isdst		Daylight Savings Time flag: >0 if DST is in effect =0 if DST is not in effect <0 if the information is not available

These members can appear in any order and there may be additional members.

The time-conversion functions are defined as:

```
struct tm *localtime(const time_t *timer);
```

and:

```
struct tm *gmtime(const time_t *timer);
```

The argument is a pointer to a time_t. The localtime() and gmtime() functions return a pointer to a structure containing time information. The next call to localtime() or gmtime() may (or may not) overwrite this structure. If you want to keep it around, copy it somewhere safe.

A simple example of localtime() is:

```
time_t      now;
struct tm   *t;

    now = time((time_t *)NULL);
    t = localtime(&now);
    (void)printf("It is now %2d:%2d:%2d on %d/%d/%d\n",
        t->tm_hour, t->tm_min, t->tm_sec,
        t->tm_mon+1, t->tm_mday, t->tm_year);
    (void)printf("Day of week: %d\n",t->tm_wday+1);
    (void)printf("Day of year: %d\n",t->tm_yday+1);
    if (t->tm_isdst > 0)
        (void)printf("Daylight savings time\n");
    else
        (void)printf("Standard time\n");
```

Notice that you need to add "1" to the month before printing it. The value in tm_mon is in the range 0 to 11.

The gmtime() function is exactly the same as localtime(), except that the time is expressed in Coordinated Universal Time (UTC). Standard C allows this function to return NULL if the time zone is unknown, but POSIX Section 8.1.1 requires that the time zone be known.

If your program needs to be ported to non-POSIX and non-UNIX systems, localtime() is more portable than gmtime().

The mktime() Function

The mktime() function is the inverse of localtime(). It converts the structure that Standard C calls a *broken-down time* to a value of type time_t. The function is defined as:

```
time_t mktime(struct tm *timeptr);
```

The mktime() function ignores the original values of tm_wday and tm_yday. On successful completion, the values of tm_wday and tm_yday are updated and the other values are set to reflect the specified calendar time. This can be used to compute the day of the week a given date falls on.

The mktime() function may or may not fail on all invalid times, for example, February 29, 1995. It is best not to give mktime() invalid input.

The strftime() Function

To print the current date or time, it is possible to use localtime() and format a string. The strftime() function, similar to sprintf(), performs this task. It converts a struct tm to a string under the guidance of a format string. The strftime() function is defined as:

```
size_t strftime(char *s, size_t maxsize,
        const char *format, const struct tm *timeptr);
```

where s points to an array of maxsize bytes. format is a format-control string and timeptr is a pointer to a structure returned by localtime() or gmtime().

Characters are copied from the format string to the array pointed to by s. A conversion specifier consists of a % followed by a character that determines the substitution. The list of conversion specifiers is strftime() conversion specifiers:

Specifier	Replaced by the locale's
%a	Abbreviated weekday name.
%A	Full weekday name.
%b	Abbreviated month name.
%B	Full month name.
%c	Date and time.
%d	Day of the month as a decimal number (01-31).
%H	Hour as a decimal number (00-23).
%I	Hour as a decimal number (01-12).
%j	Day of the year as a decimal number (001-366).

Specifier	Replaced by the locale's
%m	Month as a decimal number (01-12).
%M	Minute as a decimal number (00-59).
%p	Equivalent of AM/PM for use with a 12-hour clock.
%S	Second as a decimal number (00-61).
%U	Week of the year as a decimal number (00-53) using the first Sunday as day 1 of week 1.
%w	Weekday as a decimal number (0[Sunday]-6).
%W	Week of the year as a decimal number (00-53) using the first Monday as day 1 of week 1.
%x	Date.
%X	Time.
%y	Year without a century (00-99).
%Y	Year with century (e.g., 1991).
%z	Time zone.
%%	%

Here are some examples of format strings and possible output in the POSIX locale:

Format:	Result:
%A, %B, %d, %Y	Saturday April 13, 1991
%a %d-%b-%y	Sat 13-Apr-91
%m/%d/%y	04/13/90
%Y%m%d	19900413
%H:%M	15:25
%H:%M:%S	15:25:30
%c	Sat Apr 13 15:25:30 1991
%X on %x	3:25 PM on 4/13/91

The formats %c, %X, and %x produce strings for the current locale. They offer an easy way to produce a program that can be moved from country to country.

---

* The locales are covered in Chapter 10, *Porting to Far-off Lands*. The information in the example is the default POSIX result.

The asctime() and ctime() Functions

There are a couple of functions that are shorthand for popular routines.

The function `asctime(timeptr)` returns a pointer to a string of the form:

```
Sat Apr 13 15:25:30 1991\n\0
```

The function `ctime(timer)` is equivalent to:

```
asctime(localtime(timer))
```

The difftime() Function

The C standard defines the `difftime()` function as:

```
double difftime(time_t time1, time_t time2);
```

returning the number of seconds between `time1` and `time2` expressed as a `double`. Since POSIX defines the units of `time_t` as seconds since midnight January 1, 1970 Coordinated Universal Time, this function is not needed. A simple subtraction with a cast gives the same answer. For example, in:

```
time_t      start,end;
double      diff1, diff2;
. . .
diff1 = difftime(end,start);
diff2 = end - start;
```

`diff1` will be equal to `diff2`. Use the `difftime()` function if your code might be ported to systems which use Standard C but do not conform to POSIX.

The clock() and times() Functions

The `clock()` function defined in Standard C is defined as:

```
clock_t clock(void);
```

and returns the amount of processor time used. The standard does not define when the clock starts, so this function is used to measure the amount of processor time used between two events, say, the start and end of a complex calculation.

The `clock()` function returns a number that can be converted to seconds by dividing by `CLOCKS_PER_SEC`.

In addition to the `clock()` function, POSIX defines a more powerful function called `times()`. This is defined as:

```
clock_t times(struct tms *buffer);
```

and returns the amount of real time since the system was started.* The return value is useful for computing the elapsed time between two events. The value of a `clock_t` can be converted to seconds by dividing by the macro `CLK_TCK`.

The `struct tms` structure contains at least the following members:

Member Name	Description
`tms_utime`	User CPU time.
`tms_stime`	System CPU time.
`tms_cutime`	User time of terminated child processes.
`tms_cstime`	System time of terminated child processes.

All members have the type `clock_t` and can be converted to seconds by dividing by the symbol `CLK_TCK`. User time is time charged for the execution of user processes. System time is time charged for executing the system on behalf of the process. Which library functions charge system time and the amount that they charge will vary from implementation to implementation.

If you plan to compile your application on every target computer, dividing by `CLK_TCK` to get seconds is fine. However, if you plan to compile in one place and move your compiled binary from computer to computer, dividing by `CLK_TCK` may give the wrong answer. It is better to use the `sysconf(_SC_CLK_TCK)` function to determine this value at run time.† The `sysconf()` function is described later in this chapter.

Environment Variables

An array of strings called the *environment* is made available when the process begins. This array is pointed to by the external variable `environ`, which is defined as:

```
extern char **environ;
```

---

* The `times()` function does not really need to return the amount of real time since the system was started. It really returns the amount of real time since some arbitrary point in the past before any processes were started. Applications can count on this number increasing as they `fork()` and `exec()` new processes.

† Of course, the clever system implementer may have defined the `CLK_TCK` macro with a call to `sysconf()`, for example:

```
#define CLK_TCK ((clock_t)(__sysconf(3)))
```

He or she used `__sysconf()` instead of `sysconf()` because the `sysconf()` function is not declared in `<time.h>` and is available for the user unless `<unistd.h>` is included. The value 3 is used instead of `_SC_CLK_TCK` for the same reason.

These strings have the form `name=value`; the following names are defined by POSIX:

Name	Description
HOME	The name of the user's initial working directory.
LANG	The name of the predefined setting for locale.
LC_ALL	The default locale to use if any of the following `LC_` symbols is not defined.
LC_COLLATE	The name of the locale for collation information.
LC_CTYPE	The name of the locale for character classification.
LC_MONETARY	The name of the locale for money related information.
LC_NUMERIC	The name of the locale for numeric editing.
LC_TIME	The name of the locale for date- and time-formatting information.
LOGNAME	The name of the user's login account.
PATH	The sequence of path prefixes used by `execlp()` and `execvp()` in locating programs to run.
TERM	The user's terminal type.
TZ	Time zone information.

The environment variables having to do with locale are used for moving an application from one country to another. They are discussed in Chapter 10, *Porting to Far-off Lands*.

Of course, some variables may be missing and other environment variables may be present. Many programs look in the environment variable list for system-specific information. These programs can be fully portable and still adjust themselves to a given system. The value string contains some form of user preference information. For example:

```
mm=/usr/don/mail.rc
```

or:

```
haminfo="-call WB2UMF -grid FN42"
```

The getenv() Function

The `getenv()` function is used to look up names in the environment strings. This is defined as:

```
char *getenv(const char *name);
```

It searches the environment for name and returns a pointer to the value or NULL if name cannot be found. Like most functions that return a pointer to a string, getenv() may overwrite the information on a subsequent call.

Do not attempt to modify the string returned by getenv(); it might be a copy of the real environment variable.

The sysconf() Function

The POSIX standard is defined exclusively at the source-code level. The objective is that a conforming application can be compiled and executed on a conforming implementation.

While POSIX does not guarantee binary portability even across machines of the same make and model, it does try hard not to preclude portability either.

Traditional UNIX applications are distributed in one of two ways:

- By distributing portable source files that can be tailored to each system (most of the public domain applications fall into this category). Software distributed in source form can be tailored in many ways. For example, an installation script can create system-specific header files used to compile the application. Applications distributed by the Free Software Foundation, such as GNU C, provide a good example of this technique.

- By distributing compiled software for a specific make and model of computer. Software vendors would like to compile their software and distribute only the compiled binary because it provides the best security for the software. Software vendors would also like as much binary portability as possible.

One of the aids to binary portability is the sysconf() function. It lets an application determine the run-time value of variables in <limits.h>. The sysconf() function is defined as:

```
long sysconf(int name);
```

where name is a code for one of the system limits.[*] The codes are:

Compile-Time Macro	sysconf() name	Description
ARG_MAX	_SC_ARG_MAX	The length of the arguments for the exec() function.
_POSIX_CHILD_MAX	_SC_CHILD_MAX	The number of simultaneous processes per real user ID.

---

[*] The most common error I have seen with sysconf() and pathconf() is confusing the parameter to pass with the value returned. The parameter is always a macro, such as _SC_OPEN_MAX. The system limit is returned.

Compile-Time Macro	sysconf() name	Description
CLK_TCK	_SC_CLK_TCK	The number of clock ticks per second.
_POSIX_NGROUPS_MAX	_SC_NGROUPS_MAX	The number of simultaneous supplementary group IDs.
STREAM_MAX*	_SC_STREAM_MAX*	The maximum number of streams that one process can have open at one time. This is the same as FOPEN_MAX from the C standard.
TZNAME_MAX*	_SC_TZNAME_MAX*	The maximum number of bytes in a time zone name.
_POSIX_OPEN_MAX	_SC_OPEN_MAX	The maximum number of files that one process can have open at one time.
_POSIX_JOB_CONTROL	_SC_JOB_CONTROL	Job control functions are supported.
_POSIX_SAVED_IDS	_SC_SAVED_IDS	Each process has a saved SETUID and a saved SETGID.
_POSIX_VERSION	_SC_VERSION	Indicates the 4-digit year and 2-digit month in which the standard was approved. The integer 198808L indicates the 1988 version and the integer 199009L indicates the 1990 version.

POSIX Section 2.8.4 (2.9.4 in the 1988 version) states, "A definition of one of the values ... shall be omitted from the <limits.h> on specific implementations where the corresponding value is equal to or greater than the stated minimum, but is indeterminate." This paragraph has been interpreted in several different ways. I believe that the safest thing to do is to ignore symbols and always use the value returned by sysconf(). That is, use sysconf(_SC_OPEN_MAX) instead of _POSIX_OPEN_MAX. This will often be a more generous value.

---

* This symbol is defined in IEEE Std 1003.1-1990 but not in IEEE Std 1003.1-1988.

The pathconf() and fpathconf() Functions

Some limits vary not only from system to system but also from file to file. The pathconf() and fpathconf() functions return file-specific configuration information. They are defined as:

```
long pathconf(const char *path, int name);
```

and:

```
long fpathconf(int fildes, int name);
```

The possible values for name are:

Name	Description
_PC_LINK_MAX	Maximum value of a file's link count. If path or fildes refers to a directory, then this value applies to the entire directory.
_PC_MAX_CANON	Maximum length of a formatted input line. path or fildes must refer to a terminal.
_PC_MAX_INPUT	Maximum length of an input line. path or fildes must refer to a terminal.
_PC_NAME_MAX	Maximum length of a filename for this directory.
_PC_PATH_MAX	The maximum length of a relative pathname when this directory is the working directory. That is, the number of characters that may be appended to path and still have a valid pathname.
_PC_PIPE_BUF	Size of the pipe buffer. fildes must refer to a pipe or FIFO. path must be a FIFO.
_PC_CHOWN_RESTRICTED	The chown() system call may not be used on this file. If path or fildes refers to a directory, then this applies to all files in that directory
_PC_NO_TRUNC	Generate an error if a filename is truncated in the named directory.
_PC_VDISABLE	Allow special-character processing to be disabled. path or fildes must refer to a terminal.

The sysconf(), pathconf(), and fpathconf() functions were invented by the POSIX committee. They are not found on older systems. You must use some form of compile-time value on non-POSIX systems.

The values returned by these functions should be thought of as minimum guarantees. For example, if pathconf(".",_SC_NAME_MAX) returns 63, your application can create files with names up to 63 characters. If you read the directory with `readdir()`, you may encounter files with names greater than 63 characters. The values returned by `sysconf()` and `pathconf()` are not suitable for allocating memory. Some values may be huge.

Portability Lab

To review the contents of this chapter, try to do the following exercises:

1. This chapter gives two different ways to get the user's login name. What are they? Is there any advantage to one over the other?

2. What is the difference between the real user ID and the effective user ID?

3. What errors does `geteuid()` detect?

4. Is there a portability advantage to using `getpwuid()` instead of just reading `/etc/passwd`?

5. One way to obtain the number of groups is to call `getgroups()` with `gidsetsize` equal to zero. Another way is to use the symbol `NGROUPS_MAX`. A third way is to call `sysconf(_SC_NGROUPS_MAX)`. It is possible for all three methods to come up with a different answer. Give an example of a good use for each of the methods.

6. Give one use for the information returned by the `uname()` function.

7. Is it possible for a POSIX system to know the local time but not know the UTC time? Why or why not?

8. Write a simple program to print out the day of the week on which your birthday falls for the next 20 years.

9. The format specifier `%x` in `strftime()` prints the date. Why is this better than `%d/%m/%y`? Note: Answers of the form "it is less typing" do not count.

10. The POSIX committee is working to eliminate the use of the symbol `CLK_TCK`. Why? What can replace it?

11. What is a portable use for the information returned by `times()`?

12. What is one disadvantage of using the environment variables to provide user preference information to an application? What is one advantage?

13. The `sysconf()` function is intended to help a compiled program move from one system to another. What do you think some of the rules are to allow this kind of portability?

14. What information does the call:

    ```
    pathconf("/usr",_PC_NAME_MAX);
    ```

    return?

CHAPTER 8

Terminal I/O

The functions we have already covered (scanf(), printf(), read(), write(), and so on) are used by most applications to do I/O to a terminal. This chapter concentrates on the control functions defined in the header file <termios.h>. The vast majority of applications do not use terminal control functions. We begin by looking at the hardware and the use of tcsetattr() to modify a terminal's parameters. There is an example showing how to turn off the echoing of input on the terminal screen, a fairly typical use of the terminal control functions. Then we go through a detailed description of input processing and look at all the parameters a program can alter. We look at some examples of using a terminal port for computer-to-computer communications. Finally, we describe POSIX job control. These are functions used by the shell to control which processes get signals and which ones have access to the terminal.

The *1984 /usr/group Standard* attempted to specify a portable mechanism that application writers could use to get and set the modes of an asynchronous terminal. The intention of that committee was to provide an interface that was neither implementation-specific nor hardware-dependent. The terminal interface specification underwent more debate and revision than any other part of the POSIX standard.

The resulting interface, though it meets all of the original goals, is different from any existing system. The most dramatic change is the replacement of the ioctl() function with a collection of terminal-specific functions. The change was made for several reasons:

- The ioctl() mechanism is difficult to specify adequately due to its use of a third argument that varies in both size and type according to the second argument.

- The exact semantics of ioctl() are different on different systems.

- None of the existing implementations was adequate in an international environment.

While the functions for terminal control may be new to you, experienced UNIX programmers will see many familiar things.

Terminal Concepts

A classic terminal is a keyboard and a display (or printer) that is connected to the computer using an asynchronous communications port. From the perspective of the operating system, the important characteristic of a terminal is the communications port that connects it to the host and not the device sitting at the end of the wire. Figure 8-1 shows a typical configuration.

FIGURE 8-1. Communications hardware

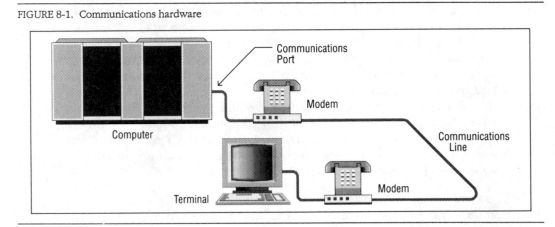

☞ Many UNIX manuals (even the POSIX standard) use the phrase "terminal parameters" in a way that might be confusing. Strictly speaking, the terminal-control library functions change the characteristics of the communications port and have no effect on the terminal. When you read a phrase like "setting the terminal speed," it means setting the speed of the communications port to match the speed of the terminal.

An asynchronous communications port can be used to talk to other computers, printers, plotters, and special I/O equipment. The programming techniques used are the same as talking to a computer terminal.

A serial device sends a character one bit at a time. Each character starts with a leading zero called the start bit. The data bits are sent one at a time, beginning with the Least Significant Bit (LSB) and ending with the Most Significant Bit (MSB). The last bit to be sent is a trailing one called the stop bit. The ASCII character D might be represented as shown in Figure 8-2.

The ASCII code uses seven data bits. The parity bit is used to make the total number of one bits even (or, on some systems, odd). The speed of transmission (the number of bits per second that are transmitted counting the start and stop bits) is called the baud rate.

If the stop bit is not a 1, then a framing error takes place. If all of the data bits are zero and there is a framing error, a break condition occurs.

FIGURE 8-2. ASCII D

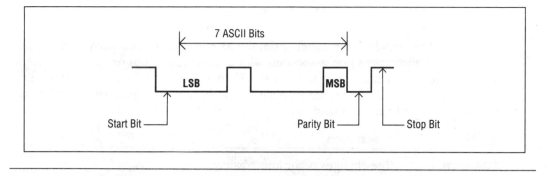

Most terminals operate in full-duplex. When you press a key, a character is sent from the terminal to the computer. When it receives the character, the computer sends the character back to the terminal where it is displayed. The process of sending characters back to the terminal is called *echoing*.

Echoing gives the computer control over the characters displayed by the terminal. Some uses of echoing are:

- A program can inhibit echo to hide the characters you type. For example, `login` inhibits echo to keep your password secret and `vi` inhibits echo to prevent commands from appearing on the screen.

- A program can echo a special sequence. For example, a backspace may echo as backspace-space-backspace to wipe out the last character you typed.

You can control echoing using the functions described in this chapter.

Setting Terminal Parameters

Terminal parameters are all manipulated through a data structure known as `struct termios`. The `tcgetattr()` function copies the parameters from the operating system into a `termios` structure and the `tcsetattr()` function copies the parameters from a `termios` structure into the operating system. First, we will look at these two functions and then we will look at the `termios` structure in detail.

The tcsetattr() and tcgetattr() Functions

The function:

```
int tcgetattr(int fildes, struct termios *ptr);
```

copies all of the information associated with `fildes` into the `struct termios` pointed to by `ptr`. The `fildes` argument must be a valid file descriptor associated with a terminal.

The function:

```
int tcsetattr(int fildes, int option,
                    struct termios *ptr);
```

copies all of the terminal parameters from the `struct termios` pointed to by `ptr` into the communications port associated with `fildes`. The `tcsetattr()` function sets every terminal parameter with one call. There is no way to selectively set terminal parameters. The `fildes` argument must be a valid file descriptor associated with a terminal. The `option` argument must be one of the following symbols:

Symbol	Description
TCSANOW	The changes occur immediately.
TCSADRAIN	The changes occur after all output written to `fildes` has been transmitted. This function may be used when changing parameters that affect output. See "Avoiding Pitfalls" on Page 161.
TCSAFLUSH	Same as `TCSADRAIN` except that, in addition to waiting for output, all input that had been received but not read is discarded.

The `tcsetattr()` function does not detect errors in the `struct termios`. If there are invalid combinations, `tcsetattr()` just does its best. If you need to know if a particular terminal attribute was correctly set, you must follow the `tcsetattr()` with a `tcgetattr()`.

The termios Structure

The `tcgetattr()` and `tcsetattr()` functions read or write all of the terminal parameters with one call. The proper way to modify terminal parameters is by reading them with `tcgetattr()`, changing the parameters of interest, and rewriting them with `tcsetattr()`.

The `termios` structure and all of the functions that operate on it are defined in `<termios.h>`. Most of the terminal parameters should not be changed by an application. These parameters can be explicitly changed by the user using a utility such as `stty`. The `termios` structure has five members and each member has flags defined by POSIX as well as system-specific flags:

Member Name	Member Type	Description
c_iflag	tcflag_t	Controls the processing of input data. There are 11 flags defined by POSIX. There is only one, ISTRIP, that may be of interest to a portable application. This flag causes input characters to be masked to seven bits.
c_oflag	tcflag_t	Controls the processing of output data. The only flag defined by POSIX, OPOST, causes system-specific output processing. There are no flags of interest to a portable application.
c_cflag	tcflag_t	Controls information related to the hardware, for example, the parity setting. There are seven flags defined by POSIX, none of interest to a portable application.
c_lflag	tcflag_t	Controls echoing and character processing. There are nine flags defined by POSIX; four of these flags may be modified by a portable application:

ECHO	Turns on echoing.
ICANON	Turns on input processing.
ISIG	Enables signals.
TOSTOP	Stops background processes if they write to the controlling terminal.

Member Name	Member Type	Description
c_cc	cc_t	An array of control characters. The size of the array is given by the symbol NCCS. Each element has a unique function described later in this chapter.

A portable application may determine what these characters are; however, it should not change them. |

System V termio and POSIX termios Structures

If you use System V, you will notice that the POSIX `termios` structure is very similar to the `termio` structure used by System V. The System V structure is:

```
struct termio
{
unsigned short  c_iflag;
unsigned short  c_oflag;
unsigned short  c_cflag;
unsigned short  c_lflag
char            c_line;
unsigned char   c_cc[NCC];
}
```

POSIX changed `unsigned short` to a defined type, `tcflag_t`, which is typically an `unsigned short` or an `unsigned long`. POSIX also changed `unsigned char` to `cc_t`. On most systems, `cc_t` is still an `unsigned char`.

POSIX also supports terminals that have different input and output baud rates; System V does not.

Converting from System V to POSIX is very easy:

- Use `<termios.h>` instead of `<termio.h>` and add an "s" to the name of the structure.

- If your program places a baud rate in the `CBAUD` field of `termio`, replace that with calls to `cfsetispeed()` and `cfsetospeed()`.

- Change calls to `ioctl()` to call `tcsetattr()` or one of the other functions described in this chapter.

- The `c_line` member of `termio`, which must be set to zero in System V, is not used in POSIX.

Example: Reading a Password

Before covering all of the details of the various terminal control functions, we will show a typical use for these functions. Let's write a function to read a password from the terminal. Here is a brief specification for this function:

1. The function will be defined as:

   ```
   int getpswd(char *buff, size_t size);
   ```

   where `buff` is a pointer to a buffer to receive the password and `size` is the size of that buffer.

   The `getpswd()` function returns the number of characters read or −1 in case of error.

2. The function should issue a prompt of `Password:`

3. The function should discard characters typed before the prompt appears (type-ahead). This will encourage the person typing the password to wait for the echo to be turned off.

4. Turn off echo.

5. Read the password from the terminal.

6. Restore echo.

Let's look at a couple of technical details:

- Prompting for a password with:

  ```
  (void)printf("Password: ");
  ```

is not enough to guarantee that the user can read it. We need to call:

```
(void)fflush(stdout);
```

to make sure that the standard I/O library issues a call to write().

In addition, we use the TCSAFLUSH option to tcsetattr() to wait for all of the characters to be sent to the terminal.

- The TCSAFLUSH option also discards type-ahead meeting item #3 in the specification for getpswd().

The code for this function is shown in Example 8-1.

EXAMPLE 8-1. getpswd.c

```
#define _POSIX_SOURCE 1

#include <termios.h>
#include <stdio.h>
#include <sys/types.h>
#include <unistd.h>

int getpswd(char *buff,unsigned size)
{
struct termios attr;        /* Used for getting and setting
                             * terminal attributes.
                             */

int              n;         /* Number of bytes read */

    (void)printf("Password: "); /* Issue the prompt */
    (void)fflush(stdout);       /* Cause the data to be written out
                                 * to the terminal
                                 */

    /*
     * Now turn off echo.
     */

    if(tcgetattr(STDIN_FILENO,&attr) != 0) return(-1);
                        /* Start by getting current
                         * attributes.  This call
                         * copies all of the terminal
                         * parameters into attr.
                         */

    attr.c_lflag &= ~(ECHO);
                        /* Turn off echo flag.
                         * NOTE: We are careful not to
                         * modify any bits except ECHO.
                         */

    if(tcsetattr(STDIN_FILENO,TCSAFLUSH,&attr) != 0)
                return(-1);
                        /* Wait for all of the data
                         * to be printed.
                         */
                        /* Set all of the terminal
                         * parameters from the (slightly)
```

```
                                 * modified struct termios.
                                 */
                                /* Discard any characters that
                                 * have been typed but
                                 * not yet read.
                                 */

        n = read(STDIN_FILENO,buff,size);
                                /* Read a line from the
                                 * terminal.
                                 */

        /*
         * Turn echo back on.
         */
        attr.c_lflag |= ECHO;
        if(tcsetattr(STDIN_FILENO,TCSANOW,&attr) != 0)
                        return(-1);

        return(n);
                                /*
                                 * Return the number of bytes
                                 * in the password
                                 */
}
```

This function uses a common trick: since all of the functions that it calls return −1 and store an error code in errno when they detect an error, all this function has to do is check for a non-zero return from the library and pass that back to the caller. This trick is easier done than said, for example:

```
        if (tcdrain(STDOUT_FILENO) != 0) return(-1);
```

Now, let's look at how input and output characters are processed.

Input Processing

When an application reads from a disk, the data is merely transferred from the disk to the program, with no special processing taking place. This is not true when data is read from a terminal. When a character is typed on a terminal, the system does some processing before handing it to the user program. This processing consists of two tasks:

- Echoing.
- Looking for special characters.

Output Processing

Various forms of output processing may be required. For example, a terminal may need a delay after a newline character to give it enough time to scroll. POSIX does not specify any standard output processing—each system is free to do what is required. In general, this freedom makes your application more portable because the system takes care of the hardware details.

Modem Control

If a terminal is connected to the host by a modem and telephone line, the program may want to get some control over the telephone connection. POSIX provides minimal modem control:

- The SIGHUP signal is sent to a program if the connection to the controlling terminal is unexpectedly lost.

- The host can also hang up on the user via the tcsetattr() function.

More elaborate modem control was not specified because it would reduce application program portability, especially in Europe. Hardware-specific functions, such as answering the phone and detecting the carrier, are left to the operating system.

Non-Canonical I/O

In normal, or canonical, mode, terminal input is processed in units of lines. Thus, a read request does not return until an entire line has been typed. At most one line is returned by a single read call.

Sometimes, you might want to read input without breaking it into lines. For example, an editor might respond to a single key press. In non-canonical mode, input bytes are not assembled into lines and erase and kill processing is not done. The read completes either after a minimum number of characters is read or after some timeout occurs.

Input Modes

The c_iflag member of the termios structure is the bitwise inclusive OR of 11 flags. The flags are:

Flag	Description
BRKINT	
IGNBRK	If BRKINT is set and IGNBRK is not set, a break condition flushes all data from the input and output queues and generates a SIGINT signal for the foreground process group. If neither BRKINT nor IGNBRK is set, a break condition is read as '\0'. If PARMRK is also set, breaks are translated into the following three-byte sequence:

                Byte 1 '\377'
                Byte 2 '\0'
                Byte 3 '\0'

Using breaks makes your program depend on particular hardware. Not all terminals can generate a break condition.

Flag	Description
IGNPAR	If IGNPAR is set, a byte with a framing or parity error (other than a break) is ignored.

Flag	Description
PARMRK	If PARMRK is set, and IGNPAR is not set, a byte with a framing or parity error is given to the application as the following three-byte sequence:

> Byte 1 '\377'
> Byte 2 '\0'
> Byte 3 **X**

where **X** is the byte with the error.

If ISTRIP is not set, a valid '\377' is given to the application as the following two-byte sequence:

> Byte 1 '\377'
> Byte 2 '\377'.

Flag	Description
INPCK	The INPCK flag enables parity checking.
ISTRIP	If set, valid input bytes are first stripped to seven bits.
INLCR	If set, a received NL character is translated into a CR character.
IGNCR	If set, a received CR is ignored.
ICRNL	If ICRNL is set and IGNCR is not set, a received CR is translated into a NL character.
IXON	If set, allows the terminal to control the flow of output from the computer. Sending a STOP character to the computer suspends output until a START character is received. If IXON is set, the START and STOP characters merely perform flow control. Your program never sees them. If IXON is not set, the characters are passed to your program as ordinary data.
IXOFF	If set, requests the computer to control the flow of data from the terminal. The system will send START and STOP characters to the terminal to prevent loss of input data.

Output Modes

The c_oflag field has one bit defined. The OPOST bit, if set, causes output data to be processed in an implementation-defined manner; otherwise the data is transmitted without change. Setting this bit makes your program less portable. For full portability, do not change the c_oflag member.

Control Modes

The `c_cflag` field is composed of the bitwise inclusive OR of the following seven flags:

Flag	Description
CLOCAL	Ignore modem status lines.
CREAD	Enable receiver. If this bit is not set, no characters are received.
CSIZE	One of the following symbols:

        CS5 for 5 bits-per-byte
        CS6 for 6 bits-per-byte
        CS7 for 7 bits-per-byte
        CS8 for 8 bits-per-byte

Flag	Description
CSTOPB	If set, two stop bits are sent; otherwise, only one is sent. Some older mechanical terminals require two stop bits, but these terminals are quite rare today.
HUPCL	If there is a user logged in on this terminal, hang up the modem when he or she logs out. If the communications port is being used for data, hang up the modem after all processes close the device.
PARENB	If set, parity generation and detection is enabled and a parity bit is added to each character.
PARODD	If both PARODD and PARENB are set, odd parity is used. If PARENB is set but PARODD is not set, even parity is used. If PARENB is not set, the setting of PARODD is ignored.

Local Modes

The `c_lflags` field contains the bitwise inclusive OR of the following nine flags:

Flag	Description
ECHO	If set, input characters are echoed back to the terminal.
ECHOE	If ECHOE and ICANON are both set, the ERASE character causes the terminal to erase the last character from the display, if possible.
ECHOK	If ECHOK and ICANON are both set, the KILL character erases the last line from the display. If the hardware does not allow the data to be erased, this flag is ignored.
ECHONL	If ECHONL and ICANON are both set, the '\n' character is echoed even if ECHO is not set.
ICANON	If set, enables canonical input processing.
ISIG	If set, the INTR, QUIT, and SUSP characters generate signals.

Flag	Description
NOFLSH	If set, the normal flush of the input and output queues on the INTR, QUIT, and SUSP characters is not done.
TOSTOP	If set and job control is supported, the signal SIGTTOU is sent to the process group of a process that tries to write to the controlling terminal if it is not in the foreground process group for that terminal. This signal, by default, stops the members of the process group.
IEXTEN	If set, implementation-defined functions are recognized from the input data. Portable programs should not set this bit.

Control Characters

Special characters are defined by the c_cc_array. The size of this array is given by the symbol NCCS in the <termios.h> header file. The meaning of the members of the c_cc array depends on the setting of the ICANON flag. If ICANON is set, the array elements have the following meanings:

Array Subscript	Description
VEOF	EOF character. The end-of-file character (usually Control-D) may be used to generate an EOF from the terminal.
VEOL	EOL character. The newline (Control-J) is the normal line delimiter.
VERASE	ERASE character. The erase character (typically backspace or delete) erases the preceding character.
VINTR	INTR character. The interrupt character (usually Control-C or DEL) generates a SIGINT. It is often used to stop a running program. See Example 8-1 to see how an application can take advantage of SIGINT.
VKILL	KILL character. The kill character (usually Control-U) deletes the entire line being typed.
VQUIT	QUIT character. The quit character (typically Control-\) generates a SIGQUIT. The POSIX standard does not specify any special action for SIGQUIT. The shell in UNIX systems uses SIGQUIT to stop the current program and generate a core file.
VSUSP	SUSP character. The suspend character (typically Control-Z) generates a SIGTSTP signal and is used to place a process in the background. See the discussion of POSIX job control later in this chapter for a description of a background process.
VSTART	START character. The start character (almost always Control-Q) is typed by the user to resume output after a stop character.

Array Subscript	Description
VSTOP	STOP character. The stop character (almost always Control-S) stops the computer from sending output to the terminal. It is useful for preventing information from scrolling off the screen faster than you can read it.

Your program probably should not change any of these special characters because:

- The control characters affect all of the processes using the terminal, including the shell. In general, you should not do things which may interfere with other processes. Disabling the INTR character is very different from ignoring SIGINT.

- You may astonish the user. For example, if you change the INTR character from Control-C to Control-I, you would confuse most people.

- The changes you make are not reset when your program exits. If your program crashes, the terminal may be left in an unusable state.

An application should not disable special characters and POSIX does not make it easy. System V suggests disabling special characters by setting them to a value unlikely to occur, say '\377'. Picking an unlikely character is not fully portable, especially in an international environment. POSIX tries to solve this problem; however, it does not do a perfect job. Here are the rules that POSIX defines:

1. If the symbol _POSIX_VDISABLE is defined in the header <unistd.h> with a value other than −1, then the value of _POSIX_VDISABLE can be used to disable special characters on all terminals.

2. If the symbol _POSIX_VDISABLE is not defined in <unistd.h> or has the value −1, pathconf(path,_PC_VDISABLE) or fpathconf(path,_PC_VDISABLE) must be used to determine the character to use, if any.

3. If pathconf() or fpathconf() return −1 with errno unchanged, the system has no suggestion for the value to use to disable special characters.

Here is some sample code that disables the interrupt character:

```
#if !defined(_POSIX_VDISABLE) || (_POSIX_VDISABLE == -1)
    /* The symbol is defined so we can just use it.
     */
    t.c_cc[VINTR] = _POSIX_VDISABLE;
#else /* The symbol is not defined */
    errno = 0;      /* Make sure we can tell
                     * if fpathconf() changes
                     * errno.
                     */
    /* See if it is defined for the terminal. */
    temp = fpathconf(tty,_PC_VDISABLE);
    if (temp != -1)
            {       /* temp is not -1.  This is
                     * the value to use to disable
                     * the interrupt character.
                     */
```

```
            t.c_cc[VINTR] = temp; /* Stuff it in. */
            return;               /* All set. */
            }
    /* We get here if fpathconf() returned -1.  If
     * errno is changed then there was a real
     * error.
     */
    if (errno != 0) PANIC;
    /* We get here is we can not disable the
     * the interrupt character.  Fall back on
     * the unlikely character.
     */
    t.c_cc[VINTR] = 0377;
#endif
    return;
```

If `ICANON` is not set, the `c_cc` array elements have the following meanings:

Array Subscript	Description
VINTR	INTR character.
VMIN	If VTIME is zero, it is the number of bytes to read. A pending read is not satisfied until enough bytes or a signal is received. If VTIME is not zero, the TIME value is used as an inter-byte timer. If TIME/10 seconds expire between characters, the read is satisfied.
VQUIT	QUIT character.
VTIME	If VMIN is zero, a read is satisfied as soon as a single byte is received or TIME/10 seconds elapse. If VMIN is not zero, the action is as described above for VMIN. If both VMIN and VTIME are zero the read() function will return as much data as possible without waiting.
VSTART	START character.
VSTOP	STOP character.
VSUSP	SUSPEND character.

AT&T System V uses the same index into the `c_cc` array for VMIN and VEOF. VTIME shares an index with VEOL. You should remember that this reuse can occur.

Speed Storing Functions

The `termios` structure also contains the input and output baud rates for the terminal. POSIX defines some functions to copy the baud rates into and out of the `termios` structure. The functions:

```
speed_t cfgetispeed(const struct termios *ptr);
speed_t cfgetospeed(const struct termios *ptr);
```

return the input and output baud rates from the structure pointed to by `ptr`. These functions blindly return the values in the structure. There is no check to see if these values are valid. The functions:

```
int cfsetispeed(struct termios *ptr, speed_t spd);
int cfsetospeed(struct termios *ptr, speed_t spd);
```

copy the value `spd` into the structure pointed to by `ptr`. These functions return zero on success and –1 on error; however, the standard does not require any error checking. These functions merely store values into a structure. The hardware is not changed until a `tcsetattr()` is done.

The type `speed_t` is defined in `<termios.h>` and is `unsigned`. Symbols of the form B*xxxx* are defined for each legal baud rate. The complete list of symbols and baud rates is given in the following table:

Symbol	Baud Rate
B0	0[*]
B50	50
B75	75
B110	110
B134	134.5[†]
B150	150
B200	200
B300	300
B600	600
B1200	1200
B1800	1800
B2400	2400
B4800	4800
B9600	9600
B19200	19200
B38400	38400

Portable programs should set both the input and the output baud rates. Split speed may or may not work for a given terminal.

---

[*] The zero baud rate disables the communications port. If there is a modem, the computer hangs up the phone.

[†] The 134.5-baud speed was used by IBM 2741-style terminals. These terminals were very popular in the late 1960s and early 70s. Since they do not use ASCII and are quite slow, they are rare today.

Line Control Functions

There are a few assorted functions for dealing with terminals. These are functions that are new with POSIX. If you must move your application to an older (non-POSIX) system, you can create these functions using `ioctl()`.

The tcsendbreak() Function

Some terminals perform a special function when they receive a break. The `tcsend-break()` function provides a POSIX application with a portable method of generating a break. Since the meaning of break varies from terminal to terminal, it is more portable to avoid this function.

The function:

```
int tcsendbreak(int fildes, int duration);
```

sends a break (a `'\0'` with a framing error). The `duration` parameter is used to indicate how long the break should be. The standard does not define the units of `duration` and the only portable value is zero. This will send a break between 250 and 500 milliseconds long.

The tcdrain() Function

The function:

```
int tcdrain(int fildes);
```

waits for all of the data written to `fildes` to be transmitted. The `fildes` argument must be a valid file descriptor associated with a terminal. This function waits only for data that has already been written with the `write()` function. If you are using the standard I/O library (`fprintf()`, `putc()`, etc.), you must first use the `fflush()` function to transmit buffered data.

This function is equivalent to using `tcsetattr()` with the TCSADRAIN flag, except no terminal parameters are set.

The tcflush() Function

The function:

```
int tcflush(int fildes, int option);
```

discards terminal input and/or output data. The exact action depends on the `option` argument:

option	Description
TCIFLUSH	Discard all data that has been received but not read.
TCOFLUSH	Discard all data that has been written but not transmitted.
TCIOFLUSH	Do both the TCIFLUSH and TCOFLUSH functions.

The tcflow() Function

The function:

```
int tcflow(int fildes, int action);
```

suspends or resumes transmission or reception of data depending on the value of `action`. The `action` argument must be one of the following symbols:

action	Description
TCOOFF	Suspend output.
TCOON	Resume output.
TCIOFF	Transmit a STOP character. This is intended to cause the terminal to stop sending data to the system.
TCION	Transmit a START character. This is intended to cause the terminal to resume sending data to the system.

Avoiding Pitfalls

There are several unfortunate attributes of the `tcsetattr()` interface:

- There may be (and almost always are) implementation-defined bits in the `struct termios`. If your program builds a `struct termios` and does a `tcsetattr()`, it may trash some implementation-defined bits.

- There is no good error reporting. For example, if you try to set a terminal to 19200 baud and the hardware does not support this speed, `tcsetattr()` does not change the line speed.

To be safe and make your program fully portable, follow these steps:

1. Use the `tcdrain()` function to wait for all output data to be transmitted.

2. Use the `tcgetattr()` function to read the current terminal settings.

3. Modify the fields in `struct termios` to make any changes that you need. Do not change any bits that are not defined in the standard.

4. Use the `tcsetattr()` function to change the terminal characteristics.

5. Read back the new terminal characteristics with `tcgetattr()`.

6. Compare the results of step 5 with the argument to step 4 and see if there were any settings that you were unable to change.

Example: Computer-to-Computer Communications

Sometimes one needs to use a terminal port for data. This is often done to talk to other computers. Let's write a simple version of the System V `cu` command. The `cu` command calls up another system. The `cu` program runs as two processes: the transmit process reads data from the standard input and passes it to the remote system; the receive process accepts data from the remote system and passes it to standard output. The System V version has many command line options and other features, but our `cu` is very simple.

There are three functions in the `cu` utility:

1. `comm_init()` gets the package started. This function opens the communications port and sets all of the terminal parameters. For computer-to-computer communications, most character processing is turned off.

2. The `listen()` function waits for data to arrive from the terminal port and calls the `write()` function for each character that is read. A `fork()` is done prior to calling `listen()`. This leaves one process to listen for data while the other process is used to transmit.

3. The `main()` function first calls `comm_init()` to establish a connection to the remote system. Next, `main()` turns off echo and canonical processing for the controlling terminal. Then, `main()` calls `listen()` as a process. Finally, `main()` reads characters from standard input and sends them to the communications port.

The code is shown in Example 8-2:

EXAMPLE 8-2. `cu.c`

```
 1 #define _POSIX_SOURCE 1
 2
 3 #include <termios.h>
 4 #include <sys/types.h>
 5 #include <sys/stat.h>
 6 #include <fcntl.h>
 7 #include <unistd.h>
 8 #include "panic.h"               /* Defines the PANIC macro */
 9
10 #define BUFFSIZE 256
11
12 static int chan = -1;            /* I/O Descriptor for the
13                                   * terminal port.
14                                   */
15
```

```
16
17 /*
18  * Setup the communications port
19  */
20 void comm_init(void)
21 {
22 struct termios t;
23
24
25     chan = open("/dev/tty01", O_RDWR|O_NOCTTY);
26     if (chan == -1) PANIC;
27     if (tcgetattr(chan, &t) != 0) PANIC;
28     t.c_cc[VMIN] = 32;              /* Wake up after 32
29                                     * characters arrive.
30                                     */
31     t.c_cc[VTIME] = 1;             /* Wake up 0.1 seconds
32                                     * after the first char
33                                     * arrives.
34                                     */
35                                    /* The combination of
36                                     * VMIN/VTIME will cause
37                                     * the program to wake up
38                                     * 0.1 seconds after the
39                                     * first character arrives
40                                     * or after 32 characters
41                                     * arrive whichever comes
42                                     * first.
43                                     */
44     t.c_iflag &= ~(BRKINT          /* Ignore break      */
45       | IGNPAR | PARMRK |          /* Ignore parity     */
46           INPCK |                  /* Ignore parity     */
47           ISTRIP |                 /* Don't mask        */
48     INLCR | IGNCR | ICRNL          /* No <cr> or <lf>   */
49       | IXON);                     /* Ignore STOP char  */
50     t.c_iflag |= IGNBRK | IXOFF;   /* Ignore BREAK
51                                     * send XON and XOFF for
52                                     * flow control.
53                                     */
54     t.c_oflag &= ~(OPOST);         /* No output flags   */
55     t.c_lflag &= ~(               /* No local flags.  In */
56         ECHO|ECHOE|ECHOK|ECHONL|  /* particular, no echo */
57         ICANON |                  /* no canonical input  */
58                                   /* processing,         */
59         ISIG |                    /* no signals,         */
60         NOFLSH |                  /* no queue flush,     */
61         TOSTOP);                  /* and no job control. */
62                                    * /
63     t.c_cflag &= (                /* Clear out old bits  */
64         CSIZE |                   /* Character size      */
65         CSTOPB |                  /* Two stop bits       */
66         HUPCL |                   /* Hangup on last close*/
67         PARENB);                  /* Parity              */
68     t.c_cflag |= CLOCAL | CREAD | CS8;
69                                   /* CLOCAL => No modem
70                                    * CREAD  => Enable
71                                    *            receiver
72                                    * CS8    => 8-bit data
73                                    */
74
```

```
 75 /* Copy input and output speeds into
 76  * struct termios t
 77  */
 78      if (cfsetispeed(&t, B9600) == -1) PANIC;
 79      if (cfsetospeed(&t, B9600) == -1) PANIC;
 80
 81 /* Throw away any input data (noise) */
 82      if (tcflush(chan, TCIFLUSH) == -1) PANIC;
 83
 84 /* Now, set the termial port attributes */
 85      if (tcsetattr(chan,TCSANOW, &t) == -1) PANIC;
 86
 87      return;
 88 }
 89
 90
 91 /*
 92  * Here is the receive process.  The call to
 93  * listen() never returns.
 94  */
 95 void listen(void)
 96 {
 97 char buf[BUFFSIZE];
 98 int  count;
 99 int  i;
100
101      while(1)                       /* Loop forever */
102          {
103          count = read(chan, &buf, BUFFSIZE);
104          if (count < 0) PANIC;
105          (void)write(STDOUT_FILENO,&buf,count);
106          }
107 }
108
109 /*
110  * Here is the main() function
111  */
112 int main(void)
113 {
114 struct termios t;
115 char          ch;
116
117      comm_init();        /* Fire up the comm port */
118
119      if (tcgetattr(STDIN_FILENO,&t) != 0) PANIC;
120                          /* Read the current terminal
121                           * parameters into t.
122                           */
123
124      t.c_lflag &= ~(ICANON | ECHO);
125                          /* Turn off the flags for
126                           * echo and canonical
127                           * input processing.
128                           */
129
130      if (fork() == 0) listen();
131                          /* Call listen() as a
132                           * new process.
133                           */
134
135
```

```
136        while (1)              /* Loop forever */
137           {
138           (void)read(STDIN_FILENO,&ch,1);
139           if (write(chan,&ch,1) != 1) PANIC;
140                             /* Copy standard input
141                              * to the comm port.
142                              */
143           }
144  }
145
146
```

Notes on cu.c:

LINE	NOTES

22   You might think that t is a poor choice for the name of a structure. Why not call it terminal_information or some other descriptive name? There are several reasons why t is an acceptable name:

- The structure is local to the comm_init() function. If the structure were global and used in many places in the program, a longer name would be used.

- The name t is almost always qualified by a structure member name, for example: t.c_iflag. The reader knows that t must be a struct termios.

- There is only one struct termios used in the function. It is not possible to become confused about which one we mean. If there were two structures, names like old_terminal_state and new_terminal_state would be better than t.

- The example looks better if statements fit on one line.

25   A more general version of this program would not build in the filename /dev/tty01 but might accept the device name as a command-line parameter.

25   Open the data port. The O_NOCTTY macro prevents this terminal from ever becoming our controlling terminal. We do not want a received Control-C to stop our process.

27   Even though we are going to explicitly set or clear every POSIX-defined option, we need to preserve any implementation-defined bits.

49   If the computer at the other end never sends binary data, IXON may be used for flow control. If any binary data is being sent, IXON must be turned off; otherwise a STOP character in the binary data might hang the program.

50   Here we are setting IXOFF to allow the system to send STOP characters to the target computer. The combination of IXON clear and IXOFF set allows the computer at the far end to send anything but assumes that it will respond to STOP and START. Our program is pretending to be a terminal on a remote system.

LINE   NOTES

105   We are not checking for errors writing to standard output. There is not much to
      do if standard output does not work.

This sample program shows how to use a communications port from an application.
There are a few practical problems:

1.   The program does not pass special characters to the target machine. If you typed
     Control-C (or whatever character is selected to generate SIGINT), the program
     stops. To be a useful application, special characters should be sent to the target
     system.

2.   If you fix problem 1, there is no way to stop the program.

3.   When problem 2 is fixed, the program should reset the terminal attributes to their
     initial states. This can be done by doing an additional tcgetattr() at program
     startup and doing a tcsetattr() prior to calling exit().

The solutions to these problems are left as an exercise to the reader.

Process Groups and Job Control

It is often useful to run multiple programs from a single terminal. One of the issues with
running multiple programs is what happens to terminal input and output. POSIX job
control is used to determine which processes have access to the terminal.

Job control is a POSIX option. There are two ways to find out if job control is supported.

- If the symbol _POSIX_JOB_CONTROL is defined in <unistd.h>, job control is
  supported.

- If the symbol _POSIX_JOB_CONTROL is not defined in <unistd.h> and
  sysconf(_SC_JOB_CONTROL) returns −1, job control is not supported and all
  processes have equal access to the controlling terminal. Since job control is
  required by FIPS 151-1, most systems do support POSIX job control.

The process group functions and signals are not used by most applications. They are
used only by the shell to allow commands to run in the background. Some complex
applications perform shell-like functions; the emacs editor is an example of such an
application. Unless you are writing that sort of application, you can ignore the job
control functions.

Your application can inadvertently subvert job-control processing by "blindly" altering
the handling of signals. A common application error is to learn how many signals the
system supports and to ignore or catch all of them. Such an application makes the
assumption that it does not know what the signal is, but knows the right action for it.
Applications written this way will not work correctly on POSIX systems.

Process Groups

A process group is a collection of related processes. There is one important attribute of a process group: it is possible to send a signal to every process in the group. Typically, when the shell creates a process to run an application, the process is placed into a new process group. As the application forks new processes, these processes are all members of the process group. There are two types of process groups: foreground and background.

Foreground Process

A foreground process has read and write access to the terminal. Every process in the foreground process group receives SIGINT, SIGQUIT, and SIGTSTP signals. The foreground process group normally consists of the process forked by the shell and all the processes that they fork.

A terminal may (or may not) have a foreground process group associated with it.

Background Process

On the other hand, if a process does not have read access to the terminal, it is a background process. Attempts by a background process to read from its controlling terminal cause its process group to be sent a SIGTTIN signal.[*] The default action of the SIGTTIN signal is to stop the process to which it is sent.

Whether a background process can write to its controlling terminal depends on the TOSTOP mode bit. If TOSTOP is not set, or the process is blocking the SIGTTOU signal, the process is allowed to write to the terminal and the signal is not sent. If the TOSTOP bit is set, all processes in the process group are sent a SIGTTOU signal.[†] The TOSTOP bit is in the c_lflags member of the **struct termios** and is set or cleared using the tcsetattr() function. An individual process can achieve the same effect as clearing the TOSTOP by setting the action for SIGTTOU to SIG_IGN.

Session

A collection of process groups is called a session. Each process group is member of a session. A newly-created process joins the session of its creator. In normal operation, the login shell creates a new session and all processes are members of that session. The login shell is the session leader.

Historical UNIX systems have a concept of an orphaned process, which is a process whose parent process has exited. When POSIX job control is in use, it is necessary to

---

[*] If the reading process is ignoring or blocking the SIGTTIN signal, or if the process group of the reading process has no controlling terminal, the read() returns −1 with errno set to EIO and no signal is sent.

[†] If the process group of the writing process has no controlling terminal, the write() returns −1 with errno set to EIO, and no signal is sent.

---

prevent processes from being stopped in response to interactions with the controlling terminal after they are no longer controlled by a job-control-cognizant program. Because signals generated by the terminal are sent to process groups and not to individual processes, and because a signal may be provoked by a process that is not orphaned, but sent to another process that is orphaned, it is necessary to define an orphaned process group. An orphaned process group is a process group in which the parent of every member is either itself a member of the group or is not a member of the group's session.

This definition of orphaned process groups ensures that a session leader's process group is always considered to be orphaned, and thus it is prevented from stopping in response to terminal signals.

Controlling Terminal

If special characters typed on a terminal keyboard generate signals, such as SIGINT, then the terminal is a controlling terminal. A terminal may belong to a process as its controlling terminal. A terminal may be the controlling terminal for at most one session.

A controlling terminal is inherited by a child during a fork() function call. A process can relinquish its controlling terminal when it creates a new session with the setsid() call. When a controlling process terminates, the controlling terminal is disassociated from the current session, allowing it to be acquired by a new session leader.

Get/Set Process Group

Each process in the system is a member of a process group. A newly-created process joins the process group of its creator. Each process group is a member of a session.

The setsid() Function

The setsid() function creates a new session. The calling process is the session group leader of this new session. The process group ID of the calling process is set equal to the process ID of the calling process. The calling process is the only process in the new group. The setsid() function takes no arguments and returns the value of the process group ID of the calling process.

This function is normally used only by the shell.

The setpgid() Function

The setpgid() function is used either to join an existing process group or create a new process group within the session of the calling process. The call is defined as:

```
int setpgid(pid_t pid, pid_t pgid)
```

and places the process with process ID pid into process group pgid.

This function is normally used only by the shell.

The tcsetpgrp() Function

This function is used to determine which process group is the foreground process group associated with a controlling terminal. The call:

```
int tcsetpgrp(int fildes, pid_t pgrp_id)
```

is used to associate the process group `pgrp_id` with the terminal fildes. On successful completion, zero is returned. Otherwise, a value of -1 is returned and errno is set to indicate the error.

The shell uses this function to move process groups into the foreground. The previous foreground process group, if any, is moved into the background.

```
tcgetpgrp()
```

The call:

```
pid_t tcgetpgrp(int fildes)
```

returns the process group ID of the foreground process group associated with the terminal fildes. If there is no foreground process group, the 1990 standards says a value greater than 1 that does not match any existing process group is returned.[*]

Portability Lab

To review the contents of this chapter, try to do the following exercises:

1. The fast file copy example program given in Chapter 5, *Advanced File Operations*, will not work if the input is from a terminal. There are at least two problems. What are they? How can they be fixed?

2. The fast file copy example program given in Chapter 5 will not work if the input is from a terminal. Will it work if the output is to a terminal?

3. Why does the computer echo characters instead of having the terminal print them directly?

4. Why would you ever want to use non-canonical I/O?

5. Why are process groups used? Why would a normal application ever use `setpgid()`?

6. What is the distinction between `setpgid()` and `tcsetpgrp()`?

7. If an asynchronous communications line is sending 7-bit ASCII characters with parity at 300 baud, how many characters are sent in one second?

---

[*] This was felt to be much more portable than returning an error.

8. When the POSIX standard says something like "setting the terminal baud rate," what baud rate are they really talking about?

9. Why might it be useful to set the ISTRIP bits in the c_iflag member of struct termios? Where might this give you problems?

10. What does the OPOST bit in the c_oflag member of struct termios do? When should a portable program set it?

11. Clearing the ISIG flag in the c_lflag member of struct termios will prevent the INTR character from generating a signal. Give another way to have a similar effect. What are the differences between the two schemes?

12. Why would you ever use the TCSADRAIN option of the tcsetattr() function?

13. When would a program use the tcdrain() function?

14. Should ordinary applications change the settings in the c_cc array? Why or why not?

CHAPTER 9

POSIX and Standard C

This chapter tells you how to use Standard C to achieve maximum portability for your POSIX applications. Some people use the name "ANSI C" for Standard C. I prefer the name Standard C to reflect its use as an international standard and not just an American National Standard. The POSIX standard is written in terms of the C programming language. It recognizes two forms of the C language support: C Standard Language-Dependent System Support and Common Usage C Language-Dependent System Support.

Common Usage C

To allow the greatest possible support for POSIX, implementors are not required to meet the C standard in implementing POSIX. They may support existing pre-standard C compilers and "use common usage as guidance." Since common usage varied from one system to another, portability of applications is reduced in this type of implementation. Common usage support is still the default on many systems; you have to work to get Standard C support.

Standard C

In a Standard C implementation, the system is required to support International Standard ISO/IEC 9899: *Information processing systems—Programming languages—C* for all required POSIX functions. Standard C adds a number of features and capabilities that are not present in Common Usage C. In general, you are better off writing new applications with Standard C. Because the definition of Standard C is more precise than Common Usage C, you will find that Standard C programs are more portable and more easily maintained. Over time, most systems and programmers will convert to Standard C. This chapter is your guide into the future.

Getting Standard C

Since Standard C is new, most systems default to pre-Standard C behavior. Typically, you must specify Standard C as a compiler option. For example, under AT&T System V.4, you specify the −Xa option on the cc command line. The GNU C compiler requires the ansi switch.* See your system documentation for details.

---

* The −pedantic switch will cause warnings for all non-standard features.

The Standard C Preprocessor

The most non-standard and least specified part of Common Usage C is the preprocessor. Operations like recognition of white space and macro replacement did not have a guaranteed ordering. Standard C eliminates this problem by supplying a rigorous definition of the preprocessing and translation process. While the committee was nailing down the exact definition, they also threw in a few new features. These features are discussed in the following sections.

Translation Phases

The standard defines eight translation phases:

1. Every trigraph in the source file is replaced. This usually has no effect. For a discussion of trigraphs, see "Character Sets" on Page 184.

2. Every backslash-newline character pair is deleted. This means that a backslash-newline can be used to continue a line in any context. In older C compilers, the backslash-newline pairs were allowed only as a way to continue a directive, a string literal, or a character constant.

3. The source file is converted into preprocessing tokens and white space.

   Each comment is replaced by a space.

4. Every preprocessing directive is handled and all macro invocations are replaced. Each file read by the #include directive is run through phases 1 to 4 and replaces the #include line.

5. Every escape sequence in character constants and string literals is interpreted.

6. Adjacent character string literals are concatenated.

7. The result of steps 1-6 is compiled.

8. All external references are resolved. The result is a complete program.

As you can see, most of the work is done in step 7. Most compilers do not perform these phases as distinct steps but fold them together. The standard does not require distinct phases; however, the result must be "as if" separate phases are used.

Macro Replacement

Traditional C compilers did not follow the simple sequence of steps described above. Instead, macros were processed on a moment-by-moment basis and the expansion of complex macros would vary from system to system. Many macros were not truly portable.

Standard C also allows many simple macros to work correctly. For example:

```
#define allen *allen
```

will replace all uses of `allen` with `*allen`. Many traditional C compilers would die in the `#define` statement and complain about macro recursion.

Conversion of Macro Arguments to Strings

There was a big argument about the correct operation of the following example:

```
#define p(a) printf("a = %d\n",a)
p(sue);
```

It could expand to either:

```
printf("sue = %d\n",sue);
```

or to:

```
printf("a = %d\n",sue);
```

Traditional C compilers gave the first result. They looked inside quoted strings for possible macro arguments. Standard C will produce the second result. String literals are not examined. To allow the intended effect of the above macro, the # operator was invented. In Standard C, you would write:

```
#define p(a) printf(#a " = %d\n",a)
```

The # sign converts the argument into a string literal. The concatenation of string literals produces the desired result.

Token Pasting

In some traditional C compilers, the code:

```
#define paste(a,b) a/**/b*
x = paste(x,1) + paste(y,2);
```

would produce:

```
x = x1 + y2;
```

By Standard C rules, this code would produce:

```
x = x 1 + y 2;
```

which is not what you want. To get the correct result, use the new Standard C ## operator. The Standard C macro would be:

---

* You cannot just put a next to b because ab is a unique symbol.

```
#define paste(a,b) a ## b
```

Since ## is a real operation and not an artifact of the preprocessor, it is not sensitive to white space.

New Directives

The #elif directive has been added as a shorthand form of the #else #if preprocessor sequence.

The identifier defined is reserved during the #if or #elif so that:

```
#if defined(NULL)
#if !defined(TRUE)
```

is equivalent to:

```
#ifdef   NULL
#ifndef  TRUE
```

In addition to the two legal ways of including a header file:

```
#include <header>
#include "file"
```

it is now legal to write:

```
#include MACRO
```

where MACRO expands to one of the first two cases.

Namespace Issues

In traditional C implementations, the contents of the various header files would vary from system to system. This caused portability problems. There was no way to protect yourself from implementation-defined symbols in the headers you used. Standard C solves this problem by defining a strict set of rules on the use of names. There are a set of names reserved to various parts of the implementation. If you avoid those names, there will be no conflicts.

Names Reserved by the C Language

The Standard C language defines a list of keywords. These have special meaning to the compiler and may not be used for any other purpose. They are:

auto	double	int	struct
break	else	long	switch
case	enum	register	typedef
char	extern	return	union
const	float	short	unsigned
continue	for	signed	void
default	goto	sizeof	volatile
do	if	static	while

Names Reserved by Header Files

The C library uses many identifiers that begin with an underscore. Although there are places where one can safely use an identifier that begins with an underscore, the rules are complex and it is better just to avoid them. Some of these are POSIX restrictions, not part of standard C.

Using #include to read a header file causes a set of symbols to be reserved. These symbols depend on the header file and are listed in the following table:

Header File	Reserved Names
<ctype.h>	All symbols starting with is or to.
<dirent.h>	All symbols starting with d_.
<errno.h>	All symbols starting with E followed by any uppercase letter or a digit.
<fcntl.h>	All symbols starting with l_.[*] Symbols starting with F_, O_, or S_ may be used if an #undef is done for each symbol prior to any other use.
<grp.h>	All symbols starting with gr_.
<limits.h>	All symbols ending with _MAX.
<locale.h>	All symbols starting with LC_ followed by an uppercase letter.
<math.h>	The names of existing math functions followed by an f or an l.
<pwd.h>	All symbols starting with pw_.
<signal.h>	All symbols starting with sa_. Symbols starting with SIG or SA_ may be used if an #undef is done for each symbol prior to any other use.
<string.h>	All symbols starting with mem, str, or wcs.
<sys/stat.h>	All symbols starting with st_. Symbols starting with S_ may be used if an #undef is done for each symbol prior to any other use.
<sys/times.h>	All symbols starting with tms_.

---

[*] That is lowercase letter "l" followed by an underscore.

Header File	Reserved Names
<termios.h>	All symbols starting with c_. Symbols starting with V, I, O, or TC may be used if an #undef is done for each symbol prior to any other use. Symbols starting with B followed by a digit may be used if an #undef is done for each symbol prior to any other use.
Any POSIX header	All symbols ending with _t.

The Header files section in the Reference Manual of this book spells out the contents of the header files in detail. The POSIX interpretation committee has ruled that POSIX 1003.1-1988 is ambiguous. A system conforming to the 1988 standard may define any POSIX symbol in any POSIX header. Systems meeting the 1990 standard must obey the stricter rules set forth in the Header Files section.

C Library Functions

The Standard C library defines a large number of functions. It is legal for a system to load every function in the library even if you do not use it in your program. You should consider the following names reserved by the Standard C library:

abort	fprintf	longjmp	strcat
abs	fputc	malloc	strchr
acos	fputs	mblen	strcoll
asctime	fread	mbstowcs	strcopy
asin	free	mbtowc	strcspn
atan	freopen	memchr	strerror
atan2	frexp	memcmp	strftime
atexit	fscanf	memcpy	strlen
atof	fsetpos	memmove	strncat
atoi	ftell	memset	strncmp
atol	fwrite	mktime	strncpy
bsearch	getc	modf	strpbrk
ceil	getchar	perror	strrchr
calloc	getenv	printf	strspn
clearerr	gets	putc	strstr
clock	gmtime	putchar	strtod
cos	isalnum	puts	strtok
cosh	isalpha	qsort	strtol
ctime	iscntrl	raise	strtoul
difftime	isdigit	rand	strxfrm
div	isgraph	realloc	system
exit	islower	remove	tan
exp	isprint	rename	tanh
fabs	ispunct	rewind	time
fclose	isspace	scanf	tmpfile
feof	isupper	setbuf	tmpnam
ferror	isxdigit	setlocale	tolower
fflush	labs	setvbuf	toupper
fgetc	ldexp	sin	ungetc
fgetpos	ldiv	sprintf	vfprintf
fgets	localeconv	sqrt	vprintf
floor	localtime	srand	vsprintf
fmod	log	strcmp	wcstombs
fopen	log10	sscanf	wctomb

POSIX Library Functions

The POSIX standard defines the following library functions:

access	fdopen	mkdir	sigpending
alarm	fork	mkfifo	sigprocmask
asctime	fpathconf	open	sigsetjmp
cfgetispeed	fstat	opendir	sigsuspend
cfgetospeed	getcwd	pathconf	sleep
cfsetispeed	getegid	pause	stat
cfsetospeed	getenv	pipe	sysconf
chdir	geteuid	read	tcdrain
chmod	getgid	readdir	tcflow
chown	getgrgid	rename	tcflush
close	getgrnam	rewinddir	tcgetattr
closedir	getgroups	rmdir	tcgetpgrp
creat	getlogin	setgid	tcsendbreak
ctermid	getpgrp	setjmp	tcsetattr
cuserid	getpid	setlocale	tcsetpgrp
dup	getppid	setpgid	time
dup2	getpwnam	setuid	times
execl	getpwuid	sigaction	ttyname
execle	getuid	sigaddset	tzset
execlp	isatty	sigdelset	umask
execv	kill	sigemptyset	uname
execve	link	sigfillset	unlink
execvp	longjmp	sisismember	utime
_exit	lseek	siglongjmp	waitpid
fcntl			write

Avoiding Pitfalls

The chances of stumbling over a reserved C or POSIX name can be minimized by following a few simple rules:

1. Start each source file with the line:

    ```
    #define _POSIX_SOURCE 1
    ```

    All symbols not defined by Standard C or the POSIX standard will be hidden, except those with leading underscores.[*]

2. Following the definition of _POSIX_SOURCE, place the #include statements for any standard header files.

3. Use #undef for any symbols that are used by your application and reserved by the header files you use.

4. After the standard #include statements, place any #include or #define statements for this application. The local definitions will redefine any symbol defined in the standard headers.

---

[*] There is also the reverse of this pitfall. If you forget the _POSIX_SOURCE but specify Standard C, all of the POSIX symbols will be hidden.

Of course, this practice will merely prevent problems from identifiers that we do not know about. We can't redefine a macro and still use its standard definition.

Here is a brief example:

```
#define _POSIX_SOURCE 1

#include <stdio.h>
#include <termios.h>
#include <limits.h>

/*
 * #undef symbols that I use in my program, but are
 *   reserved to POSIX headers.
 *   See Headers section in the reference part of
 *   this book.
 */

#undef B52          /* <termios.h> reserves B<digit> */
#undef BOMB_MAX     /* <limits.h> reserves ???_MAX */
#undef SIGMA        /* <signal.h> reserves SIG??? */

/*
 * Now, my application specific headers
 *

#include "planes.h"
#include "ships.h"

/* -
 * Now all of the #defines local to this file
 */

#define B52          "Bomber"
#define BOMB_MAX     60
#define SIGMA        2.378

rest of the program goes here. . .
```

Function Prototypes

Standard C adds some additional checking to the traditional C language. The *argument declarations* can now define the type of each argument. So, we might have a definition as follows:

```
long sum(short count, long *vect[])
```

This call defines a function called sum which returns a long. The sum( ) function has two arguments, a short called count and a pointer to an array called vect. The identifiers vect and count are for descriptive purposes only and do not go beyond the scope of sum.

If the parameter list terminates with an ellipsis (, ...), no information about the number or types of the parameters after the comma is supplied. It is used for functions with a variable number of arguments. If a function takes no arguments, the parameter list should have void as the only entry.

If a function declaration does not include arguments, as in:

```
double julie();
```

then nothing is to be assumed about the arguments of julie, and parameter checking is turned off. This allows older C programs to compile with new compilers, but it is a bad idea to use it with new programs. If the function takes arguments, declare them; if it takes no arguments, use void.

Avoiding Pitfalls

The syntax of function prototypes was borrowed almost completely from C++. Here are some rules for good use:

1. The parameters are comma separated, instead of semicolon terminated as other declarations are.

2. The last parameter in a prototype must not be followed by a comma. This is different from enum and struct where the trailing comma is optional.

3. *If you use a prototype in one place, use them every place!* The compiler is allowed to generate better code using the knowledge gained from the prototypes. For example, if your header contains:

    ```
    int myfunc(char a, unsigned short b, float f);
    ```

    but the code for myfunc is:

    ```
    myfunc()
    char a;
    unsigned short b;
    float f;
    {
        . . .
    }
    ```

    the code generated for the call to myfunc may not match what the function is expecting.

4. You do not have to use parameter names in function prototypes. However, they may make the operation of the function much clearer. Consider:

    ```
    int copy(char *,char *);
    ```

    compared to:

    ```
    int copy(char *from, char *to);
    ```

5. Do not define prototypes for the standard library functions. These functions are declared in system headers.

Writing New Programs

New programs should use new style function declarations. If you want to allow for the code to be ported to older systems that do not have Standard C compilers, the __STDC__ macro should be used, as in:

```
#ifdef __STDC__
        void myfunc(const char *src, char *dest);
#else
        myfunc();
#endif
```

The symbol __STDC__ should be defined only on systems that meet the C standard.

Maintaining Old Programs

In considering existing programs, the question is: How much code are you going to change? Depending on the answer, you have a choice of one of several strategies:

1. Do nothing. The old code should compile just fine.

2. Add function prototypes just to the headers. This will cover all calls to global functions.

3. Add function prototypes to the headers and start each source file with prototypes for its local functions.

4. Change all function declarations and definitions to use prototypes.

I suggest either 1 or 4. Although choices 2 and 3 are good compromises, they require detailed knowledge of the rules for the mixing of old and new styles.

It is a good idea to use prototypes for any functions that have POSIX types as arguments. If you call a function with an ino_t as a parameter, it will increase portability to use prototypes for that function at least.

Mixing Old and New

Mixing old and new style function definitions requires caution. The use of function prototypes allows the compiler to generate faster and smaller code and do more error checking. This code may not be compatible with old-style functions. For most purposes, it is best to avoid mixing old and new. There is one place where you need to consider mixing the two: libraries. The users of a library may want to use old or new type calls.

Here are the rules for mixing:

1. You cannot mix the Standard C ellipsis notation and old-style functions. Before Standard C, functions with a variable number of arguments were not completely portable. If your library has functions with a variable number of parameters, you must decide to either keep the old-style definitions or force all callers to use prototypes.

2. For all integral types narrower than an `int`, use `int` in the function prototype and the function itself. Functions without a prototype will widen integral types to `int`.

3. For all floating-point types, use `double` in the function definition and in the function itself. Functions without a prototype will widen floating-point types to `double`.

Using const and volatile

Standard C has added two type qualifiers to C: `const` and `volatile`. The `volatile` qualifier tells the compiler to take no shortcuts when accessing an object. Consider the fragment:

```
int a,b;
int i;
int tbl[100];
. . .

a=5;
b=3;
for (i=0; i<=99; i++)
     tbl[i] = a + b;
```

The compiler is free to observe that every element of `tbl` is set to 8 and then generate optimized code to do that quickly, maybe with a block move of some sort. If b may change in some way that the compiler cannot predict, say as the result of a signal, the optimization may not provide the correct result.

The following:

```
volatile int a,b;
```

tells the compiler not to do anything clever. The compiler will add a to b for every element of `tbl`.

A more common use for this feature is:

```
flag = 1;
while (flag)
     {
     . . .
     }
```

where `flag` is set to zero by some asynchronous event like a `SIGALARM`. If the `volatile` qualifier is not used, the compiler is not required to check the value of `flag` each time around the loop.

The `const` qualifier is much easier to understand. It says that an object of that type will not be modified. A declaration such as:

```
int copy(const char *from, char *to);
```

tells the compiler (and the human reader) that `from` is not modified by the `copy()` function. It has two advantages. First, the compiler can detect errors where `copy()` might attempt to modify `from`. Second, the compiler can generate better code both for `copy()` and for the places where `copy()` is called. Telling the compiler that a function parameter will not be modified is a good thing to do.

There is one tricky thing here. The declaration:

```
const char *sp1
```

and:

```
char *const sp2
```

do very different things. The first declaration says that `sp1` points only at characters that will not be changed through `sp1` (although they may be modified through some other pointer). The second declaration says that `sp2` is an unchanging pointer to a possibly changing `char`. The way you would declare an un-modifiable pointer to an un-modifiable `char` is with:

```
const char *const sp;
```

String Constants

A useful new feature of Standard C is that consecutive string constants are seamlessly pasted together. The statements:

```
printf("a" "bc" "def");
```

and:

```
printf("abcdef");
```

produce identical results.[*] This allows programs to be cleanly formatted. For example:

```
text = "x   "
       "  x "
       "   x";
```

is a readable way to fill in a 3x3 array.

---

[*] This is a new feature created by the ANSI C committee. Older C compilers will not support it.

It is neither required nor forbidden that identical string constants be represented by a single copy of the string in memory. So, if we have the program:

```
sue = &"This is a string";
jenn = &"This is a string";
```

some compilers set `sue` and `jenn` to the same value; other compilers set them to different values.

Data Type Conversions

When a binary arithmetic operator is presented with two operands of different type, the operands must be converted to a common type. The common type is also the type of the result. This set of conversion rules is called *usual arithmetic conversions*. The following rules are applied, in order, until one of them is satisfied:

1. If either operand has type `long double`, the other operand is converted to `long double`. The result has type `long double`.

2. If either operand has type `double`, the other operand is converted to `double`. The result has type `double`.

3. If either operand has type `float`, the other operand is converted to `float`. The result has type `float`.

4. If either operand has type `unsigned long int`, the other operand is converted to `unsigned long int`. The result has type `unsigned long int`.

5. If one operand has type `long int` and the other has type `unsigned int`, if a `long int` can represent all values of an `unsigned int`, the operand of type `unsigned int` is converted to `long int`; if a `long int` cannot represent all of the values of an `unsigned int`, both operands are converted to `unsigned long int`.

6. If either operand has type `long int`, the other operand is converted to `long int`.

7. If either operand has type `unsigned int`, the other operand is converted to `unsigned int`.

8. If none of rules 1 to 7 applies, both operands and the result must have type `int`.

A compiler may perform calculations in a wider type than absolutely necessary, if this produces smaller and faster code.[*] Calculations may also be performed in a narrower type, so long as the same end result is obtained.

---

[*] Strictly speaking, the compiler can do this even if it produces larger, slower code.

Standard C uses what is called a *value preserving* approach to integer promotion. When a value with an integer type is converted to another integer type, if the value can be represented by the new type, its value is unchanged.

When a signed integer is converted to an unsigned integer with equal or greater size, its value is unchanged. If the unsigned integer has greater size, the signed integer is first promoted to the signed integer of the correct size and then that bit pattern is converted to unsigned.

An ambiguity arises whenever an `unsigned int` and a `signed int` are operands and the `signed int` is, in fact, negative. The `signed int` becomes a very large `unsigned int`. This may be surprising or it may be exactly what the programmer has in mind. If we execute this code fragment:

```
short a;
unsigned short b,c;

    a = -10;
    b = 5;
    c = a + b;
```

c will end up with a value of 65,531 on a machine with 16-bit shorts.

Character Sets

The C programming language was created with the ASCII character set in mind. Not all computers use ASCII. Outside of the United States, some of the special characters are missing. We need a character set that will work in any country. The following characters are in the portable[*] character set:

```
ABCDEFGHIJKLMNOPQRSTUVWXYZ
abcdefghijklmnopqrstuvwxyz
0123456789
! " % & ' ( ) * + , - . / : ; < = > ? _
```

The following characters are used in C but are missing from the portable set:

```
# [ ] { } \ | ^ ~
```

In order to represent these characters, there is a set of magic escape sequences called trigraphs. A trigraph is a sequence that looks like `??x`. These trigraphs are converted into the missing characters by the C compiler. The defined trigraphs are:

```
??=        #
??(        [
??/        \
??)        ]
??'        ^
??<        {
```

---

[*] The International Organization for Standards (ISO) has defined these as an *invariant subset* of ASCII in ISO standard 646.

```
??!     |
??>     }
??-     ~
```

Question marks that do not begin a trigraph listed above are not changed. Thus, the following source line:

```
printf("What???/n");
```

is the same as:

```
printf("What?\n");
```

after `??/` is replaced by `\`.

It is ugly and awkward to type `??<` instead of `{`. You can avoid using the trigraphs if your development computer has the required special characters. It is fairly simple to write a program that will replace the special characters with the trigraphs. You can then port the files with the trigraphs to other environments.

You also need to be careful not to trip over one of the trigraphs. The statement:

```
printf("What???!\n");
```

will produce `What?|` instead of `What???!`. Chances are you want the second result. The escape sequence `\?` results in a single `?`. Escape sequences can be used to prevent unintended trigraphs in character strings. For example:

```
printf("What\?\?\?\n");
```

In fact, if it were not for the possibility that you might get a trigraph by accident, I would not even have mentioned them.

Using Floating-point Data

Standard C defines a number of additional constants for the `<float.h>` header file. In order to use them, it helps to understand how computers store floating-point data.

A `float` stores a value according to the following formula:

```
value = s X base^exp
```

The exact value for `base` depends on the computer's hardware. The popular values are 2 and 16. A computer stores a `float` in a format that looks something like:

+ −	exp	s

The number of bits used to hold the exponent (`exp`) and the fraction (`s`) change from computer to computer. The number of bits may also vary among `float`, `double`, and `long double`.

The most natural way to think of a floating-point number is in decimal. The value is given by the formula:

```
value = frac × 10 exp
```

even if no real computer uses this exact formula. Using this formula, all computers can support `exp` values from -37 to $+37$. Items of type `float` have at least 6 decimal digits in the fraction. Items of type `double` or `long double` have at least 9 decimal digits in the fraction.

The header file `<float.h>` defines symbols for the actual limits on the target computer. Your program should use these symbols instead of numeric constants. The macros[*] are:

Description	Symbol for float	Symbol for double	Symbol for long double
Radix of the exponent	FLT_RADIX	FLT_RADIX	FLT_RADIX
Number of FLT_RADIX digits in frac	FLT_MANT_DIG	DBL_MANT_DIG	LDBL_MANT_DIG
Number of decimal digits in the fraction	FLT_DIG	DBL_DIG	LDBL_DIG
Minimum exponent	FLT_MIN_EXP	DBL_MIN_EXP	LDBL_MIN_EXP
Smallest value of exp such that 10S(exp) is a valid number	FLT_MIN_10_EXP	DBL_MIN_10_EXP	LDBL_MIN_10_EXP
Maximum exponent	FLT_MAX_EXP	DBL_MAX_EXP	LDBL_MAX_EXP
Largest value of exp such that 10S(exp) is a valid number	FLT_MAX_10_EXP	DBL_MAX_10_EXP	LDBL_MAX_10_EXP
Maximum number	FLT_MAX	DBL_MAX	LDBL_MAX
Minimum number	FLT_MIN	DBL_MIN	LDBL_MIN

---

[*] These macros are most often simple defines, for example:

```
#define FLT_DIG 6
```

On some systems they may be defined as functions, as in:

```
#define FLT_DIG (__mathconf(__FLT_DIG))
```

The different definitions should have no effect on your program. All of the private symbols used by these macros must begin with two underscores to prevent conflicts with your symbols.

Description	Symbol for `float`	Symbol for `double`	Symbol for `long double`
The smallest value that can be added to 1.0 to give a distinct number	FLT_EPSILON	DBL_EPSILON	LDBL_EPSILON

Using Data Structures

This section does not deal with the Standard C/Common Use C definition, but with its implementation; specifically, this section covers the way data is stored in memory and some portability pitfalls related to data structures. Normally, programs are not sensitive to the way data is stored in memory. If you misuse a pointer or a union, however, your programs may be sensitive to the way data is stored.

Alignment

The C compiler has a great deal of freedom in assigning storage. Consider the structure:

```
struct date {
    unsigned char   day;
    unsigned char   month;
    unsigned short  year;
};
```

It has two **char** elements and a **short** element. It is possible to store this structure in four contiguous bytes:

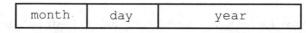

month	day	year

There is no obligation for the system to pack the data this way, but there are good reasons to insert padding.

First, the compiler may decide to round up to some convenient boundary. Some computers require that **longs** are placed only at certain storage boundaries. Other computers will give correct results with any alignment, but give faster results with preferred alignments.

Some compilers have no alignment rules. Some will start every structure on an even boundary. Others will align a structure on the same boundary as required for its most strictly aligned component. For instance, a **struct** containing only **char** members would have no alignment restrictions, while a **struct** containing a **double** is aligned on an 8-byte boundary.

On some machines it is much faster to access data aligned on 4-byte boundaries. The compiler may pad out our `date` structure to look like:

pad	pad	pad	day
pad	pad	pad	month
pad	pad	year	

This requires three times as much storage as a tightly packed structure, however, it may be much faster to access.

This packing of data is one difference between traditional Complex Instruction Set Computers (CISC) and the newer Reduced Instruction Set Computers (RISC). In general, the CISCs packed data as tightly as possible to save space. However, they also require the hardware that accesses memory to be more complex and thus slower. The RISC computers use more memory and are able to access data using fast and simple hardware.

A structure may be padded at the end to round the size up to a handy value for the computer. On some machines, it may be just up to an even boundary. On other machines, the size of a structure is a multiple of the most strictly aligned element. Thus, any structure that contains a `double` will be a multiple of 8 bytes long.

The point is that `sizeof(struct date)` can change a great deal from system to system. This should not be a problem if you do not write code that depends upon the exact size.

Do not assume that `sizeof(struct a)` and `sizeof(struct b)` will always be the same, even if they are on the system you are using for development.

Data Segment Layout

The compiler and linker may add padding between variables. The following assumption is incorrect:

```
short   a = 0;
short   b = 0;
/* assert(&a + sizeof(a) == &b) */
```

Some linkers and compilers place uninitialized variables in a separate segment. Thus:

```
short   a = 0;
short   b;        /* uninitalized */
short   c = 0;
```

may result in b being placed a great distance from a or c.

Big-endian vs. Little-endian

There are many possible ways to pack chars into a short and shorts into a long. There are two very popular schemes and most computers use one or the other: big-endian or little-endian.

Let's assume we have a 16-bit computer that stores two 8-bit bytes in a word.

The least significant bit is on the right and the most significant bit is on the left. The decimal number 600 is stored in binary as:[*]

00000001	00101100

There are two possible ways to store the string `"ab"` in those 2 bytes.

'a'	'b'

'b'	'a'

The first case is called "big-endian" and the second "little-endian." If the union:

```
union foo {
short      num;
char       ch[2];
};
```

had 600 stored in num, on big-endian machines ch[0] would contain 00000001 binary and on little-endian machines ch[0] would contain 00101100 binary.

When we go to 32-bit words, the picture gets even worse. Big-endian looks like:

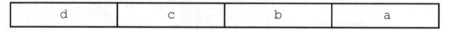

a	b	c	d

and little-endian looks like:

d	c	b	a

The IBM System/360, introduced in 1964, was big-endian. All of the follow-on IBM mainframes have also been big-endian. The IBM-PC is little-endian. Digital Equipment Corporation introduced the PDP-11 in 1969 as the first little-endian machine. The follow-on VAX series is also little-endian. The world of micro-computers has been split between the little-endian Intel family (8080, 8086, 8028, 80386, 80486, etc.) and the big-endian Motorola family (68000, 68010, 68020, 68030, 88100, etc.). Some chips are used

---

[*] This is a 16-bit number. Do not assume anything about byte addresses. When the computer uses this information as a short, it gets the bits in the order shown.

both ways. For example, the MIPS R2000 is big-endian in boxes sold by MIPS and Silicon Graphics and little-endian in boxes sold by Digital Equipment Corp.

The bottom line is: programs must not depend on the way data is stored in memory. It is not possible to transfer binary data blindly between two computer systems even if the same CPU chip is used.

Internationalization

Standard C adds a number of internationalization features that include multi-byte characters, wide characters, and new conversion functions. These are covered in detail in the next chapter.

Portability Lab

To review the contents of this chapter, try to do the following exercises:

1. What is the difference between ANSI C and Standard C?

2. Given the macro:

    ```
    #define list(a,b) printf(#a "=%d\n" #b "=%d\n",a,b);
    ```

    what does:

    ```
    list(howard,harriet)
    ```

    expand into?

3. What does the ## operator do?

4. If you define the function `log` in your program, what portability risks do you run?

5. Should you `#include` systems headers before application headers? Does it matter? Why or why not?

6. What can you say about a function defined by the following prototype:

    ```
    void eniwel(const int i, const int *i, ...);
    ```

7. What is the difference between a function defined by:

    ```
    julie();
    ```

    and:

    ```
    int julie(void);
    ```

8. When would you need to use the `volatile` attribute?

9. What does this do?

    ```
    wchr = '??';
    ```

10. Given the structure:

```
struct time {
    unsigned char  hours;
    unsigned char  minutes;
    unsigned char  seconds;
};
```

may the compiler pack this structure into 3 bytes? May the compiler insert pad bytes between `hours` and `minutes`? May the compiler store `seconds` at a lower address than `hours`?

CHAPTER 10

Porting to Far-off Lands

The C programming language and the UNIX system were invented by people who speak English, and the intended users all spoke English. The seven-bit ASCII code was capable of holding every character anyone really needed. As C and UNIX grew into international standards, the demand grew for them to address the needs of the world outside of New Jersey.

☞ If you are in the United States and you are sure you will never have to port your software to other countries or cultures, then you can skip this chapter.*

Some Definitions

Before we get too far into the subject, it is worth defining some terms.

Internationalization

A program written for a specific culture and following a set of local customs may be difficult to move elsewhere. It is possible to write programs which make no assumptions about language, local customs, or coded character set. Such programs are said to be *internationalized*. That is, internationalization means making our software location neutral.

Localization

Making a program specific to any particular language, cultural convention, and codeset is referred to as *localization*. In the ideal situation, no changes in program logic are required: all localization is done by compiling with the correct library and including the proper data files.

Locale

We need a specific term to refer to a set of language and cultural rules. POSIX calls it a *locale*. A program must be able to determine its locale and "do the right thing."

---

* Of course, you may be wrong. I have lots of horror stories about people who knew that their software was only for the domestic market only to have the boss come in with the big deal they just closed in Saudi Arabia. Then there was the person who discovered that Puerto Rico was part of the United States.

Locale Control

A number of things can vary from one locale to the next. Before I discuss the programming techniques to use, we should understand the problem we are up against.

Character and Codeset

The character set for the United States is based on seven-bit characters defined by the American Standard Code for Information Interchange (ASCII). For many locales, additional characters are required, such as: œ ø å ß ç and ¿. The 8-bit International Standard code ISO 8859-1:1987 has enough special characters to handle major Western European languages. Because the low-order seven bits of ISO 8859 are the same as ASCII, most data files can be exchanged.

It is important that our programs be "eight-bit clean." Programs that use the 0200 bit of characters as some form of internal flag fail in eight-bit locales.

The problem is more difficult in Asia, where the character set might consist of thousands of characters. Clearly, eight bits cannot do the job. Characters with more than eight bits per character, (called *wide characters*) and characters that consist of a sequence of eight-bit bytes, (called *multi-byte characters*) provide support for Asian languages. These are covered later in this chapter.

Messages

One obvious thing to fix is hardcoded messages. Statements such as:

```
printf("Hello, World\n");
```

will not work well in places where the correct output is something like:

```
Bonjour tout le monde
```

The mechanism used to solve this problem is called a *message catalog*. The message catalog provides an external file of messages that can be translated without access to the source code.

Unfortunately, POSIX does not yet have a message catalog facility. Such a facility is part of the X/Open Portability Guide and is included as part of AT&T UNIX System V.4.0. This facility is covered later in this chapter in the Section entitled "Native Language Messages."

Representation of Numbers

Different cultures have different ways of representing numbers. The most common are the English (12,345.67) and the French (12.345,67). The decimal point and the comma are interchanged.

In Asia, four-digit groups are preferred (e.g., 1,2345.67).

Currency

Currency symbols vary both in terms of the character used and in its position.

Dates

The format of dates and times is not universally defined. January 9, 1990 may be written as 1/9/90 in the United States and as 9.1.90 in Germany.

The use of AM and PM is also not universal. Some locals use 24-hour time. Some use a colon (:) between the hour and the minutes and others use a dot (.).

Setting the Current Locale

A program needs to select its locale. A single program might be capable of operating in a large number of places. A user may want to switch from locale to locale based on what he or she is doing. The `setlocale()` function is used to select the locale. This is defined as:

```
char *setlocale(int category, const char *locale);
```

The `category` argument is a symbolic constant and tells the `setlocale()` function which items to set. The effect of the locale settings is described in the next section. The choices are:

LC_COLLATE   Changes the behavior of the `strcoll()` and `strxfrm()` functions.

LC_CTYPE   Changes the behavior of the character-handling functions: `isalpha()`, `isgraph()`, `islower()`, `isprint()`, `ispunct()`, `isspace()`, `isupper()`, `toupper()`, and `tolower()`; and of the multi-byte functions: `mblen()`, `mbtowc()`, `wctomb()`, `mbstowcs()`, and `wcstombs()`.

LC_MONETARY   Changes the information returned by `localeconv()`.

LC_MESSAGES   Changes the language in which messages are displayed.

LC_NUMERIC   Changes the radix character for numeric conversions.

LC_TIME   Changes the behavior of the `strftime()` function.

LC_ALL   Changes all of the above.

The `locale` argument is the name of a locale. There are a few special locale names:

"C"   Makes everything work as defined in the C standard. No locale-specific actions take place.

"POSIX"   Has the same effect as `"C"`.

" "   Selects the native locale. This is done using the following steps:

1. If LC_ALL is defined in the environment and is not null, the value of LC_ALL is used.

2. If there is a variable defined in the environment with the same name as the category and which is not null, the value specified by that environment variable is used.

3. If LANG is defined in the environment and is not null, the value of LANG is used.

If the resulting value is the same as a supported locale, that name is used. If the value does not name a supported locale (and is not null), setlocale() returns a NULL pointer, and the locale is not changed by this call. If no nonnull environment variable is present, the exact behavior of setlocale() is implementaion defined.

Setting all of the categories by using LC_ALL as the first argument is similar to successively setting each individual category of the locale, except that all error checking is done before any actions are performed.

NULL   Returns the current locale without changing it.

At program startup:

```
setlocale(LC_ALL,"C");
```

is performed before main() is called. If your program uses the library functions according to the guidelines in this chapter, you can start the program with:

```
setlocale(LC_ALL,"");
```

and do the best job possible in the local environment.

The setlocale() function returns a pointer to the name of the current locale for the selected category. If setlocale() is given an unknown locale, NULL is returned.

You might wonder what effect setting the locale has on functions like printf(). The answer is, none at all. While you can set LC_MONETARY and LC_NUMERIC, the printf() family of functions is not required to use the information you supply. Most implementations format numbers for the United Stated even if the locale is set elsewhere. On some systems, printf() will format numbers based on locale.

Character-handling Functions

Some of the character-handling functions are sensitive to the locale. They will report different results for different national character sets.

The isalpha(), islower(), and isupper() Functions

These functions may expand the set of alphabetic characters to include native language characters like ç, å, and so on. These characters do not have values between 'a' and 'z'.

The toupper() and tolower() Functions

Not all lowercase letters have corresponding upper-case letters. For example, the lowercase German ß becomes SS in uppercase. The `toupper()` and `tolower()` functions assume that a one-to-one mapping exists. They will return the input character if there is no way to convert it.

The isspace() Function

A native language, such as Japanese, may have specific white space characters beyond the standard set.

The strcoll() Function

The `strcoll()` function compares two strings in the native language character set and reports which is greater. The function is defined by:

```
int strcoll(const char *s1, const char *s2);
```

and returns a number that is less than, equal to, or greater than zero, depending on whether the string pointed to by s1 is less than, equal to, or greater than the string pointed by s2.

In the "C" locale, `strcoll()` is equivalent to `strcmp()`. In other locales, `strcoll()` must compensate for the rules of the native language. Most locales can be accommodated using a one-to-one mapping that inserts characters like å in the correct place. In some cases, a one-to-many mapping is required for characters like the German ß. There are also many-to-one mappings like the Spanish "ll," which is sorted right after "l".

The strxfrm() Function

The use of `strcoll()` can be quite slow if a great deal of transformation is required and many comparisons are going to be made. The `strxfrm()` function performs the transformation required by `strcoll()` and leaves the result in a form where `strcmp()` can be used.

In the "C" locale, `strxfrm()` merely copies the string and is almost equivalent to `strncpy()`. The difference is that `strxfrm()` returns the length of the transformed string which may be different from the length of the source.

In applications where many comparisons must be made, a sort say, using `strxfrm()` and `strcmp()` can provide a performance enhancement over using `strcoll()`. There is no untransform function to recover the source string. It must be kept around if you are going to need it again. Also, the transformation is implementation-dependent so that even two systems operating on German may produce different transformations.

The strerror() and perror() Functions

The `strerror()` and `perror()` functions may produce native language messages even in the `"C"` locale.

The strftime() Function

The `strftime()` function is covered in detail in Chapter 7, *Obtaining Information at Run–time*. One of its features is the ability to generate locale-specific dates and times. For example, the format string `"%c"` may produce:

```
Friday April 13, 1990  3:25 PM
```

in one locale and:

```
viernes abril 13 1990 15.25
```

in another locale. The `"%x"` format produces a native date (no time) and the `"%X"` produces a native time (no date).

Native Language Messages

One important task of a program is to translate messages into the native language. There is no provision in Standard C or POSIX to provide this capability. There is an existing method that is part of the X/Open Portability Guide[*] and is available on many systems including AT&T System V.4 and OSF/1. In late 1990 the POSIX working group concluded that it would be premature to adopt any messaging proposal because:

- No proposal represented significant historical practice.

- All proposals had been developed with a primary focus on character terminals. The group felt that the rapidly rising importance of windowing might require a proposal that explicitly considered messaging in windows.

- All proposals seemed clumsy.

In my opinion, the working group abdicated their responsibility in the face of a difficult problem. Since this is an important capability for building portable applications, I have decided to describe the X/Open functions even though they are not part of POSIX.

---

[*] The X/Open Portability Guide is published by Prentice-Hall. Volume 3: XSI Supplementary Definitions covers internationalization. See the Related Documents section in the Reference Manual of this book.

Message Catalogs

The basic mechanism for language-independent messages is a message catalog. It consists of a file, external to your code, that can be translated to provide messages in other languages. A message ID is used to look up the message in the catalog.

The message text file has the form:

```
$set n
i message-i
j message-j
k message-k
$set m
l message-l
    . . .
```

Each message is identified by a set number and a message within that set. The usual backslash escape sequences may be used.

Sets are often used to break messages into blocks of normal messages, error messages, and so on. They can also be used to indicate which source module uses the message.

By default, there is no quoting and messages are delimited by white space as in:

```
$set 0
1 Hello, World\n
2 Goodbye, World\n
3 Have a nice day. . .
```

The `$quote c` command makes c a quote character. It can be used to include leading or trailing white space in a message. For example:

```
$quote "
$set 0
1 " Hello, World\n"
2 " Goodbye, World\n"
3 " Have a nice day . . . "
```

To speed retrieval, the message text is compiled into binary with the `gencat` utility. This command takes two arguments, the name of the catalog to be created and the input text file:

```
gencat catalog  text
```

The generated catalog is in a machine-specific format and is not portable. The text file, of course, is portable (at least, on systems with the same code set).

The catopen() Function

The `catopen()` routine is used to make a message catalog available to your program. The function is defined as:

```
#include <nl_types.h>
nl_catd catopen(char *name, int oflag);
```

The argument `name` points to a string used to locate the catalog. If the string contains a "`/`" it is assumed to be the full path for the message catalog. Otherwise, the environment variable `NLSPATH` is used with the string pointed to by `name` substituted for `%N`. The `oflag` argument must be zero.

The `catopen()` function returns a number of type `nl_catd` for use with subsequent calls to `catgets()` and `catclose()`. If an error takes place, `-1` is returned and `errno` is set to indicate the error.

The catgets() Function

The `catgets()` function is used to pull strings out of a message catalog. The function is defined as:

```
#include <nl_types.h>
char *catgets(nl_catd catd, int set_id, int msg_id,
    char *s);
```

where `catd` is the value returned by `catopen()`, `set_id` is used to identify a block of messages, `msg_id` is used to identify a particular message within a set, and `s` is a pointer to a default string. The `catgets()` function returns a pointer to a message. If `catgets()` has a problem locating the message, `s` is returned. No errors are detected.

A typical use of `catgets()` is:

```
printf(catgets(catd,0,1,"Hello, World\n"));
```

which might print out:

```
Bonjour tout le monde
```

in France.

The catclose() Function

When you are done with the message catalog, the call `catclose(catd)` closes the catalog. No errors are detected.

Local Numeric Formatting

Various information for formatting numbers is made available in the `lconv` structure. This structure is defined in `<locale.h>` and contains the following members:

Type	Member Name	Default	Description
char *	decimal_point	"."	The character used to format non-monetary quantities.

Type	Member Name	Default	Description
char *	thousands_sep	" "	The character used to separate groups of digits in non-monetary quantities.
char *	grouping	" "	A string whose elements indicate the size of each group of digits in non-monetary quantities.
			Each character is examined:
			0 repeat the previous element for the remainder of the digits.
			1..CHAR_MAX-1 the number of digits in the current group.
			CHAR_MAX no further grouping is to be performed.
char *	int_curr_symbol	" "	International currency symbol for the current locale (e.g., NOK for Norway).
char *	currency_symbol	" "	Local currency symbol for the current locale (e.g., Kr for Norway).
char *	mon_decimal_point	" "	The decimal point for monetary quantities.
char *	mon_thousands_sep	" "	The character used to separate groups of digits for monetary quantities.
char *	mon_grouping	" "	A string whose elements indicate the size of each group of digits in monetary quantities.
char *	positive_sign	" "	The string used to indicate a nonnegative valued monetary quantity (e.g., "+", "DB", or " ").
char *	negative_sign	" "	The string used to indicate a negative valued monetary quantity (e.g., "-", or, "CR").
char	int_frac_digits	CHAR_MAX	Number of digits after the decimal point for internationally formatted monetary quantities.
char	frac_digits	CHAR_MAX	Number of digits after the decimal point for formatted monetary quantities.

Type	Member Name	Default	Description
char	p_cs_precedes	CHAR_MAX	1 if the currency symbol precedes nonnegative monetary quantities; zero if it goes after them.
char	p_sep_by_space	CHAR_MAX	1 if there is a space between the currency symbol and the digits in nonnegative monetary quantities. Zero if there is no space.
char	n_cs_precedes	CHAR_MAX	1 if the currency symbol precedes negative monetary quantities. Zero if it goes after them.
char	n_sep_by_space	CHAR_MAX	1 if there is a space between the currency symbol and the digits in negative monetary quantities. Zero if there is no space.
char	p_sign_posn	CHAR_MAX	Position of the positive sign in monetary quantities:

$0 \rightarrow$ Surround with ( ).

$1 \rightarrow$ Sign string precedes the quantity and the currency symbol.

$2 \rightarrow$ Sign string succeeds the quantity and the currency symbol.

$3 \rightarrow$ Sign string precedes the currency symbol.

$4 \rightarrow$ Sign string immediately after the currency symbol.

Type	Member Name	Default	Description
char	n_sign_posn	CHAR_MAX	Position of the positive sign in monetary quantities; has the same codes as p_sign_posn.

The localeconv() function returns a pointer to this structure. It is defined as:

```
struct lconv *localeconv(void);
```

There are no arguments and no errors are detected. Do not modify the returned structure, which may be overwritten by subsequent calls to localeconv() or setlocale().

Asian Languages

The ISO 8859-1:1987 8-bit code handles most Western European languages. Other eight-bit codes will support Hebrew, Arabic, or Russian. Asian languages present a problem. For example, the Japanese language in Japanese is 日本語. Since many thousands of characters are required to support the Japanese or Chinese languages, eight bits are not enough.

One could try to use a phonetic English system to represent information inside the computer. Using the English alphabet does not work very well, because a given symbol may have several readings, and a given sound maps into a large number of symbols. Many characters are pronounced *ko* or *shi*. Proper names may merge when converted to a phonetic spelling.*

You are forced to keep track of all of the symbols.

Multi-byte Characters

One way to support extended characters without breaking lots of programs is to use escape codes. We assume that information is stored in a sequence of eight-bit bytes. The interpretation of these bytes depends on a *shift state*. A special byte or series of special bytes are used to establish the shift state. Thus, the character with a value of 65 might be "A" in one shift state and "¥" in another shift state.

Multi-byte encodings are useful for I/O in general and terminal I/O in particular. They are also useful for programs that deal with strings without looking at them. For example:

```
printf("¥\n");
```

works just fine with no special additions to the C compiler.

The only important rule is that the null character (\0) must never be used as part of the multi-byte encodings.

A major disadvantage of this scheme is that the shift state must be kept around someplace. Extracting a substring may have unintended side effects; functions like strcat() would need to be made much smarter. The usual assumption is that every string starts in a default shift state and any required escapes are inserted in the front.

Wide Characters

The more straightforward (but much less C-like) way to extend the character set is to use more bits per character. Standard C defines the type wchar_t as a wide character. The

---

* To make matters more complicated, the Japanese use three phonetic alphabets in addition to the large set of Chinese (*kanji*) characters: the Latin alphabet called *romaji*, an alphabet for words of foreign origin called *katakana*, and an alphabet for words of true Japanese origin called *hiragana*.

`wchar_t` has enough bits to store all possible symbols without the need for escapes or a shift state.

Wide characters may also be more efficient for storing text that is mostly in the extended character set. Several implementations of AT&T System V.4 have defined `wchar_t` as a 32-bit data item. This requires four bytes per character and is not very efficient.

Working with Multi-byte and Wide Characters

Multi-byte and wide characters are optimized for different purposes. Multi-byte characters are variable size and optimized for compactness. Wide characters are fixed size and optimized for random access. The Standard C library provides a set of functions for converting between wide characters and multi-byte characters. They are all defined in the `<stdlib.h>` header file.

The mbtowc() Function

The `mbtowc()` function converts a single multi-byte character to a wide character. The function is defined as:

```
int mbtowc(wchar_t *pwc, const char *s, size_t n);
```

where `s` points to an array of at most `n` bytes. If the array contains a valid multi-byte character, the corresponding wide character is stored in the `wchar_t` pointed to by `pwc`. The function returns the number of bytes in the multi-byte character or −1 if the encoding is not valid.

If `s` is a null pointer, a special case of `mbtowc()` is used. In this case, no conversion is performed and a non-zero value is returned if multi-byte characters have a state dependent encoding; zero is returned if they do not.

The mbstowcs() Function

A multi-byte-character-encoded string can be converted to a wide-character string using the `mbstowcs()` function. This is defined as:

```
size_t mbstowcs(wchar_t *pwc, const char *s, size_t n);
```

and converts the string pointed to by `s` into at most `n`-wide characters stored in the array pointed to by `pwc`. The function returns the number of wide characters stored or −1 if an invalid code in encountered.

The wctomb() Function

The `wctomb()` function converts a wide character to a multi-byte character. It is defined as:

```
size_t wctomb(char *s, wchar_t wchar);
```

and stores the character sequence required to represent `wchar` in the string pointed to by `s`. Any required shift characters are included. The function returns the number of bytes stored in `s`. If `s` is a null pointer, the `wctomb()` returns the same special value as `mbtowc()` with a null pointer.

The wcstombs() Function

The `wctombs()` function converts a wide-character string to a multi-byte-character string. It is defined as:

```
int wcstombs(char *s, const wchar_t *pwcs, size_t n);
```

and converts the null-terminated, wide-character string pointed to by `pwcs` into a null-terminated, multi-byte-character string pointed to by `s`. At most, `n` bytes are stored into the string `s`. The `wcstombs()` function returns the number of bytes stored in `s`, not counting the final null byte. If an invalid wide character is encountered, -1 is returned.

The mblen() Function

The `mblen()` function returns the number of bytes in a multi-byte character. The function:

```
mblen(const char *s, size_t n);
```

is exactly the same as:

```
mbtowc((wchar_t *)0, s, n);
```

except that the shift state of `mbtowc()` is not changed.

Portability Lab

To review the contents of this chapter, try to do the following exercises:

1. What is the key distinction between internationalization and localization?

2. What does "eight-bit clean" mean?

3. What is the C locale? What is the default locale?

4. When would the `strcoll()` function give a different answer from the `strcmp()` function? Which function is, in general, faster?

5. What can you do with the output of `strxfrm()`? Is there any other use for the output?

6. Is Poland in the C locale? Why or why not?

7. One way to support multiple languages would be to write a translate function. This function is called with:

   ```
   printf(translate("Have a nice day. . .\n"));
   ```

   and uses the English string as a key into a file to find the translation. The file might look like:

   ```
   ENGLISH:  message 1
   FRENCH:   message 1
   GERMAN:   message 1
           . . .
   ENGLISH:  message n
   FRENCH:   message n
   GERMAN:   message n
   ```

   The `translate()` function merely returns a pointer to the correct text.

   Write the `translate()` function.

   What are some of the pros and cons of this scheme?

8. Write a program to convert an amount of money stored in a `double` into a character string using the information returned by the `localconv()` function.

9. Given the multi-byte and wide-character functions, write a complete Japanese word processor. If you cannot do it, what information do you need?

Library Functions

Library Functions

This section lists all of the library functions in the ANSI C and POSIX library. The table is in strict alphabetical order. The reader does not need to know if a function is a macro, a system call, or a true library function. Every function is listed in its proper place. For example, the calloc() *function is listed at its correct place in the Cs and not hidden under* malloc(). *The descriptions are self-standing; if you look up* creat(), *you are not told to see* open() *for details. You are told that* open() *is a more general function than* creat(). *You may also want to look up* open(), *but the description of the* creat() *function is complete.*

Format:

Each function is described in the following format:

function name — One-line description of the function.

Synopsis:

The C language prototype for the function, with a list of all of the header files that must be included when this function is used.

Arguments:

Gives a description of each argument. In many cases the language is not quite as precise as the standard. For example, if an argument is defined as char *path, the description might say:

path   The path of the file to use.

instead of the more precise:

path   A pointer to a character array representing the path to be used.

Since the programmer is likely to write something like /usr/don/foo.bar, the short description is better. If confusion is likely, the more precise description is used.

Returns:

Describes the value returned.

Errors:

Lists the error codes that this function is required to detect. It may also detect other errors. The error codes are described in the Error Code section.

The entries for some functions, such as `fprintf()`, do not list error codes, but these functions do detect errors. The standards do not require any particular error code and error codes can differ from system to system.

Description:

Provides a complete description of this function.

Reference:

The "American National Standard for Information Systems—Programming Language C" is abbreviated "C."

The "IEEE Standard Portable Operating System Interface for Computer Environments" is abbreviated "P."

The section of the appropriate standard is indicated as P *s.s.s.s* or C *s.s.s.s.* A few functions are covered in both documents. In general, the POSIX standard adds additional requirements to the definition in the ANSI C standard.

Conversions:

Provides compatibility hints for bringing existing programs into compliance with the POSIX standard. The following abbreviations are used:

SysV:	All releases of AT&T System V.
SVR1:	System V Release 1.
SVR2:	System V Release 2.
SVR3:	System V Release 3.
SVR4:	System V Release 4.

These may be combined, as in SVR1-3 to mean System V Release 1 to 3.

BSD:	Berkeley Software Distribution 4.2 and 4.3.
BSD 4.2:	Berkeley Software Distribution 4.2.
BSD 4.3:	Berkeley Software Distribution 4.3.
XPG3:	X/Open Portability Guide Issue 3.

Notes:

Adds any general comments when needed, otherwise you can add your own annotations. OSF/1 and SVR4 supply every interface in this chapter.

abort() — Causes abnormal process termination.

Synopsis:

```
#include <stdlib.h>
void abort(void);
```

Arguments:

None.

Returns:

Never returns.

Description:

The abort() function causes abnormal program termination unless the signal SIGABRT is being caught and the signal handler does not return. If the abort() function causes program termination, it has the effect of calling fclose() on every open stream.

If your program blocks or ignores the SIGABRT signal, the abort() function will still override it.

Reference:

C 4.10.4.1 and P 8.2.3.12

Conversions:

BSD and SVR1-2 generate SIGIOT instead of SIGABRT and return int instead of void. SVR3 returns int instead of void. SVR4 is conforming.

Notes:

The abort() function will not return even if the SIGABRT signal is caught or ignored.

Catching the SIGABRT signal is a way to do application-specific cleanup. Programs should terminate shortly after getting a SIGABRT.

abs ( ) —Computes the absolute value of an integer.

Synopsis:

```
#include <stdlib.h>
int abs(int j);
```

Arguments:

j

Returns:

Absolute value of j.

Description:

The abs ( ) function computes the absolute value of the integer argument.

Reference:

C 4.10.6.1

Conversions:

Add to the list of included headers:

```
#include <stdlib.h>
```

Notes:

Trying to take the absolute value of the most negative integer is not defined.

`access()`—Tests for file accessibility.

Synopsis:

```
#include <unistd.h>
int access(const char *path, int amode);
```

Arguments:

path	Pointer to the name of file to be checked.
amode	Bitwise OR of the access permissions to be checked (R_OK for read, W_OK for write, X_OK for execute, and F_OK for existence).

Returns:

0	If access is allowed.
−1	On error with `errno` set to indicate the error. If access is not allowed, `errno` will be set to EACCES.

Errors:

EACCES, EINVAL, ENAMETOOLONG, ENOENT, ENOTDIR, EROFS

Description:

The `access()` function checks the accessibility of the file named by the `path` argument for the permissions indicated by `amode`, using the real user ID in place of the effective user ID and the real group ID in place of the effective group ID.

Reference:

P 5.6.3.1

Conversions:

Add to the list of headers:

```
#include <unistd.h>
```

SVR1–2 used 4, 2, 1, and 0 instead of the symbols R_OK, W_OK, X_OK, and F_OK, respectively. Change these values to symbols.

BSD and newer releases of SysV used both the symbols and the values. Make sure your program uses only these symbols.

Notes:

access ( ) uses the real UID, not the effective UID. It is not a general utility for finding out "Can I do this?" before doing a call. It is used by SETUID programs to check their actions.

Some historical implementations of access ( ) do not check the file's access correctly when the real user ID of the process is the superuser. In particular, they indicate that the file may be executed without regard to whether the file is executable. The standards allow this behavior.

acos( )—Computes the principal value of arc cosine.

Synopsis:

```
#include <math.h>
double acos(double x);
```

Arguments:

x

Returns:

Arc cosine of x in the range 0 to π radians.

Errors:

EDOM

Description:

The acos( ) function computes the principal value of arc cosine. A domain error occurs for arguments less than –1 or greater than +1.

Reference:

C 4.5.2.1

Notes:

The acos( ) function returns a result in the range 0 to π while the asin( ) function returns a result in the range $-\pi/2$ to $+\pi/2$.

`alarm()`—Schedules an alarm.

Synopsis:

```
#include <unistd.h>
unsigned int alarm(unsigned int seconds);
```

Arguments:

seconds   Number of elapsed seconds before signal.

Returns:

Number of seconds left in previous request or zero if no previous `alarm()` request.

Description:

The `alarm()` functions causes the system to send the calling process a SIGALARM signal after a specified number of seconds elapse.

There can be only one outstanding alarm request at any given time. A call to `alarm()` will reschedule any previous unsignaled request. An argument of zero causes any previous requests to be canceled.

Reference:

P 3.4.1.3

Conversions:

Add to the list of headers:

```
#include <unistd.h>
```

Notes:

The SIGALARM may be delayed by other system activity.

The default action for SIGALARM is to terminate the process.

Some systems allow the signal to occur up to one second early.

The `alarm()` function uses ordinary wall-clock time. This time is measured in the ordinary, human way and is not related to *real-time*, *virtual-time*, or any other form of computer time.

The maximum portable argument is 65,535.

See example on Page 116.

`asctime()`—Converts a time structure to a string.

Synopsis:

```
#include <time.h>
char *asctime(const struct tm *timeptr);
```

Arguments:

`timeptr`   Pointer to a struct `tm` returned by `gmtime()` or `localtime()`.

Returns:

Pointer to string.

Description:

The `asctime()` function converts the time in the structure pointed to by `timeptr` into a string of the form:

```
Sun Oct 21 19:54:52 1990\n\0
```

Reference:

C 4.12.3.1

Conversions:

BSD used the header `<sys/time.h>` for this function.

Notes:

The string returned may be in static storage. Each call overwrites the results of the previous call.

The string returned does NOT depend on the current locale. It is always in English.

`asin()`—Computes the principal value of the arc sine.

Synopsis:

```
#include <math.h>
double asin(double x);
```

Arguments:

> x

Returns:

> Arc sine of x in the range $-\pi/2$ to $+\pi/2$ radians.

Errors:

> EDOM

Description:

> The `asin()` function computes the principal value of the arc sine. A domain error occurs for arguments less than −1 or greater than +1.

Reference:

> C 4.5.2.2

Notes:

> The `acos()` function returns a result in the range 0 to π while the `asin()` function returns a result in the range $-\pi/2$ to $+\pi/2$.

assert()—Aborts the program if assertion is false.

Synopsis:

```
#include <assert.h>
void assert(int expression);
```

Arguments:

expression   If zero the assert function will crash the application by printing an error message and calling abort().

Returns:

No value is returned.

Description:

The assert() macro puts tests into programs. If expression is false the assert() macro writes a message with the line and file of the failing assert() on stderr and calls abort(). The exact format of the message varies widely.

Example:

```
assert(start < end);
for (i=start; i<=end; i++)
    {
    . . .

    }
```

Reference:

C 4.2.1.1

Notes:

assert() is implemented as a macro. If the macro NDEBUG is defined, then calls to assert() are ignored. For example, use statements like:

```
assert(i > j);
```

in places where you assume that i must be greater the j. Define NDEBUG after all of the bugs have been eliminated from the program.

Do not use expressions with side-effects! Statements like:

```
assert(i++ < 100);
```

will not increment i when NDEBUG is defined. Programs that fail only when the debug features are turned off greatly shorten the life of the programmers who write them.

Do not pass a pointer to `assert()`. Use

```
assert(ptr != null);
```

instead of

```
assert(ptr);
```

`atan()` —Computes the principal value of the arc tangent.

Synopsis:

```
#include <math.h>
double atan(double x);
```

Arguments:

x

Returns:

Arc tangent of x in the range $-\pi/2$ to $+\pi/2$ radians.

Description:

The `atan()` function computes the principal value of the arc tangent.

Reference:

C 4.5.2.3

Notes:

atan2() —Computes the principal value of the arc tangent of y/x.

Synopsis:

```
#include <math.h>
double atan2(double y, double x);
```

Arguments:

x and y.

Returns:

Arc tangent of y/x.

Errors:

EDOM

Description:

The atan2() function computes the principal value of the arc tangent of y/x, using the signs of both arguments to determine the quadrant of the return value. A domain error can occur if both arguments are zero.

Reference:

C 4.5.2.4

Notes:

The function atan(y/x) generates an error when x is equal to zero. The call atan2(y,x) returns $\pm^\pi/_2$, depending on the sign of y.

atexit( )—Registers a function to be called at normal program termination.

Synopsis:

```
#include <stdlib.h>
int atexit(void (*func)(void));
```

Arguments:

func   Pointer to function to be called.

Returns:

0 on success and non-zero on failure.

Description:

The function func( ) will be called without arguments at normal program termination.

The functions registered by atexit( ) are called in the reverse order of their registration.

Reference:

C 4.10.4.2

Conversions:

This function is new in Standard C. It is not included in BSD or System V prior to SVR4.

Notes:

At least 32 functions can be registered with atexit( ).

This function is required by Standard C and is not part of the POSIX standard.

atof() —Converts a text string to double.

Synopsis:

```
#include <stdlib.h>
double atof(const char *nptr);
```

Arguments:

nptr   Points to the character string to convert.

Returns:

The converted value.

Description:

The atof() function converts the initial portion of the string pointed to by nptr to double. The behavior is the same as strtod(nptr, (char **)NULL) except that atof() does not detect errors.

Reference:

C 4.10.1.1

Conversions:

Add to the list of headers:

```
#include <stdlib.h>
```

Notes:

See strtod() for the general case.

atoi( )—Converts a text string to integer.

Synopsis:

```
#include <stdlib.h>
int atoi(const char *nptr);
```

Arguments:

nptr   Pointer to text string.

Returns:

Converted value.

Description:

The atoi( ) function converts the initial portion of the string pointed to by nptr to int. The behavior is the same as strtol(nptr, (char **)NULL, 10) except that atoi( ) does not detect errors.

Reference:

C 4.10.1.2

Conversions:

Add to the list of headers:

```
#include <stdlib.h>
```

Notes:

See strtol( ) for the general case.

atol() —Converts a text string to long integer.

Synopsis:

```
#include <stdlib.h>
long int atol(const char *nptr);
```

Arguments:

nptr   Pointer to a text string.

Returns:

Converted value.

Description:

The atol() function converts the initial portion of the string pointed to by nptr to long. The behavior is the same as strtol(nptr, (char **)NULL, 10) except that atol() does not detect errors.

Reference:

C 4.10.1.3

Conversions:

Add to the list of headers:

```
#include <stdlib.h>
```

Notes:

See strtol() for the general case.

bsearch() —Searches a sorted array.

Synopsis:

```
#include <stdlib.h>
void *bsearch(const void *key, const void *base, size_t nmemb,
size_t size, int (*compar)(const void *, const void *));
```

Arguments:

key	Pointer to the element to match.
base	Pointer to the start of the array.
nmemb	Number of elements in the array.
size	Size of each element.
compar	Pointer to a comparison function called with a pointer to a key and a pointer to an array element, in that order. It returns a number less than zero, equal to zero, or greater than zero, depending on the relative order.

Returns:

Pointer to the matching element or NULL if no match is found.

Description:

The bsearch() function searches an array for an element that matches a key. The elements must all have a fixed size and the array must be sorted (see qsort()) according to the comparison function.

If there are multiple elements that match the key, the element returned is unspecified.

Example:

```
/*
 * Score structures contain the student's name
 *   and test score.
 */
struct score
    {
    char student_name[25];
    int  test_score;
    };

/* Class is an array of scores */
struct score class[50];
```

```
/*
 * Comparison function to use with bsearch
 */
int comp_name(const void *key, const void *test)
{
     return(strcmp((char *) key,((struct score *) test) -> student_name));
}

/*
 * Return the score for a student (-1 if not found)
 *
int lookup_score(const char *name)
{
struct score *ptr;

     ptr = (struct score *)bsearch(
          (void*)name,             /* key */
          &score[0],               /* base */
          50,                      /* number of elements */
          sizeof(struct score),/* size */
          comp_name);              /* comparison function */
     if (ptr == NULL) return(-1);
     return(ptr -> test_score);
}
```

Reference:

C 4.10.5.1

Conversions:

Add to the list of headers:

```
#include <stdlib.h>
```

BSD does not support **bsearch( )**.

Notes:

This function is required by Standard C and is not part of the POSIX standard.

calloc( )—Allocates and zeroes memory.

Synopsis:

```
#include <stdlib.h>
void *calloc(size_t nmemb, size_t size);
```

Arguments:

nmemb   Number of elements to allocate.

size   Size of each element.

Returns:

Pointer to the allocated space or NULL if no space can be found.

Description:

The calloc( ) function allocates space for an array of nmemb elements of size bytes. The allocated space is filled with zeros. If the space does not need to be zeroed the malloc( ) function may be used.

The call calloc(100,1) allocates and zeroes 100 bytes.

Reference:

C 4.10.3.1

Conversions:

Add to the list of headers:

```
#include <stdlib.h>
```

BSD and SVR1-3 use unsigned for size and nmemb.

Notes:

The calloc( ) function initializes the allocated space to all zero bits. This may not be the same as floating-point zero or the NULL macro.

ceil()—Computes the smallest integer greater than or equal to x.

Synopsis:

```
#include <math.h>
double ceil(double x);
```

Arguments:

x

Returns:

Smallest integral value not less than **x**, expressed as a **double**.

Description:

Rounds the argument up to the next integer value. The result is still in floating-point format. For example:

```
ceil(1.0000) returns 1.0000
ceil(1.0001) returns 2.0000
ceil(1.9999) retruns 2.0000
```

Conversions:

C 4.5.6.1

Notes:

The resulting value may not fit into an **int** or even a **long**.

cfgetispeed()—Reads terminal input baud rate.

Synopsis:

```
#include <termios.h>
speed_t cfgetispeed(const struct termios *p);
```

Arguments:

p   Pointer to a `struct termios`.

Returns:

Code for the baud rate.

Description:

The `cfgetispeed()` function returns a code for the terminal speed stored in a `struct termios`. The codes are defined in `<termios.h>` by the macros B0, B50, B75, B110, B134, B150, B200, B300, B600, B1200, B1800, B2400, B4800, B9600, B19200, and B38400.

The `cfgetispeed()` function does not do anything to the hardware. It merely returns the value stored by a previous call to `tcgetattr()`.

Reference:

P 7.1.2.7.1

Conversions:

This function is new to POSIX. BSD and System V required the application to store device-dependent information and use the `ioctl()` function to pass that information to the system. That code should be replaced by this function. See `tcsetattr()` for more information.

This function is not supported in BSD or SVR1-3.

Notes:

Baud rates are defined by symbols, such as B110, B1200, B2400. The actual number returned for any given speed may change from system to system.

See Chapter 8, *Terminal I/O*, for more information.

`cfgetospeed()`—Reads terminal output baud rate.

Synopsis:

```
#include <termios.h>
speed_t cfgetospeed(const struct termios *p);
```

Arguments:

p   Pointer to a `struct termios`.

Returns:

Code for the baud rate.

Description:

The `cfgetospeed()` function returns a code for the terminal speed stored in a `struct termios`. The codes are defined in `<termios.h>` by the macros `B0`, `B50`, `B75`, `B110`, `B134`, `B150`, `B200`, `B300`, `B600`, `B1200`, `B1800`, `B2400`, `B4800`, `B9600`, `B19200`, and `B38400`.

The `cfgetospeed()` function does not do anything to the hardware. It merely returns the value stored by a previous call to `tcgetattr()`.

Reference:

P 7.1.2.7.1

Conversions:

This function is new to POSIX. BSD and System V required the application to store device-dependent information and use the `ioctl()` function to pass that information to the system. That code should be replaced by this function. See `tcsetattr()` for more information.

This function is not supported in BSD or SVR1-3.

Notes:

Baud rates are defined by symbols, such as `B110`, `B1200`, `B2400`. The actual number returned for any given speed may change from system to system.

See Chapter 8, *Terminal I/O*, for more information.

`cfsetispeed()`—Sets terminal input baud rate.

Synopsis:

```
#include <termios.h>
int cfsetispeed(struct termios *p, speed_t speed);
```

Arguments:

p   Pointer to a `struct termios`.

speed   Code for the desired speed.

Returns:

Zero on success and −1 on error.

Description:

The `cfsetispeed()` function stores a code for the terminal speed stored in a `struct termios`. The codes are defined in `<termios.h>` by the macros B0, B50, B75, B110, B134, B150, B200, B300, B600, B1200, B1800, B2400, B4800, B9600, B19200, and B38400.

The `cfsetispeed()` function does not do anything to the hardware. It merely stores a value for use by `tcsetattr()`.

Reference:

P 7.1.2.7.1

Conversions:

This function is new to POSIX. BSD and System V required the application to store device-dependent information and use the `ioctl()` function to pass that information to the system. That code should be replaced by this function. See `tcsetattr()` for more information.

This function is not supported in BSD or SVR1-3.

Notes:

This function merely stores a value in the `termios` structure. It does not change the terminal speed until a `tcsetattr()` is done. It does not detect impossible terminal speeds.

See Chapter 8, *Terminal I/O*, for more information.

cfsetospeed( ) —Sets terminal output baud rate.

Synopsis:

```
#include <termios.h>
int cfsetospeed(struct termios *p, speed_t speed);
```

Arguments:

p   Pointer to a `struct termios`.

speed   Code for the desired speed.

Returns:

Zero on success and −1 on error.

Description:

The `cfsetospeed()` function stores a code for the terminal speed stored in a `struct termios`. The codes are defined in `<termios.h>` by the macros B0, B50, B75, B110, B134, B150, B200, B300, B600, B1200, B1800, B2400, B4800, B9600, B19200, and B38400.

The `cfsetospeed()` function does not do anything to the hardware. It merely stores a value for use by `tcsetattr()`.

Reference:

P 7.1.2.7.1

Conversions:

This function is new to POSIX. BSD and System V required the application to store device-dependent information and use the `ioctl()` function to pass that information to the system. That code should be replaced by this function. See `tcsetattr()` for more information.

This function is not supported in BSD or SVR1-3.

Notes:

This function merely stores a value in the `termios` structure. It does not change the terminal speed until a `tcsetattr()` is done. It does not detect impossible terminal speeds.

See Chapter 8, *Terminal I/O*, for more information.

chdir( )—Changes the current working directory.

Synopsis:

```
#include <unistd.h>
int chdir(const char *path);
```

Arguments:

> path   Pointer to the name of the new directory.

Returns:

> Zero on success and −1 on failure.

Errors:

> EACCES, ENAMETOOLONG, ENOENT, ENOTDIR

Description:

> The chdir( ) function causes the directory named by path to become the current working directory; that is, the starting point for searches of pathnames not beginning with a slash.
>
> If chdir( ) detects an error, the current working directory is not changed.

Reference:

> P 5.2.1.1

Conversions:

> Add to the list of headers:
>
> > ```
> > #include <unistd.h>
> > ```

Notes:

chmod( )—Changes file mode.

Synopsis:

```
#include <sys/types.h>
#include <sys/stat.h>
int chmod(const char *path, mode_t mode);
```

Arguments:

    path   Pointer to pathname of the file to modify.

    mode   New permission bits, S_ISUID and S_ISGID.

Returns:

Zero on success and −1 on failure.

Errors:

EACCES, ENAMETOOLONG, ENOENT, ENOTDIR, EPERM, EROFS

Description:

Set the file permission bits, the set user ID bit, and the set group ID bit for the file named by path to mode. If the effective user ID does not match the owner of the file and the calling process does not have the appropriate privileges, chmod( ) returns −1 and sets errno to EPERM.

Reference:

P 5.6.4.1

Conversions:

SVR1–2 and BSD did not specify symbols for the mode bits; they gave absolute values. Change these to symbols using the following key:

Value	Symbol	Meaning
04000	S_ISUID	Set user ID on execution.
02000	S_ISGID	Set group ID on execution.
00400	S_IRUSR	Allow the owner to read the file.
00200	S_IWUSR	Allow the owner to write the file.
00100	S_IXUSR	Allow the owner to execute the file.

Value	Symbol	Meaning
00040	S_IRGRP	Allow a process with a group ID that matches the file's group to read the file.
00020	S_IWGRP	Allow a process with a group ID that matches the file's group to write the file.
00010	S_IXGRP	Allow a process with a group ID that matches the file's group to execute the file.
00004	S_IROTH	Allow anyone to read the file.
00002	S_IWOTH	Allow anyone to write the file.
00001	S_IXOTH	Allow anyone to execute the file.

BSD and SVR1-3 used int for mode instead of mode_t

Notes:

S_ISUID and S_ISGID may be ignored on some implementations.

Do not attempt to set any bits not listed above.

chown ( ) —Changes the owner and/or group of a file.

Synopsis:

```
#include <sys/types.h>
#include <unistd.h>
int chown(const char *path, uid_t owner, gid_t group);
```

Arguments:

path   Pointer to path name of the file to modify.

owner   New owner ID.

group   New group ID.

Returns:

Zero on success and −1 on failure.

Errors:

EACCES, EINVAL, ENAMETOOLONG, ENOENT, ENOTDIR, EPERM, EROFS

Description:

The user ID and group ID of the file named by path are set to owner and path, respectively.

For regular files, the set group ID (S_ISGID) and set user ID (S_ISUID) bits are cleared.

Some systems consider it a security violation to allow the owner of a file to be changed. If users are billed for disk space usage, loaning a file to another user could result in incorrect billing. The chown ( ) function may be restricted to privileged users for some or all files. The group ID can still be changed to one of the supplementary group IDs.

Reference:

P 5.6.5.1

Conversions:

Add to the list of headers:

```
#include <unistd.h>
```

SVR1-3 and BSD used int for owner and group.

Notes:

This function may be restricted for some files. The `pathconf()` function can be used to test the `_PC_CHOWN_RESTRICTED` flag.

clearerr( )—Clears end-of-file and error indicators for a stream.

Synopsis:

```
#include <stdio.h>
void clearerr(FILE *stream);
```

Arguments:

stream   File to use.

Returns:

No value is returned.

Description:

The error and end-of-file indicators for stream are cleared.

Reference:

C 4.9.10.1

Notes:

clock( )—Determines processor time used.

Synopsis:

```
#include <time.h>
clock_t clock(void);
```

Arguments:

None.

Returns:

The processor time used or −1 if unknown.

Description:

The clock( ) function returns an approximation of the amount of CPU time used by the program. The value returned has a type of clock_t. To convert a clock_t to seconds, divide by the macro CLOCKS_PER_SECOND.

Reference:

C 4.12.2.1

Conversions:

This function is not supported in BSD.

SVR1–2 return long.

SVR3 used the header <sys/types.h>.

Notes:

The standards say nothing about when the timer for the clock( ) function is reset. It may not be reset while your process is running. To measure how much time your program used, call clock( ) at the start of your program and again at the end. The difference between the two values is the answer.

This function is required by Standard C and is not part of the POSIX standard.

close()—Closes a file.

Synopsis:

```
#include <unistd.h>
int close(int fildes);
```

Arguments:

fildes   The file descriptor to close.

Returns:

Zero on success and −1 on failure.

Errors:

EBADF, EINTR

Description:

The close() function deallocates the file descriptor named by fildes and makes it available for reuse. All outstanding record locks owned by this process for the file are unlocked.

If it is the last file descriptor that refers to a given file, the following additional steps are taken:

1. Any remaining pipe or FIFO data is discarded.

2. If the link count of the file is zero, the space occupied by the file is freed and the file is no longer accessible.

Reference:

P 6.3.1.1

Conversions:

Add to the list of headers:

```
#include <unistd.h>
```

Notes:

A signal can interrupt the close() function. In that case, close() returns −1 with errno set to EINTR. The file may or may not be closed.

`closedir()`—Ends directory read operation.

Synopsis:

```
#include <sys/types.h>
#include <dirent.h>
int closedir(DIR *dirp);
```

Arguments:

> `dirp`   Pointer returned by `opendir()`.

Returns:

> Zero on success and −1 on failure.

Errors:

> EBADF

Description:

> The directory stream associated with `dirp` is closed. The value in `dirp` may not be usable after a call to `closedir()`.

Reference:

> P 5.1.2.1

Conversions:

> BSD used the header `<sys/dir.h>`, which must be replaced by `<dirent.h>`. The BSD `struct direct` must be replaced by the POSIX equivalent `struct dirent`. BSD also provided the `seekdir()` and `telldir()` functions that are not supported by POSIX.

> SVR1–2 did not provide this function. SVR1–2 programs read directories as ordinary files. Directory entries are 14-byte names and 2-byte I-node numbers. These programs must be changed to use `readdir()`.

Notes:

> The argument to `closedir()` must be a pointer returned by `opendir()`. If it is not, the results are not portable and most likely unpleasant.

cos ( ) —Computes the cosine function.

Synopsis:

```
#include <math.h>
double cos(double x);
```

Arguments:

x

Returns:

Cosine of x.

Description:

Computes the cosine of x. The result will be between −1 and +1.

Reference:

C 4.5.2.5

Notes:

cosh( ) —Computes the hyperbolic cosine function.

Synopsis:

```
#include <math.h>
double cosh(double x);
```

Arguments:

x

Returns:

Hyperbolic cosine of **x**.

Errors:

ERANGE

Description:

Computes the hyperbolic cosine of **x**. This function occurs in numerical solutions to partial differential equations.

Reference:

C 4.5.3.2

Notes:

`creat()`—Creates a new file or rewrites an existing one.

Synopsis:

```
#include <sys/types.h>
#include <sys/stat.h>
#include <fcntl.h>
int creat(const char *path, mode_t mode);
```

Arguments:

path Pointer to path of the file to be created.

mode Permission bits for the new file.

Returns:

A file descriptor or −1 on error.

Errors:

EACCES, EEXIST, EINTR, EISDIR, EMFILE, ENAMETOOLONG, ENFILE, ENOENT, ENOSPC, ENOTDIR, EROFS

Description:

The function call:

```
creat(path,mode);
```

is equivalent to:

```
open(path, O_WRONLY|O_CREAT|O_TRUNC, mode);
```

It opens a file for writing. If the file does not exist, it is created with the permission bits set from mode and the owner and group IDs are set from the effective user and group ID of the calling process. If the file exists, it is truncated to zero length but the owner and group IDs are not changed. The file descriptor returned by `creat()` may be used only for writing.

Reference:

P 5.3.2.1

Conversions:

Make sure the required headers are included.

SVR1–2 used int for mode.

`ctermid()` —Generates terminal pathname.

Synopsis:

```
#include <stdio.h>
#include <unistd.h>
char *ctermid(char *s);
```

Arguments:

s   Pointer to an buffer to hold the terminal pathname. If NULL, a buffer in the `ctermid()` function is used.

Returns:

A pointer to the string.

Description:

The `ctermid()` function returns a string that, when used as a pathname, refers to the current controlling terminal for the current process. If a pathname cannot be determined, an empty string is returned.

The symbolic constant `L_ctermid` is the maximum length of the buffer.

Reference:

P 4.7.1.1

Conversions:

BSD does not support this function.

Notes:

The string returned may not uniquely identify a terminal (e.g., `/dev/tty`).

There is no guarantee that your program can open the terminal.

ctime() —Formats a calendar time.

Synopsis:

```
#include <time.h>
char *ctime(const time_t *timer);
```

Arguments:

timer   Pointer to a local time value.

Returns:

Pointer to the resulting string.

Description:

Converts a time stored as a time_t into a string of the form:

```
Mon Nov 19 14:59:51 1990\n\0
```

Reference:

C 4.12.3.2

Conversions:

BSD and SVR1-3 used long for timer.

The BSD header file <sys/time.h> must be changed to <time.h>.

Notes:

The string returned by ctime() may be overwritten by a subsequent call.

ctime() is equivalent to:

```
asctime(localtime(timer))
```

cuserid()—Gets user name.

Synopsis:

```
#include <stdio.h>
char *cuserid(char *s);
```

Arguments:

    s   Pointer to an array of L_cuserid bytes to return the user name or NULL to use a static array in the cuserid() function.

Returns:

    Pointer to the name string.

Description:

This function returns either the user name associated with the real user ID or the user name associated with the effective user ID. This function is included in the 1988 version of POSIX but removed from the 1990 version. Programs should use one of three alternative calls:

1. getlogin() to return the user's login name.

2. getpwuid(geteuid()) to return the user name associated with the effective user ID.

3. getpwuid(getuid()) to return the user name associated with the real user ID.

Reference:

    P 4.2.4.1

Notes:

    Do not use this function.

`difftime()` —Computes the difference between two times.

Synopsis:

```
#include <time.h>
double difftime(time_t time1, time_t time0);
```

Arguments:

time1   Ending calendar time.

time0   Starting calendar time.

Returns:

The number of seconds between `time0` and `time1`.

Description:

The `difftime()` function returns the number of seconds between `time0` and `time1` expressed as a `double`.

Reference:

C 4.12.2.2

Conversions:

This function is new in Standard C. It is not included in BSD or System V prior to SVR4.

Notes:

This function is required by Standard C and is not part of the POSIX standard.

div() —Computes the quotient and remainder of an integer division.

Synopsis:

```
#include <stdlib.h>
div_t div(int numer, int denom);
```

Arguments:

numer   Numerator.

denom   Denominator.

Returns:

A structure of type `div_t`.

Description:

The `div()` function divides `numer` by `denom` in a portable manner. If the division is inexact, the resulting quotient is the integer of lesser magnitude than the algebraic quotient (round towards zero).

The `div()` function returns a structure of type `div_t` with two members, `quot` and `rem`. Use `div(a,b).quot` instead of `a/b` if the quotient must be rounded the same way on all systems. Use `div(a,b).rem` to obtain the remainder of dividing `a` by `b`.

Reference:

C 4.10.6.2

Conversions:

This function is new in Standard C. It is not included in BSD or System V prior to SVR4.

Notes:

This function is required by Standard C and is not part of the POSIX standard.

dup ( ) —Duplicates an open file descriptor.

Synopsis:

```
#include <unistd.h>
int dup(int fildes);
```

Arguments:

fildes   File descriptor to duplicate.

Returns:

File descriptor that refers to the same file as **fildes** or **−1** on error.

Errors:

EBADF, EINTR

Description:

The call:

```
fid = dup(fildes);
```

is equivalent to:

```
fid = fcntl(fildes, F_DUPFD, 0);
```

This returns the lowest numbered available file descriptor. This new descriptor refers to the same open file as the original descriptor and shares any locks.

Reference:

P 6.2.1.1

Conversions:

Add to the list of headers:

```
#include <unistd.h>
```

Notes:

dup2() —Duplicates an open file descriptor.

Synopsis:

```
#include <unistd.h>
int dup2(int fildes, int fildes2);
```

Arguments:

fildes   File descriptor to duplicate.

fildes2   Desired new file descriptor.

Returns:

File descriptor that refers to the same file as fildes or −1 on error.

Errors:

EBADF, EINTR

Description:

Except for error detection, the call:

```
fid = dup2(fildes, fildes2);
```

is equivalent to:

```
close(fildes2);
fid = fcntl(fildes, F_DUPFD, fildes2);
```

In other words, close the file associated with fildes2, if any. Assign a new file descriptor with the value fildes2. This new descriptor refers to the same open file as fildes and shares any locks.

Reference:

P 6.2.1.1

Conversions:

Add to the list of headers:

```
#include <unistd.h>
```

This function was not supported in SVR1–2.

`execl()` —Executes a file.

Synopsis:

```
#include <unistd.h>
int execl(const char *path, const char *arg, ...);
```

Arguments:

`path`	Pointer to the path name for new process image file.
`arg0,...,argn`	Arguments to pass to new process.

Returns:

−1 on error with `errno` set.

Never returns on success.

Errors:

E2BIG, EACCES, ENAMETOOLONG, ENOENT, ENOTDIR, ENOEXEC, ENOMEM

Description:

This function replaces the current process image with a new process image. When a C program is executed as a result of this call, it is entered as if called by:

```
main(argc,argv)
```

where `argc` is the argument count and `argv` is an array of character pointers to the arguments themselves. In addition, the variable:

```
extern char **environ;
```

is initialized as a pointer to an array of character pointers to the environment strings. The `argv` and `environ` arrays are each terminated by a NULL pointer. The NULL pointer terminating the `argv` array is not counted in `argc`.

The `path` argument identifies the new process image file.

The argument `arg` and the subsequent ellipses can be thought of as `arg0`, `arg1`, `arg2`, ..., `argN`.

The environment for the new process is taken from the current process.

The number of bytes available for the combined argument list and environment list is given by the ARG_MAX macro in `<limits.h>`. This value is usually greater than 4096.

Files with the `FD_CLOEXEC` flag set are closed. All other file descriptors remain unchanged. Directory streams are closed.

Signals set to be caught by the calling process are set to the default action in the new process. Other signals are unchanged.

If the set user ID bit of the new process image file is set, the effective user ID of the new process is set to the owner of the new process image file. The set group ID bit causes a similar action with the effective group ID.

All other process attributes (process ID, real user ID, current working directory, etc.) are inherited by the new program.

Reference:

P 3.1.2.1

Conversions:

Add to the list of headers:

```
#include <unistd.h>
```

Notes:

The last argument must be `(char *)NULL`.

See Example on Page 103.

execle()—Executes a file.

Synopsis:

```
#include <unistd.h>
int execle(const char *path, const char *arg, ...);
```

Arguments:

path	Pointer to the path name for new process image file.
arg0,...,argn−1	Pointer to arguments to pass to new process.
argn	Pointer to an array of pointers to the environment strings.

Returns:

−1 on error with errno set.

Never returns on success.

Errors:

E2BIG, EACCES, ENAMETOOLONG, ENOENT, ENOTDIR, ENOEXEC, ENOMEM

Description:

This function replaces the current process image with a new process image. When a C program is executed as a result of this call, it is entered as if called by:

```
main(argc,argv)
```

where argc is the argument count and argv is an array of character pointers to the arguments themselves. In addition, the variable:

```
extern char **environ;
```

is initialized as a pointer to an array of character pointers to the environment strings. The argv and environ arrays are each terminated by a NULL pointer. The NULL pointer terminating the argv array is not counted in argc.

The path argument identifies the new process image file.

The argument arg and the subsequent ellipses can be thought of as arg0, arg1, arg2, ..., argN.

The final non-NULL argument is a pointer to an array of environment string pointers. This array is terminated by a NULL pointer.

The number of bytes available for the combined argument list and environment list is given by the `ARG_MAX` macro in `<limits.h>`. This value is usually greater than 4096.

Files with the `FD_CLOEXEC` flag set are closed. All other file descriptors remain unchanged. Directory streams are closed.

Signals set to be caught by the calling process are set to the default action in the new process. Other signals are unchanged.

If the set user ID bit of the new process image file is set, the effective user ID of the new process is set to the owner of the new process image file. The set group ID bit causes a similar action with the effective group ID.

All other process attributes (process ID, real user ID, current working directory, etc.) are inherited by the new program.

Reference:

P 3.1.2.1

Conversions:

Add to the list of headers:

```
#include <unistd.h>
```

Notes:

This is the same as `execl()` except for the final non-NULL argument.

The last argument must be `(char *)NULL`.

execlp() —Executes a file.

Synopsis:

```
#include <unistd.h>
int execlp(const char *file, const char *arg, ...);
```

Arguments:

file   Pointer to the filename for new process image file. If file does not
                contain a / then **execlp()** searches the list of directories defined
                by the PATH environment variable.

arg0,...,argn   Pointer to arguments to pass to new process.

Returns:

−1 on error with **errno** set.

Never returns on success.

Errors:

E2BIG, EACCES, ENAMETOOLONG, ENOENT, ENOTDIR, ENOEXEC, ENOMEM

Description:

This function replaces the current process image with a new process image. When a C
program is executed as a result of this call, it is entered as if called by:

```
main(argc,argv)
```

where **argc** is the argument count and **argv** is an array of character pointers to the
arguments themselves. In addition, the variable:

```
extern char **environ;
```

is initialized as a pointer to an array of character pointers to the environment strings. The
argv and **environ** arrays are each terminated by a NULL pointer. The NULL pointer
terminating the **argv** array is not counted in **argc**.

The **path** argument identifies the new process image file.

The argument **arg** and the subsequent ellipses can be thought of as arg0, arg1, arg2,
..., argN.

The environment for the new process is taken from the current process.

The number of bytes available for the combined argument list and environment list is given by the `ARG_MAX` macro in `<limits.h>`. This value is usually greater than 4096.

Files with the `FD_CLOEXEC` flag set are closed. All other file descriptors remain unchanged. Directory streams are closed.

Signals set to be caught by the calling process are set to the default action in the new process. Other signals are unchanged.

If the set user ID bit of the new process image file is set, the effective user ID of the new process is set to the owner of the new process image file. The set group ID bit causes a similar action with the effective group ID.

All other process attributes (process ID, real user ID, current working directory, etc.) are inherited by the new program.

Reference:

P 3.1.2.1

Conversions:

Add to the list of headers:

```
#include <unistd.h>
```

Notes:

The last argument must be `(char *)NULL`.

execv( )—Executes a file.

Synopsis:

```
#include <unistd.h>
int execv(const char *path, char *const argv[]);
```

Arguments:

path   Pointer to the path name for new process image file.

argv   Pointer to an array of arguments to pass to new process.

Returns:

−1 on error with errno set.

Never returns on success.

Errors:

E2BIG, EACCES, ENAMETOOLONG, ENOENT, ENOTDIR, ENOEXEC, ENOMEM

Description:

This function replaces the current process image with a new process image. When a C program is executed as a result of this call, it is entered as if called by:

```
main(argc,argv)
```

where argc is the argument count and argv is an array of character pointers to the arguments themselves. In addition, the variable:

```
extern char **environ;
```

is initialized as a pointer to an array of character pointers to the environment strings. The argv and environ arrays are each terminated by a NULL pointer. The NULL pointer terminating the argv array is not counted in argc.

The path argument identifies the new process image file.

The argument argv is an array of character pointers to null-terminated strings. The last member of this array must be NULL. These strings constitute the argument list available to the new process. The value in argv[0] is usually the name of the file for the new process.

The environment for the new process is taken from the current process.

The number of bytes available for the combined argument list and environment list is given by the `ARG_MAX` macro in `<limits.h>`. This value is usually greater than 4096.

Files with the `FD_CLOEXEC` flag set are closed. All other file descriptors remain unchanged. Directory streams are closed.

Signals set to be caught by the calling process are set to the default action in the new process. Other signals are unchanged.

If the set user ID bit of the new process image file is set, the effective user ID of the new process is set to the owner of the new process image file. The set group ID bit causes a similar action with the effective group ID.

All other process attributes (process ID, real user ID, current working directory, etc.) are inherited by the new program.

Reference:

P 3.1.2.1

Conversions:

Add to the list of headers:

```
#include <unistd.h>
```

Notes:

execve( )—Executes a file.

Synopsis:

```
#include <unistd.h>
int execve(const char *path, char *const argv[], char *const *envp);
```

Arguments:

path	Pointer to the path name for new process image file.
argv	Pointer to an array of arguments to pass to new process.
envp	Pointer to an array of character pointers to the environment strings.

Returns:

−1 on error with `errno` set.

Never returns on success.

Errors:

E2BIG, EACCES, ENAMETOOLONG, ENOENT, ENOTDIR, ENOEXEC, ENOMEM

Description:

This function replaces the current process image with a new process image. When a C program is executed as a result of this call, it is entered as if called by:

```
main(argc,argv)
```

where `argc` is the argument count and `argv` is an array of character pointers to the arguments themselves. In addition, the variable:

```
extern char **environ;
```

is initialized as a pointer to an array of character pointers to the environment strings. The `argv` and `environ` arrays are each terminated by a NULL pointer. The NULL pointer terminating the `argv` array is not counted in `argc`.

The argument `argv` is an array of character pointers to null-terminated strings. The last member of this array must be NULL. These strings constitute the argument list available to the new process. The value in `argv[0]` is usually the name of the file for the new process.

The argument `envp` is a pointer to an array of environment string pointers. This array is terminated by a NULL pointer.

The environment for the new process is taken from the current process.

The number of bytes available for the combined argument list and environment list is given by the `ARG_MAX` macro in `<limits.h>`. This value is usually greater than 4096.

Files with the `FD_CLOEXEC` flag set are closed. All other file descriptors remain unchanged. Directory streams are closed.

Signals set to be caught by the calling process are set to the default action in the new process. Other signals are unchanged.

If the set user ID bit of the new process image file is set, the effective user ID of the new process is set to the owner of the new process image file. The set group ID bit causes a similar action with the effective group ID.

All other process attributes (process ID, real user ID, current working directory, etc.) are inherited by the new program.

Reference:

P 3.1.2.1

Conversions:

Add to the list of headers:

```
#include <unistd.h>
```

Notes:

execvp()—Executes a file.

Synopsis:

```
#include <unistd.h>
int execvp(const char *file, char *const argv[]);
```

Arguments:

file   Pointer to the filename for new process image file. If file does not contain a / then `execlp()` searches the list of directories defined by the `PATH` environment variable.

argv   Pointer to an array of arguments to pass to new process.

Returns:

−1 on error with `errno` set.
Never returns on success.

Errors:

E2BIG, EACCES, ENAMETOOLONG, ENOENT, ENOTDIR, ENOEXEC, ENOMEM

Description:

This function replaces the current process image with a new process image. When a C program is executed as a result of this call, it is entered as if called by:

```
main(argc,argv)
```

where `argc` is the argument count and `argv` is an array of character pointers to the arguments themselves. In addition, the variable:

```
extern char **environ;
```

is initialized as a pointer to an array of character pointers to the environment strings. The `argv` and `environ` arrays are each terminated by a `NULL` pointer. The `NULL` pointer terminating the `argv` array is not counted in `argc`.

The `file` argument is used to construct a pathname that identifies the new process image file. If the `file` argument contains a slash, `file` is used as the pathname. Otherwise, the path prefix for this file is obtained by a search of the directories passed as the environment variable `PATH`.

The argument `argv` is an array of character pointers to null-terminated strings. The last member of this array must be `NULL`. These strings constitute the argument list available to the new process. The value in `argv[0]` is usually the name of the file for the new process.

The environment for the new process is taken from the current process.

The number of bytes available for the combined argument list and environment list is given by the `ARG_MAX` macro in `<limits.h>`. This value is usually greater than 4096.

Files with the `FD_CLOEXEC` flag set are closed. All other file descriptors remain unchanged. Directory streams are closed.

Signals set to be caught by the calling process are set to the default action in the new process. Other signals are unchanged.

If the set user ID bit of the new process image file is set, the effective user ID of the new process is set to the owner of the new process image file. The set group ID bit causes a similar action with the effective group ID.

All other process attributes (process ID, real user ID, current working directory, etc.) are inherited by the new program.

Reference:

P 3.1.2.1

Conversions:

Add to the list of headers:

```
#include <unistd.h>
```

Notes:

`exit()`—Causes normal program termination.

Synopsis:

```
#include <stdlib.h>
void exit(int status);
```

Arguments:

status   Value to be returned to the parent.

Returns:

No value is returned.

Description:

The `exit()` function causes normal program termination. The following steps are taken, in order:

1. All functions registered with `atexit()` are called in reverse order of their registration.

2. All open streams are flushed and closed. All files created by the `tmpfile()` function are removed.

3. `_exit(status)` is called.

Reference:

C 4.10.4.3

Conversions:

Add to the list of headers:

```
#include <stdlib.h>
```

Notes:

Do not call `exit()` from a function registered by `atexit()`.

For maximum portability, use only the `EXIT_SUCCESS` and `EXIT_FAILURE` macros for `status`.

_exit( )—Terminates a process.

Synopsis:

```
#include <unistd.h>
void _exit(int status);
```

Arguments:

status   Termination status.

Returns:

Never returns to caller.

Description:

Takes the following actions:

1. Close all open files and directory streams.

2. If the parent of this process is executing a wait( ) or waitpid( ), it wakes up and is given status. If the parent is not waiting, the status is saved for a future call to wait( ) or waitpid( ).

3. A SIGCHLD signal is sent to the parent.[*]

4. If the process is a controlling process, the SIGHUP signal is sent to each process in the foreground process group and the terminal is disassociated from the session.

5. Children of the terminating process are assigned new parents.

Reference:

P 3.2.2.1

Conversions:

Add to the list of headers:

```
#include <unistd.h>
```

Notes:

---

[*] Unless the implementation does not support SIGCHLD.

exp ( ) —Computes the exponential function.

Synopsis:

```
#include <math.h>
double exp(double x);
```

Arguments:

x

Returns:

e^x

Errors:

ERANGE

Description:

Compute the exponential function of **x**.

Reference:

C 4.5.4.1

Notes:

`fabs()`—Computes the absolute-value function.

Synopsis:

```
#include <math.h>
double fabs(double x);
```

Arguments:

x

Returns:

Absolute value of x.

Description:

If x is positive return x else return −x.

Reference:

C 4.5.6.2

Notes:

fclose()—Closes an open stream.

Synopsis:

```
#include <stdio.h>
int fclose(FILE *stream);
```

Arguments:

stream   Pointer to object to close.

Returns:

Zero if the operation is succeeds, EOF if it fails.

Description:

Any unwritten buffered data for stream is written to the file; any unread buffered data for stream is discarded. Any system resources that were automatically allocated are de-allocated.

Reference:

C 4.9.5.1 & P 8.2.3.2

Notes:

fcntl() —Manipulates an open file descriptor.

Synopsis:

```
#include <sys/types.h>
#include <fcntl.h>
#include <unistd.h>
int fcntl(int fildes, int cmd, ...);
```

Arguments:

fildes   File descriptor.

cmd   Command.

...   Additional command specific arguments.

Returns:

Depends on cmd. In all cases, −1 is returned on error.

Errors:

EACCES, EAGAIN, EBADF, EDEADLK, EINTR, EINVAL, EMFILE, ENOLCK

Description:

This multi-purpose function operates on a file descriptor. The file descriptor is the first argument. The second argument is a macro defined in <fcntl.h>. The action depends on this macro.

> F_DUPFD

Returns the lowest available (not open) file descriptor greater than or equal to the third argument. The new file descriptor refers to the same open file as fildes, and shares any locks.

The FD_CLOEXEC flag for the new descriptor is cleared, so the new descriptor will not be closed on a call to an **exec** function.

> F_GETFD

Returns the FD_CLOEXEC flag associated with fildes.

> F_SETFD

Sets or clears the FD_CLOEXEC flag for a file descriptor. The **exec()** family of functions will close all file descriptors with the FD_CLOEXEC FLAG set.

The correct way to modify the FD_CLOEXEC flag is first to read the flags with F_GETFD. Then, modify the FD_CLOEXEC bit and rewrite the flags with F_SETFD.

```
flags = fcntl(fd, F_GETFD);  /* Get flags */
flags |= FD_CLOEXEC;         /* Set FD_CLOEXEC */
fcntl(fd, F_SETFD, flags);   /* Load new settings */
```

This method allows the application to tolerate implementation-defined flags.

F_GETFL

Returns the file status flags for the file associated with fildes. Unlike F_GETFD, these flags are associated with the file and shared by all descriptors. The following flags are returned:

O_APPEND   Append mode.

O_NONBLOCK   Do not block waiting for data to become available.

O_RDONLY   File is open for reading only.

O_RDWR   File is open for reading and writing.

O_WRONLY   File is open for writing only.

F_SETFL   Set the file status flags from the third argument. The only bits that can be modified with this function are O_APPEND and O_NONBLOCK. Use a read-modify-write to update the flags (see F_SETFL above).

F_GETLK   The third argument must be a pointer to a struct flock. This structure is taken as a description of a lock. If there is a lock which would prevent this lock from being locked, it is returned in the struct flock. If there are no locks which would prevent this lock from being locked, the l_type member is set to F_UNLCK.

F_SETLK   The third argument must be a pointer to a struct flock. The lock is set or cleared according to the function code in the l_type member. If the lock is busy, fcntl() returns −1 and sets errno to EACCES or EAGAIN.

F_SETLKW   The third argument must be a pointer to a struct flock. The lock is set or cleared according to the function code in the l_type member. If the lock is busy, fcntl() waits for it to be unlocked.

Reference:

P 6.5.2.1

Conversions:

Add to the list of headers:

```
#include <unistd.h>
```

SVR3 returns EAGAIN instead of EACCES to indicate a locked file.

The SVR3 flock structure contained the following members:

```
short   l_type;
short   l_whence;
long    l_start;
long    l_len;
short   l_pid;
```

POSIX uses off_t for l_start and l_len. It also uses pid_t for l_pid, while on many POSIX systems pid_t is a long.

The BSD flock() function must be converted to fcntl().

Notes:

F_GETFD   There may be bits other the FD_CLOEXEC returned by this function. You can mask off unwanted bits, for example:

```
flag = fcntl(fd,FD_GETFD) & FD_CLOEXEC;
```

F_SETFD / F_SETFL

Do not set the flags directly. Use a read-modify-write to update the flags. See above.

F_GETLK / F_SETLK / F_SETLKW

File locks are not inherited through fork() but are inherited through one of the exec() functions.

Closing a file descriptor releases all locks held by the process for that file even if there are other file descriptors open for this file.

See discussion on Page 92.

fdopen() —Opens a stream on a file descriptor.

Synopsis:

```
#include <stdio.h>
FILE *fdopen(int fildes, const char *type);
```

Arguments:

    fildes   File descriptor.

    type   Pointer to a character string identical to the mode argument to **fopen()** (e.g., "**r**" for read and "**w**" for write).

Returns:

A pointer to a stream or **NULL** on error.

Description:

The **fdopen()** function associates a stream with a file descriptor. The **FILE** may be used with **stdio** functions, such as **printf()** and **fread()**.

The file position is set to the file offset associated with the file descriptor. The error indicator and end-of-file indicator are cleared.

Reference:

P 8.2.2.1

Notes:

The **fdopen()** function is not required to detect an invalid file descriptor.

`feof()`—Tests the end-of-file indicator for a stream.

Synopsis:

```
#include <stdio.h>
int feof(FILE *stream);
```

Arguments:

stream   Pointer to file to test.

Returns:

Nonzero if and only if the end-of-file indicator is set for **stream**.

Description:

Tests the end-of-file indicator for stream.

Reference:

C 4.9.10.2

Notes:

ferror()—Tests the error indicator for a stream.

Synopsis:

```
#include <stdio.h>
int ferror(FILE *stream);
```

Arguments:

stream   Pointer to file to test.

Returns:

Nonzero if and only if the error indicator is set for **stream**.

Description:

Test the error indicator for **stream**.

Reference:

C 4.9.10.3

Notes:

fflush( )—Updates stream.

Synopsis:

```
#include <stdio.h>
int fflush(FILE *stream);
```

Arguments:

stream   Pointer to the stream to update. If NULL is used, all open files are updated.

Returns:

EOF on error and zero on success.

If an error occurs, a code is stored in errno to identify the error.

Description:

If stream refers to an output stream or an update stream in which the most recent operation was not input, any unwritten data is written to the file. The action of fflush( ) on input streams or streams where the most recent operation was a read is undefined.

If stream is NULL, the fflush( ) operation is performed on all streams where it is defined.

Reference:

C 4.9.5.2 & P 8.2.3.4

Notes:

`fgetc()` —Reads a character from a stream.

Synopsis:

```
#include <stdio.h>
int fgetc(FILE *stream);
```

Arguments:

stream   Pointer to file to read.

Returns:

Character converted to an `int`. `EOF` is returned on error or end-of-file.

Description:

Obtains from `stream` the next character, if any, as an `unsigned char` converted to `int`. Advance the file position.

Reference:

C 4.9.7.1 & P 8.2.3.5

Notes:

`fgetpos()`—Gets the current file position.

Synopsis:

```
#include <stdio.h>
int fgetpos(FILE *stream, fpos_t *pos);
```

Arguments:

stream   Pointer to file to use.

pos   Pointer to file position indicator.

Returns:

A file position is written into pos and zero is returned. Nonzero is returned on error.

Description:

Stores the current value of the file position for **stream** into the object pointed to by **pos**.

Reference:

C 4.9.9.1

Conversions:

This function is new in Standard C. It is not included in BSD or System V prior to SVR4.

Notes:

This function is required by Standard C. It is not part of the POSIX standard.

The format of an **fpos_t** is unspecified.

fgets()—Reads *n* characters from a stream.

Synopsis:

```
#include <stdio.h>
char *fgets(char *s, int n, FILE *stream);
```

Arguments:

s   Pointer to array to read into.

n   Number of characters to read.

stream   Pointer to file to read.

Returns:

If there is no error, s is returned. If an error occurred, NULL is returned and a code is stored in errno to identify the error.

Description:

Reads at most one less that the number of characters specified by n from stream into the array s. No additional characters are read after a newline character or after end-of-file. If a newline character is read, it is stored in the array. A null character is written immediately after the last character read into the array.

Reference:

C 4.9.7.2 & P 8.2.3.5

Notes:

fileno() —Maps a stream pointer to a file descriptor.

Synopsis:

```
#include <stdio.h>
int fileno(FILE *stream);
```

Arguments:

stream   Stream pointer.

Returns:

A file descriptor or −1 on error. If an error occurs, a code is stored in errno to identify the error.

Description:

The fileno() function returns the integer file descriptor associated with stream.

Reference:

P 8.2.1.1

Notes:

fileno(stdin) returns 0.

fileno(stdout) returns 1.

fileno(stderr) returns 2.

If stream is invalid fileno() may or may not detect the error.

floor()—Computes the largest integer not greater than *x*.

Synopsis:

```
#include <math.h>
double floor(double x);
```

Arguments:

x

Returns:

The integer part of x expressed as a **double**.

Description:

Truncates the argument to an integer. For example, floor(2.0000), floor(2.0001), and floor(2.9999) all return 2.0000.

Reference:

C 4.5.6.3

Notes:

fmod() —Computes the remainder of x/y.

Synopsis:

```
#include <math.h>
double fmod(double x, double y);
```

Arguments:

x and y

Returns:

Remainder of x/y expressed as a double.

Description:

Computes the value of x - (y * i), where i is the largest integer such that, if y is nonzero, the result has the same sign as x and a magnitude less than y. The arguments x and y and the returned value are all doubles. The call fmod(15.00,4.00) returns 3.00.

Reference:

C 4.5.6.4

Notes:

If y is zero, fmod() may or may not detect an error.

`fopen()`—Opens a stream.

Synopsis:

```
#include <stdio.h>
FILE *fopen(const char *filename, const char *mode);
```

Arguments:

filename   Pointer to path of file to open.

mode   Pointer to a character string:

"r"   for read.

"w"   for write.

"a"   for append (all writes are at end-of-file).

"r+" for update (reading and writing; all existing data is preserved).

"w+" truncate to zero length and open for update.

"a+" for append update (read any place but all writes are at end-of-file).

Returns:

Pointer to the object controlling the stream or NULL if the operation failed.

Description:

Opens the file whose name is pointed to by `filename` and associates a stream with it.

Reference:

C 4.9.5.3 & P 8.2.3.1

Notes:

Opening a file with append mode causes all writes to be forced to the current end-of-file. This is true even if an `fseek()` operation attempts to change the file position.

If a file is open for reading and writing (mode "r+", "w+", "a+"), an `fflush()`, `fseek()`, `fsetpos()`, or `rewind()` must be done when changing from output to input.

The `mode` argument may have a `b` as the second or third character to indicate binary. This has no effect on POSIX systems but can be useful for portability.

`fork()`—Creates a process.

Synopsis:

```
#include <sys/types.h>
#include <unistd.h>
pid_t fork(void);
```

Arguments:

None.

Returns:

−1 on error.
On success, the PID of the child is returned to the parent and zero is returned to the child.

Errors:

EAGAIN, ENOMEM

Description:

The `fork()` function creates a new process (the child) that is an exact copy of the calling process except:

1. The child process has a new unique process ID.

2. The child process has the process ID of the caller as its parent process ID.

3. The child has a copy of the parent's file descriptors. Each descriptor refers to the same open files as the corresponding descriptor of the parent.

4. The child has its own copy of the parent's open directory stream.

5. The timers returned by the `times()` function are reset for the child.

6. File locks are not inherited by the child.

7. Pending alarms are cleared for the child.

8. There are no pending signals for the child.

Reference:

P 3.1.1.1

Conversions:

Add to the list of headers:

```
#include <unistd.h>
```

BSD and SVR1-3 return `int` instead of `pid_t`.

Notes:

The interaction of `fork()` and `readdir()` is not well defined. Do not attempt to share a directory stream between the parent and child.

See example on Page 103.

fpathconf()—Gets configuration variable for an open file.

Synopsis:

```
#include <unistd.h>
long fpathconf(int fildes, int name);
```

Arguments:

fildes	Open file descriptor.
name	Symbolic constant.

Returns:

If fildes is invalid, −1 is returned and errno is set to indicate the error. If the implementation has no limit for the requested item, −1 is returned and errno is not changed. Otherwise, the limit is returned.

Errors:

EINVAL, EBADF

Description:

Returns a configuration limit for an open file. The fildes argument is an open file descriptor. The possible values for name are:

Name	Description
_PC_LINK_MAX	Maximum value of a file's link count. If fildes refers to a directory then this value applies to the entire directory.
_PC_MAX_CANON	Maximum length of a formatted input line. fildes must refer to a terminal.
_PC_MAX_INPUT	Maximum length of an input line. fildes must refer to a terminal.
_PC_NAME_MAX	Maximum length of a filename for this directory.
_PC_PATH_MAX	The maximum length of a relative pathname when this directory is the working directory.
_PC_PIPE_BUF	Size of the pipe buffer. fildes must refer to a pipe or FIFO.
_PC_CHOWN_RESTRICTED	The chown() system call may not be used on this file. If path or fildes refer to a directory, then this applies to all files in that directory.

Name	Description
_PC_NO_TRUNC	Attempting to create a file in the named directory will fail with ENAMETOOLONG if the filename would be truncated.
_PC_VDISABLE	Allow special character processing to be disabled. `fildes` must refer to a terminal.

Reference:

P 5.7.1.1

Conversions:

This function is new to POSIX. It allows a portable application to determine the quantity of a resource, or the presence of an option, at execution time.

Older applications either use a fixed amount of a resource or attempt to deduce the amount of resource available using the error returns from various functions.

Notes:

The value returned by _PC_PATH_MAX is not useful for allocating storage. Files with paths longer than _PC_PATH_MAX may exist.

fprintf()—Writes formatted text to a stream.

Synopsis:

```
#include <stdio.h>
inf fprintf(FILE *stream, const char *format, ...);
```

Arguments:

stream	File to be written.
format	Format string.
...	Additional arguments.

Returns:

Number of characters written. Negative value if an error occurred.

Description:

The fprintf() function converts its arguments to a character string and writes that string to stream.

The format is a character string that contains zero or more directives. Each directive fetches zero or more arguments to fprintf. Each directive starts with the % character. After the %, the following appear in sequence:

flags   Zero or more of the following flags (in any order):

–   Will cause this conversion to be left-justified. If the – flag is not used, the result will be right-justified.

+   The result of a signed conversion will always begin with a sign. If the + flag is not used, the result will begin with a sign only when negative values are converted.

space   This is the same as + except a space is printed instead of a plus sign. If both the *space* and the + flags are used, the + wins.

The result is converted to an alternate form. The details are given below for each conversion.

width   An optional *width* field. The exact meaning depends on the conversion being performed. See the table on the next page.

prec		An optional *precision*. The *precision* indicates how many digits will be printed to the right of the decimal point. If the *precision* is present, it is preceded by a decimal point (.). If the decimal point is given with no precision, the precision is assumed to be zero. A precision argument may be used only with the e, E, f, g, and G conversions.	
type		An optional h, l, or L. The h causes the argument to be converted to short prior to printing. The l specifies that the argument is a long int. The L specifies that the argument is a long double.	
format		A character that specifies the conversion to be performed.	

The conversions are given by the following table:

	Description	Meaning of *width*	Meaning of # flag
i or d	An int argument is converted to a signed decimal string.	Specifies the minimum number of characters to appear. If the value is smaller, padding is used. The default is 1. The result of printing zero with a width of zero is no characters.	UNDEFINED.
o	An unsigned int argument is converted to unsigned octal.	Same as i.	Increase the precision to force the first digit to be a zero.
u	An unsigned int argument is converted to unsigned decimal.	Same as i.	UNDEFINED.
x	An unsigned int argument is converted to unsigned hexadecimal. The letters abcdef are used.	Same as i.	Prefix non-zero results with 0x.
X	Same as x except the letters ABCDEF are used.	Same as i.	Prefix non-zero results with 0X.

	Description	Meaning of *width*	Meaning of # flag
f	A `double` argument is converted to decimal notation in the `[-]ddd.ddd` format.	Minimum number of characters to appear. May be followed by a period and the number of digits to print after the decimal point. If a decimal point is printed, at least one digit will appear to the left of the decimal.	Print a decimal point even if no digits follow.
e	A `double` argument is converted in the style `[-]d.ddde dd`. The exponent will always contain at least two digits. If the value is zero, the exponent is zero.	Same as `f`.	Same as `f`.
E	Same as `e` except `E` is used instead of `e`.	Same as `f`.	Same as `f`.
g	Same as `f` or `e`, depending on the value to be converted. The `e` style is used only if the exponent is less than –4 or greater than the precision.	Same as `f`.	Same as `f`.
G	Same as `g` except an `E` is printed instead of `e`.	Same as `f`.	Same as `f`.
c	An `int` argument is converted to an `unsigned char` and the resulting character is written.	UNDEFINED.	UNDEFINED.

	Description	Meaning of *width*	Meaning of # flag
s	An argument is assumed to be char *. Characters up to (but not including) a terminating null are written.	Specifies the maximum number of characters to be written.	UNDEFINED.
p	An argument must be a pointer to void. The pointer is converted to a sequence of printable characters in an implementation-defined manner. This is not very useful for a portable program.	UNDEFINED.	UNDEFINED.
n	An argument should be a pointer to an integer which is *written* with the number of characters written to. Nothing is written to the output stream by this directive.	UNDEFINED.	UNDEFINED.

Reference:

C 4.9.7.3

Conversions:

Change \07 in format to \a.

Notes:

See "Pitfalls" on Page 42.

fputc ( ) —Writes a character to a stream.

Synopsis:

```
#include <stdio.h>
int fputc(int c, FILE *stream);
```

Arguments:

c   Character to write.

stream   Pointer to file to write into.

Returns:

The character written or EOF on error.

Description:

Write the character c (converted to unsigned char) to stream and update the file position. If stream was opened in append mode, the character is appended to the file.

Reference:

C 4.9.7.3 & P 8.2.3.6

Notes:

fputs( )—Writes a string to a stream.

Synopsis:

```
#include <stdio.h>
int fputs(const char *s, FILE *stream);
```

Arguments:

    s   String to write.

    stream   Pointer to file to write.

Returns:

    EOF on error or a non-negative value.

Description:

The character string pointed to by s is written to stream. The terminating null is not written.

Reference:

    C 4.9.7.4 & P 8.2.3.6

Notes:

fread() —Reads an array from a stream.

Synopsis:

```
#include <stdio.h>
size_t fread(void *ptr, size_t size, size_t nmemb, FILE *stream);
```

Arguments:

ptr   Pointer to array to read into.

size   Size of one array member.

nmemb   Number of array members to read.

stream   Pointer to file to read from.

Returns:

Number of elements read or EOF on error.

Description:

Reads in the array pointed to by ptr, up to nmemb elements whose size is specified by size, from stream. The file position of the stream is advanced by the number of characters read. If an error occurs, the file position is indeterminate. If a partial element is read, its value is indeterminate.

Reference:

C 4.9.8.1 & P 8.2.3.5

Conversions:

BSD and SVR1-2 use int for size and nmemb.

Notes:

If size or nmemb is zero, fread() returns zero without reading anything.

`free()`—Deallocates dynamic memory.

Synopsis:

```
#include <stdlib.h>
void free(void *ptr);
```

Arguments:

ptr   Pointer returned by a previous call to `calloc()`, `malloc()`, `realloc()`.

Returns:

No value is returned.

Description:

The `free()` function causes the space pointed to by `ptr` to be made available for allocation. If `ptr` is NULL, nothing happens.

Reference:

C 4.10.3.2

Conversions:

Add to the list of headers:

```
#include <stdlib.h>
```

Notes:

If `ptr` is not a value returned by `calloc()`, `malloc()`, `realloc()`, or if multiple attempts are made to free the same block, the program is not portable.

`freopen()`—Closes and then opens a stream.

Synopsis:

```
#include <stdio.h>
FILE *freopen(const char *filename, const char *mode, FILE *stream);
```

Arguments:

`filename` Pointer to path of the file to open.

`mode`   Pointer to file mode string.

`stream`   Pointer to stream to use.

Returns:

`stream`, unless the operation failed. In that case, `NULL` is returned.

Description:

The call:

```
stream = freopen(file, mode, stream);
```

is equivalent to:

```
fclose(stream);
stream = fopen(file,mode);
```

Reference:

C 4.9.5.4 & P 8.2.3.3

Notes:

frexp() —Breaks a floating-point number into a fraction and integer.

Synopsis:

```
#include <math.h>
double frexp(double value, int *exp);
```

Arguments:

value   Floating-point value.

exp   Pointer to an int to be returned by frexp().

Returns:

A value x, such that, $\frac{1}{2} \leq x < 1$ and value = x 2^{exp}.

Description:

Compute a value x, such that, $\frac{1}{2} \leq x < 1$ and value = x 2^{exp}. If value is zero, both parts of the result are zero.

Reference:

C 4.5.4.2

Notes:

See ldexp() for the inverse function.

The frexp() function may be inefficient on nonbinary architectures.

fscanf()—Reads formatted input from a stream.

Synopsis:

```
#include <stdio.h>
int fscanf(FILE *stream, const char *format, ...);
```

Arguments:

stream	Pointer to file to read.
format	Pointer to control string.
...	Pointers to variables to store into.

Returns:

EOF if an error took place before any characters were read. Otherwise, the number of input items assigned is returned.

Description:

Reads input from stream under control of format.

The format string contains ordinary text and conversion specifiers. Each directive starts with the % character. After the %, the following appear in sequence:

star	An optional assignment-suppressing character *.
width	An optional decimal integer that specifies the maximum field width.
type	An optional h, l, or L indicating the size of the receiving object. The exact meaning depends on the conversion. See the table below.
format	A character that specifies the type of conversion to perform.

The conversions are given by the following table:

	Description	Meaning of *size* flags
d	Matches an optionally signed decimal integer. The subject is defined as the longest initial subsequence of the input string, starting with the first non-white-space character that is of the expected form.	none → int h → short l → long
	The expected form is an optional plus or minus sign followed by a sequence of the digits 0 through 9.	

	Description	Meaning of *size* flags
o	Same as d except only the digits 0 to 7 are allowed.	none → `unsigned int` h → `unsigned short` l → `unsigned long`
u	Same as d except the argument is pointer to an unsigned value. Note: leading minus sign is legal.	Same as o.
x	Same as d except the argument is a pointer to an unsigned value and the letters A to F are valid. Note: a leading minus is legal.	Same as o.
e f g	Matched an optionally signed floating-point number. The number may be in any format which is acceptable as a floating-constant, but no floating suffix is allowed.	none → `float` l → `double` L → `long double`
s	Matches a sequence of non-white-space characters. Note: Use %nc to match exactly n characters.	UNDEFINED.
[	Matches a sequence of characters from a set of expected characters. The conversion specifier includes all subsequent characters in the `format` string, up to and including the matching right bracket (]). The characters between the brackets comprise the set of expected characters (the *scanset*). If the character following the left bracket is a circumflex (^), the scanset contains all characters that do not appear between the brackets. If the conversion specifier begins with [ ] or [^], the right bracket is included in the scanset and the next right bracket ends the specification. Some systems allow specifications of the form [a–z], meaning all characters between a and z. This depends on the codeset used and is not portable.	UNDEFINED.

	Description	Meaning of *size* flags
c	Matches a sequence of characters. The field width determines how many characters are matched. If there is no field width, one character is matched.	UNDEFINED.
	NOTE: The format %nc matches n characters. The format %ns matches up to n non-white-space characters.	
p	Matches a pointer. The only portable use is to read back a pointer written by the %p directive to fprintf during the execution of this program.	UNDEFINED.
n	Does not match anything. The corresponding argument is written with the number of characters read from the input stream so far by this call to fscanf().	UNDEFINED.
%	Match a single %.	UNDEFINED.

Reference:

C 4.9.6.2 & P 8.2.3.7

Notes:

See "Pitfalls" on Page 47.

fseek() —Sets file position.

Synopsis:

```
#include <stdio.h>
int fseek(FILE *stream, long int offset, int whence);
```

Arguments:

stream   Pointer to file to be positioned.

offset   File position.

whence   One of the following macros:

         SEEK_SET   absolute offset.

         SEEK_CUR   relative to current position.

         SEEK_END   relative to end of file.

Returns:

Zero on success and nonzero on failure.

Description:

Set the file position, measured in bytes from the beginning of the file, by adding offset to the value specified by whence.

A successful call to fseek() clears the end-of-file indicator and undoes any effects of ungetc(). The next operation on an update stream may be either input or output.

Reference:

C 4.9.9.2 & P 8.2.3.7

Conversions:

Replace numeric constants with macros using the following key:

0   SEEK_SET

1   SEEK_CUR

2   SEEK_END

`fsetpos()`—Sets the file position for a stream.

Synopsis:

```
#include <stdio.h>
int fsetpos(FILE *stream, const fpos_t *pos);
```

Arguments:

stream   File to use.

pos   Value returned by `fgetpos()`.

Returns:

Zero on success and nonzero on failure.

Description:

Set the file position indicator for `stream` from the object pointed to by `pos`. The object pointed to by `pos` must have been obtained by a prior call to `fgetpos()`.

A successful call to `fsetpos()` clears the end-of-file indicator and undoes any effects of `ungetc()`. The next operation on an update stream may be either input or output.

Reference:

C 4.9.9.3

Conversions:

This function is new in Standard C. It is not included in BSD or System V prior to SVR4.

Notes:

This function is required by Standard C. It is not part of the POSIX standard.

`fstat()`—Gets file status.

Synopsis:

```
#include <sys/types.h>
#include <sys/stat.h>
int fstat(int fildes, struct stat *buf);
```

Arguments:

fildes   Open file descriptor for file.

buf   Pointer to an object of type struct `stat` where the file information will be written.

Returns:

Zero on success and −1 on failure.
If an error occurs, a code is stored in `errno` to identify the error.

Errors:

EBADF

Description:

The `fstat()` function obtains information about the file associated with `fildes` and writes it to the area pointed to by the `buf` argument.

Reference:

P 5.6.2.1

Conversions:

System V has an `st_rdev` member in the `stat` structure which POSIX does not support. BSD and SVR4 have `st_rdev`, `st_blksize`, and `st_blocks` members which POSIX does not support.

Many older programs use `short` or `unsigned short` for many `stat` structure members. These must be changed to the POSIX types (`dev_t`, `ino_t`, and so on). See `stat` in the Data Structures section.

`ftell()`—Gets the position indicator for a stream.

Synopsis:

```
#include <stdio.h>
long int ftell(FILE *stream);
```

Arguments:

stream   Pointer to file to use.

Returns:

Current file position or −1L on error.

Description:

Returns the current value of the file position indicator associated with `stream`. The value is the number of bytes from the beginning of the file.

Reference:

C 4.9.9.4 & P 8.2.3.6

Notes:

The `ftell()` function will fail for files with more than `LONG_MAX` bytes. The `fgetpos()` function is more general.

The underlying function is `lseek()`.

`fwrite()`—Writes an array to a stream.

Synopsis:

```
#include <stdio.h>
size_t fwrite(const void *ptr, size_t size, size_t nmemb, FILE *stream);
```

Arguments:

`ptr`	Pointer to array to write.
`size`	Size of each array element.
`nmemb`	Number of array elements.
`stream`	Pointer to file to write into.

Returns:

Number of elements successfully written.

Description:

Writes, from the array pointed to by `ptr`, up to `nmemb` elements whose size is specified by `size`, to `stream`. The file position indicator is advanced by the number of bytes written. If an error occurs, the resulting file position is indeterminate.

Reference:

C 4.9.8.2 & P 8.2.3.6

Conversions:

BSD and SVR1–2 use `int` for `size` and `nmemb`.

Notes:

getc()—Reads a character from a stream.

Synopsis:

```
#include <stdio.h>
int getc(FILE *stream);
```

Arguments:

stream   Pointer to file to read.

Returns:

Character converted to int or EOF on error or end-of-file.

Description:

Obtains the next byte, if any, as an unsigned char converted to int from stream and advances the file position indicator.

This function is equivalent to fgetc(), except that it is implemented as a macro which may evaluate stream more than once. Do not use an expression with side effects for stream.

Reference:

C 4.9.7.5 & P 8.2.3.5

Notes:

This function may be coded as an "unsafe" macro. That is, it may evaluate the argument more than once. This will produce non-portable results for arguments like file++.

getchar()—Reads a character from standard input.

Synopsis:

```
#include <stdio.h>
int getchar(void);
```

Arguments:

None.

Returns:

Character converted to `int` or `EOF` on error.

Description:

The `getchar()` function is equivalent to `getc(stdin)`.

Reference:

C 4.9.7.6 & P 8.2.3.5

Notes:

`getcwd( )`—Gets current working directory.

Synopsis:

```
#include <unistd.h>
char *getcwd(char *buf, size_t size);
```

Arguments:

buf   Pointer to a place to store the current working directory.

size   Size of the array pointed to by buf.

Returns:

buf on success and NULL on error.

Errors:

EINVAL, ERANGE, EACCES

Description:

The getcwd( ) function copies the absolute pathname of the current working directory to the character array pointed to by buf. The size argument is the number of bytes available in buf.

Reference:

P 5.2.2.1

Conversion:

Add to the list of headers:

```
#include <unistd.h>
```

System V uses int for size. BSD has a similar function called getwd( ).

Notes:

There is no way to determine the maximum string length that getcwd( ) may need to return. Applications should tolerate getting ERANGE and allocate a larger buffer. See Example 2-4 on Page 30.

It is possible for getcwd( ) to return EACCES if, say, login puts the process into a directory without read access.

The 1988 standard uses int instead of size_t for the second parameter.

getegid( )—Gets effective group ID.

Synopsis:

```
#include <sys/types.h>
#include <unistd.h>
gid_t getegid(void);
```

Arguments:

None.

Returns:

Effective group ID.

Description:

The getegid( ) function returns the effective group ID of the calling process.

Reference:

P 4.2.1.1

Conversion:

Add to the list of headers:

```
#include <unistd.h>
```

BSD returns int.

SVR1-3 return unsigned short.

Notes:

See Example 7-1 on Page 129.

getenv()—Gets the environment variable.

Synopsis:

```
#include <stdlib.h>
char *getenv(const char *name);
```

Arguments:

name   Pointer to the name to match.

Returns:

A pointer to the string associated with the matched name or NULL if there is no match.

Description:

The getenv() function searches the environment list for a string that matches the string pointed to by name. The strings are of the form name=value. The pointer returned points to value.

Reference:

C 4.10.4.4 & P 4.6.1.1

Conversion:

Add to the list of headers:

```
#include <stdlib.h>
```

Notes:

The string returned by `getenv()` may be overwritten by a subsequent call. Do not attempt to modify the string returned by `getenv()`. The following names are defined:

HOME	The initial working directory.
LANG	Predefined setting for locale.
LC_COLLATE	The name of the locale for collating.
LC_CTYPE	The name of the locale for `char` functions.
LC_MONETARY	The name of the locale for editing money.
LC_NUMERIC	The name of the locale for editing numbers.
LOGNAME	The login account.
PATH	The search path for the `exec()` functions.
TERM	The terminal type.
TZ	The timezone information.

geteuid()—Gets effective user ID.

Synopsis:

```
#include <sys/types.h>
#include <unistd.h>
uid_t geteuid(void);
```

Arguments:

None.

Returns:

Effective user ID.

Description:

The geteuid() function returns the effective user ID.

Reference:

P 4.2.1.1

Conversion:

Add to the list of headers:

```
#include <unistd.h>
```

BSD returns int.

SVR1-3 return unsigned short.

Notes:

See Example 7-1 on Page 129.

`getgid( )` —Gets real group ID.

Synopsis:

```
#include <sys/types.h>
#include <unistd.h>
gid_t getgid(void);
```

Arguments:

None.

Returns:

Real group ID.

Description:

The `getgid( )` function returns the real group ID.

Reference:

P 4.2.1.1

Conversion:

Add to the list of headers:

```
#include <unistd.h>
```

BSD returns `int`.

SVR1-3 return `unsigned short`.

Notes:

See Example 7-1 on Page 129.

getgrgid()—Reads groups database based on group ID.

Synopsis:

```
#include <grp.h>
struct group *getgrgid(gid_t gid);
```

Arguments:

gid   Group ID to lookup.

Returns:

A pointer to a group structure or NULL on error.

Description:

The getgrgid() function looks up the supplied group ID and returns a pointer to a struct group.

Reference:

P 9.2.1.1

Conversion:

BSD used int for gid. BSD's struct group also included a gr_passwd member, not supported by POSIX.

SVR1-3 did not provide this function. Code that reads /etc/groups must be replaced by calls to this function.

Notes:

The return value may (or may not) point to static data that is overwritten by each call.

See Example 7-1 on Page 129.

getgrnam( )—Reads group database based on group name.

Synopsis:

```
#include <grp.h>
struct group *getgrnam(const char *name);
```

Arguments:

name   Pointer to name of the group to lookup.

Returns:

A pointer to a group structure or NULL on error.

Description:

The getgrnam( ) function looks up the supplied group name and returns a pointer to a struct group.

Reference:

P 9.2.1.1

Conversion:

BSD's struct group also included a gr_passwd member, not supported by POSIX.

SVR1-3 did not provide this function. Code that reads /etc/groups must be replaced by calls to this function.

Notes:

The return value may (or may not) point to static data that is overwritten by each call.

getgroups()—Gets supplementary group IDs.

Synopsis:

```
#include <sys/types.h>
#include <unistd.h>
int getgroups(int gidsetsize, gid_t grouplist[]);
```

Arguments:

gidsetsize   Size of the grouplist array. If zero, getgroups() returns the number of entries required.

grouplist   Pointer to array to store group IDs.

Returns:

The number of supplementary group IDs returned. On error, −1 is returned.

Errors:

EINVAL

Description:

The getgroups() function fills in the array grouplist with the supplementary groups IDs of the calling process. The gidsetsize argument specifies the number of elements in the supplied array. The actual number of elements used is returned.

If gidsetsize is zero, getgroups() returns the number of supplemental group IDs associated with the calling process.

Reference:

P 4.2.3.1

Conversion:

Replace BSD's #include <sys/param.h> with #include <unistd.h>.

This function is not supported in SVR1-3.

Notes:

If `gidsetsize` is greater than zero but less than the number of supplementary group IDs, −1 is returned and `errno` is set to `EINVAL`. The `grouplist` array may (or may not) have been modified.

The effective group ID may (or may not) be returned by `getgroups()`. Use `getegid()` to make sure you have all the information.

See Example 7-1 on Page 129.

The macro `NGROUPS_MAX` may not be a constant.

getlogin()—Gets user name.

Synopsis:

```
#include <unistd.h>
char *getlogin(void);
```

Arguments:

None.

Returns:

Pointer to a string containing the user's login name.

Description:

The getlogin() function returns a pointer to the user's login name. The same user ID may be shared by several login names. The string returned by getlogin() may be used as an argument to getpwnam() to get the user database information.

Reference:

P 4.2.4.1

Conversion:

Add to the list of headers:

```
#include <unistd.h>
```

This function was not supported on SVR1-3.

Notes:

On some systems, a user will have several login names but one user ID. For example, k_lewine might log in using the Korn shell and c_lewine the C shell.

getpgrp( )—Gets process group ID.

Synopsis:

```
#include <sys/types.h>
#include <unistd.h>
pid_t getpgrp(void);
```

Arguments:

None.

Returns:

Process group ID.

Description:

Returns the process group ID for the calling process.

Reference:

P 4.3.1.1

Conversion:

Add to the list of headers:

```
#include <unistd.h>
```

BSD returns `int`. The BSD `getpgrp( )` function takes a process ID as an argument. In practice, this is never used and is not supported by POSIX.

SVR1-3 return `unsigned short`.

Notes:

getpid( )—Gets process ID.

Synopsis:

```
#include <sys/types.h>
#include <unistd.h>
pid_t getpid(void);
```

Arguments:

None.

Returns:

Process ID.

Description:

Returns the process ID for the calling process.

Reference:

P 4.1.1.1

Conversion:

Add to the list of headers:

```
#include <unistd.h>
```

BSD returns `int`.

SVR1-3 returns `unsigned short`.

Notes:

getppid( )—Gets parent process ID.

Synopsis:

```
#include <sys/types.h>
#include <unistd.h>
pid_t getppid(void);
```

Arguments:

None.

Returns:

Parent's process ID.

Description:

Returns the process ID of the process that created the calling process.

Reference:

P 4.1.1.1

Conversion:

Add to the list of headers:

```
#include <unistd.h>
```

BSD returns int.

SVR1-3 returns unsigned short.

Notes:

Parent may no longer exist.

`getpwnam()`—Reads user database based on user name.

Synopsis:

```
#include <pwd.h>
struct passwd *getpwnam(const char *name);
```

Arguments:

name   Pointer to the name to lookup.

Returns:

A pointer to a `passwd` structure or `NULL` on error.

Description:

The `getpwnam()` function looks up the supplied user name and returns a pointer to a `struct passwd`.

Reference:

P 9.2.2.1

Conversion:

BSD's `struct passwd` also included `pw_comment`, `pw_quota`, and `pw_gecos` members, not supported by POSIX.

SVR1-3 did not provide this function. Code that reads `/etc/passwd` must be replaced by calls to this function.

Notes:

getpwuid( )—Reads user database based on user ID.

Synopsis:

```
#include <pwd.h>
struct passwd *getpwuid(uid_t uid);
```

Arguments:

uid   User ID to lookup.

Returns:

A pointer to a passwd structure or NULL on error.

Description:

The getpwuid( ) function looks up the supplied user ID and returns a pointer to a struct passwd.

Reference:

P 9.2.2.1

Conversion:

BSD used int for uid. BSD's struct passwd also included pw_comment, pw_quota, and pw_gecos members, not supported by POSIX.

SVR1-3 did not provide this function. Code that reads /etc/passwd must be replaced by calls to this function.

Notes:

See Example 7-1 on Page 129.

gets() —Reads a string from standard input.

Synopsis:

```
#include <stdio.h>
char *gets(char *s);
```

Arguments:

s   Pointer to array to store into.

Returns:

s on success and NULL on failure.

Description:

Read characters from stdin into the array pointed to by s until a newline is read or end-of-file is encountered. Any newline read is discarded and a null character is written after the last character is read into the array.

Reference:

C 4.9.7.7 & P 8.2.3.5

Notes:

This function is not equivalent to fgets(stdin,s). There is no checking to see if the input characters fit in the array, and is thus very dangerous. Use fgets() instead.

getuid()—Gets real user ID.

Synopsis:

```
#include <sys/types.h>
#include <unistd.h>
uid_t getuid(void);
```

Arguments:

None.

Returns:

Real user ID.

Description:

The getuid() function returns the user ID of the calling process.

Reference:

P 4.2.1.1

Conversion:

Add to the list of headers:

```
#include <unistd.h>
```

BSD returns int.

SVR1-3 returns unsigned short.

Notes:

gmtime()—Breaks down a timer value into a `time` structure in Coordinated Universal Time (UTC).

Synopsis:

```
#include <time.h>
struct tm *gmtime(const time_t *timer);
```

Arguments:

timer   `time_t` returned by `time()`.

Returns:

A pointer to a `struct tm`.

Description:

The `gmtime()` function breaks down the time in the `time_t` pointed to by `timer` into year, month, day, hours, minutes, seconds, etc., and stores the information in a `struct tm`. A pointer to the `struct tm` is returned.

Reference:

C 4.12.3.3

Conversion:

BSD used the header `<sys/time.h>` instead of `<time.h>`.

BSD and SVR1-3 used `long` for timer.

Notes:

See `localtime()`.

See description on Page 133.

isalnum( )—Tests for alphabetic or numeric character.

Synopsis:

```
#include <ctype.h>
int isalnum(int c);
```

Arguments:

c   Character to be tested.

Returns:

Non-zero (true) if the argument is an uppercase or lowercase letter or a digit.

Description:

The call isalnum(c) is equivalent to isalpha(c) || isdigit(c).

Reference:

C 4.3.1.1

Notes:

`isalpha()`—Tests for alphabetic character.

Synopsis:

```
#include <ctype.h>
int isalpha(int c);
```

Arguments:

c   Character to be tested.

Returns:

Non-zero (true) if the argument is an uppercase or lowercase letter.

Description:

The `isalpha()` function returns true if the argument is an alphabetic character in the current locale. In the "`C`" or "`POSIX`" locale `isalpha(c)` is equivalent to `isupper(c) || islower(c)`.

Reference:

C 4.3.1.2

Notes:

isatty( )—Determines if a file descriptor is associated with a terminal.

Synopsis:

```
#include <unistd.h>
int isatty(int fildes);
```

Arguments:

    fildes   File descriptor to test.

Returns:

    1 if **fildes** refers to a terminal and zero if it does not.

Description:

    The **isatty( )** function returns 1 if **fildes** is a valid file descriptor associated with a terminal, zero otherwise.

Reference:

    P 4.7.2.1

Conversion:

    Add to the list of headers:

```
#include <unistd.h>
```

Notes:

iscntrl( )—Tests for control character.

Synopsis:

```
#include <ctype.h>
int iscntrl(int c);
```

Arguments:

    c   Character to be tested.

Returns:

    Non-zero (true) if the argument is a control character.

Description:

    The iscntrl( ) function returns non-zero if the argument is a control character in the current locale.

Reference:

    C 4.3.1.3

Notes:

`isdigit()`—Tests for decimal-digit character.

Synopsis:

```
#include <ctype.h>
int isdigit(int c);
```

Arguments:

    c   Character to be tested.

Returns:

Non-zero (true) if the argument is a decimal-digit character.

Description:

The `isdigit()` returns non-zero if the argument is one of `'0'`, `'1'`, `'2'`, `'3'`, `'4'`, `'5'`, `'6'`, `'7'`, `'8'`, or `'9'`.

Reference:

C 4.3.1.4

Notes:

isgraph()—Tests for printing character.

Synopsis:

```
#include <ctype.h>
int isgraph(int c);
```

Arguments:

c   Character to be tested.

Returns:

Non-zero (true) if the argument is any printing character except space.

Description:

The isgraph() function returns non-zero for any character except ' '.

Reference:

C 4.3.1.5

Conversion:

Not supported in BSD 4.2, but added in 4.3.

Notes:

`islower()`—Tests for lowercase character.

Synopsis:

```
#include <ctype.h>
int islower(int c);
```

Arguments:

    c   Character to be tested.

Returns:

Non-zero (true) if the argument is a lowercase letter.

Description:

The `islower()` function returns non-zero if the argument is a lowercase letter in the current locale.

Reference:

C 4.3.1.6

Notes:

`isprint()`—Tests for printing character.

Synopsis:

```
#include <ctype.h>
int isprint(int c);
```

Arguments:

c   Character to be tested.

Returns:

Non-zero (true) if the argument is any printing character including space.

Description:

The `isprint()` function tests for any printing character including a space in the current locale.

Reference:

C 4.3.1.7

Notes:

ispunct()—Tests for punctuation.

Synopsis:

```
#include <ctype.h>
int ispunct(int c);
```

Arguments:

c   Character to be tested.

Returns:

Non-zero (true) if the argument is an printing character which is not a space, an upper-case letter, a lowercase letter, or a digit.

Description:

The call ispunct(c) is equivalent to ((c != ' ') && !isalnum(c))

Reference:

C 4.3.1.8

Notes:

`isspace()`—Tests for white-space character.

Synopsis:

```
#include <ctype.h>
int isspace(int c);
```

Arguments:

c   Character to be tested.

Returns:

Non-zero (true) if the argument is a standard or implementation defined white-space character.

Description:

The `isspace()` function returns non-zero if the argument is a white-space character in the current locale. In the "`C`" or "`POSIX`" locales, the white-space characters are: space, form-feed (`'\f'`), newline (`'\n'`), carriage return (`'\r'`), horizontal tab (`'\t'`), and vertical tab (`'\v'`).

Reference:

C 4.3.1.9

Notes:

`isupper()`—Tests for uppercase alphabetic character.

Synopsis:

```
#include <ctype.h>
int isupper(int c);
```

Arguments:

  `c`   Character to be tested.

Returns:

Non-zero (true) if the argument is an uppercase letter.

Description:

The call `isupper(c)` is equivalent to `(!iscntrl(c) && !isdigit(c) && !ispunct(c) && !isspace(c))`.

Reference:

C 4.3.1.10

Notes:

isxdigit()—Tests for hexadecimal-digit character.

Synopsis:

```
#include <ctype.h>
int isxdigit(int c);
```

Arguments:

    c   Character to be tested.

Returns:

Non-zero (true) if the argument is one of:

0 1 2 3 4 5 6 7 8 9 a b c d e f A B C D E F

Description:

The isxdigit() function returns non-zero if the argument is one of:

0 1 2 3 4 5 6 7 8 9 a b c d e f A B C D E F

Reference:

C 4.3.1.11

Conversion:

Not supported in BSD 4.2, but added in 4.3.

Notes:

`kill()`—Sends a signal to a process.

Synopsis:

```
#include <sys/types.h>
#include <signal.h>
int kill(pid_t pid, int sig);
```

Arguments:

pid   Process ID of the process or processes to be signalled.

sig   Signal number to deliver.

Returns:

Zero on success and –1 on failure.

If an error occurs, a code is stored in `errno` to identify the error.

Errors:

EINVAL, EPERM, ESRCH

Description:

The `kill()` function sends a signal to a process or a group of processes specified by `pid`. If the signal is zero, error checking is performed but no signal is actually sent. This can be used to check for a valid `pid`.

If `pid` is greater than zero, `sig` is sent to the process whose process ID is `pid`. If `pid` is negative, `sig` is sent to all processes whose process group ID is equal to the absolute value of `pid`.

If the `kill()` function causes a signal to be generated for the calling process, and if `sig` is not blocked, either `sig` or another pending unblocked signal will be delivered before the `kill()` function returns.

Reference:

P 3.3.2.1

Conversion:

BSD and SVR1-3 use `int` for `pid`.

Notes:

See `raise()` to signal the current process. `pid` must not be –1.

---

labs()—Computes the absolute value of a long integer.

Synopsis:

```
#include <stdlib.h>
long int labs(long int j);
```

Arguments:

j

Returns:

Absolute value of j.

Description:

If j is greater than or equal to zero, j is returned; else −j is returned.

Reference:

C 4.10.6.3

Conversion:

This function is new in Standard C. It is not included in BSD or System V prior to SVR4.

Notes:

This function is required by Standard C. It is not part of the POSIX standard.

ldexp( )—Multiplies a floating-point number by a power of 2.

Synopsis:

```
#include <math.h>
double ldexp(double x, int exp);
```

Arguments:

x   Arbitrary value.

exp   Integer exponent.

Returns:

x^{exp}

Errors:

ERANGE

Description:

The ldexp( ) function multiplies a floating-point number by an integral power of 2.

Reference:

C 4.5.4.3

Notes:

See frexp( ) for the inverse function.

The ldexp( ) function may lose precision on nonbinary architectures.

`ldiv()`—Computes the quotient and remainder of integer division.

Synopsis:

```
#include <stdlib.h>
ldiv_t ldiv(long int numer, long int denom);
```

Arguments:

numer   Numerator.

denom   Denominator.

Returns:

A structure of type `ldiv_t`.

Description:

The `ldiv()` function divides `numer` by `denom` in a portable manner. If the division is inexact, the resulting quotient is the integer of lesser magnitude than the algebraic quotient (round towards zero).

The `ldiv()` function returns a structure of type `ldiv_t` with two members, `quot` and `rem`. Use `ldiv(a,b).quot` instead of `a/b` if the quotient must be rounded the same way on all systems. Use `ldiv(a,b).rem` to obtain the remainder of dividing a by b.

Reference:

C 4.10.6.2

Conversion:

This function is new in Standard C. It is not included in BSD or System V prior to SVR4.

Notes:

This function is required by Standard C. It is not part of the POSIX standard.

link( )—Creates a link to a file.

Synopsis:

```
#include <unistd.h>
int link(const char *existing, const char *new);
```

Arguments:

existing Pointer to path name of an existing file.

new   Pointer to additional path name to link to the same data.

Returns:

Zero on success and –1 on failure.

If an error occurs, a code is stored in errno to identify the error.

Errors:

EACCES, EEXIST, EMLINK, ENAMETOOLONG, ENOENT, ENOSPC, ENOTDIR, EPERM, EROFS, EXDEV

Description:

The link( ) function atomically creates a new link for an existing file and increments the link count for the file.

If the link( ) function fails, no directories are modified.

The existing argument should not be a directory.

The caller may (or may not) need permission to access the existing file.

Reference:

P 5.3.4.1

Conversion:

Add to the list of headers:

```
#include <unistd.h>
```

`localeconv()`—Gets rules to format numeric quantities for the current locale.

Synopsis:

```
#include <locale.h>
struct lconv *localeconv(void);
```

Arguments:

None.

Returns:

Pointer to a `struct lconv`.

Description:

The `localeconv()` returns a pointer to a `struct lconv` for the current locale.

Reference:

C 4.4.2.1

Conversion:

This function is new in Standard C. It is not included in BSD or System V prior to SVR4.

Notes:

See Chapter 10, *Porting to Far-off Lands,* for a complete description of `localeconv()` and the merits of using it.

`localtime()` —Breaks down a timer value into a time structure in local time.

Synopsis:

```
#include <time.h>
struct tm *localtime(const time_t *timer);
```

Arguments:

timer   Pointer to a `time_t` value returned by `time()`.

Returns:

Pointer to a `struct tm`.

Description:

The `localtime()` function converts a `time_t` pointed to by `timer` into year, month, day, hours, minutes, seconds, etc., and stores the information in a `struct tm`. A pointer to the `struct tm` is returned. The current time can be obtained with the `time()` function.

Reference:

C 4.12.3.4 & P 8.1.1

Conversion:

BSD used the headed `<sys/time.h>` instead of `<time.h>`.

SVR1-3 and BSD used `long` for `timer`.

Notes:

The data returned by `localtime()` may be overwritten by a subsequent call.

See discussion on Page 133.

Also see `gmtime()`.

`log()`—Computes the natural log function.

Synopsis:

```
#include <math.h>
double log(double x);
```

Arguments:

x

Returns:

Natural log of x.

Errors:

EDOM, ERANGE

Description:

Returns a number ln, such that $x = e^{ln}$.

Reference:

C 4.5.4.4

Notes:

log10() —Computes the base-ten logarithm function.

Synopsis:

```
#include <math.h>
double log10(double x);
```

Arguments:

x

Returns:

Base-ten logarithm of x.

Errors:

EDOM, ERANGE

Description:

Returns a number lc, such that, $x = 10^{lc}$. The argument must be positive.

Reference:

C 4.5.4.5

Notes:

`longjmp()`—Restores the calling environment.

Synopsis:

```
#include <setjmp.h>
void longjmp(jmp_buf env, int val);
```

Arguments:

env   Information saved by `setjmp()`.

val   Value to return to caller of `setjmp()`.

Returns:

`val` is returned to the caller of `setjmp()`.

Description:

The `longjump()` function restores the environment saved in `env` by a previous call to `setjmp()`.

The values of variables in automatic storage which are not qualified by `volatile` are indeterminate.

Reference:

C 4.6.2.1

Notes:

POSIX does not specify if `setjmp()` does or does not save signal masks. If you want to save signal masks, use `sigsetjmp()`/`siglongjmp()`.

WINNER OF THE MOST ASTONISHING FEATURE AWARD: If val is set to 0, 1 is returned instead!

lseek( ) —Repositions read/write file offset.

Synopsis:

```
#include <sys/types.h>
#include <unistd.h>
off_t lseek(int fildes, off_t offset, int whence);
```

Arguments:

fildes   File descriptor to be repositioned.

offset   New offset.

whence   One of the following codes:

     SEEK_SET   Set offset to offset.

     SEEK_CUR   Add offset to current position.

     SEEK_END   Add offset to current file size.

Returns:

The new offset. In case of error, ((off_t)-1) is returned.

Errors:

EBADF, ESPIPE

Description:

The lseek( ) function sets the file offset for the file description associated with fildes as follows:

SEEK_SET   Set offset to offset.

SEEK_CUR   Add offset to current position.

SEEK_END   Add offset to current file size.

Reference:

P 6.5.3.1

Conversion:

Add to the list of headers:

```
#include <unistd.h>
```

Replace numeric constants with macros using the following key:

```
0    SEEK_SET
1    SEEK_CUR
2    SEEK_END
```

SVR1-3 returns `long` instead of `off_t`. `offset` is also `long` instead of `off_t`.

BSD uses `int` for `offset` and also returns `int`. The BSD symbols `L_SET`, `L_INCR`, and `L_XTND` must be replaced by `SEEK_SET`, `SEEK_CUR`, and `SEEK_END`.

Notes:

Some devices are incapable of performing seek operations.

The `lseek( )` function allows the file offset to be set beyond the end of the existing data in the file.

`malloc()`—Allocates dynamic memory.

Synopsis:

```
#include <stdlib.h>
void *malloc(size_t size);
```

Arguments:

size   Number of bytes to allocate.

Returns:

A pointer to the allocated space or NULL if no space is available.

Description:

The `malloc()` function allocates `size` bytes and returns a pointer to the allocated space. The memory is not cleared.

Reference:

C 4.10.3.3

Conversion:

Add to the list of headers:

```
#include <stdlib.h>
```

SVR1-3 and BSD use `unsigned` for `size`.

SVR1-3 uses the header `<malloc.h>` which is no longer required.

Notes:

`malloc()` does not zero the storage it allocates. If a program depends on the contents of the allocated storage, the results are not portable.

`mblen()`—Determines the number of bytes in a character.

Synopsis:

```
#include <stdlib.h>
int mblen(const char *s, size_t n);
```

Arguments:

s	Pointer to string to scan.
n	Number of bytes to examine.

Returns:

The number of bytes that comprise the character.

Description:

This is equivalent to `mbtowc ((wchat_t *)0, s, n)` except the shift state of the `mbtowc` function is not affected.

Reference:

C 4.10.7.1

Conversion:

This function is new in Standard C. It is not included in BSD or System V prior to SVR4.

Notes:

See Chapter 10, *Porting to Far-off Lands*, for a description of multibyte characters.

This function is required by Standard C but is not part of the POSIX standard.

mbstowcs()—Converts a multibyte string to a wide-character string.

Synopsis:

```
#include <stdlib.h>
size_t mbstowcs(wchar_t *pwcs, const char *s, size_t n);
```

Arguments:

pwcs   Pointer to the resulting wide-character string.

s   Pointer to the input multibyte character string.

n   Maximum number of wide characters to store.

Returns:

The number of wide characters stored or −1 if s contains an invalid character.

Description:

The mbstowcs() function converts a sequence of multibyte characters that begins in the initial shift state from the array pointed to by s into a sequence of wide characters and stores up to n wide characters into the array pointed to by pwcs.

Reference:

C 4.10.8.1

Conversion:

This function is new in Standard C. It is not included in BSD or System V prior to SVR4.

Notes:

See Chapter 10, *Porting to Far-off Lands*, for a description of wide characters and multibyte characters.

The source and destination must not overlap.

This function is required by Standard C and is not part of the POSIX standard.

`mbtowc()`—Converts a multibyte character to a wide character.

Synopsis:

```
#include <stdlib.h>
int mbtowc(wchar_t *pwc, const char *s, size_t n);
```

Arguments:

pwc Pointer to the wide character.

s   Pointer to the multibyte character.

n   Maximum number of bytes to examine.

Returns:

The number of bytes in character or –1 if the character is not valid.

Description:

If s is not NULL, the `mbtowc()` function determines the number of bytes that are contained in the multibyte character pointed to by s. It then determines a code value of type wchar_t that corresponds to the multibyte character. If the multibyte character is valid and pwc is not NULL, the code is stored in the wchar_t pointed to by pwc.

At most, n bytes of s will be examined.

Reference:

C 4.10.7.2

Conversion:

This function is new in Standard C. It is not included in BSD or System V prior to SVR4.

Notes:

See Chapter 10, *Porting to Far-off Lands*, for a description of wide and multibyte characters.

This function is required by Standard C and is not part of the POSIX standard.

memchr () —Scans memory for a byte.

Synopsis:

```
#include <string.h>
void *memchr(const void *s, int c, size_t n);
```

Arguments:

s	Pointer to the source string.
c	Character to look for.
n	Maximum number of bytes to examine.

Returns:

A pointer to the located character or NULL.

Description:

The memchr () function converts c to **unsigned char** and scans the first n bytes of s. The first byte (interpreted as **unsigned char**) to match c stops the operation. A pointer to the matching byte is returned.

Reference:

C 4.11.5.1

Conversion:

Add to the list of headers:

```
#include <string.h>
```

SVR1-3 used **int** for n instead of **size_t**.

This function is not supported in BSD.

Notes:

This function is required by Standard C. It is not part of the POSIX standard.

If a constant is used for n, typecast it to **size_t**, as in (**size_t**) 26.

`memcmp()`—Compares two memory objects.

Synopsis:

```
#include <string.h>
int memcmp(const void *s1, const void *s2, size_t n);
```

Arguments:

s1   Pointer to object 1.

s2   Pointer to object 2.

n   Number of bytes to compare.

Returns:

An `int` that is greater than, equal to, or less than zero according to the relative order of `s1` and `s2`.

That is, if `s1 > s2`, `memcmp()` will return a positive value.

Description:

Compares the first n bytes of `s1` with the first n bytes of `s2`. Returns an `int` that is greater than, equal to, or less than zero according to the relative order of `s1` and `s2`.

Reference:

C 4.11.4.1

Conversion:

Add to the list of headers:

```
#include <stdlib.h>
```

SVR1-3 used `int` for n instead of `size_t`.

This function is not supported in BSD.

Notes:

This function is required by Standard C and is not part of the POSIX standard.

If a constant is used for n, typecast it to `size_t`, as in `(size_t)13`.

memcpy()—Copies non-overlapping memory objects.

Synopsis:

```
#include <string.h>
void *memcpy(void *s1, const void *s2, size_t n);
```

Arguments:

s1	Pointer to the destination.
s2	Pointer to the source.
n	Number of bytes to move.

Returns:

s1

Description:

Copies n bytes from s2 into s1.

Reference:

C 4.11.2.1

Conversion:

Add to the list of headers:

```
#include <stdlib.h>
```

SVR1-3 used int for n instead of size_t.

This function is not supported in BSD.

Notes:

If the strings might overlap, use memmove().

This function is required by Standard C. It is not part of the POSIX standard.

If a constant is used for n, typecast it to size_t, as in (size_t)13.

memmove( ) —Copies (possibly overlapping) memory objects.

Synopsis:

```
#include <string.h>
void *memmove(void *s1, const void *s2, size_t n);
```

Arguments:

s1	Pointer to the destination.
s2	Pointer to the source.
n	Number of bytes to move.

Returns:

s1

Description:

Copies n characters from s2 to s1. Copying takes place as if the n characters are first moved into a temporary array and then into the destination.

Reference:

C 4.11.2.2

Conversion:

This function is new in Standard C. It is not included in BSD or System V prior to SVR4.

Notes:

This function is required by Standard C and is not part of the POSIX standard.

If a constant is used for n, typecast it to **size_t**, as in **(size_t)13**.

memset() —Fills memory with a constant byte.

Synopsis:

```
#include <string.h>
void *memset(void *s, int c, size_t n);
```

Arguments:

s	Pointer to the region of memory to fill.
c	Fill byte.
n	Number of bytes to store.

Returns:

s

Description:

Copies c into the first n characters of s.

Reference:

C 4.11.6.1

Conversion:

Add to the list of headers:

```
#include <string.h>
```

SVR1-3 used int for n instead of size_t.

This function is not supported in BSD.

Notes:

This function is required by Standard C. It is not part of the POSIX standard.

If a constant is used for n, typecast it to size_t, as in (size_t)13.

mkdir( )—Makes a directory.

Synopsis:

```
#include <sys/types.h>
#include <sys/stat.h>
int mkdir(const char *path, mode_t mode);
```

Arguments:

path   Pointer to name of the directory to create.

mode   Directory permission bits.

Returns:

Zero on success and −1 on failure.

If an error occurs, a code is stored in **errno** to identify the error.

Errors:

EACCES, EEXIST, EMLINK, ENAMETOOLONG, ENOENT, ENOSPC, ENOTDIR, EROFS

Description:

The mkdir( ) function creates a new directory named **path**. The permission bits (modified by the file creation mask)* are set from **mode**. The owner and group IDs for the directory are set from the effective user ID and group ID.

The new directory may (or may not) contain entries for **.** and **..** but is otherwise empty.

Reference:

P 5.4.1.1

Conversion:

SVR1-2 used mknod( ) to create directories.

BSD and SVR3 use int for mode.

---

* See umask( ).

mkfifo( )—Makes a FIFO special file.

Synopsis:

```
#include <sys/types.h>
#include <sys/stat.h>
int mkfifo(const char *path, mode_t mode);
```

Arguments:

path	Path name of the FIFO to create.
mode	FIFO permission bits.

Returns:

Zero on success and −1 on failure.

If an error occurs a code is stored in errno to identify the error.

Errors:

EACCES, EEXIST, ENOENT, ENOSPC, ENOTDIR, EROFS

Description:

The mkfifo( ) function creates a new FIFO special file named path. The permission bits (modified by the file creation mask)* are set from mode. The owner and group IDs for the FIFO are set from the effective user ID and group ID.

Reference:

P 5.4.2.1

Conversion:

SVR1-3 used mknod( ) to create FIFOs.

BSD does not support this function.

Notes:

---

* See umask( ).

mktime() —Converts time formats.

Synopsis:

```
#include <time.h>
time_t mktime(struct tm *timeptr);
```

Arguments:

timeptr   Pointer to a struct tm.

Returns:

The calendar time encoded as a time_t. On invalid input, (time-t) −1 is returned.

Description:

The mktime() function converts the local time in the struct tm pointed to by timptr to a time_t. The values of tm_wday and tm_yday are ignored. If tm_isdst is greater than zero, mktime() assumes that daylight savings time is in effect. If tm_isdst is equal to zero, mktime() assumes that daylight savings time is not in effect. If tm_isdst is negative, the mktime() function will attempt to determine if daylight savings time is in effect for the specified time. The struct tm pointed to by timeptr is updated with valid values.

Reference:

C 4.12.2.3 & P 8.1.1

Conversion:

This function is new in Standard C. It is not included in BSD or System V prior to SVR4.

Notes:

The mktime() function is not required to reject invalid dates. For example, November 55th may be equivalent to December 25th.

modf ( )—Breaks a value into integral and fractional parts.

Synopsis:

```
#include <math.h>
double modf(double value, double *iptr);
```

Arguments:

value   Arbitrary value.

iptr   Pointer to a double to hold result.

Returns:

Fractional part of value. Store the integer part of value in the double pointed to by iptr.

Description:

The modf ( ) function breaks value into integral and fractional parts. The integral part is stored into the double pointed to by iptr. The fractional part is returned. For example, modf (123 . 4567 , &foo) stores 123 . 0 into foo and returns 0 . 4567.

Reference:

C 4.5.4.6

Notes:

open( )—Opens a file.

Synopsis:

```
#include <sys/types.h>
#include <sys/stat.h>
#include <fcntl.h>
int open(const char *path, int oflag, ...);
```

Arguments:

path   Pointer to path of the file to open.

oflag   Symbolic flags.

...   Permission bits to use if a file is created. This argument is called the file's mode and has type mode_t.

Returns:

A file descriptor or −1 on error.

Errors:

EACCES, EEXIST, EINTR, EISDIR, EMFILE, ENAMETOOLONG, ENFILE, ENOENT, ENOSPC, ENOTDIR, ENXIO, EROFS

Description:

The open( ) function establishes a connection between a file and a file descriptor. The file descriptor is a small integer that is used by I/O functions to reference the file. The path argument points to the pathname for the file.

The oflag argument is the bitwise inclusive OR of the values of symbolic constants. The programmer must specify exactly one of the following three symbols:

O_RDONLY   Open for reading only.

O_WRONLY   Open for writing only.

O_RDWR   Open for reading and writing.

Any combination of the following symbols may also be used:

O_APPEND   Set the file offset to the end-of-file prior to each write.

O_CREAT   If the file does not exist, allow it to be created. This flag indicates that the mode argument is present in the call to open().

O_EXCL   This flag may be used only if O_CREAT is also set. It causes the call to open() to fail if the file already exists.

O_NOCTTY   If path identifies a terminal, this flag prevents that terminal from becoming the controlling terminal for this process. See Chapter 8 for a description of terminal I/O.

O_NONBLOCK   Do not wait for the device or file to be ready or available. After the file is open, the read() and write() calls return immediately. If the process would be delayed in the read or write operation, -1 is returned and errno is set to EAGAIN instead of blocking the caller.

O_TRUNC   This flag should be used only on ordinary files opened for writing. It causes the file to be truncated to zero length.

Upon successful completion, open() returns a non-negative file descriptor.

Reference:

P 5.3.1.1

Conversion:

BSD used the flag O_NDELAY to mark file descriptors so that a process would not block when doing I/O to them. A read() or write() that would block for data returns zero and sets errno to EWOULDBLOCK.

System V also has the O_NDELAY flag, however, there is no way to distinguish between no data available and end-of-file.

To allow implementations to continue to support existing applications, POSIX uses a new flag O_NONBLOCK for non-blocking I/O. If no data is available, POSIX gives the error EAGAIN.

Notes:

opendir()—Opens a directory.

Synopsis:

```
#include <sys/types.h>
#include <dirent.h>
DIR *opendir(const char *dirname);
```

Arguments:

dirname   Pointer to the name of the directory to read.

Returns:

A pointer for use with `readdir()` and `closedir()` or, if an error took place, NULL.

Errors:

EACCES, ENAMETOOLONG, ENOENT, ENOTDIR, EMFILE, ENFILE

Description:

The `opendir()` function opens a directory stream corresponding to the directory named in the `dirname` argument. The stream is positioned at the first entry.

Reference:

P 5.1.2.1

Conversion:

BSD used the header `<sys/dir.h>`, which must be changed to `<dirent.h>`. The BSD `struct direct` must be replaced by the POSIX equivalent `struct dirent`. BSD also provided the `seekdir()` and `telldir()` functions that are not supported by POSIX.

SVR1-2 did not provide this function. SVR1-2 programs read directories as ordinary files. Directory entries are 14-byte names and 2-byte I-node numbers. These programs must be changed to use `readdir()`.

Notes:

See "Complete Example" on Page 77.

`pathconf()` —Gets configuration variables for a path.

Synopsis:

```
#include <unistd.h>
long pathconf(const char *path, int name);
```

Arguments:

path   Pointer to path name of file.

name   Symbolic constant.

Returns:

If `name` or `path` is invalid, `-1` is returned and `errno` is set to indicate the error. If the implementation has no limit for the requested item, `-1` is returned and `errno` is not changed. Otherwise, the limit is returned.

Errors:

EINVAL, EACCES, EINVAL, ENAMETOOLONG, ENOENT, ENOTDIR

Description:

The `pathconf()` function returns a configuration limit.

The possible values for `name` are:

name	Description
_PC_LINK_MAX	The maximum value of a file's link count. If `path` refers to a directory, then this value applies to the entire directory.
_PC_MAX_CANON	The maximum length of a formatted input line. `path` must refer to a terminal.
_PC_MAX_INPUT	The maximum length of an input line. `path` must refer to a terminal.
_PC_NAME_MAX	The maximum length of a filename for this directory.
_PC_PATH_MAX	The maximum length of a relative pathname when this directory is the working directory; that is, the number of characters that may be appended to `path` and still have a valid pathname.
_PC_PIPE_BUF	The size of the pipe buffer. `path` must be a FIFO.

name	Description
_PC_CHOWN_RESTRICTED	
	The chown() system call may not be used on this file. If path or fildes refers to a directory, then this applies to all files in that directory.
_PC_NO_TRUNC	Attempting to create a file in the named directory will fail with ENAMETOOLONG if the filename would be truncated.
_PC_VDISABLE	Allow special character processing to be disabled. path or fildes must refer to a terminal.

Reference:

P 5.7.1.1

Conversion:

This function is new to POSIX. It allows a portable application to determine the quantity of a resource, or the presence of an option, at execution time.

Older applications either use a fixed amount of resource or attempt to deduce the amount of resource available using the error returns from various functions.

Notes:

The value returned by _PC_PATH_MAX is not useful for allocating storage. Files with paths longer than _PC_PATH_MAX may exist.

pause()—Suspends process execution.

Synopsis:

```
#include <unistd.h>
int pause(void);
```

Arguments:

None.

Returns:

−1 on error.

There is no successful completion return value.

Errors:

EINTR

Description:

The pause( ) function suspends the calling process until the delivery of a signal whose action is to either execute a signal-catching function or to terminate the process.

If the signal-catching function returns, pause( ) returns −1 and sets errno to EINTR. There is no "success" return.

Reference:

P 3.4.2.1

Conversion:

Add to the list of headers:

```
#include <unistd.h>
```

Notes:

perror() —Prints an error message.

Synopsis:

```
#include <stdio.h>
void perror(const char *s);
```

Arguments:

s   Pointer to string to print in front of error message.

(implicit) errno   Error number to convert.

Returns:

No value is returned.

Description:

The perror() function converts the error number in errno to an error message. If s is not NULL, the string pointed to by s is written to stderr followed by a colon and a space. Then the error message is written followed by a newline.

Reference:

C 4.9.10.4 & P 8.2.3.8

Notes:

`pipe()`—Creates an interprocess channel.

Synopsis:

```
#include <unistd.h>
int pipe(int fildes[2]);
```

Arguments:

fildes   Array of two integers: `fildes[0]` is the read end of the pipe and `fildes[1]` is the write end of the pipe.

Returns:

Zero on success and −1 on failure.

If an error occurs, a code is stored in `errno` to identify the error.

Description:

The `pipe()` function creates a pipe, placing a descriptor for the read end of the pipe into `fildes[0]` and for the write end of the pipe into `fildes[1]`. The `O_NONBLOCK` and `FD_CLOEXEC` flags are clear on both descriptors (you can use `fcntl()` to set them).

Data can be written to `fildes[1]` and read from `fildes[0]`. A read on `fildes[0]` accesses the data written to `fildes[1]` on a first-in-first-out basis.

Reference:

P 6.1.1.1

Conversion:

Add to the list of headers:

```
#include <unistd.h>
```

Notes:

pow( )—Computes x raised to the power y.

Synopsis:

```
#include <math.h>
double pow(double x, double y);
```

Arguments:

    x   Base.

    y   Power.

Returns:

    x^y

Errors:

    EDOM, ERANGE

Description:

    The function pow(x,y) returns x^y. A domain error occurs if x is negative and y is not an integral value.

Reference:

    C 4.5.5.1

Notes:

`printf()`—Writes formatted text to the standard output stream.

Synopsis:

```
#include <stdio.h>
int printf(const char *format, ...);
```

Arguments:

format   Pointer to format string.

...   Variables to be written.

Returns:

The number of characters written, or negative if an error occurred.

Description:

The `printf()` function writes output to `stdout` under control of the string pointed to by `format`.

The format is a character string that contains zero or more directives. Each directive fetches zero or more arguments to `printf()`. Each directive starts with the `%` character. After the `%`, the following appear in sequence:

flags   Zero or more of the following flags (in any order):

         –   Will cause this conversion to be left-justified. If the – flag is not used, the result will be right-justified.

         +   The result of a signed conversion will always begin with a sign. If the + flag is not used, the result will begin with a sign only when negative values are converted.

         space   This is the same as + except a space is printed instead of a plus sign. If both the *space* and the + flags are used, the + wins.

         #   The result is converted to an alternate form. The details are given below for each conversion.

width   An optional *width* field. The exact meaning depends on the conversion being performed.

prec   An optional *precision*. The precision indicates how many digits will be printed to the right of the decimal point. If the *precision* is present, it is preceded by a decimal point(`.`). If the decimal point is given with no precision, the precision is assumed to be zero. A precision argument may be used only with the e, E, f, g, and G conversions.

type   An optional h, l, or L. The h causes the argument to be converted to short prior to printing. The l specifies that the argument is a long int. The L specifies that the argument is a long double.

format   A character that specifies the conversion to be performed.

The conversions are given by the following table:

	Description	Meaning of *width*	Meaning of # flag
i or d	An int argument is converted to a signed decimal string.	Specifies the minimum number of characters to appear. If the value is smaller, padding is used. The default is 1. The result of printing zero with a width of zero is no characters.	UNDEFINED.
o	An unsigned int argument is converted to unsigned octal.	Same as i.	Increase the precision to force the first digit to be a zero.
u	An unsigned int argument is converted to unsigned decimal.	Same as i.	UNDEFINED.
x	An unsigned int argument is converted to unsigned hexadecimal. The letters abcdef are used.	Same as i.	Prefix non-zero results with 0x.
X	Same as x except the letters ABCDEF are used.	Same as i.	Prefix non-zero results with 0X.
f	A double argument is converted to decimal notation in the [-]ddd.ddd format.	Minimum number of characters to appear. May be followed by a period and the number of digits to print after the decimal point. If a decimal point is printed, at least one digit will appear to the left of the decimal.	Print a decimal point even if no digits follow.

	Description	Meaning of *width*	Meaning of # flag
e	A `double` argument is converted in the style `[-]d.ddde dd` The exponent will always contain at least two digits. If the value is zero, the exponent is zero.	Same as `f`.	Same as `f`.
E	Same as `e` except `E` is used instead of `e`.	Same as `f`.	Same as `f`.
g	Same as `f` or `e`, depending on the value to be converted. The `e` style is used only if the exponent is less than −4 or greater than the precision.	Same as `f`.	Same as `f`.
G	Same as `g` except an `E` is printed instead of `e`.	Same as `f`.	Same as `f`.
c	An `int` argument is converted to an `unsigned char` and the resulting character is written.	UNDEFINED.	UNDEFINED.
s	An argument is assumed to be `char *`. Characters up to (but not including) a terminating null are written.	Specifies the maximum number of characters to be written.	UNDEFINED.
p	An argument must be a pointer to `void`. The pointer is converted to a sequence of printable characters in an implementation-defined manner. This is not very useful for a portable program.	UNDEFINED.	UNDEFINED.

	Description	Meaning of *width*	Meaning of # flag
n	An argument should be a pointer to an integer which is *written* with the number of characters written to the output stream so far. Nothing is written to the output stream by this directive.	UNDEFINED.	UNDEFINED.

Reference:

C 4.9.6.3 & P 8.2.3.6

Conversion:

Change \07 in `format` to \a.

Notes:

See "Pitfalls" on Page 42.

`putc()`—Writes a character to a stream.

Synopsis:

```
#include <stdio.h>
int putc(int c, FILE *stream);
```

Arguments:

c   Character to write.

stream   Pointer to an open stream to write into.

Returns:

The character written. If an error occurs, EOF is returned.

Description:

Write the character c, converted to an unsigned char, to stream at the position indicated by the file position indicator and advance the indicator.

The putc() function is equivalent to fputc(), except putc() may be a macro which may evaluate stream more than once, so the argument should not have side effects.

Reference:

C 4.9.7.8 & P 8.2.3.6

Notes:

This function may be coded as an "unsafe" macro; that is, it may evaluate the arguments more than once. This will produce non-portable results for arguments like x++.

`putchar()`—Writes a character to standard output.

Synopsis:

```
#include <stdio.h>
int putchar(int c);
```

Arguments:

c

Returns:

The character written or EOF on error.

Description:

The call `putchar(c)` is equivalent to `putc(c,stdout)`.

Reference:

C 4.9.7.9 & P 8.2.3.6

Notes:

`puts()`—Writes a string to standard output.

Synopsis:

```
#include <stdio.h>
int puts(const char *s);
```

Arguments:

s   Pointer to the string to write.

Returns:

EOF on error; otherwise, a nonnegative value.

Description:

Write the string pointed to by s to `stdout` and append a newline character. The terminating null is not written.

Reference:

C 4.9.7.10 & P 8.2.3.6

Notes:

The call `puts(s)` is not exactly equivalent to `fputs(s,stdout)` because `puts()` adds a new line and `fputs()` does not.

qsort() —Sorts an array.

Synopsis:

```
#include <stdlib.h>
void qsort(void *base, size_t nmemb, size_t size,
int (*compar)(const void *,const void *));
```

Arguments:

base	Pointer to the start of the array.
nmemb	Number of members in the array.
size	Size of each element in the array.
compar	Pointer to a function with two arguments that point to the objects being compared. The function returns an int less than, equal to, or greater than zero depending on the relative order of the two arguments.

Returns:

No value is returned.

Description:

The qsort() function sorts an array with nmemb elements of size size. The base argument points to the start of the array. The compar function is called with pointers to two array elements and returns an int less than, equal to, or greater than zero depending on the relative order of the two arguments.

Example:

```
/*
 * Score structures contain the student's name
 *   and test score.
 */
struct score
     {
     char student_name[25];
     int  test_score;
     };

/* Class is an array of scores */
struct score class[50];

/*
 * Comparison function to use with qsort
 */
int comp_elements(const void * t1,
                  const void *s2)
```

```
    {
         return( strcmp(((struct score *) s1) -> student_name,
                        ((struct score *) s2) -> student_name));
    }

    /*
     * Sort the score array for later use by bsearch()
     *
    void sort_score(void)
    {
    struct score *ptr;

         qsort(
              &score[0],                /* base */
              50,                     / /* number of elements */
              sizeof(struct score),    /* size of one element */
              comp_elements);          /* comparison function */
         return;
    }
```

Reference:

C 4.10.5.2

Conversion:

Add to the list of headers:

```
    #include <stdlib.h>
```

SVR1-3 use unsigned for size and nmemb.

BSD used int for size and nmemb.

Notes:

raise()—Sends a signal.

Synopsis:

```
#include <signal.h>
int raise(int sig);
```

Arguments:

sig   Signal number.

Returns:

Zero on success, nonzero on failure.

Description:

The call raise(sig) is equivalent to kill(getpid(),sig).

Reference:

C 4.7.2.1

Conversion:

This function is new in Standard C. It is not included in BSD or System V prior to SVR4.

Notes:

See kill() for the more general case.

This function is required by Standard C. It is not part of the POSIX standard.

rand()—Returns a random number.

Synopsis:

```
#include <stdlib.h>
int rand(void);
```

Arguments:

None.

Returns:

A value between 0 and RAND_MAX.

Description:

The rand() function returns a pseudo-random integer between 0 and RAND_MAX.

Reference:

C 4.10.2.1

Conversion:

Add to the list of headers:

```
#include <stdlib.h>
```

Notes:

If the srand() function is not called, rand() will return the same sequence of random numbers every time your program is run.

The rand() function is not completely portable in the sense that different implementations will produce different sequences. This should not be a problem.

This function is required by Standard C. It is not part of the POSIX standard.

`read()`—Reads from a file.

Synopsis:

```
#include <unistd.h>
int read(int fildes, void *buf, unsigned int nbyte);
```

Arguments:

fildes   File descriptor open for reading.

buf   Pointer to the place where the data should be read.

nbyte   Maximum number of bytes to read.

Returns:

The number of bytes actually read or −1 on error.

Errors:

EAGAIN, EBADF, EINTR, EIO

Description:

The `read()` function reads `nbyte` bytes from the file associated with `fildes` into the buffer pointed to by `buf`.

The `read()` function returns the number of bytes actually read and placed in the buffer. This will be less than `nbyte` if:

- The number of bytes left in the file is less than `nbyte`.

- The `read()` request was interrupted by a signal.

- The file is a pipe or FIFO or special file with less than `nbytes` immediately available for reading.

When attempting to read from any empty pipe or FIFO:

- If no process has the pipe open for writing, zero is returned to indicate end-of-file.

- If some process has the pipe open for writing and O_NONBLOCK is set, −1 is returned and `errno` is set to EAGAIN.

- If some process has the pipe open for writing and O_NONBLOCK is clear, `read()` waits for some data to be written or the pipe to be closed.

When attempting to read from a file other than a pipe or FIFO and no data is available:

- If O_NONBLOCK is set, −1 is returned and `errno` is set to EAGAIN.

- If O_NONBLOCK is clear, `read()` waits for some data to become available.

- The O_NONBLOCK flag is ignored if data is available.

Reference:

P 6.4.1.1

Conversion:

Add to the list of headers:

```
#include <unistd.h>
```

Notes:

The standard adopted by the International Organization for Standards (ISO/IEC 9945) has a slightly different definition for `read()`. They use:

```
ssize_t read(int fildes, void *buf, size_t nbyte)
```

where `ssize_t` is a new system data type used by functions that return a size in bytes or an error code. Also, note the change of `unsigned int` to `size_t` for `nbyte`.

The standard does not specify the file offset after an error is returned.

If a `read()` is interrupted by a signal after it has read some data, it returns either the number of bytes read or −1 with `errno` set to EINTR. The POSIX standard allows this to vary from system to system or even from read to read.

`readdir()`—Reads a directory.

Synopsis:

```
#include <sys/types.h>
#include <dirent.h>
struct dirent *readdir(DIR *dirp);
```

Arguments:

> `dirp`   Pointer returned by `opendir()`.

Returns:

> A pointer to an object of type `struct dirent` or, in case of error, NULL.

Errors:

> **EBADF**

Description:

> The `readdir()` function returns a pointer to a `structure dirent` representing the next directory entry from the directory stream pointed to by `dirp`. On end-of-file, NULL is returned.

> The `readdir()` function may (or may not) return entries for `.` or `..` Your program should tolerate reading dot and dot-dot but not require them.

> The data pointed to by `readdir()` may be overwritten by another call to `readdir()` for the same directory stream. It will not be overwritten by a call for another directory stream.

Reference:

> P 5.1.2.1

Conversion:

> BSD used the header `<sys/dir.h>`. This must be changed to `<dirent.h>`. The BSD `struct direct` must be replaced by the POSIX equivalent `struct dirent`. BSD also provided the `seekdir()` and `telldir()` functions. These are not supported by POSIX.

> SVR1-2 did not provide this function. SVR1-2 programs read directories as ordinary files. Directory entries are 14-byte names and 2-byte I-node numbers. These programs must be changed to use `readdir()`.

Notes:

See "Complete Example" on Page 77.

Filenames returned by `readdir()` may contain any character including spaces, tabs, and newlines. There will be at least one character before the terminating null.

The `readdir()` function may not see files created after the most recent call to `opendir()` or `rewinddir()` for this directory stream.

The `readdir()` function returns NULL both on error and at the end of a directory. If you need to tell the difference, use code similar to the following:

```
errno = 0;      /* Zero out errno */
ptr = readdir(dirp);
if (ptr == NULL)
    {
    if (errno == 0)
        {
        Code to process end-of-file goes here.
        }
    else
        {
        Code to process errors goes here.
        }
```

realloc()—Changes the size of a memory object.

Synopsis:

```
#include <stdlib.h>
void *realloc(void *ptr, size_t size);
```

Arguments:

ptr   Pointer returned by a previous call to `calloc()`, `malloc()`, or `realloc()`.

size   New size.

Returns:

A pointer to the (possibly moved) allocated space.

Description:

The `realloc()` function changes the size of the object pointed to by `ptr` to `size`. If `size` is larger than the current size of the object, the newly allocated space is not initialized. The call `realloc(NULL,size)` is equivalent to `malloc(size)`. The call `realloc(ptr,(size_t)0)` is equivalent to `free(ptr)`.

Reference:

C 4.10.3.4

Conversion:

Add to the list of headers:

```
#include <stdlib.h>
```

BSD and SVR1-2 use `unsigned` for `size`.

Notes:

If `ptr` is not a pointer returned by `malloc()`, `calloc()`, or `realloc()` or has been deallocated with `free()` or `realloc()`, the results are not portable and are probably disastrous.

remove( )—Removes a file from a directory.

Synopsis:

```
#include <stdio.h>
int remove(const char *filename);
```

Arguments:

filename   Pointer to filename to delete.

Returns:

Zero on success and non-zero on failure.

If an error occurs a code is stored in errno to identify the error.

Errors:

EACCES, EBUSY, EMNAMETOOLONG, ENOENT, ENOTDIR, EPERM, EROFS

Description:

The remove( ) function comes from Standard C and has the same effect as unlink( ); namely, the string pointed to by filename can no longer be used to access a file.

Use the rmdir( ) function to delete directories.

Reference:

C 4.9.4.1 & P 8.2.4

Conversion:

This function is new in Standard C. It is not included in BSD or System V prior to SVR4.

Notes:

See unlink( ) for another function to delete files.

rename() —Renames a file.

Synopsis:

```
#include <unistd.h>
int rename(const char *old, const char *new);
```

Arguments:

old   Pointer to a path name of an existing file.

new   Pointer to a new path name for the file.

Returns:

Zero on success and −1 on failure.

If an error occurs a code is stored in errno to identify the error.

Errors:

EACCES, EBUSY, EEXIST, EINVAL, EISDIR, EMLINK, ENAMETOOLONG, ENOENT, ENOSPC, ENOTDIR, ENOTEMPTY, EROFS, EXDEV

Description:

The rename() function causes the file known by old to now be known as new.

Ordinary files may be renamed to ordinary files, and directories may be renamed to directories; however, files cannot be converted using rename(). The new pathname may not contain a path prefix of old.

Reference:

C 4.9.4.2 & P 5.5.3.1

Conversion:

Add to the list of headers:

```
#include <unistd.h>
```

This function is not supported in SVR1-3.

Notes:

If a file already exists by the name new, it is removed. The `rename()` function is atomic. If the `rename()` detects an error, no files are removed. This guarantees that the `rename("x", "x")` does not remove x.

You may not rename dot or dot-dot.

UNIX systems return the error code `EXDEV` if the file must be copied from one file system to another. The `rename()` function does not do the copying. The POSIX standard allows `rename()` to copy files but does not require it.

The 1990 standard adds the requirement that if `rename()` returns −1, the old and new files must be unchanged.

`rewind()`—Sets the file position to the beginning of the file.

Synopsis:

```
#include <stdio.h>
void rewind(FILE *stream);
```

Arguments:

stream   File to rewind.

Returns:

No value is returned.

Description:

The call `rewind(stream)` is equivalent to:

```
(void)fseek(stream, 0L, SEEK_SET);
```

except the error indicator for the stream is also cleared.

Reference:

C 4.9.9.5

Notes:

rewinddir()—Resets the readdir() pointer.

Synopsis:

```
#include <sys/types.h>
#include <dirent.h>
void rewinddir(DIR *dirp);
```

Arguments:

dirp   Pointer returned by opendir().

Returns:

No value is returned.

Description:

The rewinddir() function resets the position associated with the directory stream pointed to by dirp. It also causes the directory stream to refer to the current state of the directory.

Reference:

P 5.1.2.1

Conversion:

BSD used the header <sys/dir.h>. This must be changed to <dirent.h>. The BSD struct direct must be replaced by the POSIX equivalent struct dirent. BSD also provided the seekdir() and telldir() functions. These are not supported by POSIX.

SVR1-2 did not provide this function. SVR1-2 programs read directories as ordinary files. Directory entries are 14-byte names and 2-byte I-node numbers. These programs must be changed to use readdir().

Notes:

If dirp is not a pointer returned by opendir(), the results are undefined.

rmdir()—Removes a directory.

Synopsis:

```
#include <unistd.h>
int rmdir(const char *path);
```

Arguments:

> path   Pointer to the path name of the directory to remove.

Returns:

> Zero on success and –1 on failure. If an error occurs, a code is stored in errno to iden-
> tify the error.

Errors:

> EACCES, EBUSY, EEXIST, ENOTEMPTY, ENAMETOOLONG, ENOENT, ENOTDIR, EROFS

Description:

> If the directory named by path is empty* it is removed. If the system considers the
> directory to be "in use," –1 is returned and errno is set to EBUSY. This means that you
> may (or may not) be able to remove a directory that is the current working directory of
> a process.

Reference:

> P 5.5.2.1

Conversion:

> Add to the list of headers:
>
> ```
> #include <unistd.h>
> ```
>
> SVR1-2 do not support this function. SVR3 includes this function.

Notes:

> When the path argument names a directory that is not empty, BSD gives the error
> ENOTEMPTY, while System V gives the error EEXIST. The standard allows either of
> these errors to be returned.

---

* An empty directory may contain entries for dot and dot-dot.

scanf( )—Reads formatted text from standard input stream.

Synopsis:

```
#include <stdio.h>
int scanf(const char *format, ...);
```

Arguments:

format   Control string.

...   Variables to store into.

Returns:

EOF if an error occurred prior to any data being read. Otherwise, the number of variables stored is returned.

Description:

The `scanf()` function reads from standard input under control of `format`. The call `scanf(format,args)` is equivalent to `fscanf(stdin,format,args)`.

The `format` string contains ordinary text and conversion specifiers. Each directive starts with the % character. After the %, the following appear in sequence:

star   An optional assignment-suppressing character *.

width   An optional decimal integer that specifies the maximum field width.

type   An optional h, l, k, or L indicating the size of the receiving object. The exact meaning depends on the conversion. See the table on the next page.

format   A character that specifies the type of conversion to perform.

The conversions are given by the following table:

	Description	Meaning of *size* flags
d	Matches an optionally signed decimal integer. The subject is defined as the longest initial subsequence of the input string, starting with the first non-white-space character that is of the expected form.	none → int h → short l → long
	The expected form is an optional plus or minus sign followed by a sequence of the digits 0 through 9.	
i	Same as d except the expected form is the same as an integer constant in Standard C. It may be a decimal constant, an octal constant, or a hexadecimal constant. Each may be preceded with an optional plus or minus sign.	Same as d.
	A decimal constant begins with a non-zero digit followed by zero or more digits in the range 0 to 9.	
	An octal constant begins with a leading zero followed by zero or more of the digits 0 through 9.	
	A hexadecimal constant begins with 0x or 0X followed by one or more of the digits 0 to 9 and the letters A to F.	
o	Same as d except only the digits 0 to 7 are allowed.	none → unsigned int h → unsigned short l → unsigned long
u	Same as d except the argument is a pointer to an unsigned value. Note: a leading minus sign is legal.	Same as o.
x	Same as d except the argument is a pointer to an unsigned value and the letters A to F are valid. Note: a leading minus sign is legal.	Same as o.
e f g	Matches an optionally signed floating-point number. The number may be in any format which is acceptable as a floating constant, but no floating suffix is allowed.	none → float l → double L → long double

	Description	Meaning of *size* flags
s	Matches a sequence of non-white-space characters.	UNDEFINED.
	Note: Use %nc to match exactly n characters.	
[	Matches a sequence of characters from a set of expected characters. The conversion specifier includes all subsequent characters in the format string, up to and including the matching right bracket (]). The characters between the brackets comprise the set of expected characters (the *scanset*). If the character following the left bracket is a circumflex (^), the scanset contains all characters that do not appear between the brackets. If the conversion specifier begins with [ ] or [^], the right bracket is included in the scanset and the next right bracket ends the specification.	UNDEFINED.
	Some systems allow specifications of the form [a-z], meaning all characters between a and z. This depends on the codeset used and is not portable.	
c	Matches a sequence of characters. The field width determines how many characters are matched. If there is no field width, one character is matched.	UNDEFINED.
	NOTE: The format %nc matches n characters. The format %ns matches up to n non-white-space characters.	
p	Matches a pointer. The only portable use is to read back a pointer written by the %p directive to fprintf during the execution of this program.	UNDEFINED.
n	Does not match anything. The corresponding argument is written with the number of characters read from the input stream so far by this call to fscanf( ).	UNDEFINED.
%	Matches a single %.	UNDEFINED.

Reference:

    C 4.9.6.4 & P 8.2.3.5

Notes:

    See "Pitfalls" on Page 47.

setbuf()—Determines how a stream will be buffered.

Synopsis:

```
#include <stdio.h>
void setbuf(FILE *stream, char *buf);
```

Arguments:

stream   Pointer to a freshly-opened stream.

buf   Pointer to a buffer.

Returns:

No value is returned.

Description:

The call **setbuf(stream,buf)** is equivalent to:

```
if (buf == NULL)
  (void)setvbuf(stream,NULL,_IONBF,BUFSIZE);
else
  (void)setvbuf(stream,buf,_IOFBF,BUFSIZE);
```

Reference:

C 4.9.5.5

Notes:

setgid( )—Sets group ID.

Synopsis:

```
#include <sys/types.h>
#include <unistd.h>
int setgid(gid_t gid);
```

Arguments:

gid   New group ID.

Returns:

Zero on success and −1 on failure. If an error occurs, a code is stored in `errno` to identify the error.

Errors:

EINVAL, EPERM

Description:

If the process has appropriate privileges, the real group ID, the effective group ID, and the saved set-group-ID are set to `gid`.

If the process does not have appropriate privileges and the symbol `_POSIX_SAVED_IDS` is defined in `<unistd.h>` and `gid` is equal to the real group ID or the saved set-group-ID, the effective group ID is set to `gid`; the real group ID and the saved set-group-ID are unchanged.

If the process does not have appropriate privileges and the symbol `_POSIX_SAVED_IDS` is not defined in `<unistd.h>` and `gid` is equal to the real group ID, the effective group ID is set to `gid`; the real group ID is unchanged.

If the process does not have appropriate privileges and is not trying to set the effective group ID back to the real or saved value, −1 is returned and `errno` is set to EPERM.

Reference:

P 4.2.2.1

Conversion:

Add to the list of headers:

```
#include <unistd.h>
```

Notes:

This function depends on the user's privileges in an implementation-defined manner. Do not use it in fully portable programs.

setjmp( )—Saves the calling environment for use by longjmp( ).

Synopsis:

```
#include <setjmp.h>
int setjmp(jmp_buf env);
```

Arguments:

env   Variable of type jmp_buf suitable for holding the information needed to restore the calling environment.

Returns:

Zero if returning directly; non-zero if returning via longjmp( ).

Description:

The setjmp( ) macro saves the calling environment in the env argument for later use by longjmp( ).

The setjmp( ) macro must be used in one of the following places:

- The entire controlling expression of a switch, while, if, or for statement.

- One operand of a relational or equality operator with the other operand an integral constant, with the resulting expression being the entire controlling expression of a selection of iteration statement.

- The operand of a unary ! operator with the resulting expression being the entire controlling expression of a selection or iteration statement.

- The entire expression of a statement.

Examples of valid use:

```
if (setjmp(env)) { ... }
while (setjmp(env) != 0) { ... }
switch (setjmp(env)) { ... }
setjmp(env);
(void)setjmp(env);
if (!setjmp(env)) { ... }
```

Examples of invalid use:

```
x = setjmp(env) + 3;
if (retry_flag && setjmp(env)) { ... }
printf("setjmp returned =%d\n",setjmp(env));
setjmp(env1) + setjmp(env2);
```

Reference:

C 4.6.1.1

Notes:

setjmp( )/longjmp( ) make programs hard to understand and maintain. Try to find an alternative.

setjmp( ) is a macro and may not exist as a real function.

POSIX does not specify if setjmp( ) does or does not save signal masks. If you want to save signal masks, use sigsetjmp( )/siglongjmp( ).

`setlocale()`—Sets or queries a program's locale.

Synopsis:

```
#include <locale.h>
char *setlocale(int category, const char *locale);
```

Arguments:

`category`   One of the following macros:

`LC_ALL` for the entire locale.

`LC_COLLATE` affects `strcoll()` and `strxfrm()`.

`LC_CTYPE` affects character-handling functions.

`LC_MONETARY` affects `localeconv()`.

`LC_NUMERIC` affects the decimal point character.

`LC_TIME` affects `strftime()`.

`locale`   Pointer to a string that specifies the implementation-defined native environment.

Returns:

A pointer to the string for the new locale, or `NULL` if the request cannot be honored. This string should not be modified by the program and may be overwritten by a subsequent call.

Description:

The `setlocale()` function is used to change or query the program's current locale or part of the locale. If `locale` is `"C"` or `"POSIX"`, the locale is set to the portable locale. If `locale` is `" "` the locale is set to whatever default locale was selected for the system. The system behaves as if `setlocale(LC_ALL, "C")` is called prior to calling `main()`.

Reference:

C 4.4.1.1 & P 8.1.2.1

Conversion:

This function is new in Standard C. It is not included in BSD or System V prior to SVR4.

Notes:

Chapter 10, *Porting to Far-off Lands*, covers locales and internationalization.

`setpgid()` —Sets process group ID for job control.

Synopsis:

```
#include <sys/types.h>
#include <unistd.h>
int setpgid(pid_t pid, pid_t pgid);
```

Arguments:

pid   Process to set.

pgid   New process group ID.

Returns:

Zero on success and –1 on failure.

If an error occurs, a code is stored in `errno` to identify the error.

Errors:

EACCES, EBUSY,* EINVAL, ENOSYS, EPERM, ESRCH

Description:

The process group ID of the process with process ID `pid` is set to `pgid`. If `pid` is zero, the current process is used. If `pgid` is zero, the `pid` of the affected process is used.

If the macro `_POSIX_JOB_CONTROL` is defined in `<unistd.h>`, the `setpgid()` function works as described above. If it is not defined, `setpgid()` may work as described above or may fail.

Reference:

P 4.3.3.1

Conversion:

This function is a cross between the System V `setpgrp()` and BSD 4.3 `setpgrp()`.

Notes:

This function is used by special programs like the shell. It is not used by ordinary applications.

---

* Added in 1990 standard.

setsid()—Creates a session and sets the process group ID.

Synopsis:

```
#include <sys/types.h>
#include <unistd.h>
pid_t setsid(void);
```

Arguments:

None.

Returns:

-1 on error, or the process group ID of the caller on success.

Errors:

EPERM

Description:

If the calling process is not a process group leader, the setsid() function creates a new session. The calling process is the session leader of the new session, the process group leader of the new process group, and has no controlling terminal. The process group ID of the calling process is set to the process ID of the calling process. The calling process is the only process in the new process group and the only process in the new session.

Reference:

P 4.3.2.1

Conversion:

This function is a cross between the System V setpgrp() and BSD 4.3 setpgrp().

Notes:

This function is used by special programs like the shell. It is not used by ordinary applications.

setuid( )—Sets the user ID.

Synopsis:

```
#include <sys/types.h>
#include <unistd.h>
int setuid(uid_t uid);
```

Arguments:

uid   New user ID.

Returns:

Zero on success and −1 on failure.

If an error occurs, a code is stored in `errno` to identify the error.

Errors:

EINVAL, EPERM

Description:

If the process has appropriate privileges, then the real user ID, the effective user ID, and the saved set-user-ID are set to `uid`.

If the symbol `_POSIX_SAVED_IDS` is defined in `<unistd.h>` and the process does not have appropriate privileges and `uid` is equal to the real user ID or the saved set-user-ID, the effective user ID is set to `uid`; the real user ID and the saved set-user-ID are unchanged.

If the symbol `_POSIX_SAVED_IDS` is not defined in `<unistd.h>` and the process does not have appropriate privileges and `uid` is equal to the real user ID, the effective user ID is set to `uid`; the real user ID is unchanged.

If the process does not have appropriate privileges and is not trying to set the effective user ID back to the real or saved value, −1 is returned and `errno` is set to EPERM.

Reference:

P 4.2.2.1

Conversion:

Add to the list of headers:

```
#include <unistd.h>
```

SVR1-3 and BSD used `int` for `uid`.

Notes:

This function depends on the user's privileges in an implementation-defined manner. Do not use it in fully portable programs.

`setvbuf()`—Determines buffering for a stream.

Synopsis:

```
#include <stdio.h>
int setvbuf(FILE *stream, char *buf, int mode, size_t size);
```

Arguments:

`stream`	Pointer to a freshly opened stream.
`buf`	Pointer to a character array to use as an I/O buffer.
`mode`	One of:
	`_IOFBF` for full buffering.
	`_IOLBF` for line buffering.
	`_IONBF` for no buffering.
`size`	Size of `buf`.

Returns:

Zero if the operation succeeds, nonzero if it fails.

Description:

The `setvbuf()` function determines how `stream` will be buffered and allows a buffer to be supplied. If `buf` is not `NULL`, it points to an array of `size` bytes used to buffer the file. The system may (or may not) use the buffer.

The `setvbuf()` function should be used only after `stream` has been opened and before any other operation is performed on the stream. The `mode` argument determines how `stream` will be buffered. The system may (or may not) honor the request.

The idea behind `setvbuf()` is to allow portable applications to attempt to improve efficiency; however, the library is not required to honor the request if that would introduce additional overhead.

Reference:

C 4.9.5.6

Conversion:

SVR1-3 use `int` for `size.`

BSD uses the `setbuffer()` function.

Notes:

This function is required by Standard C. It is not part of the POSIX standard.

sigaction( )—Examines and changes signal action.

Synopsis:

```
#include <signal.h>
int sigaction(int sig, const struct sigaction *act,
struct sigaction *oact);
```

Arguments:

sig	Signal number.
act	Pointer to a structure specifying new signal action.
oact	Pointer to a structure to be filled in with the old action.

Returns:

Zero on success and −1 on failure.

If an error occurs, a code is stored in errno to identify the error.

Errors:

EINVAL

Description:

The sigaction( ) function allows the calling process to examine and/or specify the action to be associated with a specific signal.

The sigaction structure, defined by the header <signal.h>, includes the following members:

Member Type	Member Name	Description
void(*)()	sa_handler	SIG_DFL for the default action
		or:
		SIG_IGN to ignore this signal
		or:
		pointer to the signal-catching function.
sigset_t	sa_mask	Additional signals to be blocked during the execution of the signal-catching function.

Member Type	Member Name	Description
int	sa_flags	This member is used only for the SIGCHLD signal. If the value SA_NOCLDSTOP is used, then SIGCHLD will not be generated when children stop.
		There may be other flags defined by a particular implementation. A portable program should not use them.

The sigaction() function sets the structure pointed to by oact to the old action for signal sig and then takes the action indicated by the structure pointed to by act. If the act argument is NULL, sigaction() returns the current signal status in oact, but does not change it. If the oact argument is NULL, nothing is returned. The call sigaction(sig,NULL,NULL) can be used to see if sig is a valid signal number on this system.

There may be additional members in a given implementation's struct sigaction. Portable programs are guaranteed that these members will not affect them. To use implementation-defined members, system-specific flags must be set.

Reference:

P 3.3.4.1

Conversion:

This is similar to the BSD sigvec() function. The major difference is that the BSD sv_mask is an int, while the POSIX sa_mask is a sigset_t. This allows for more than 32 signals.

Notes:

sigaddset() —Adds a signal to a signal set.

Synopsis:

```
#include <signal.h>
int sigaddset(sigset_t *set, int signo);
```

Arguments:

set   Pointer to the signal set.

signo   Signal number to add.

Returns:

Zero on success and −1 on failure.

If an error occurs, a code is stored in errno to identify the error.

Errors:

EINVAL

Description:

Adds signo to the signal set pointed to by set.

Reference:

P 3.3.3.1

Conversion:

This function is a POSIX invention. It provides a portable way to support more than 32 signals. Replace code like:

```
mask |= 1<<SIGSEGV;
```

with:

```
sigaddset(&mask, SIGSEGV);
```

Notes:

sigdelset() —Removes a signal from a signal set.

Synopsis:

```
#include <signal.h>
int sigdelset(sigset_t *set, int signo);
```

Arguments:

set   Pointer to the signal set.

signo   Signal number to delete.

Returns:

Zero on success and -1 on failure.

If an error occurs, a code is stored in **errno** to identify the error.

Errors:

EINVAL

Description:

Removes **signo** from the signal set pointed to by **set**.

Reference:

P 3.3.3.1

Conversion:

This function is a POSIX invention. It provides a portable way to support more than 32 signals. Replace code like:

```
mask &= ~(1<<SIGSEGV);
```

with:

```
sigdelset(&mask, SIGSEGV);
```

Notes:

`sigemptyset()`—Creates an empty signal set.

Synopsis:

```
#include <signal.h>
int sigemptyset(sigset_t *set);
```

Arguments:

set   Pointer to the signal set.

Returns:

Zero on success and –1 on failure.

If an error occurs, a code is stored in `errno` to identify the error.

Description:

Sets the signal set pointed to by `set` to empty.

Reference:

P 3.3.3.1

Conversion:

This function is a POSIX invention. It provides a portable way to support more than 32 signals. Replace code like:

```
mask = 0;
```

with:

```
sigemptyset(&mask);
```

Notes:

sigfillset()—Creates a full set of signals.

Synopsis:

```
#include <signal.h>
int sigfillset(sigset_t *set);
```

Arguments:

set   Pointer to the signal set.

Returns:

Zero on success and −1 on failure.

If an error occurs, a code is stored in errno to identify the error.

Description:

Fills the signal set pointed to by set with all valid signals.

Reference:

P 3.3.3.1

Conversion:

This function is a POSIX invention. It provides a portable way to support more than 32 signals. Replace code like:

```
mask = -1;
```

with:

```
sigfillset(&mask);
```

Notes:

sigismember()—Tests a signal set for a selected member.

Synopsis:

```
#include <signal.h>
int sigismember(const sigset_t *set, int signo);
```

Arguments:

set   Pointer to the signal set.

signo   Signal number to test.

Returns:

1 if the selected signal is a member of the set.

0 if the selected signal is not a member of the set.

−1 on error.

Errors:

EINVAL

Description:

Tests whether signo is a member of the signal set pointed to by set.

Reference:

P 3.3.3.1

Conversion:

This function is a POSIX invention. It provides a portable way to support more than 32 signals. Replace code like:

```
if(mask & (1<<SIGSEGV))  . . .
```

with:

```
if(sigismember(&mask, SIGSEGV)) . . .
```

Notes:

siglongjmp()—Goes to and restores signal mask.

Synopsis:

```
#include <setjmp.h>
void siglongjmp(sigjmp_buf env, int val);
```

Arguments:

env	Environment saved by sigsetjmp().
val	Value to return to the caller of sigsetjmp().

Returns:

val is returned to the caller of setjmp().

Description:

The siglongjump() function restores the environment saved in env by a previous call to sigsetjmp().

The values of variables in automatic storage that are not qualified by volatile are indeterminate.

Reference:

P 8.3.1.1

Conversion:

This function is a POSIX invention. BSD and System V differ on saving signals with setjmp().

POSIX Function	BSD Function	SysV Function
N/A	_setjmp()	setjmp()
N/A	_longjmp()	longjmp()
sigsetjmp()	setjmp()	N/A
siglongjmp()	longjmp()	N/A

Notes:

If val is set to 0, 1 is returned instead!

`signal()`—Specifies signal handling.

Synopsis:

```
#include <signal.h>
void (*signal(int sig, void(*func)(int)))(int);
```

Arguments:

> `sig`   Signal number.
>
> `func`   Pointer to a function that is called with a single integer parameter (the signal number).

Returns:

> The value of `func` from the previous call to `signal()`.

Description:

> The `signal()` function comes from the C Standard. It should be used for applications which need to be portable to non-POSIX systems. POSIX applications should use `sigaction()`.
>
> The `sig` argument is a signal number. The `func` argument is a pointer to a signal-catching function or one of the following macros:
>
> `SIG_DFL`   To set the signal to the default action.
>
> `SIG_IGN`   To ignore the signal.
>
> For example:
>
> ```
> signal(SIGINT,SIG_IGN);
> ```
>
> causes the interrupt key (usually Control-C) to be ignored, and:
>
> ```
> signal(SIGSEGV,oops);
> ```
>
> causes the function `oops(SIGSEGV)` to be called on illegal memory references.

Reference:

> C 4.7.1.1

Conversion:

> Change `signal()` to `sigaction()`.

Notes:

This function is required by Standard C. It is not part of the POSIX standard. Programs written for POSIX should use `sigaction()` instead of `signal()`.

sigpending()—Examines pending signals.

Synopsis:

```
#include <signal.h>
int sigpending(sigset_t *set);
```

Arguments:

set   Pointer to a place to return the set of pending signals.

Returns:

Zero on success and −1 on failure.

If an error occurs, a code is stored in errno to identify the error.

Description:

The sigpending() function stores the set of signals that are blocked from delivery and pending for the calling process in the sigset_t pointed to by set. Individual signals may be tested with sigismember().

Reference:

P 3.3.6.1

Conversion:

This function is a POSIX invention.

Notes:

`sigprocmask()`—Examines and changes blocked signals.

Synopsis:

```
#include <signal.h>
int sigprocmask(int how, const sigset_t *set, sigset_t *oset);
```

Arguments:

how   Indicates the type of change.

set   Pointer to new set.

oset   Pointer to a place to return the old set.

Returns:

Zero on success and –1 on failure.

If an error occurs, a code is stored in `errno` to identify the error.

Errors:

EINVAL

Description:

The `sigprocmask()` function is used to examine and/or change the calling process's signal mask. If `set` is not NULL, it points to a set of signals to be changed. The `how` argument indicates the changes to make:

SIG_BLOCK   Add the signals to the process mask.

SIG_UNBLOCK   Remove the signals from the process mask.

SIG_SETMASK   Set the process mask to `set`.

If `oset` is not NULL, the previous signal mask is stored into the `sigset_t` pointed to by `oset`.

If the call to `sigprocmask()` unblocks any signals, at least one signal will be delivered before `sigprocmask()` returns.

Reference:

P 3.3.5.1

Conversion:

This is a more general version of the BSD `sigblock()` and `sigsetmask()` functions. Convert those functions to `sigprocmask()`.

Notes:

It is not possible to block `SIGKILL` or `SIGSTOP`. Attempting to block them does not cause an error.

If any of the `SIGFPE`, `SIGILL`, or `SIGSEGV` signals are generated while they are blocked, the results are not portable.

If a `sigprocmask()` is done in a signal-catching function, returning from that function may undo the work of `sigprocmask()` by restoring the original pending signal mask.

sigsetjmp()—Saves state for siglongjmp().

Synopsis:

```
#include <setjmp.h>
int sigsetjmp(sigjmp_buf env, int savemask);
```

Arguments:

env   Buffer to save the current environment.

savemask   If non-zero, the current signal mask is saved as part of the environment.

Returns:

Zero if returning directly; non-zero if returning via siglongjmp().

Description:

The sigsetjmp() macro saves the calling environment in the env argument for later use by siglongjmp().

The sigsetjmp() macro must be used in one of the following places:

- The entire controlling expression of a switch, while, if, or for statement.

- One operand of a relational or equality operator with the other operand an integral constant, with the resulting expression being the entire controlling expression of a selection of iteration statement.

- The operand of a unary ! operator with the resulting expression being the entire controlling expression of a selection or iteration statement.

- The entire expression of a statement.

Examples of valid use:

```
if (sigsetjmp(env)) { ... }
while (sigsetjmp(env) != 0) { ... }
switch (sigsetjmp(env)) { ... }
sigsetjmp(env);
(void)sigsetjmp(env);
if (!sigsetjmp(env)) { ... }
```

Examples of invalid use:

```
x = sigsetjmp(env) + 3;
if (retry_flag && sigsetjmp(env)) { ... }
printf("sigsetjmp returned =%d\n",sigsetjmp(env));
sigsetjmp(env1) + sigsetjmp(env2);
```

Reference:

P 8.3.1.1

Conversion:

This function is a POSIX invention. BSD and System V differ on saving signals with
`setjmp()`.

POSIX Function	BSD Function	SysV Function
N/A	`_setjmp()`	`setjmp()`
N/A	`_longjmp()`	`longjmp()`
`sigsetjmp()`	`setjmp()`	N/A
`siglongjmp()`	`longjmp()`	N/A

POSIX does not specify if `setjmp()` does or does not save signal masks. If you want
to save signal masks, use `sigsetjmp()/siglongjmp()`.

Notes:

sigsuspend( ) —Waits for a signal.

Synopsis:

```
#include <signal.h>
int sigsuspend(const sigset_t *sigmask);
```

Arguments:

sigmask   Pointer to signal mask.

Returns:

-1 upon being interrupted by a signal with errno set to EINTR.

There is no return value for successful completion.

Errors:

EINTR

Description:

The sigsuspend( ) function replaces the process' signal mask with the set of signals pointed to by the argument sigmask and then suspends the process until delivery of a signal whose action is either to execute a signal-catching function or to terminate the process.

Reference:

P 3.3.7.1

Conversion:

This is the same as the BSD sigpause( ) function, except that sigsuspend( ) uses a sigset_t for sigmask and can support greater than 32 signals.

Notes:

`sin()`—Computes the sine function.

Synopsis:

```
#include <math.h>
double sin(double x);
```

Arguments:

x

Returns:

The sine of x.

Description:

Computes the sine of x. The result will be between -1.00 and $+1.00$.

Reference:

C 4.5.2.6

Notes:

sinh( )—Computes the hyperbolic sine of **x**.

Synopsis:

```
#include <math.h>
double sinh(double x);
```

Arguments:

    x

Returns:

    Hyperbolic sine of **x**.

Description:

    Computes the hyperbolic sine of **x**. This function occurs in numerical solutions to partial differential equations.

Reference:

    C 4.5.3.2

Notes:

`sleep()`—Delays process execution.

Synopsis:

```
#include <unistd.h>
unsigned int sleep(unsigned int seconds);
```

Arguments:

seconds   Number of seconds to sleep.

Returns:

Zero is returned if the requested time has elapsed.

If `sleep()` is interrupted by a signal, the number of unslept seconds is returned.

Description:

The `sleep()` function causes the current process to be suspended until `seconds` have elapsed or a signal is delivered.

Reference:

P 3.4.3.1

Conversion:

Add to the list of headers:

```
#include <unistd.h>
```

Notes:

`sleep()` may sleep for longer than the amount of time requested.

The maximum portable value for `seconds` is 65,535 (a little over 18 hours).

The `sleep()` library function may (or may not) use `SIGALRM` to do the work. Thus, mixing `sleep()` and `alarm()` may cause problems. Also, blocking `SIGALRM` may cause your program to oversleep.

`sprintf()`—Formats a string.

Synopsis:

```
#include <stdio.h>
int sprintf(char *s, const char *format, ...);
```

Arguments:

s	Pointer to place to store result.
format	Pointer to format string.
...	Variables to format.

Returns:

Length of resulting string.

Description:

The `sprintf()` function formats a string in the same way the `printf()` and `fprintf()` do except that `sprintf()` stores the formatted string in the buffer pointed to by s instead of writing it to a file.

The format is a character string that contains zero or more directives. Each directive fetches zero or more arguments to `sprintf`. Each directive starts with the % character. After the %,the following appear in sequence:

flags	Zero or more of the following flags (in any order):

	−	Will cause this conversion to be left-justified. If the − flag is not used, the result will be right-justified.
	+	The result of a signed conversion will always begin with a sign. If the + flag is not used, the result will begin with a sign only when negative values are converted.
	space	This is the same as + except a space is printed instead of a plus sign. If both the *space* and the + flags are used, the + wins.
	#	The result is converted to an alternate form. The details are given below for each conversion.

width	An optional *width* field. The exact meaning depends on the conversion being performed.
prec	An optional *precision*. The *precision* indicates how many digits will be printed to the right of the decimal point. If the *precision* is present, it is preceded by a decimal point(.). If the decimal point is given with no

precision, the precision is assumed to be zero. A precision argument may be used only with the e, E, f, g, and G conversions.

type   An optional h, l, or L. The h causes the argument to be converted to short prior to printing. The l specifies that the argument is a long int. The L specifies that the argument is a long double.

format   A character that specifies the conversion to be performed.

The conversions are given by the following table:

	Description	Meaning of *width*	Meaning of # flag
i or d	An int argument is converted to a signed decimal string.	Specifies the minimum number of characters to appear. If the value is smaller, padding is used. The default is 1. The result of printing zero with a width of zero is no characters.	UNDEFINED.
o	An unsigned int argument is converted to unsigned octal.	Same as i.	Increase the precision to force the first digit to be a zero.
u	An unsigned int argument is converted to unsigned decimal.	Same as i.	UNDEFINED.
x	An unsigned int argument is converted to unsigned hexadecimal. The letters abcdef are used.	Same as i.	Prefix non-zero results with 0x.
X	Same as x except the letters ABCDEF are used.	Same as i.	Prefix non-zero results with 0X.

	Description	Meaning of *width*	Meaning of # flag
f	A `double` argument is converted to decimal notation in the `[-]ddd.ddd` format.	Minimum number of characters to appear. May be followed by a period and the number of digits to print after the decimal point. If a decimal point is printed, at least one digit will appear to the left of the decimal.	Print a decimal point even if no digits follow.
e	A `double` argument is converted in the style `[-]d.ddde dd` The exponent will always contain at least two digits. If the value is zero, the exponent is zero.	Same as `f`.	Same as `f`.
E	Same as `e` except `E` is used instead of `e`.	Same as `f`.	Same as `f`.
g	Same as `f` or `e` depending on the value to be converted. The `e` style is used only if the exponent is less than -4 or greater than the precision.	Same as `f`.	Same as `f`.
G	Same as `g` except an `E` is printed instead of `e`.	Same as `f`.	Same as `f`.
c	An `int` argument is converted to an `unsigned char` and the resulting character is written.	UNDEFINED.	UNDEFINED.

	Description	Meaning of *width*	Meaning of # flag
s	An argument is assumed to be char *. Characters up to (but not including) a terminating null are written.	Specifies the maximum number of characters to be written.	UNDEFINED.
p	An argument must be a pointer to void. The pointer is converted to a sequence of printable characters in an implementation-defined manner. This is not very useful for a portable program.	UNDEFINED.	UNDEFINED.
n	An argument should be a pointer to an integer which is *written* with the number of characters written to the output stream so far. Nothing is written to the output stream by this directive.	UNDEFINED.	UNDEFINED.

Reference:

C 4.9.6.5

Conversion:

Change \07 in format to \a.

Notes:

See "Pitfalls" on Page 47.

`sqrt()`—Computes the square root function.

Synopsis:

```
#include <math.h>
double sqrt(double x);
```

Arguments:

x

Returns:

$\sqrt{x}$

Errors:

EDOM

Description:

The `sqrt()` function computes the square root of **x**.

Reference:

C 4.5.5.2

Notes:

srand( )—Sets a seed for the **rand( )** function.

Synopsis:

```
#include <stdlib.h>
void srand(unsigned int seed);
```

Arguments:

seed   Integer which determines the sequence of random numbers returned by the **rand( )** function.

Returns:

No value is returned.

Description:

The **srand( )** function is used to seed the **rand( )** function. If **srand( )** is called with the same value, the sequence of pseudo-random numbers is repeated.

A popular way to start a random sequence is with **srand((unsigned int)timer(NULL));**

Reference:

C 4.10.2.2

Conversion:

Add to the list of headers:

```
#include <stdlib.h>
```

Notes:

The **srand( )** function is not portable in the sense that different machines will generate different random sequences for the same seed. For typical applications (games), it is not a problem.

sscanf( )—Parses a string.

Synopsis:

```
#include <stdio.h>
int sscanf(const char *s, const char *format, ...);
```

Arguments:

s	Pointer to string to parse.
format	Pointer to control string.
...	Variables to store into.

Returns:

The number of items assigned. If an error occurs prior to any items being assigned, EOF is returned.

Description:

The sscanf( ) function is similar to scanf( ) and fscanf( ) except that input comes from the buffer pointed to by s instead of a file.

The format string contains ordinary text and conversion specifiers. Each directive starts with the % character. After the %, the following appear in sequence:

star	An optional assignment-suppressing character *.
width	An optional decimal integer that specifies the maximum field width.
type	An optional h, l, or L indicating the size of the receiving object. The exact meaning depends on the conversion. See the following table.
format	A character that specifies the type of conversion to perform.

The conversions are given by the following table:

	Description	Meaning of *size* flags
d	Matches an optionally signed decimal integer. The subject is defined as the longest initial subsequence of the input string, starting with the first non-white-space character that is of the expected form.	none → `int` h → `short` l → `long`
	The expected form is an optional plus or minus sign followed by a sequence of the digits 0 through 7.	
i	Same as d except the expected form is the same as an integer constant in Standard C. It may be a decimal constant, an octal constant, or a hexadecimal constant. Each may be preceded with an optional plus or minus sign.	Same as d.
	A decimal constant begins with a non-zero digit followed by zero or more digits in the range 0 to 9.	
	An octal constant begins with a leading zero followed by zero or more of the digits 0 through 9.	
	A hexadecimal constant begins with 0x or 0X followed by one or more of the digits 0 to 9 and the letters A to F or a to f.	
o	Same as d except only the digits 0 to 7 are allowed.	none → `unsigned int` h → `unsigned short` l → `unsigned long`
u	Same as d except the argument is a pointer to an unsigned value. Note: a leading minus sign is legal.	Same as o.
x	Same as d except the argument is a pointer to an unsigned value and the letters A to F are valid. Note: a leading minus is legal.	Same as o.
e f g	Matched an optionally signed floating-point number. The number may be in any format which is acceptable as a floating constant, but no floating suffix is allowed.	none → `float` l → `double` L → `long double`

	Description	Meaning of *size* flags
s	Matches a sequence of non-white-space characters. Note: Use %nc to match exactly n characters.	UNDEFINED.
[	Matches a sequence of characters from a set of expected characters. The conversion specifier includes all subsequent characters in the format string, up to and including the matching right bracket (]). The characters between the brackets comprise the set of expected characters (the *scanset*). If the character following the left bracket is a circumflex (^) the scanset contains all characters that do not appear between the brackets. If the conversion specifier begins with [ ] or [^], the right bracket is included in the scanset and the next right bracket ends the specification. Some systems allow specifications of the form [a–z], meaning all characters between a and z. This depends on the codeset used and is not portable.	UNDEFINED.
c	Matches a sequence of characters. The field width determines how many characters are matched. If there is no field width, one character is matched. NOTE: The format %nc matches n characters. The format %ns matches up to n non-white-space characters.	UNDEFINED.
p	Matches a pointer. The only portable use is to read back a pointer written by the %p directive to fprintf ( ) during the execution of this program.	UNDEFINED.
n	Does not match anything. The corresponding argument is written with the number of characters read from the input stream so far by this call to fscanf ( ).	UNDEFINED.
%	Matches a single % .	UNDEFINED.

Reference:

C 4.9.6.6

Notes:

See "Pitfalls" on Page 47.

`stat( )`—Gets information about a file.

Synopsis:

```
#include <sys/types.h>
#include <sys/stat.h>
int stat(const char *path, struct stat *buf);
```

Arguments:

    `path`   Path name of file to research.

    `buf`   Pointer to an object of type `struct stat` where the file information will be written.

Returns:

Zero on success and −1 on failure.

If an error occurs, a code is stored in `errno` to identify the error.

Errors:

`EACCES, EBADF, ENAMETOOLONG, ENOENT, ENOTDIR`

Description:

The `path` argument points to a pathname for a file. Read, write, or execute permission for the file is not required, but all directories listed in `path` must be searchable. The `stat( )` function obtains information about the named file and writes it to the area pointed to by `buf`.

Reference:

P 5.6.2.1

Conversion:

System V has an `st_rdev` member in the `stat` structure. POSIX does not support this member.

BSD and SVR4 have `st_rdev`, `st_blksize`, and `st_blocks` members. POSIX does not support these.

Many older programs use `short` or `unsigned short` for many `stat` structure members. These must be changed to the POSIX types (`dev_t`, `ino_t`, and so on). See `stat` in Appendix B on Page 551.

`strcat()`—Concatenates two strings.

Synopsis:

```
#include <string.h>
char *strcat(char *s1, const char *s2);
```

Arguments:

s1   Pointer to destination.

s2   Pointer to source.

Returns:

s1

Description:

The `strcat()` function appends a copy of the source (including the terminating null character) to the destination. The first character of `s2` overwrites the null at the end of `s1`. The source and destination may not overlap.

Reference:

C 4.11.3.1

Notes:

strchr()—Scans a string for a character.

Synopsis:

```
#include <string.h>
char *strchr(const char *s, int c);
```

Arguments:

s   Pointer to the source string.

c   Character to look for.

Returns:

A pointer to the matched character or NULL.

Description:

The strchr() function returns a pointer to the first occurrence of c in s. If c is zero, a pointer to the terminating null character is returned.

Reference:

C 4.11.5.2

Notes:

strcmp()—Compares two strings.

Synopsis:

```
#include <string.h>
int strcmp(const char *s1, const char *s2);
```

Arguments:

s1   Pointer to string 1.

s2   Pointer to string 2.

Returns:

An int that is greater than, equal to, or less than zero according to the relative order of s1 and s2; that is, if s1 > s2, strcmp() returns a positive value.

Description:

Compares s1 with s2.

Reference:

C 4.11.4.2

Notes:

strcoll( )—Compares two strings using the current locale.

Synopsis:

```
#include <string.h>
int strcoll(const char *s1, const char *s2);
```

Arguments:

s1   Pointer to string 1.

s2   Pointer to string 2.

Returns:

An int that is greater than, equal to, or less than zero according to the relative order of s1 and s2; that is, if s1 > s2, strcoll( ) returns a positive value.

Description:

Compares s1 to s2. In the "C" or "POSIX" locale, strcoll( ) is equivalent to strcmp( ). The LC_COLLATE environment variable determines the locale for strcoll( ).

Reference:

C 4.11.4.3

Conversion:

This function is new in Standard C. It is not included in BSD or System V prior to SVR4.

Notes:

This function is required by Standard C. It is not part of the POSIX standard.

See Chapter 10, *Porting to Far-off Lands*, for a discussion of locales.

`strcpy()`—Copies a string.

Synopsis:

```
#include <string.h>
char *strcpy(char *s1, const char *s2);
```

Arguments:

s1   Pointer to destination.

s2   Pointer to source.

Returns:

s1

Description:

The string pointed to by s2 (including the terminating null character) is copied into the array pointed to by s1. There is no checking to see if s2 is large enough. The two strings may not overlap.

Reference:

C 4.11.2.3

Notes:

strcspn()—Searches a string for characters which are not in the second string.

Synopsis:

```
#include <stdlib.h>
size_t strcspn(const char *s1, const char *s2);
```

Arguments:

s1   Pointer to the subject string.

s2   Pointer to the set of break characters.

Returns:

The number of initial characters in s1 that are not in the string pointed to by s2.

Description:

The strcspn() function computes the length of the maximum initial segment of the string pointed to by s1 which consists entirely of characters not in the string pointed to by s2.

Reference:

C 4.11.5.3

Conversion:

Add to the list of headers:

```
#include <stdlib.h>
```

This function is not supported in BSD.

Notes:

strerror()—Converts an error number to a string.

Synopsis:

```
#include <string.h>
char *strerror(int errnum);
```

Arguments:

errnum   Error number.

Returns:

A pointer to the string.

Description:

The `strerror()` function maps the error code in `errnum` into an error message string.

Reference:

C 4.11.6.2

Conversion:

This function is new in Standard C. It is not included in BSD or System V prior to SVR4.

Notes:

The string returned by `strerror()` may be overwritten by a subsequent call.

The exact error message returned differs from system to system.

This function is required by Standard C and is not part of the POSIX standard.

strftime()—Formats date/time.

Synopsis:

```
#include <time.h>
size_t *strftime(char *s, size_t maxsize, const char *format,
const struct tm *timeptr);
```

Arguments:

s	Pointer to the output character string.
maxsize	Maximum number of bytes to be stored into s.
format	Pointer to format string.
timeptr	Pointer to a struct tm.

Returns:

The number of characters stored in s or zero if the result is larger than maxsize.

Description:

The strftime() function converts a struct tm to a string under the guidance of a format string. The argument s points to an array of maxsize bytes. The format argument is a pointer to a format control string and timeptr is a pointer to a structure returned by localtime() or gmtime().

Characters are copied from the format string to the array pointed to by s. A conversion specifier consists of a % followed by a character that determines the substitution. The list of conversion specifiers is:strftime() conversion specifiers, as shown in the following table.

Specifier	Replaced by the locales
%a	Abbreviated weekday name.
%A	Full weekday name.
%b	Abbreviated month name.
%B	Full month name.
%c	Date and time formatted for the current locale.
%d	Day of the month as a decimal number (01-31).
%H	Hour as a decimal number (00-23).
%I	Hour as a decimal number (01-12).

Specifier	Replaced by the locales
%j	Day of the year as a decimal number (001-366).
%m	Month as a decimal number (01-12).
%M	Minute as a decimal number (00-59).
%p	Equivalent of AM/PM for use with a 12-hour clock.
%S	Second as a decimal number (00-61).
%U	Week of the year as a decimal number (00-53) using the first Sunday as day 1 of week 1.
%w	Weekday as a decimal number (0[Sunday]-6).
%W	Week of the year as a decimal number (00-53) using the first Monday as day 1 of week 1.
%x	Date.
%X	Time.
%y	Year without a century (00-99).
%Y	Year with century (e.g. 1990).
%z	Time zone.
%%	%.

Here are some examples of format strings and possible output in the **"POSIX"** locale:

The format:	May produce:
%A %B %d, %Y	Friday April 13, 1990
%a %d-%b-%y	Fri 13-Apr-90
%m/%d/%y	04/13/90
%Y%m%d	19900413
%H:%M	15:25
%H:%M:%S	15:25:30
%c	Fri Apr 13 15:25:30 1990
%X on %x	3:25 PM on 4/13/90

The formats %c, %X, and %x produce strings for the current locale. This is an easy way to produce a program that can be moved from country to country.

Reference:

C 4.11.6.2

Conversion:

This function is new in Standard C. It is not included in BSD or System V prior to SVR4.

`strlen()`—Computes the length of a string.

Synopsis:

```
#include <string.h>
size_t strlen(const char *s);
```

Arguments:

s   Pointer to the string.

Returns:

The length of s.

Description:

Computes the length of the string pointed to by s, not counting the terminating null character.

Reference:

C 4.11.6.3

Notes:

`strncat()` —Concatenates two counted strings.

Synopsis:

```
#include <string.h>
char *strncat(char *s1, const char *s2, size_t n);
```

Arguments:

s1   Pointer to a string.

s2   Pointer to a string to be appended to s1.

n   Number of characters.

Returns:

s1

Description:

Append up to n characters from s2 to the end of s1. The null character at the end of s2 and any characters that follow it are not appended. The first character from s2 over-writes the null at the end of s1. The strings may not overlap.

A terminating null is always appended to the result. Therefore, the maximum number of characters that can end up in the array pointed to by s1 is `strlen(s1)+n+1`.

Reference:

C 4.11.3.2

Conversion:

SVR1-2 and BSD use `int` for n.

Notes:

If a constant is used for n, typecast it to `size_t`, as in `(size_t)13`.

strncmp( )—Compares two counted strings.

Synopsis:

```
#include <string.h>
char *strncmp(char *s1, const char *s2, size_t n);
```

Arguments:

s1   Pointer to string 1.

s2   Pointer to string 2.

n   Maximum number of bytes to compare.

Returns:

An int that is greater than, equal to, or less than zero according to the relative order of s1 and s2; that is, if s1 > s2, strncmp( ) returns a positive value.

Description:

Compares s1 to s2. The comparison stops after n characters are compared or a null is encountered.

Reference:

C 4.11.3.2

Conversion:

SVR1-2 and BSD use int for n.

Notes:

If a constant is used for n, typecast it to size_t, as in (size_t)13.

`strncpy()`—Copies a counted string.

Synopsis:

```
#include <string.h>
char *strncpy(char *s1, const char *s2, size_t n);
```

Arguments:

    s1   Pointer to destination.

    s2   Pointer to source.

    n   Number of bytes to move.

Returns:

    s1

Description:

Copy up to n characters from s2 to s1. The copy operation stops when a null character is copied. The strings may not overlap.

If there is no null in the first n characters of s2, the result will not be null terminated.

Reference:

C 4.11.2.4

Conversion:

SVR1-2 and BSD use int for n.

Notes:

If s2 is shorter than n bytes, null bytes are appended to s1 until n bytes have been stored.

If a constant is used for n, typecast it to size_t, as in (size_t)13.

`strpbrk()`—Searches a string for any of a set of characters.

Synopsis:

```
#include <string.h>
char *strpbrk(const char *s1, const char *s2);
```

Arguments:

s1   Pointer to the subject string.

s2   Pointer to the list of delimiters.

Returns:

Pointer to a character in s1 which matches one of the characters in s2 or NULL if there is no match.

Description:

Locate the first occurrence in s1 of any of the characters in s2.

Reference:

C 4.11.5.4

Conversion:

This function is not supported in BSD.

Notes:

`strrchr()`—Locates the last occurrence of a character in a string.

Synopsis:

```
#include <string.h>
char *strrchr(const char *s, int c);
```

Arguments:

s   Pointer to the string to scan.

c   Character to look for.

Returns:

Pointer to the last occurrence of c in s or NULL if there is no match.

Description:

Locate the last occurrence of c in s.

Reference:

C 4.11.5.5

Conversion:

This function is not supported in BSD.

Notes:

`strspn()`—Searches a string for any of a set of characters.

Synopsis:

```
#include <string.h>
size_t strspn(const char *s1, const char *s2);
```

Arguments:

s1   Pointer to the subject string.

s2   Pointer to the characters to search for.

Returns:

The number of characters in the initial segment of s1 which consist only of characters from s2.

Description:

The `strspn()` function computes the length of the maximum initial segment of s1 which consists entirely of characters from s2.

Reference:

C 4.11.5.6

Conversion:

This function is not supported in BSD.

Notes:

`strstr()`—Locates a substring.

Synopsis:

```
#include <string.h>
char *strstr(const char *s1, const char *s2);
```

Arguments:

s1   Pointer to the subject string.

s2   Pointer to the substring to locate.

Returns:

A pointer to the located string or NULL.

Description:

The `strstr()` function locates the first occurrence in s1 of the string s2. The terminating null characters are not compared.

Reference:

C 4.11.5.7

Conversion:

This function is not supported in BSD.

Notes:

strtod( )—Converts a string to double.

Synopsis:

```
#include <stdlib.h>
double strtod(const char *nptr, char **endptr);
```

Arguments:

nptr   Points to the start of the string.

endptr   If not NULL, points to a place where a pointer to the final string is stored.

Returns:

The converted value.

Description:

The strtod( ) function converts the string pointed to by nptr to double, using the following algorithm:

1. Remove leading white space by testing characters with the isspace( ) function.

2. Remove an optional + or – character.

3. Remove a nonempty sequence of digits containing an optional decimal point character.

4. Remove an optional exponent consisting of an e or E followed by an optional sign followed by a nonempty sequence of digits.

5. If endptr is not NULL, store a pointer to the first unrecognized character (which may be the final null character) in the pointer pointed to by endptr.

6. Convert the characters scanned in steps 2 to 4 to double and return the result.

If the locale is not "C" or "POSIX", additional formats may be acceptable for floating point numbers.

Reference:

C 4.10.1.4

Conversion:

Add to the list of headers:

```
#include <stdlib.h>
```

This function is not supported in BSD.

Notes:

See `atof()` for a less general case.

This function is required by Standard C and is not part of the POSIX standard.

strtok()—Breaks a string into tokens.

Synopsis:

```
#include <string.h>
char *strtok(char *s1, const char *s2);
```

Arguments:

s1   Pointer to the string to search. If **s1** is NULL, **strtok()** uses a saved pointer from the previous call.

s2   Delimiter list.

Returns:

A pointer to the first character of the token or NULL if there are no more tokens.

Description:

Break the string **s1** into tokens delimited by **s2**. The first call should have **s1** as the first argument. Subsequent calls should have NULL as the first argument. The separator string, **s2**, may be different from call to call.

The first call scans **s1** for a sequence of characters not contained in **s2**. If there are no such characters, NULL is returned. If something is found, it is the first token.

The **strtok()** function then scans the remaining characters for a character that is in **s2**. If there is no such character, there is only one token in the string. If a character is found, it is overwritten with a null character to terminate the current token. A pointer to the following character is saved for the next call to **strtok()**.

Reference:

C 4.11.5.8

Conversion:

This function is not supported in BSD.

Notes:

strtol()—Converts a string to long int.

Synopsis:

```
#include <stdlib.h>
long int strtol(const char *nptr, char **endptr, int base);
```

Arguments:

nptr   Points to the start of the string.

endptr If not NULL, points to a place where a pointer to the final string is stored.

base   Radix of input; if base is zero, the rules for a C language constant are used.

Returns:

The converted value.

Description:

The strtol() function converts the string pointed to by nptr to long using the following algorithm:

1. Remove leading white space by testing characters with the isspace() function.

2. Remove an optional + or – character.

3. If base is zero, remove a constant using the rules of the C programming language (inital 0x or 0X for hex, initial 0 for octal, etc.).

4. If base is between 2 and 36, remove a series of characters in the specified radix. The characters a (or A) to z (or Z) are used for 10 to 35.

5. If endptr is not NULL, store a pointer to the first unrecognized character (which may be the final null character) in the pointer pointed to by endptr.

6. Convert the characters scanned in steps 2 to 4 to long and return the result.

If the locale is not "C" or "POSIX", additional formats may be acceptable.

Reference:

C 4.10.1.5

Conversion:

Add to the list of headers:

```
#include <stdlib.h>
```

This function is not supported in BSD.

Notes:

See `atoi( )`.

This function is required by Standard C. It is not part of the POSIX standard.

strtoul()—Converts a string to unsigned long int.

Synopsis:

```
#include <stdlib.h>
unsigned long int strtoul(const char *nptr, char **endptr, int base);
```

Arguments:

nptr   Points to the start of the string.

endptr   If not NULL, points to a place where a pointer to the final string is stored.

base   Radix of input; if base is zero, the rules for a C language constant are used.

Returns:

The converted value.

Description:

The strtoul() function converts the string pointed to by nptr to long using the following algorithm:

1. Remove leading white space by testing characters with the isspace() function.

2. Remove an optional + or – character. That's right, a minus sign is legal!

3. If base is zero, remove a constant using the rules of the C programming language (inital 0x or 0X for hex, initial 0 for octal, etc.).

4. If base is between 2 and 36, scan of a series of characters in the specified radix. The characters a (or A) to z (or Z) are used for 10 to 35.

5. If endptr is not NULL, store a pointer to the first unrecognized character (which may be the final null character) in the pointer pointed to by endptr.

6. Convert the characters scanned in steps 2 to 4 to long and return the result.

If the locale is not "C" or "POSIX", additional formats may be acceptable for floating-point numbers.

Reference:

C 4.10.1.6

Conversion:

This function is new in Standard C. It is not included in BSD or System V prior to SVR4.

Notes:

This function is required by Standard C. It is not part of the POSIX standard.

`strxfrm()`—Transforms strings using rules for locale.

Synopsis:

```
#include <string.h>
size_t strxfrm(char *s1, const char *s2, size_t n);
```

Arguments:

s1	Pointer to output string.
s2	Pointer to input string.
n	Maximum number of bytes to store into s1.

Returns:

The number of bytes required to store the output string (not including the terminating null). If this value is greater than n, s1 is indeterminate.

Description:

The use of `strcoll()` can be quite slow if a great deal of transformation is required and many comparisons are going to be made. The `strxfrm()` function performs the transformation required by `strcoll()` and leaves the result in a form where `strcmp()` can be used.

In the "POSIX" or "C" locale, `strxfrm()` merely copies the string and is almost equivalent to `strncpy()`. The difference is that `strxfrm()` returns the length of the transformed string which may be different from the length of the source.

In applications where many comparisons must be made, a sort, say, using `strxfrm()` and `strcmp()` can provide a performance enhancement over using `strcoll()`. There is no untransform function to recover the source string. It must be kept around if you are going to need it again. Also, the transformation is implementation-dependent so that even two systems operating on German may produce different transformations.

Reference:

C 4.11.4.5

Conversion:

This function is new in Standard C. It is not included in BSD or System V prior to SVR4.

Notes:

The expression `strxfrm(NULL, s, (size_t) 0)+1` returns the number of bytes required to store the transform of `s`.

This function is required by Standard C and is not part of the POSIX standard.

`sysconf()`—Gets system configuration information.

Synopsis:

```
#include <unistd.h>
long sysconf(int name);
```

Arguments:

name   Symbolic constant.

Returns:

A value or −1 on error.

Errors:

EINVAL

Description:

The `sysconf()` function provides a method for the application to determine the current value for a system limit or option.

The possible values for `name` are shown in the following table.

Compile-Time Macro	sysconf() name	Description
ARG_MAX	_SC_ARG_MAX	The length of the arguments for the `exec()` function.
_POSIX_CHILD_MAX	_SC_CHILD_MAX	The number of simultaneous processes per real user ID.
CLK_TCK	_SC_CLK_TCK	The number of clock ticks per second.
_POSIX_NGROUPS_MAX	_SC_NGROUPS_MAX	The number of simultaneous supplementary group IDs.
STREAM_MAX[*]	_SC_STREAM_MAX[*]	The maximum number of streams that one process can have open at one time. This is the same as FOPEN_MAX from the C standard.
TZNAME_MAX[*]	_SC_TZNAME_MAX[*]	The maximum number of bytes in a timezone name.

---

[*] This symbol is in IEEE std 1003.1-1990 but not in IEEE std 1003.1-1988

Compile-Time Macro	sysconf() name	Description
_POSIX_OPEN_MAX	_SC_OPEN_MAX	The maximum number of files that one process can have open at one time.
_POSIX_JOB_CONTROL	_SC_JOB_CONTROL	Job control functions are supported.
_POSIX_SAVED_IDS	_SC_SAVED_IDS	Each process has a saved set-user-ID and a saved set-group-ID.
_POSIX_VERSION	_SC_VERSION	Indicates the 4-digit year and 2-digit month that the standard was approved.
		The integer 198808L indicates the 1988 version and the integer 199009L indicates the 1990 version.

Reference:

P 4.8.1.1

Conversion:

This function is new to POSIX. It allows a portable application to determine the quantity of a resource, or the presence of an option, at execution time.

Older applications either use a fixed amount of resource or attempt to deduce the amount of resource available using the error returns from various functions.

Notes:

sysconf() returns –1 without changing errno if name is not defined on the system.

See Chapter 7, *Obtaining Information at Run–time,* for a discussion of sysconf() and pathconf().

system( )—Executes a command.

Synopsis:

```
#include <stdlib.h>
int system(const char *string);
```

Arguments:

string   Pointer to the command to execute.

Returns:

An implementation-defined value.

Description:

The string argument is passed to a shell to be executed.

Reference:

C 4.10.4.5

Conversion:

Add to the list of headers:

```
#include <stdlib.h>
```

Notes:

Programs that use the system( ) function are not, in general, portable.

This function is required by Standard C. It is not part of the POSIX.1 standard. The POSIX.2 standard provides several hundred pages of documentation on the arguments to system( ).

`tan()`—Computes the tangent of **x**.

Synopsis:

```
#include <math.h>
double tan(double x);
```

Arguments:

x

Returns:

Tangent of **x**.

Description:

The `tan()` function returns the tangent of the argument.

Reference:

C 4.5.2.7

Notes:

The tangent function produces machine-specific results for values close to $\pi/2$.

`tanh()`—Computes the hyperbolic tangent of **x**.

Synopsis:

```
#include <math.h>
double tanh(double x);
```

Arguments:

x

Returns:

Hyperbolic tangent of **x**.

Description:

The `tanh()` function computes the hyperbolic tangent of **x**. This may be the least useful function in the entire library.

Reference:

C 4.5.3.3

Notes:

tcdrain( )—Waits for all output to be transmitted to the terminal.

Synopsis:

```
#include <termios.h>
#include <unistd.h>
int tcdrain(int fildes);
```

Arguments:

fildes   File descriptor that must refer to a terminal.

Returns:

Zero on success and −1 on failure.

If an error occurs, a code is stored in errno to identify the error.

Errors:

EBADF, EINTR, ENOTTY

Description:

The tcdrain( ) function waits until all output written to fildes has been transmitted.

Reference:

P 7.2.2.1

Conversion:

This is one of a group of functions designed to replace the System V and BSD ioctl( ) function. The ioctl( ) function is very general and hard to specify in a portable way. POSIX defines a function for each supported sub-function of ioctl( ). In general, you can replace existing ioctl( ) functions with one of the tc*( ) functions.

Notes:

`tcflow()` —Suspends/restarts terminal output.

Synopsis:

```
#include <termios.h>
#include <unistd.h>
int tcflow(int fildes, int action);
```

Arguments:

fildes   File descriptor which must refer to a terminal.

action   One of the following symbolic constants:

TCOOFF   To suspend output.

TCOON   To restart output.

TCIOFF   To transmit a stop character intended to cause the terminal to stop sending data to the system.

TCION   To transmit a start character intended to cause the terminal to resume sending data.

Returns:

Zero on success and −1 on failure.

If an error occurs, a code is stored in `errno` to identify the error.

Errors:

EBADF, EINTR, ENOTTY

Description:

The `tcflow()` function suspends transmission or reception of data for `fildes` depending on `action`.

Reference:

P 7.2.2.1

Conversion:

This is one of a group of functions designed to replace the System V and BSD `ioctl()` function. The `ioctl()` function is very general and hard to specify in a portable way. POSIX defines a function for each supported sub-function of `ioctl()`. In general, you can replace existing `ioctl()` functions with one of the `tc*()` functions.

Notes:

See Chapter 8, *Terminal I/O*, for more information.

tcflush()—Discards terminal data.

Synopsis:

```
#include <termios.h>
#include <unistd.h>
int tcflush(int fildes, int queue_selector);
```

Arguments:

fildes	File descriptor which must refer to a terminal.
queue_selector	One of the following constants:

TCIFLUSH	To discard input data.
TCOFLUSH	To discard output data.
TCIOFLUSH	To discard all data.

Returns:

Zero on success and −1 on failure.

If an error occurs, a code is stored in errno to identify the error.

Errors:

EBADF, EINVAL, ENOTTY

Description:

The tcflush() function discards any data written to fildes but not yet transmitted and/or data received for fildes but not yet read according to queue_selector.

Reference:

P 7.2.2.1

Conversion:

This is one of a group of functions designed to replace the System V and BSD ioctl() function. The ioctl() function is very general and hard to specify in a portable way. POSIX defines a function for each supported sub-function of ioctl(). In general, you can replace existing ioctl() functions with one of the tc*() functions.

Notes:

See Chapter 8, *Terminal I/O*, for more information.

`tcgetattr( )`—Gets terminal attributes.

Synopsis:

```
#include <termios.h>
#include <unistd.h>
int tcgetattr(int fildes, struct termios *tp);
```

Arguments:

`fildes`   File descriptor that must refer to a terminal.

`tp`   Pointer to a structure where the information will be returned.

Returns:

Zero on success and −1 on failure.

If an error occurs, a code is stored in `errno` to identify the error.

Errors:

EBADF, ENOTTY

Description:

The `tcgetattr()` gets the parameters associated with the terminal referred to by `fildes` and stores them into the `termios()` structure pointed to by `termios_p`.

Reference:

P 7.2.1.1

Conversion:

This is one of a group of functions designed to replace the System V and BSD `ioctl()` function. The `ioctl()` function is very general and hard to specify in a portable way. POSIX defines a function for each supported sub-function of `ioctl()`. In general, you can replace existing `ioctl()` functions with one of the `tc*()` functions.

Notes:

Chapter 8, *Terminal I/O*, covers terminal I/O and `tcgetattr()/tcsetattr()` in great detail.

tcgetpgrp()—Gets foreground process group ID.

Synopsis:

```
#include <sys/types.h>
#include <unistd.h>
pid_t tcgetpgrp(int fildes);
```

Arguments:

fildes   File descriptor that must refer to a terminal.

Returns:

Process ID of the foreground process group associated with the terminal or –1 on error.

Errors:

EBADF, EINTR, ENOTTY

Description:

The tcgetpgrp() function returns the value of the process group ID of the foreground process group associated with the terminal.

Added in IEEE Std 1003.1-1990: if there is no foreground process group, return a value greater than 1 that does not match an existing process group.

If the macro _POSIX_JOB_CONTROL is defined in <unistd.h>, the tcgetpgrp() works as described above. If _POSIX_JOB_CONTROL is not defined, tcgetpgrp() may work as described above or may fail.

Reference:

P 7.2.3.1

Conversion:

This is one of a group of functions designed to replace the System V and BSD ioctl() function. The ioctl() function is very general and hard to specify in a portable way. POSIX defines a function for each supported sub-function of ioctl(). In general, you can replace existing ioctl() functions with one of the tc*() functions.

The tcgetpgrp() function is identical to the BSD ioctl() function TIOCGPGRP; except tcgetpgrp() requires that the terminal must be the controlling terminal for the calling process.

Notes:

If a background process calls `tcgetpgrp()`, the function works; however, the information may be changed by a foreground process.

`tcsendbreak( )` —Sends a break to a terminal.

Synopsis:

```
#include <termios.h>
#include <unistd.h>
int tcsendbreak(int fildes, int duration);
```

Arguments:

fildes   File descriptor that must refer to a terminal.

duration Length of the break.

Returns:

Zero on success and −1 on failure.

If an error occurs, a code is stored in `errno` to identify the error.

Errors:

EBADF, ENOTTY

Description:

The `tcsendbreak( )` function sends a stream of zero bits for a specific duration. If `duration` is zero, the break is between 250 and 500 milliseconds long. The `fildes` argument must refer to a terminal using asynchronous serial data transmission.

The POSIX standard does not specify the units for `duration`, so non-zero values are not portable.

Reference:

P 7.2.2.1

Conversion:

This is one of a group of functions designed to replace the System V and BSD `ioctl( )` function. The `ioctl( )` function is very general and hard to specify in a portable way. POSIX defines a function for each supported sub-function of `ioctl( )`. In general, you can replace existing `ioctl( )` functions with one of the `tc*( )` functions.

Notes:

The exact length of the break and the units of `duration` are implementation-defined. Zero is the only portable value.

tcsetattr( )—Sets terminal attributes.

Synopsis:

```
#include <termios.h>
#include <unistd.h>
int tcsetattr(int fildes, int options, const struct termios *tp);
```

Arguments:

fildes   File descriptor which must refer to a terminal.

options   One of the following:

TCSANOW   To change the terminal attributes immediately.

TCSADRAIN   To change them after all output has been transmitted.

TCSAFLUSH   To change them after all output has been transmitted;
              all input that has not been read will be discarded.

Returns:

Zero on success and −1 on failure.

If an error occurs, a code is stored in errno to identify the error.

Errors:

EBADF, EINTR, EINVAL, ENOTTY

Description:

The tcsetattr( ) function loads the parameters for the terminal associated with
fildes from the struct termios pointed to by tp.

Reference:

P 7.2.1.1

Conversion:

This is one of a group of functions designed to replace the System V and BSD ioctl( )
function. The ioctl( ) function is very general and hard to specify in a portable way.
POSIX defines a function for each supported sub-function of ioctl( ). In general, you
can replace existing ioctl( ) functions with one of the tc*( ) functions.

Notes:

The tcsetattr() function returns success even if not all the requested attributes can be set. A tcgetattr() can be used to determine the parameters that were actually changed. Chapter 8, *Terminal I/O*, covers tcsetattr() in great detail.

tcsetpgrp()—Sets foreground process group ID.

Synopsis:

```
#include <sys/types.h>
#include <unistd.h>
int tcsetpgrp(int fildes, pid_t pgrpid);
```

Arguments:

fildes   File descriptor which must refer to a terminal.

pgrpid   New foreground process group ID associated with the terminal.

Returns:

Zero on success and –1 on failure.

If an error occurs, a code is stored in errno to identify the error.

Errors:

EBADF, EINVAL, ENOSYS, ENOTTY, EPERM

Description:

The tcsetpgrp() function sets the foreground process group ID for the controlling terminal to pgrpid. The fildes argument must refer to the controlling terminal for the calling process and the controlling terminal must be currently associated with the session of the calling process. The value of pgrp id must match a process group ID of a process in the same session as the calling process.

If the macro _POSIX_JOB_CONTROL is defined in <unistd.h>, the tcsetpgrp() works as described above. If _POSIX_JOB_CONTROL is not defined, tcsetpgrp() may work as described above or may fail.

Reference:

P 7.2.4.1

Conversion:

This is one of a group of functions designed to replace the System V and BSD ioctl() function. The ioctl() function is very general and hard to specify in a portable way. POSIX defines a function for each supported sub-function of ioctl(). In general, you can replace existing ioctl() functions with one of the tc*() functions.

time()—Determines the current calendar time.

Synopsis:

```
#include <time.h>
time_t time(time_t *timer);
```

Arguments:

timer   Pointer to a time_t. If this is not NULL, time() will store the return value.

Returns:

The current calendar time.

Description:

The time() function returns the number of seconds since 00:00 Coordinated Universal Time (UTC) on January 1, 1970. If timer is not NULL, the time is stored into the time_t pointed to by timer.

Reference:

C 4.12.2.4 & P 4.5.1.1

Conversion:

SVR1-2 and BSD return long and use long for timer.

Notes:

The ANSI C standard merely indicates that time_t is a numeric type capable of representing times. POSIX adds the requirement that the time() function return the number of seconds since 00:00 Coordinated Universal Time (UTC) on January 1, 1970.

times()—Gets process times.

Synopsis:

```
#include <sys/times.h>
clock_t times(struct tms *buffer);
```

Arguments:

buffer   Pointer to a structure to hold the returned information.

Returns:

Elapsed real time.

Description:

The times() function stores process times for the calling process into the struct tms pointed to by buffer.

The struct tms structure contains at least the following members:

Member Name	Description
tms_utime	User CPU time.
tms_stime	System CPU time.
tms_cutime	User time of terminated child processes for which a wait() or waitpid() has been done.
tms_cstime	System time of terminated child processes for which a wait() or waitpid() has been done.

All members have the type clock_t and can be converted to seconds by dividing by the symbol CLK_TCK. User time is time charged for the execution of user processes. System time is time charged for executing the system on behalf of the process. Which library functions charge system time and the amount that they charge will vary from implementation to implementation.

Reference:

P 4.5.2.1

Conversion:

SVR1-3 returns long.

`tmpfile()`—Creates a temporary file.

Synopsis:

```
#include <stdio.h>
FILE *tmpfile(void);
```

Arguments:

None.

Returns:

An open temporary file. The file is open for update with the "wb+" mode.

Description:

The `tmpfile()` function opens a temporary file that will be removed automatically when it is closed or at program termination. The file is opened with "wb+" mode.

Reference:

C 4.9.4.3 & P 8.2.3.9

Conversion:

This function is not supported in BSD.

Notes:

If the program terminates abnormally, the file may not be removed.

`tmpnam( )` —Generates a string that is a valid non-existing file name.

Synopsis:

```
#include <stdio.h>
char *tmpnam(char *s);
```

Arguments:

> s Pointer to an array of L_tmpnam characters or NULL.

Returns:

The argument s. If s was NULL, `tmpnam( )` returns a pointer to a static buffer.

Description:

The `tmpnam( )` function generates a string that is a valid filename and that is not the name of an existing file. The `tmpnam( )` function generates a different name each time it is called, up to TMP_MAX times.

Reference:

C 4.9.4.4

Conversion:

The BSD `mktemp( )` function must be replaced by `tmpnam( )`.

Notes:

POSIX does not specify the method used to generate the unique name.

tolower( )—Converts uppercase to lowercase.

Synopsis:

```
#include <ctype.h>
int tolower(int c);
```

Arguments:

c   Character to be converted.

Returns:

If c can be converted to lowercase, the converted character is returned. If not, c is returned.

Description:

The uppercase argument is converted to lowercase and returned.

Reference:

C 4.3.2.1

Conversion:

This function is not documented in BSD 4.2. It was added in BSD 4.3.

Notes:

`toupper()`—Converts lowercase to uppercase.

Synopsis:

```
#include <ctype.h>
int toupper(int c);
```

Arguments:

c   Character to be converted.

Returns:

If c can be converted to uppercase, the converted character is returned. If not, c is returned.

Description:

The lowercase argument is converted to uppercase and returned.

Reference:

C 4.3.2.2

Conversion:

This function is not documented in BSD 4.2. It was added in BSD 4.3.

Notes:

In some non-English locales, there are lowercase letters with no matching uppercase letter; for example, ß in German.

ttyname()—Determines a terminal pathname.

Synopsis:

```
#include <unistd.h>
char *ttyname(int fildes);
```

Arguments:

fildes   File descriptor.

Returns:

Pointer to a character string containing the pathname of the terminal associated with fildes or NULL if fildes does not refer to a terminal.

Description:

The ttyname() function returns a pointer to a string containing a null-terminated pathname of the terminal associated with fildes. The return value may point to static data that is overwritten by each call.

Reference:

P 4.7.2.1

Conversion:

Add to the list of headers:

```
#include <unistd.h>
```

Notes:

`tzset()`—Sets the timezone from environment variables.

Synopsis:

```
#include <time.h>
void tzset(void);
```

Arguments:

None.

Returns:

No value is returned.

Description:

The `tzset()` function uses the value of the environment variables `TZ` to set the time conversion information used by `localtime()`, `ctime()`, `strftime()`, and `mktime()`. If `TZ` is absent from the environment, a default timezone is used. This is most often Coordinated Universal Time (UTC).

The external variable `tzname[0]` is set to a pointer to the name of the standard timezone and the external variable `tzname[1]` is set to a pointer to the name of the daylight savings timezone.

Reference:

P 8.3.2.1

Conversion:

This function is not supported in BSD.

Notes:

umask( )—Sets a file creation mask.

Synopsis:

```
#include <sys/types.h>
#include <sys/stat.h>
mode_t umask(mode_t cmask);
```

Arguments:

cmask   Permission bits to turn off in created files.

Returns:

The previous mask.

Description:

The umask( ) function sets the process file creation mask to cmask. The file creation mask is used during open( ), creat( ), mkdir( ), and mkfifo( ) calls to turn off permission bits in the mode argument. Bit positions that are set in cmask are cleared in the mode of the created file.

The file creation mask is inherited across fork( ) and exec( ) calls. This makes it possible to alter the default permission bits of created files.

Reference:

P 5.3.3.1

Conversion:

BSD and SVR1-3 return int and use int for cmask.

Notes:

The cmask argument should have only permission bits set. All other bits should be zero.

uname ( ) —Gets system name.

Synopsis:

```
#include <sys/utsname.h>
int uname(struct utsname *name);
```

Arguments:

name   Pointer to a structure to hold the result.

Returns:

Zero on success and –1 on failure.

If an error occurs, a code is stored in errno to identify the error.

Description:

The uname ( ) function provides information about the system you are using. The information is fairly minimal. The name argument is a pointer to a struct utsname to be filled in by the uname ( ) call.

The struct utsname is defined in the header file <sys/utsname.h> as a set of null-terminated character arrays. The structure contains the following members:

Member Name	Description
sysname	Name of this operating system.
nodename	Name of this node within a network. Note: There is no guarantee that this name can be used for anything.
release	Current release level of this implementation.
version	Current version level of this release.
	While POSIX provides the release level and version, it never defines them.
machine	Name of the hardware type the system is running on.

As with most POSIX structures, these members may be in any order and there may be other members present.

Reference:

P 4.4.1.1

Conversion:

This function is not supported in BSD.

Notes:

The strings returned by `uname ( )` are useful for messages; they are not useful for much else.

`ungetc()`—Pushes a character back onto a stream.

Synopsis:

```
#include <stdio.h>
int ungetc(int c, FILE *stream);
```

Arguments:

c   Character to push back.

stream   Pointer to the file being read.

Returns:

c on success and EOF on failure.

Description:

Push the character c, converted to `unsigned char`, back onto `stream`. The pushed-back characters will be returned in reverse order. The file associated with `stream` is unchanged. Only one push-back is guaranteed. If `ungetc()` is called too many times it may fail.

If the value of c is EOF, the operation fails without doing anything to `stream`.

The end-of-file indicator is cleared. The value of the file position indicator after the pushed-back characters are read is the same as before they were pushed back.

Reference:

C 4.9.7.11

Notes:

It is possible to put back a different character from the one that was read.

`unlink()`—Removes a directory entry.

Synopsis:

```
#include <unistd.h>
int unlink(const char *path);
```

Arguments:

path   Pointer to path name of file to delete.

Returns:

Zero on success and −1 on failure.

If an error occurs, a code is stored in `errno` to identify the error.

Errors:

EACCES, EBUSY, ENAMETOOLONG, ENOENT, ENOTDIR, EPERM, EROFS

Description:

The `unlink()` function removes the link named by `path` and decrements the link count of the file referenced by the link. When the link count goes to zero and no process has the file open, the space occupied by the file is freed and the file is no longer accessible.

Reference:

P 5.5.1.1

Conversion:

Add to the list of headers:

```
#include <unistd.h>
```

Notes:

See `remove()` for an alternate name for this function.

`utime()` —Sets file access and modification times.

Synopsis:

```
#include <sys/types.h>
#include <utime.h>
int utime(const char *path, const struct utimbuf *times);
```

Arguments:

path   Pointer to name of file to update.

times   Pointer to a structure with the new access and modification times; if NULL, the current time is used.

Returns:

Zero on success and –1 on failure.

If an error occurs, a code is stored in `errno` to identify the error.

Errors:

EACCES, ENAMETOOLONG, ENOENT, ENOTDIR, EPERM, EROFS

Description:

The `utime()` function sets the access and modification times for the file named by path. The tm argument is either NULL or a pointer to a `utimbuf` structure. If the tm argument is NULL, the access and modification times are set to the current time.

If the tm argument is not NULL, it is assumed to be a pointer to a `utimbuf` structure. This contains the following members:

actime   Access time.

modtime   Modification time.

Both members have type `time_t`.

Reference:

P 5.6.6.1

Conversion:

SVR1-3 did not use `<utime.h>` and stated that the structure `utimbuf` must be defined as:

```
struct utimbuf {
        time_t actime;
        time_t modtime;
};
```

BSD did not use a `struct` but an array of 2 `time_t` elements.

Notes:

This is one of the few functions where a structure is used as an argument and there is no function to initialize the structure. It is a good idea to zero out the entire structure before using it.

va_arg()—Gets the next argument.

Synopsis:
```
#include <stdarg.h>
type va_arg(va_list ap, type);
```

Arguments:

ap   Same variable initialized by va_start().

type   Type of the return.

Returns:

The next argument.

Description:

The va_arg() macro expands to an expression that has the type and value of the next argument in the call. The parameter ap must be the same as the va_list ap initialized by va_start(). Each call to va_arg() updates ap so that the next call will access the next argument. The argument must have a type of **type**.

The va_arg() macro must not be called after the last argument is accessed.

Example:
```
#include <stdarg.h>

/*
 * Function to return the sum of a variable list of args
 */
int vsum(int count, ...)
{
int         sum = 0;            /* The sum */
int         i;                  /* Temp */
va_list     ap;                 /* Arg pointer */

        va_start(ap,count);     /* Setup for va_arg() */
    for (i=0; i<count; i++)
        {
        sum += va_arg(ap, int);
                }
    va_end(ap);
    return(sum);
}
```

Reference:

C 4.8.1.2

Conversion:

BSD used the header <varargs.h> instead of <stdarg.h>.

Notes:

Use with va_start( ) and va_end( ).

This function is required by Standard C and is not part of the POSIX standard.

va_end()—Ends variable argument list.

Synopsis:

```
#include <stdarg.h>
void va_end(va_list ap);
```

Arguments:

ap   Same variable initialized by va_start().

Returns:

No value is returned.

Description:

The va_end() macro facilitates a normal return from a function with a variable argument list. The va_end() macro must be used after a va_start() and before returning from the function. Programs that call va_start() without calling va_end() are not maximally portable.

Reference:

C 4.8.1.3

Conversion:

BSD used the header <varargs.h> instead of <stdarg.h>.

Notes:

In most implementations, va_end() does not do anything. However, if it is omitted the program is non-conforming and not maximally portable.

See va_arg() for an example.

This function is required by Standard C and is not part of the POSIX standard.

va_start() —Starts a variable argument list.

Synopsis:

```
#include <stdarg.h>
void va_start(va_list ap, parmN);
```

Arguments:

ap	Pointer to be initialized.
parmN	Rightmost parameter in the function definition (the one just before the ...).

Returns:

No value is returned. The pointer ap is set for use by va_arg().

Description:

The va_start() macro is invoked before using the va_arg() macro. The parameter parmN is the argument just before the (...) in the function prototype. The parmN argument may not be an array, may not have register storage class, may not be a function, or may not be a type incompatible with default argument promotions.

Reference:

C 4.8.1.1

Conversion:

BSD used the header <varargs.h> instead of <stdarg.h>.

Notes:

See va_arg() for an example.

This function is required by Standard C and is not part of the POSIX standard.

vfprintf( )—Writes formatted text with a variable argument list.

Synopsis:

```
#include <stdarg.h>
#include <stdio.h>
int vfprintf(FILE *stream, const char *format, va_list arg);
```

Arguments:

stream   Pointer to file to write.

format   Pointer to format string.

arg   Variable argument list initialized by va_start( ).

Returns:

The number of characters written, or negative if an error occurred.

Description:

The vfprintf( ) function is equivalent to fprintf( ), with the variable argument list replaced by arg. The va_start( ) macro must be called for arg prior to calling vfprintf( ). The va_end( ) macro must be called prior to returning from the function.

Example:

```
#include <stdarg.h>
#include <stdio.h>

/*
 * Write a message to stderr and to a log file
 */
void errmsg(char *fmt, ...)
{
va_list     ap;

    va_start(ap, fmt);
    vfprintf(stderr, fmt, ap);
    va_end(ap);

    va_start(ap, fmt);
    vfprintf(logfile, fmt, ap);
    va_end(ap);

    return;
}
```

Reference:

C 4.9.6.7

Conversion:

Change \07 in `format` to \a.

This function is not supported in BSD or SVR1.

Notes:

This function is required by Standard C and is not part of the POSIX standard.

`vprintf()`—Write formatted text to standard output with a variable argument list.

Synopsis:

```
#include <stdio.h>
int vprintf(const char *format, va_list arg);
```

Arguments:

format   Pointer to format string.

arg   Pointer to a variable argument list initialized by `va_start()`.

Returns:

The number of characters written, or negative if an error occurred.

Description:

The `vprintf()` function is equivalent to `printf()`, with the variable argument list replaced by `arg`. The `va_start()` macro must be called for `arg` prior to calling `vprintf()`. The `va_end()` macro must be called prior to returning from the function.

Reference:

C 4.9.6.8

Conversion:

Change \07 in `format` to \a.

This function is not supported in BSD or SVR1.

Notes:

See `vfprintf()` for an example.

vsprintf() —Write formatted text to a string with a variable argument list.

Synopsis:

```
#include <stdio.h>
int vsprintf(char *s, const char *format, va_list arg);
```

Arguments:

s	Pointer to array to store into.
format	Pointer to format string.
arg	Variable argument list initialized by va_start().

Returns:

The number of characters stored in s.

Description:

The vsprintf() function is equivalent to sprintf(), with the variable argument list replaced by arg. The va_start() macro must be called for arg prior to calling vsprintf(). The va_end() macro must be called prior to returning from the function.

Reference:

C 4.9.6.9

Conversion:

Change \07 in format to \a.

This function is not supported in BSD or SVR1.

Notes:

See vfprintf() for an example.

This function is required by Standard C. It is not part of the POSIX standard.

`wait()`—Waits for process termination.

Synopsis:

```
#include <sys/types.h>
#include <sys/wait.h>
pid_t wait(int *statloc);
```

Arguments:

stat_loc   Pointer to an integer where the status will be stored.

Returns:

Process ID of the child whose status is being reported, or –1 on error.

Errors:

ECHILD, EINTR

Description:

The `wait()` function suspends execution of the calling process until status information for one of its terminated children is available, or until delivery of a signal whose action is either to execute a signal-catching function or to terminate the process. If status information is available prior to the call to `wait()`, it returns immediately.

The `wait()` function returns the process ID of the child. If the argument `stat_loc` is not NULL, information is stored in the location pointed to by `stat_loc`. If the child returned a value of zero from `main()` or passed a value of zero to `exit()`, the value stored in the location pointed to by `stat_loc` will be zero. The status value can be interpreted using the macros shown in the following table.

Macro	Description
WIFEXITED(stat_value)	Evaluates to a non-zero value if status was returned for a child that terminated normally.
WEXITSTATUS(stat_value)	Evaluates to the low-order eight bits of the `status` argument that the child passed to `exit()`, or the value the child process returned from `main()`. This macro can be used only if `WIFEXITED` returned a non-zero value.
WIFSIGNALED(stat_value)	Evaluates to a non-zero value if status was returned for a child that terminated due to a signal that was not caught.

Macro	Description

WTERMSIG(stat_value)

Evaluates to the number of the signal that caused the termination of the process. This macro can be used only if **WIFSIGNALED** returned a non-zero value.

WIFSTOPPED(stat_value)

Evaluates to a non-zero value if the status was returned for a child that is currently stopped. The **waitpid()** function with the **WUNTRACED** option is the only way this value can be returned.

WSTOPSIG(stat_value)

Evaluates to the number of the signal that caused the child process to stop. This macro can be used only if **WIFSTOPPED** returned a non-zero value.

Reference:

P 3.2.1.1

Conversion:

SVR1-3 and BSD return **int**.

Notes:

`waitpid()`—Waits for process termination.

Synopsis:

```
#include <sys/types.h>
#include <sys/wait.h>
pid_t waitpid(pid_t pid, int *stat_loc, int options);
```

Arguments:

pid   Child process whose status is requested; –1 for any process or zero for any member of this process group.

stat_loc   Pointer to an integer where the status will be stored.

options   Inclusive OR of zero or more of:

        WNOHANG

        WUNTRACED

Returns:

Process ID of the child for which status is being reported or –1 on error.

Zero is returned if the WNOHANG option is used and no status is available.

Errors:

ECHILD, EINTR, EINVAL

Description:

The `pid` argument is either:

–1   To wait for any child process; this is the same as `wait()`.

positive   To wait for the specific child whose process ID is equal to `pid`.

zero   To wait for any child process whose process group ID is equal to that of the calling process.

less than –1 To wait for any child process whose process group ID is equal to the absolute value of `pid`.

Process groups are normally used only by shells supporting job control and not ordinary applications.

The `options` argument is constructed from the bitwise OR of zero or more of the following flags, defined in the header `<sys/wait.h>`:

WNOHANG   Causes the `waitpid()` function not to suspend execution of the calling process if status is not immediately available for any of the child processes specified by `pid`. In this case, zero is returned.

WUNTRACED   Reports to the calling process the status of any child processes specified by `pid` that are stopped, and whose status has not yet been reported since they stopped. It is normally used only by the shell program to support job control.

Reference:

P 3.2.1.1

Conversion:

This is similar to the BSD `wait3()` function.

Notes:

wcstombs()—Converts a wide character string to a multibyte character string.

Synopsis:

```
#include <stdlib.h>
size_t wcstombs(char *s, const wchar_t *pwcs, size_t n);
```

Arguments:

s	Pointer to the resulting multibyte character string.
pwcs	Pointer to the input wide character string.
n	Maximum number of bytes to store in s.

Returns:

The number of bytes stored in s (including the terminating null character), or −1 if the input string contains an invalid wide character.

Description:

The wcstombs() function converts a sequence of codes that corresponds to multibyte characters from the array pointed to by pwcs into a sequence of multibyte characters that begins in the initial shift state and stores these characters into the array pointed to by s. The conversion stops after n bytes are stored or if a null character is stored.

The array pointed to by pwcs and the array pointed to by s may not overlap.

Reference:

C 4.10.8.2

Conversion:

This function is new in Standard C. It is not included in BSD or System V prior to SVR4.

Notes:

See Chapter 10, *Porting to Far-off Lands*, for a description of wide and multibyte characters.

This function is required by Standard C and is not part of the POSIX standard.

wctomb( )—Converts a wide character to a multibyte character.

Synopsis:

```
#include <stdlib.h>
int wctomb(char *s, wchar_t wchar);
```

Arguments:

s   Pointer to the resulting string.

wchar   Wide character to convert.

Returns:

The number of bytes in the resulting multibyte character, or −1 if wchar is not valid.

Description:

The wctomb( ) function determines the number of bytes needed to represent the multibyte character corresponding to wchar (including any change in shift state). If s is not NULL, wctomb( ) stores the multibyte character representation in the array pointed to by s. At most, MB_CUR_MAX characters are stored. If wchar is zero, wctomb( ) is placed into the initial shift state.

Reference:

C 4.10.7.3

Conversion:

This function is new in Standard C. It is not included in BSD or System V prior to SVR4.

Notes:

See Chapter 10, *Porting to Far-off Lands*, for a description of wide and multibyte characters.

This function is required by Standard C and is not part of the POSIX standard.

`write()`—Writes to a file.

Synopsis:

```
#include <unistd.h>
int write(int fildes, const void *buf, unsigned int nbyte);
```

Arguments:

fildes   File descriptor open for writing.

buf   Pointer to the data to be written.

nbyte   Number of bytes to write.

Returns:

The number of bytes written, or −1 to indicate an error.

Errors:

EAGAIN, EBADF, EFBIG, EINTR, EIO, ENOSPC, EPIPE

Description:

The `write()` function writes `nbyte` bytes from the array pointed to by `buf` into the file associated with `fildes`.

If `nbyte` is zero and the file is a regular file, the `write()` function returns zero and has no other effect. If `nbyte` is zero and the file is a special file, the results are not portable.

If the O_APPEND flag is set, all writes are forced to the current end of file.

The `write()` function returns the number of bytes written. This number will be less than `nbyte` if there is an error. It will never be greater than `nbyte`.

If a write is interrupted by a signal, it will either return −1 with `errno` set to EINTR or it will return the non-zero number of bytes written. A `write()` to a pipe will never return EINTR if it has transferred any data and `nbyte` is less than PIPE_BUF.

After a `write()` to a regular file has successfully returned, any successful `read()` from each byte position in the file that was modified by that `write()` will return the data that was written by the `write()`. A subsequent `write()` to the same byte will overwrite the file data. If a `read()` of a file data can be proven (by any means) to occur after a `write()` of that data, it must reflect that `write()`, even if the calls are made by different processes. A similar requirement applies to multiple write operations to the same file position.*

When writing to a file descriptor (other than a pipe of FIFO) that supports non-blocking I/O and cannot accept the data immediately:

1. If O_NONBLOCK is clear, write() will block until the data can be accepted.

2. If O_NONBLOCK is set, write() will write as much as possible and return the number of bytes written. If no bytes can be written, it returns -1 with errno set to EAGAIN.

When writing to a pipe or FIFO:

1. If O_NONBLOCK is clear, write() will block until the data can be accepted. On completion it will return nbyte.

2. If O_NONBLOCK is set, the write() will operate according to the following table.

	No space is available	Less than nbyte available	nbyte or more available
nbyte less than or equal to PIPE_BUF	Return -1 with errno set to EAGAIN.	Return -1 with errno set to EAGAIN.	Atomic write of nbyte.
nbytes greater than PIPE_BUF	Return -1 with errno set to EAGAIN.	Return a number less than nbyte or -1 with errno set to EAGAIN.	Return a number less than or equal to nbyte or -1 with errno set to EAGAIN.

Reference:

P 6.4.2.1

Conversion:

Add to the list of headers:

```
#include <unistd.h>
```

---

* POSIX makes this requirement because some applications depend on it. It may seem obvious to the casual reader that a write() by one process followed by a read() by another should return the data written. On some networked file systems with caching, this may not be true. Those systems are not POSIX-conforming. A future version of POSIX may relax this requirement and/or provide a new function which has looser requirements for serialized operation.

Notes:

The 1990 standard has a slightly different definition for `write()`. It uses:

```
ssize_t write(int fildes, void *buf, size_t nbyte)
```

The `ssize_t` is a new POSIX type for a signed `size_t`. The `nbyte` argument was quietly changed from `unsigned int` to `size_t`.

`ssize_t` is a new system data type used by functions that return a size in bytes or an error code.

Appendices

APPENDIX A

Header Files

This appendix describes the contents of the header files found on a system that supports Standard C and POSIX. The macros, types, structures, and functions defined in each header file are listed.

Description of Tables

Both the C and POSIX standards are concerned with namespace pollution. Namespace pollution is defining symbols that are not expected by an application. Applications indicate which symbols they are expecting by defining feature-test macros. The tables in this appendix have three columns.

- The first column lists symbols defined by the C standard. These symbols are visible whenever the header file is included; no feature tests are required to make these symbols visible.

- The second column lists additional symbols that will be defined when the macro _POSIX_SOURCE is defined prior to the #include statement.

- The third column lists symbols that are optional when _POSIX_SOURCE is defined. Applications should tolerate these symbols being present but must not depend on them.*

Some headers reserve additional symbols. These symbols are indicated under *Notes:* POSIX also reserves all symbols which end with _t, as in size_t.

If you do not define _POSIX_SOURCE do not include headers which contain only POSIX symbols. A header contains only POSIX symbols if all of its symbols are in the "_POSIX_SOURCE defined" column; for example, <termios.h>.

---

* The POSIX Interpretation Committee has ruled that implementations conforming to the 1988 revision of the standard may include any POSIX symbol in any POSIX header. The 1990 revision will enforce the "may include" column.

Yes, there is a logical fourth column for symbols which are optional when _POSIX_SOURCE is not defined. There are no such symbols and I have left that column out.

`assert.h`   The `<assert.h>` header defines the `assert()` macro. This is used for debugging.

	Always Defined	When `_POSIX_SOURCE` Defined	
		Must contain:	*May contain:*
Macros:	`assert`		

Notes: Tests the macro `NDEBUG`.

ctype.h   The <ctype.h> header defines the Standard C character classification
                 functions. These may also be macros.

	Always Defined	When **_POSIX_SOURCE** Defined	
		Must contain:	*May contain:*
Functions:	isalnum() isalpha() iscntrl() isdigit() isgraph() islower() isprint() ispunct() isspace() isupper() isxdigit() tolower() toupper()		

Notes: Reserves all symbols beginning with **is** or **to**.

`dirent.h`   The `<dirent.h>` header defines the functions and data structures used for reading directories portably.

	Always Defined	When _POSIX_SOURCE Defined	
		Must contain:	*May contain:*
Types:		`DIR`	
Structures:		`dirent`	

Functions:		`closedir()`
		`opendir()`
		`readdir()`
		`rewinddir()`	

Notes: Any application that uses this header file should not declare any symbols that begin with d_.

errno.h   The <errno.h> header defines all of the error codes used by an
implementation. May contain many more macros of the form Exxxxx.

	Always Defined	When _POSIX_SOURCE Defined	
		Must contain:	*May contain:*
Macros:	EDOM	E2BIG	
	ERANGE	EACCES	
		EAGAIN	
		EBADF	
		EBUSY	
		ECHILD	
		EDEADLK	
		EDOM	
		EEXIST	
		EFAULT	
		EFBIG	
		EINTR	
		EINVAL	
		EIO	
		EISDIR	
		EMFILE	
		EMLINK	
		ENAMETOOLONG	
		ENFILE	
		ENODEV	
		ENOENT	
		ENOEXEC	
		ENOLCK	
		ENOMEM	
		ENOSPC	
		ENOSYS	
		ENOTDIR	
		ENOTEMPTY	
		ENOTTY	
		ENXIO	
		EPERM	
		EPIPE	
		ERANGE	
		EROFS	
		ESPIPE	
		ESRCH	
		EXDEV	

Notes: The external variable errno is declared as an int.

Applications should not declare any symbols that begin with an E followed
by an uppercase letter or digit.

fcntl.h   The <fcntl.h> function defines the creat(), fcntl(), and open() functions along with the macros used by those functions.

	Always Defined	When _POSIX_SOURCE Defined	
		Must contain:	*May contain:*
Macros:		FD_CLOEXEC	SEEK_CUR
		F_DUPFD	SEEK_END
		F_GETFD	SEEK_SET
		F_GETFL	S_IRGRP
		F_GETLK	S_IROTH
		F_RDLCK	S_IRUSR
		F_SETFD	S_IRWXG
		F_SETFL	S_IRWXO
		F_SETLK	S_IRWXU
		F_SETLKW	S_ISBLK
		F_UNLCK	S_ISCHR
		F_WRLCK	S_ISDIR
		O_ACCMODE	S_ISFIFO
		O_APPEND	S_ISGID
		O_CREAT	S_ISREG
		O_EXCL	S_ISUID
		O_NOCTTY	S_IWGRP
		O_NONBLOCK	S_IWOTH
		O_RDONLY	S_IWUSR
		O_RDWR	S_IXGRP
		O_TRUNC	S_IXOTH
		O_WRONLY	S_IXUSR
Structures:		flock	
Functions:		creat()	
		fcntl()	
		open()	

Notes: Applications should not declare any symbols that start with l_.

Applications must #undef all symbols that begin with F_, S_, or O_.

float.h   The `<float.h>` function defines a number of floating-point constants useful for portable applications.

	Always Defined	When _POSIX_SOURCE Defined	
		Must contain:	*May contain:*
Macros:	DBL_DIG DBL_EPSILON DBL_MANT_DIG DBL_MAX DBL_MAX_10_EXP DBL_MAX_EXP DBL_MIN DBL_MIN_10_EXP DBL_MIN_EXP FLT_DIG FLT_EPSILON FLT_MANT_DIG FLT_MAX FLT_MAX_10_EXP FLT_MAX_EXP FLT_MIN FLT_MIN_10_EXP FLT_MIN_EXP FLT_RADIX FLT_ROUNDS LDBL_DIG LDBL_EPSILON LDBL_MANT_DIG LDBL_MAX LDBL_MAX_10_EXP LDBL_MAX_EXP LDBL_MIN LDBL_MIN_10_EXP LDBL_MIN_EXP		

grp.h   The <grp.h> function defines the struc group returned by the group
         database functions getgrid() and getgrnam().

	Always Defined	When _POSIX_SOURCE Defined	
		Must contain:	*May contain:*
Structures:		group	
Functions:		getgrgid() getgrnam()	

Notes: Applications shall not declare any symbols that begin with gr_.

limits.h   The `<limits.h>` function defines implementation limits.

	Always Defined	When `_POSIX_SOURCE` Defined
		Must contain:
Macros:	CHAR_BIT	ARG_MAX[‡]
	CHAR_MIN	CHILD_MAX[†]
	CHAR_MAX	LINK_MAX[†]
	INT_MIN	MAX_CANON[†]
	INT_MAX	MAX_INPUT[†]
	LONG_MIN	NAME_MAX[†]
	LONG_MAX	NGROUPS_MAX
	MB_LEN_MAX	OPEN_MAX[†]
	SCHAR_MIN	PATH_MAX[†]
	SCHAR_MAX	PIPE_BUF[†]
	SHRT_MIN	SSIZE_MAX[*]
	SHRT_MAX	STREAM_MAX[‡*]
	UCHAR_MAX	TZNAME_MAX[*]
	UINT_MAX	_POSIX_ARG_MAX
	ULONG_MAX	_POSIX_CHILD_MAX
	USHRT_MAX	_POSIX_LINK_MAX
		_POSIX_MAX_CANON
		_POSIX_MAX_INPUT
		_POSIX_NAME_MAX
		_POSIX_NGROUPS_MAX
		_POSIX_OPEN_MAX
		_POSIX_PATH_MAX
		_POSIX_PIPE_BUF
		_POSIX_SSIZE_MAX[*]
		_POSIX_STREAM_MAX[*]
		_POSIX_TZNAME_MAX[*]

Notes: * indicates macros added to `<limits.h>` by the 1990 revision to the standard.

† indicates macros that may be omitted from `<limits.h>` on implementations where `pathconf()` must be used.

‡ indicates macros that may be omitted from `<limits.h>` on implementations where `sysconf()` must be used.

Applications should not declare any symbols that end **_MAX**.

locale.h   The <locale.h> function defines symbols used by the internationalization
functions setlocale() and localeconv().

	Always Defined	When _POSIX_SOURCE Defined	
		Must contain:	*May contain:*
Macros:	LC_ALL LC_COLLATE LC_CTYPE LC_MONETARY LC_NUMERIC LC_TIME NULL		
Structures:	lconv		
Functions:	setlocale() localeconv()		

Notes: Applications should #undef any symbols that they #define which begin
with LC_ followed by an upper-case letter.

`math.h`   The <math.h> function defines the Standard C math functions.

	Always Defined	When _POSIX_SOURCE Defined	
		Must contain:	*May contain:*
Macros:	HUGE_VAL		
Functions:	acos()		
	asin()		
	atan2()		
	atan()		
	ceil()		
	cos()		
	cosh()		
	exp()		
	fabs()		
	floor()		
	fmod()		
	frexp()		
	ldexp()		
	log10()		
	log()		
	modf()		
	pow()		
	sin()		
	sinh()		
	sqrt()		
	tan()		
	tanh()		

pwd.h
The <pwd.h> function defines `struct passwd` used by the user database reading functions `getpwnam()` and `getpwuid()`.

	Always Defined	When _POSIX_SOURCE Defined	
		Must contain:	*May contain:*
Structures:		`passwd`	
Functions:		`getpwnam()` `getpwuid()`	

Notes:
Applications should not declare any symbols that begin with pw_.

setjmp.h   The <setjmp.h> function defines the symbols used by longjmp(),
            siglongjmp(), setjmp(), and sigsetjmp().

	Always Defined	When _POSIX_SOURCE Defined	
		Must contain:	*May contain:*
Macros:	longjmp* setjmp*		sigsetjmp* siglongjmp*
Types:	jmp_buf	sigjmp_buf	
Functions:	longjmp()* setjmp()		sigsetjmp()* siglongjmp()*

Notes: * May be defined as macros or functions.

signal.h   The <signal.h> function defines both the symbols used by Standard C signals and by POSIX signals.

	Always Defined	When _POSIX_SOURCE Defined	
		Must contain:	*May contain:*
Macros:	SIG_DFL SIG_ERR SIG_IGN SIGABRT SIGFPE SIGILL SIGINT SIGSEGV SIGTERM	SA_NOCLDSTOP SIG_BLOCK SIG_SETMASK SIG_UNBLOCK SIGARLM SIGCHLD SIGCONT SIGHUP SIGKILL SIGPIPE SIGQUIT SIGSTOP SIGTSTP SIGTTIN SIGTTOU SIGUSR1 SIGUSR2	
Types:	sig_atomic_t	sigset_t	
Structures:		sigaction	
Functions:	raise() signal()	kill() sigaction() sigaddset() sigdelset() sigemptyset() sigfillset() sigismember() sigpending() sigprocmask() sigsuspend()	

Notes: Applications must not declare any symbols that begin with sa_. All symbols that begin with SIG or SA_ must be #undefed prior to use.

stdarg.h   The `<stdarg.h>` function defines macros to support functions with a variable number of arguments.

	Always Defined	When `_POSIX_SOURCE` Defined	
		Must contain:	*May contain:*

Macros:	`va_arg`
	`va_end`
	`va_list`
	`va_start`		

stddef.h   The <stddef.h> function defines a few symbols which are required by
            Standard C.

	Always Defined	When _POSIX_SOURCE Defined	
		Must contain:	*May contain:*
Macros:	NULL offsetof		
Types:	ptrdiff_t size_t wchar_t		

stdio.h   The <stdio.h> function defines the symbols used by the standard I/O package.

	Always Defined	When _POSIX_SOURCE Defined	
		Must contain:	*May contain:*
Macros:	BUFSIZ EOF FILENAME_MAX FOPEN_MAX L_tmpnam NULL SEEK_CUR SEEK_END SEEK_SET TMP_MAX stderr stdin stdout _IOFBF _IOLBF _IONBF	L_ctermid STREAM_MAX	L_cuserid
Types:	fpos_t size_t FILE		
Functions:	clearerr() fclose() feof() ferror() fflush() fgetc() fgetpos() fgets() fopen() fprintf() fputc() fputs() fread() freopen() fscanf() fseek() fsetpos() ftell() fwrite() getc()	fdopen() fileno()	

	Always Defined	When _POSIX_SOURCE Defined	
		Must contain:	*May contain:*
	getchar()		
	gets()		
	perror()		
	printf()		
	putc()		
	putchar()		
	puts()		
	remove()		
	rename()		
	rewind()		
	scanf()		
	setbuf()		
	setvbuf()		
	sprintf()		
	sscanf()		
	tmpfile()		
	tmpnam()		
	ungetc()		
	vfprintf()		
	vprintf()		
	vsprintf()		

stdlib.h   The <stdlib.h> function defines a set of miscellaneous functions from the Standard C library.

	Always Defined	When _POSIX_SOURCE Defined	
		Must contain:	*May contain:*
Macros:	EXIT_FAILURE EXIT_SUCCESS MB_CHR_MAX NULL RAND_MAX		
Types:	div_t ldiv_t size_t wchar_t		
Functions:	abort() abs() atexit() atof() atoi() atol() bsearch() calloc() div() exit() free() getenv() labs() ldiv() malloc() mblen() mbstowcs() mbtowc() qsort() rand() realloc() srand() strtod() strtol() strtoul() system() wcstombs() wctomb()		

string.h   The <string.h> function defines the Standard C string functions.

	Always Defined	When _POSIX_SOURCE Defined	
		Must contain:	*May contain:*
Macros:	NULL		
Types:	size_t		
Functions:	memchr( ) memcmp( ) memcpy( ) memmove( ) memset( ) strcat( ) strchr( ) strcmp( ) strcoll( ) strcpy( ) strcspn( ) strerror( ) strlen( ) strncat( ) strncmp( ) strncpy( ) strpbrk( ) strrchr( ) strspn( ) strstr( ) strtok( ) strxfrm( )		

Notes: Reserves symbols that begin with mem, str, or wcs.

sys/stat.h The <sys/stat.h> function defines the chmod(), fstat(), mkdir(), mkfifo(), stat(), and umask() functions and the structures and symbols used by those functions.

	Always Defined	When _POSIX_SOURCE Defined	
		Must contain:	*May contain:*
Macros:		S_IRGRP S_IROTH S_IRUSR S_IRWXG S_IRWXO S_IRWXU S_ISBLK S_ISCHR S_ISDIR S_ISFIFO S_ISGID S_ISREG S_ISUID S_IWGRP S_IWOTH S_IWUSR S_IXGRP S_IXOTH S_IXUSR	
Structures:		stat	
Functions:		chmod() fstat() mkdir() mkfifo() stat() umask()	

Notes: Applications should not declare any symbols that begin with st_.

Applications must #undef all symbols that begin with S_ prior to use.

sys/times.h The <sys/times.h> function defines the times() function for reporting process runtimes.

	Always Defined	When _POSIX_SOURCE Defined	
		Must contain:	*May contain:*
Types:	clock_t		
Structures:	tms		
Functions:	times()		.

Notes: Applications should not declare any symbols that begin with tms_.

`sys/types.h` The `<sys/types.h>` function defines all of the POSIX fundamental types.

	Always Defined	When _POSIX_SOURCE Defined	
		Must contain:	*May contain:*
Types:		dev_t gid_t ino_t mode_t nlink_t off_t pid_t size_t ssize_t* uid_t	

Notes: * `ssize_t` was added in the 1990 revision and is used for the value returned by `read( )` and `write( )`. It is a number of bytes or an error code.

sys/utsname.h   The <sys/utsname.h> function defines the uname() function and
the struct utsname it returns.

	Always Defined	When **_POSIX_SOURCE** Defined	
		Must contain:	*May contain:*
Structures:		utsname	
Functions:		uname()	

sys/wait.h The <sys/wait.h> function defines the wait() and waitpid() functions and macros to manipulate process termination status.

	Always Defined	When _POSIX_SOURCE Defined	
		Must contain:	*May contain:*
Macros:		WEXITSTATUS WIFEXITED WIFSIGNALED WIFSTOPPED WNOHANG WSTOPSIG WTERMSIG WUNTRACED	
Functions:		wait() waitpid()	

termios.h   The <termios.h> function defines the POSIX terminal interface.

	Always Defined	When _POSIX_SOURCE Defined	
		Must contain:	*May contain:*
Macros:		B0	
		B50	
		B75	
		B110	
		B134	
		B150	
		B200	
		B300	
		B600	
		B1200	
		B1800	
		B2400	
		B4800	
		B9600	
		B19200	
		B38400	
		BRKINT	
		CLOCAL	
		CREAD	
		CS5	
		CS6	
		CS7	
		CS8	
		CSIZE	
		CSTOPB	
		ECHO	
		ECHOE	
		ECHOK	
		ECHONL	
		HUPCL	
		ICANON	
		ICRNL	
		IEXTEN	
		IGNBRK	
		IGNCR	
		IGNPAR	
		IGNLCR	
		INPCK	
		ISIG	
		ISTRIP	
		IXOFF	
		IXON	
		NCCS	
		NOFLSH	

	Always Defined	When _POSIX_SOURCE Defined	
		Must contain:	*May contain:*
		OPOST PARENB PARMRK PARODD TCIFLUSH TCIOFF TCIOFLUSH TCION TCOFLUSH TCOOFF TCOON TCSADRAIN TCSAFLUSH TCSANOW TOSTOP VEOF VEOL VERASE VINTR VKILL VMIN VQUIT VSTART VSTOP VSUSP VTIME	
Types:		cc_t speed_t tcflag_t	
Structures:		termios	
Functions:		cfgetispeed() cfgetospeed() cfsetispeed() cfsetospeed() tcdrain() tcflow() tcflush() tcgetattr() tcsendbreak() tcsetattr()	

Notes: Applications should not declare any symbols that begin with c_.

Applications must #undef all symbols that they #define which begin with V, I, O, TC, or B[0-9] prior to use.

time.h   The <time.h> function defines the Standard C and POSIX time functions.

	Always Defined	When _POSIX_SOURCE Defined	
		Must contain:	*May contain:*
Macros:	CLOCKS_PER_SEC NULL	CLK_TCK	
Types:	clock_t size_t time_t		
Structures:	tm		
Functions:	asctime() clock() ctime() difftime() gmttime() localtime() mktime() strftime() time()	tzset()	

Notes: This header also declares the external variable tzname.

Applications shall not declare any symbols that begin with tm_.

unistd.h   The <unistd.h> function defines miscellaneous POSIX macros and
            functions.

	Always Defined	When _POSIX_SOURCE Defined
		Must contain:
Macros:		F_OK
		R_OK
		SEEK_CUR
		SEEK_END
		SEEK_SET
		STDERR_FILENO
		STDIN_FILENO
		STDOUT_FILENO
		W_OK
		X_OK
		_PC_CHOWN_RESTRICTED
		_PC_MAX_CANNON
		_PC_MAX_INPUT
		_PC_NAME_MAX
		_PC_NO_TRUNC
		_PC_PATH_MAX
		_PC_PIPE_BUF
		_PC_VDISABLE
		_POSIX_CHOWN_RESTRICTED
		_POSIX_JOB_CONTROL
		_POSIX_NO_TRUNC
		_POSIX_SAVED_IDS
		_POSIX_VDISABLE
		_POSIX_VERSION
		_SC_ARG_MAX
		_SC_CHILD_MAX
		_SC_CLK_TCK
		_SC_JOB_CONTROL
		_SC_NGROUPS_MAX
		_SC_OPEN_MAX
		_SC_SAVED_IDS
		_SC_STREAM_MAX
		_SC_TZNAME_MAX
		_SC_VERSION
Types:	size_t	
	ssize_t	
Functions:		_exit()
		access()
		alarm()
		chdir()

Always Defined	When _POSIX_SOURCE Defined
	Must contain:
	dup2()
	dup()
	execl()
	execle()
	execlp()
	execv()
	execve()
	execvp()
	fork()
	fpathconf()
	getcwd()
	getegid()
	geteuid()
	getgid()
	getgroups()
	getlogin()
	getpgrp()
	getpid()
	getppid()
	getuid()
	isatty()
	link()
	lseek()
	pathconf()
	pause()
	pipe()
	read()
	rmdir()
	setgid()
	setpgid()
	setsid()
	setuid()
	sleep()
	sysconf()
	tcgetpgrp()
	tcsetpgrp()
	ttyname()
	unlink()
	write()
	cuserid()

utime.h   The <utime.h> function defines the function to set file access times and the structure it uses.

	Always Defined	When _POSIX_SOURCE Defined	
		Must contain:	May contain:
Structures:		utimbuf	
Functions:		utime()	

APPENDIX B

Data Structures

This section contains a list of all of the data structures defined by POSIX or by Standard C. You must remember the following:

1. The members of these structures may be in any order. Your programs should not assume that they are in the order given here.

2. The structures may contain additional members. Your programs should ignore these members.

3. These structures are defined in the standard header listed. You must include this header to declare the structure. Do not declare the structure yourself.

4. You may use these names for your own structures in files that do not include the standard header. For example, you can have your own structure called `stat` in a file that does not include `<stat.h>`. You should avoid this practice.

`dirent`	Defines the directory information returned by the `readdir()` function.
See:	Chapter 4, *Files and Directories* [Also examples in Chapters 2 and 7].
Header File:	`<dirent.h>`

Member Name	Member Type	Description
`d_name`	`char[]`	Null terminated filename.

`div_t`	Defines the result of the `div()` function from the Standard C library.
See:	Description of `div()` in functions section and example in Chapter 2.
Header File:	`<stdlib.h>`

Member Name	Member Type	Description
`quot`	`int`	Quotient.
`rem`	`int`	Remainder.

`flock`	Controls the advisory record locking operations of the `fcntl()` function.
See:	Chapter 5, *Advanced File Operations.*
Header File:	`<fcntl.h>`

Member Name	Member Type	Description
`l_type`	`short`	One of the macros F_RDLCK, F_WRRLCK or F_UNLCK.
`l_whence`	`short`	Flag for starting offset. One of the macros SEEK_CUR, SEEK_END, or SEEK_SET.
`l_start`	`off_t`	Relative offset in bytes.
`l_len`	`off_t`	Size (zero means to EOF).
`l_pid`	`pid_t`	Process ID of the process holding the lock.

`group`	Defines the information returned by functions that read the group's database.
See:	Chapter 7, *Obtaining Information at Run–time.*
Header File:	`<grp.h>`

Member Name	Member Type	Description
`gr_name`	`char *`	The name of the group.
`gr_gid`	`gid_t`	The group number.
`gr_mem`	`char **`	A null-terminated vector of pointers to the member names.

lconv	Defines the internationalization information returned by the `localeconv()` function.
See:	Chapter 10, *Porting to Far-off Lands*.
Header File:	`<locale.h>`

Member Name	Member Type	Description
decimal_point	char *	The decimal-point character for nonmonetary quantities.
thousands_sep	char *	The character used to separate groups of digits.
grouping	char *	A string whose elements indicate the size of each group.
int_curr_symbol	char *	The international currency symbol.
currency_symbol	char *	The local currency symbol.
mon_decimal_point	char *	The decimal-point character for monetary quantities.
mon_thousands_sep	char *	The character used to separate groups of digits in monetary quantities.
mon_grouping	char *	A string whose elements indicate the size of each group.
positive_sign	char *	The string for non-negative monetary quantities.
negative_sign	char *	The string for negative monetary quantities.
int_frac_digits	char	Number of digits after the decimal point in international monetary quantities.
frac_digits	char	Number of digits after the decimal point in monetary quantities.
p_cs_precedes	char	1 if the currency symbol comes first in non-negative monetary quantities.
p_sep_by_space	char	1 if the currency symbol has a space between the symbol and the number in non-negative monetary quantities.
n_cs_precedes	char	1 if the currency symbol comes first in negative monetary quantities.
n_sep_by_space	char	1 if the currency symbol has a space between the symbol and the number in negative monetary quantities.
p_sign_posn	char	Position of positive_sign.
n_sign_posn	char	Position of negative_sign.

ldiv_t   Defines the information returned by the ldiv() function.

See: Description of ldiv() in the Functions section.

Header File: <stdlib.h>

Member Name	Member Type	Description
quot	long	Quotient.
rem	long	Remainder.

passwd   Defines the information returned by the functions that read the user database.

See: Chapter 7, *Obtaining Information at Run–time.*

Header File: <pwd.h>

Member Name	Member Type	Description
pw_name	char *	User name.
pw_uid	uid_t	User ID number.
pw_gid	gid_t	Group ID number.
pw_dir	char *	Initial working directory.
pw_shell	char *	Initial user program.

sigaction		Defines the information given to and returned by the sigaction() function.
See:		Chapter 6, *Working with Processes.*
Header File:		<signal.h>

Member Name	Member Type	Description
sa_handler	void(*)()	A pointer to a signal-catching function or the symbolic constant SIG_DFL or SIG_IGN.
sa_mask	sigset_t	Additional set of signals to be blocked during the execution of the signal-catching function.
sa_flags	int	Special flags.
		The only flag currently defined is SA_NOCLDSTOP. This flag prevents a SIGCHLD signal from being generated when children stop.

stat		Defines the file status information returned by the stat() and fstat() functions.
See:		Chapter 4, *Files and Directories* [also used in examples in Chapters 2, 5, 6, 8, and 9].
Header File:		<sys/stat.h>

Member Name	Member Type	Description
st_mode	mode_t	File mode.
st_ino	ino_t	File serial number.
st_dev	dev_t	ID of the device containing this file.
st_nlink	nlink_t	Number of links.
st_uid	uid_t	User ID of the file's owner.
st_gid	gid_t	Group ID of the file's owner.
st_size	off_t	The file size in bytes (may not be valid for special files).
st_atime	time_t	Time of last access.
st_mtime	time_t	Time of last data modification.
st_ctime	time_t	Time of last file status change.

`termios`	Defines the information used to control terminals. This is returned by `tcgetattr()` and used as an argument to `tcsetattr()`.
See:	Chapter 8, *Terminal I/O.*
Header File:	`<termios.h>`

Member Name	Member Type	Description
`c_iflag`	`tcflag_t`	Input modes.
`c_oflag`	`tcflag_t`	Output modes.
`c_cflag`	`tcflag_t`	Control flags.
`c_lflag`	`tcflag_t`	Local modes.
`c_cc`	`cc_t`	An array of NCCS elements which define various control characters.

`tm`	Defines the various components of the time information returned by `localtime()` and `gmttime()`. This is the argument to the `mktime()` function.
See:	Chapter 7, *Obtaining Information at Run–time.*
Header File:	`<time.h>`

Member Name	Member Type	Description
`tm_sec`	`int`	Seconds after the minute.
`tm_min`	`int`	Minutes after the hour.
`tm_hour`	`int`	Hours since midnight.
`tm_mday`	`int`	Day of month.
`tm_mon`	`int`	Month.
`tm_wday`	`int`	Day of week
`tm_year`	`int`	Years since 1900.
`tm_yday`	`int`	Days since January 1.
`tm_isdst`	`int`	Positive: Daylight savings. Zero: Standard time. Negative: Unknown.

`tms`   Defines the information returned by the `times()` function.

See: Chapter 7, *Obtaining Information at Run–time.*

Header File: `<sys/times.h>`

Member Name	Member Type	Description
`tms_utime`	`clock_t`	User CPU time.
`tms_stime`	`clock_t`	System CPU time.
`tms_cutime`	`clock_t`	User time of terminated child processes.
`tms_cstime`	`clock_t`	System time of terminated child processes.

`utimbuf`   Defines the argument to the `utime()` function.

See: Chapter 4, *Files and Directories* [Also example in Chapter 2].

Header File: `<utime.h>`

Member Name	Member Type	Description
`actime`	`time_t`	Access time.
`modtime`	`time_t`	Modification time.

`utsname`   Defines the system identification information returned by the `uname()` function.

See: Chapter 7, *Obtaining Information at Run–time.*

Header File: `<sys/utsname.h>`

Member Name	Member Type	Description
`sysname`	`char[]`	Name of operating system.
`nodename`	`char[]`	Name of this node.
`release`	`char[]`	Current release level.
`version`	`char[]`	Current version of this release.
`machine`	`char[]`	Name of the hardware that the system is running on.

APPENDIX C

Error Codes

This appendix lists, in alphabetical order, the defined error codes and the functions that must produce them. All functions may return error codes in addition to the ones presented here, and these error codes may be returned for reasons other than the ones listed here. This list is useful for portable applications. Debugging should be done with the documentation for the system that is being used for the debug process.

E2BIG   The number of bytes used by the new process image's argument list and environment list is greater than the system limit of ARG_MAX bytes.

Used by: execl(), execle(), execlp(), execv(), execve(), execvp()

EACCES   Search permission is denied for a directory in a file's path prefix.

Used by: access(), chdir(), chmod(), chown(), execl(), execle(), execv(), execve(), execvp(), fcntl(), getcwd(), link(), mkdir(), mkfifo(), open(), opendir(), pathconf(), rename(), rmdir(), setpgid(), stat(), unlink(), utime()

EAGAIN   The O_NONBLOCK flag is set for a file descriptor and the process would be delayed in the I/O operation.

The fork() function returns EAGAIN if the system lacks the resources to create another process.

Used by: fcntl(), fork(), read(), write()

EBADF   Invalid file descriptor.

Used by: close(), closedir(), dup(), dup2(), fcntl(), lseek(), pathconf(), read(), readdir(), stat(), tcdrain(), tcflow(), tcflush(), tcgetpgrp(), tcsendbreak(), tcsetattr(), tcsetpgrp(), write()

EBUSY   The directory is in use.

Used by: rename(), rmdir(), unlink()

ECHILD There are no children or a process or process group number does not specify a child of this process.

    Used by: `wait( )`, `waitpid( )`

EDEADLK An `fcntl` with function `F_SETLKW` would cause a deadlock.

    Used by: `fcntl( )`

EDOM An input argument was outside the defined domain of a mathematical function.

    Used by: `acos( )`, `asin( )`, `atan2( )`, `atan( )`, `ceil( )`, `cos( )`, `cosh( )`, `exp( )`, `fabs( )`, `floor( )`, `fmod( )`, `frexp( )`, `ldexp( )`, `log10( )`, `log( )`, `modf( )`, `pow( )`, `sin( )`, `sinh( )`, `sqrt( )`, `tan( )`, `tanh( )`

EEXIST The named file already exists.

The `rmdir( )` function may return **EEXIST** on an attempt to delete a non-empty directory. It may also return **ENOTEMPTY**.

    Used by: `link( )`, `mkdir( )`, `mkfifo( )`, `open( )`, `rename( )`, `rmdir( )`

EFAULT The system detected an invalid address in attempting to use an argument of a function call.

    Used by: No functions are required to detect this condition.

EFBIG An attempt was made to write to a file that exceeds the maximum file size.

    Used by: `write( )`

EINTR Function was interrupted by a signal.

    Used by: `close( )`, `dup( )`, `dup2( )`, `fcntl( )`, `open( )`, `pause( )`, `read( )`, `sigsuspend( )`, `tcdrain( )`, `tcflow( )`, `tcflush( )`, `tcsetattr( )`, `wait( )`, `waitpid( )`, `write( )`

EINVAL Invalid argument.

    Used by: `access( )`, `chown( )`, `fcntl( )`, `fpathconf( )`, `getcwd( )`, `getgroups( )`, `kill( )`, `lseek( )`, `pathconf( )`, `rename( )`, `setgid( )`, `setpgid( )`, `setuid( )`, `sigaction( )`, `sigaddset( )`, `sigdelset( )`, `sigismember( )`, `sysconf( )`, `tcsetattr( )`, `tcsetpgrp( )`, `waitpid( )`

EIO	Input or output error.
Used by:	`read()`, `write()`

EISDIR	Attempt to open a directory for writing or to rename a file to be a directory.
Used by:	`open()`, `rename()`

EMFILE	Too many file descriptors are in use by this process.
Used by:	`fcntl()`, `open()`, `opendir()`

EMLINK	The number of links would exceed `LINK_MAX`.
Used by:	`link()`, `mkdir()`, `rename()`

ENAMETOOLONG

Length of a filename string exceeds `PATH_MAX` and `_POSIX_NO_TRUNC` is in effect.

Used by: `access()`, `chdir()`, `chmod()`, `chown()`, `execl()`, `execle()`, `execlp()`, `execv()`, `execve()`, `execvp()`, `link()`, `mkdir()`, `mkfifo()`, `open()`, `opendir()`, `pathconf()`, `rename()`, `rmdir()`, `stat()`, `unlink()`, `utime()`

ENFILE	Too many files are currently open in the system.
Used by:	`creat()`, `open()`, `opendir()`

ENODEV No such device.

Attempt to perform an inappropriate function to a device; for example, reading from a line-printer.

Used by: No functions are required to detect this error.

ENOENT A file or directory does not exist.

Used by: `chdir()`, `chmod()`, `chown()`, `execl()`, `execle()`, `execlp()`, `execv()`, `execve()`, `execvp()`, `link()`, `mkdir()`, `mkfifo()`, `open()`, `opendir()`, `pathconf()`, `rename()`, `rmdir()`, `stat()`, `unlink()`, `utime()`

ENOEXEC   An attempt was made to execute a file that is not in the correct format.

Used by: `execl( ), execle( ), execv( ), execve( )`

ENOLCK   No locks available.

Used by: `fcntl( )`

ENOMEM   No memory available.

Used by: `execl( ), execle( ), execlp( ), execv( ), execve( ), execvp( ),`
`fork( )`

ENOSPC   No space left on disk.

Used by: `link( ), mkdir( ), mkfifo( ), open( ), rename( ), write( )`

ENOSYS   Function not implemented.

Used by: `setpgid( ), tcgetpgrp( ), tcsetpgrp( )`

ENOTDIR   A component of the specified pathname was not a directory when a
directory was expected.

Used by: `access( ), chdir( ), chmod( ), chown( ), execl( ), execle( ),`
`execlp( ), execv( ), execve( ), execvp( ), link( ), mkdir( ),`
`mkfifo( ), open( ), opendir( ), pathconf( ), rename( ), rmdir( ),`
`stat( ), unlink( ), utime( )`

ENOTEMPTY   Attempt to delete or rename a non-empty directory. NOTE: dot (`.`) and
dot-dot (`..`) may be present in an empty directory; no other files are
allowed.

Used by: `rename( ), rmdir( )`

ENOTTY   Terminal control function attempted for a file that is not a terminal.

Used by: `tcdrain( ), tcflow( ), tcflush( ), tcgetattr( ), tcgetpgrp( ),`
`tcsendbreak( ), tcsetattr( ), tcsetpgrp( )`

ENXIO   No such device. This error may also occur when a device is not ready, for
example, a tape drive is off-line.

Used by: `open( )`

EPERM	Operation is not permitted. Process does not have the appropriate privileges or permissions to perform the requested operation.
Used by:	chmod( ), chown( ), kill( ), link( ), setgid( ), setpgid( ), setsid( ), setuid( ), tcsetpgrp( ), unlink( ), utime( )

EPIPE	Attempt to write to a pipe or FIFO with no reader.
Used by:	write( )

ERANGE	Result is too large.
Used by:	getcwd( )
	acos( ), asin( ), atan2( ), atan( ), ceil( ), cos( ), cosh( ), exp( ), fabs( ), floor( ), fmod( ), frexp( ), ldexp( ), log10( ), log( ), modf( ), pow( ), sin( ), sinh( ), sqrt( ), tan( ), tanh( )

EROFS	Read-only file system.
Used by:	access( ), chmod( ), chown( ), link( ), mkdir( ), mkfifo( ), open( ), rename( ), rmdir( ), unlink( ), utime( )

ESPIPE	An lseek( ) was issued on a pipe or FIFO.
Used by:	lseek( )

ESRCH	No such process.
Used by:	kill( ), setpgid( )

EXDEV	Attempt to link a file to another file system.
Used by:	link( ), rename( )

APPENDIX D

Porting from BSD and System V

You may want to convert programs to POSIX which were written for Berkeley Software Distribution (BSD) or AT&T UNIX System V. Chapter 2, Developing POSIX Applications, contains a discussion of the porting process, along with an example. The Functions section of the Reference Manual lists the differences between historic implementations and the POSIX and C standards. What about functions that are not in Standard C or POSIX? There are several alternatives:

1. The function can be replaced by one or more functions from the standard libraries; the replacements are listed in this appendix. For example, the BSD hypot(x,y) function can be written as:

    ```
    sqrt(x*x + y*y);
    ```

2. The function can be coded using ordinary C. For example, the BSD isascii() function can be written as:

    ```
    int isascii(int c)
    {
    if ((c < 0200) || (c == EOF)) return(1);
    if (c >= 0) return(1);
    return(0);
    }
    ```

    In the following pages, these functions are labeled "Ordinary C."

3. The function can be deleted completely, for example, nice() or endpwent() in the following pages, these are labeled "Not Needed."

4. For many calls, there is no equivalent. These are administrative functions, such as, mount() or sync(); functions which are not portable, such as swab() or valloc(); or functions which have no POSIX equivalent, such as symlink() or readv(). I have not listed these functions; therefore, if you don't see a function in the following pages, you can assume that there is no replacement.

In most cases, the replacement is not exact. Read the description of the replacement function and decide if the changes are important to your application.

BSD Functions

Function	Replace with:
alloca()	malloc() and free()
bcmp()	memcmp()
bcopy()	memcpy()
bzero()	memset()
cabs()	sqrt(x*x + y*y)
ecvt()	sprintf()
endgrent()	Not Needed
endpwent()	Not Needed
fcvt()	sprintf()
ffs()	Ordinary C
flock()	fcntl()
gamma()	Ordinary C
gcvt()	sprintf()
getdtablesize()	sysconf(_SC_OPEN_MAX)
getpass()	Ordinary C
getpw()	getpwent()
gettimeofday()	localtime() and time()
getwd()	getcwd()
hypot()	sqrt()
index()	strchr()
initstate()	srand()
insque()	Ordinary C
ioctl()	tcsetattr(), tcgetattr(), cfgetispeed(), cfgetospeed(), cfsetispeed(), cfsetospeed()
isascii()	Ordinary C
j0()	Ordinary C
j1()	Ordinary C
jn()	Ordinary C
killpg()	kill() with a negative process group number
mknod()	mkdir() or mkfifo()
nice()	Not Needed
pclose()	close()
popen()	pipe(), fdopen(), fork(), system(), wait()
random()	rand()

Function	Replace with:
remque()	Ordinary C
rindex()	strrchr()
scandir()	readdir(), malloc(), qsort()
seekdir()	opendir() followed by n calls to readdir()
setbuffer()	setvbuf()
setgrent()	Not Needed
setitimer()	alarm()
setlinebuf()	setvbuf()
setpwent()	Not Needed
setregid()	setgid() and setegid()
setreuid()	setuid() and seteuid()
setstate()	srand()
sigblock()	sigprocmask()
sigpause()	sigsuspend()
sigsetmask()	sigprocmask()
sigvec()	sigpending()
srandom()	srand()
timezone()	localtime()
utimes()	utime()
utimes()	utime()
valloc()	malloc()
vfork()	fork()
vhangup()	tcsetattr()
wait3()	waitpid()
y0()	Ordinary C
y1()	Ordinary C
yn()	Ordinary C

System V Functions

Function	Replace with:
drand48()	rand()
erand48()	rand()
erfc()	Ordinary C
erf()	Ordinary C
ftw()	opendir(), readdir(), closedir()
gamma()	Ordinary C
getopt()	Ordinary C
getw()	fread() or multiple calls to getc()
hcreate()	Ordinary C
hdestroy()	Ordinary C
hsearch()	Ordinary C
hypot()	sqrt(x*x + y*y)
ioctl()	tcsetattr(), tcgetattr(), cfgetispeed(), cfgetospeed(), cfsetispeed(), cfsetospeed()
isascii()	Ordinary C
j0()	Ordinary C
j1()	Ordinary C
jn()	Ordinary C
jrand48()	rand()
lfind()	Ordinary C
lockf()	fcntl()
lrand48()	rand()
lsearch()	Ordinary C
mknod()	mkdir() or mkfifo()
popen()	pipe(), fdopen(), fork(), system(), wait()
remque()	Ordinary C
srand48()	srand()
tdelete()	Ordinary C
tfind()	Ordinary C
tsearch()	Ordinary C
twalk()	Ordinary C
y0()	Ordinary C
y1()	Ordinary C
yn()	Ordinary C

APPENDIX E

Changes and Additions in Standard C

Standard C contains a number of changes from the traditional C compiler used on many systems. Since there was no prior standard, and many compiler vendors wanted to adopt these extensions, these changes might already exist in a compiler even if it does not completely meet the standard.

Preprocessor

The following features were added to the preprocessor:

- ## added for concatenation of tokens.
- # added for creation of strings.
- #pragma added. Any use of #pragma is non-portable.
- #elif added.
- Parameters inside strings are not replaced.
- Splicing lines with \ is allowed everywhere.

Character Set

The following features were added to the character set:

- Trigraphs added. This may break old programs which have a string containing ??.
- wchar_t added for wide-character strings.
- char may be signed or unsigned with the use of the corresponding keyword.

Identifiers

- Minimum significance of internal identifiers increased to 31 characters.
- All names which begin with an underscore (_) followed by another underscore or a capital letter are reserved by the system.
- Including a system header may cause some names to be reserved.

Keywords

The following keywords were added:

- `void`
- `const`
- `volatile`
- `signed`
- `enum`

Operators

- The assignment operators −=, +=, and so on are treated as single tokens. No whitespace is allowed between the characters.
- Unary + added.
- `sizeof` yields `size_t` instead of `unsigned int`.
- The & operator may always be applied to arrays.
- The & operator may never be used with an object declared as a `register`.

Strings

- List of \x escapes expanded and better defined.
- Adjacent string literals are concatenated.
- String constants may be placed in read-only memory.

Constants

- U and L added as integer suffixes
- F and L added for floating constants.
- L may be used to specify a wide-character constant or a string of wide-characters. For example, L'å' or L"300¥".

Structures, Unions, and Arrays

- Unions may be initialized.
- Automatic structures and unions may be initialized.
- Character arrays with an explicit size may be initialized with exactly that many characters.

switch Statements

The controlling expression, and the case labels, of a `switch` may have any integral type.

Headers

- `<limits.h>` added.

- `<float.h>` added.

- `<stddef.h>` added.

- `<stdlib.h>` added.

- `<stdarg.h>` added.

- `<locale.h>` and the functions it defines were added.

- No header specified by the C Standard may require that any other header be included. That is, the headers are *self-sufficient.*

- Any header specified by the C Standard may be included multiple times without causing problems. That is, the headers are *idempotent.*

Pointers

- `void *` added as the generic pointer type.

- A pointer to a function may be used without an explicit `*`.

- Pointers may point just beyond the end of an array.

Functions

- Structures may be passed to functions and returned by functions.

- Function prototypes and type checking added.

Arithmetic

- The usual arithmetic conversions were changed to use the smallest type which can hold the result.

- Shifting by a `long` count does not coerce the shifted operand to `long`.

APPENDIX F

Federal Information Processing Standard 151-1

The U.S. Government has adopted IEEE Standard 1003.1-1988 (POSIX.1) as a Federal Information Processing Standard for use in computer systems procurement. Notice of the adoption was published in the Federal Register, Volume 54, Number 70, Thursday, April 13, 1989. The text of the notice follows:

The IEEE P1003.1 Standard defines a C language source code level interface to an operating system environment. IEEE Standard P1003.1-1988 refers to and is a complement to draft ANSI standard X3J11/88-102 C Language which is under development by the Accredited Standards Committee X3. The IEEE P1003.1 requires specific areas of the ANSI X3J11/88-102 C Language to complete the environment specification for portable application software.

The following modifications to IEEE Standard 1003.1-1988 for Portable Operating System Interface for Computer Environments are required for implementations for POSIX that are acquired by Federal agencies:

- Inconsistencies with `CLK_TCK` exist between the IEEE Standard 1003.1-1988 and the referenced ANSI/X3.159-198x Programming language C Standard draft 13 May 1988 (X3J11/88-102). This inconsistency shall be resolved in the ratified C Standard. Until the C Standard is ratified, `CLK_TCK` is to be treated as a POSIX-only symbol.

- The implementation shall support the POSIX option `_POSIX_CHOWN_RESTRICTED`.

- The implementation shall support the option `NGROUPS_MAX` greater than or equal to eight (8), thus providing multiple groups.

- The implementation shall support the setting of the group-ID of a file (when it is created) to that of its parent directory.

- The implementation shall support the functionality associated with the feature `_POSIX_SAVED_IDS`.

- The implementation shall support the functionality associated with the feature `_POSIX_VDISABLE`.

- The implementation shall support the option `_POSIX_JOB_CONTROL`.

- The implementation shall support the functionality associated with the feature `_POSIX_NO_TRUNC`.

- In section 6.4.1.2, the sentence "If a `read()` is interrupted by a signal after it has successfully written some data, either it shall return -1 with `errno` set to EINTR, or it shall return the number of bytes read" shall be deleted and replaced by the sentence, "If a `read()` is interrupted by a signal after it has successfully read some data, it shall return the number of bytes read."

  In section 6.4.2.2, the sentence "If a `write()` is interrupted by a signal after it has successfully read some data, either it shall return -1 with `errno` set to EINTR, or it shall return the number of bytes written" shall be deleted and replaced by the sentence, "If a `write()` is interrupted by a signal after it has successfully read some data, it shall return the number of bytes written."

- The environment for the login shell shall contain the environment variables HOME and LOGNAME as defined in Section 2.7.

This standard is effective October 13, 1989. This standard is compulsory and binding for use in all solicitations and contracts for new operating systems where POSIX-like interfaces are required.

APPENDIX G

Answers to Selected Exercises

Chapter 3

1. The program will print:

```
0000017
       17
17
```

2. Use the `%hd` format specifier when printing a `short`. Use the `%ld` format specifier when printing a `long`. The use of `%d` can cause portability problems when you print a variable with an implementation defined type, for example, `pid_t`.

4. The `putc()` function is equivalent to `fputc()`, except `putc()` may be a macro which may evaluate `stream` more than once. The call `puts(s)` is not exactly equivalent to `fputs(s,stdout)` because `puts()` adds a new line and `fputs()` does not.

5. On some systems, it matches all uppercase letters. It is not part of Standard C and does not work on systems that do not use ASCII.

6. The input string can be larger than the allocated storage. If the input string is too long, it will overwrite other variables and cause the program to fail.

7. `gets()` may be a macro.

8. The input string can be larger than the allocated storage. If the input string is too long, it will overwrite other variables and cause the program to fail. However, if you can depend on the length of the input strings, `gets()` can safely be used.

9. On POSIX systems there is no difference. On some operating systems, the `"wb"` indicates that the file is binary and no character processing is done.

10. It allows you to check for errors.

11. It writes 100 two-byte `shorts` from `array` to `outfile`.

12. `fwrite(array,sizeof(short),100,outfile);`

13. The `fsetpos()` function works for files longer than `LONG_MAX` bytes. It can also be faster.

14. The first case tells the person (or program) reading the source that the return value from `printf()` is being explicitly ignored. There should be no difference in the operation of the resulting program.

Chapter 4

2. See 3.

3. This program creates the directories for Exercise 2 and then deletes them:

```c
#define _POSIX_SOURCE 1

#include <stdio.h>
#include <stdlib.h>
#include <unistd.h>
#include <sys/stat.h>
#include <sys/types.h>

/*
 * Make as may directories as possible
 */
void make_directories(void)
{
long    ndirs=0;
char    *cwd;

/* First select a safe place to start */
if (chdir("/tmp") != 0)
{
    perror("chdir /tmp failed");
    return;
}
while (1)          /* Loop forever */
{
    if (mkdir("dir",0777) == -1)
        break;    /* Could not create directory */
    ndirs++;      /* Count it as made */
    if (chdir("dir") != 0) /* Make new directory
                            * the working directory
                            */
        break;                 /* Could not do it */
}
fprintf(stderr,"\nCreated %d directories\n",ndirs);
perror("Error was: ");
return;
}

/*
 * Delete the mess we made
 */

void zapem(void)
{
/* Start back at the top */
if (chdir("/tmp") != 0)
{
    perror("chdir to /tmp failed");
    return;
}
/* Loop down to the bottom */
while (chdir("dir") == 0) ;

/* Loop going  up one level and delete this directory */
while (chdir("..") == 0)
    if (rmdir("dir") != 0) return;
```

```
        return;
}


int     main()
{
        make_directories();
        zapem();
        return(EXIT_SUCCESS);
}
```

4. A program may need to know if two links point to the same file.

5. Applications may need to refer to the same file by different names.

6. The `unlink()` function deletes a file when the last user has closed it. There is no portable way to tell when this happens.

7. See page 70.

8. It is the execute permission bit for the file's owner.

9. Macros are more portable than values.

10. No.

11. It might be possible to make the system think that files were created by someone else. On systems that have disk quotas, you can give away files to avoid having them charged to your disk quota. It also might be possible to cover your tracks when replacing a system file with a Trojan Horse.

    The only completely portable use for `chown()` is to change the group of a file to the effective group ID of the caller or to a member of its group set.

12. Some programs, for example `cpio`, need to set the file's access and modification times to restore the file to a previous state.

14. The `dirent` structure may (or may not) contain members other than d_name. There is no portable way to access them, however, you can look in `dirent.h` to see if there are any extra members on your system.

15. Add the declaration:

    ```
    long long_ino;  /* Temp to make ino_t a long */
    ```

    The modified section should look like this:

    ```
    /*
     * Print out the name of the current directory with
     * leading spaces.
     */
    for (i=1; i <= indent; i++) (void)printf(" ");
    (void)printf("%s",name);

    /* Now open the directory for reading */
    current_directory = opendir(name);
    if (current_directory == NULL)
    ```

```
        {
        (void)perror("Can not open directory");
        return;
        }
    if (stat(name,&status) != 0) PANIC; /* Get file serial number */
    long_ino = (long)status.st_ino;      /* Convert to known size  */
    (void)printf(" %ld\n",long_ino);     /* Print it */
```

16. If the files "." and ".." were not ignored, the function would loop forever.

Chapter 5

1. Your function would, most likely, be slower than the library function. Most system vendors have spent a great deal of time tuning the library functions for performance.

2. If the O_EXCL flag is not set, O_CREAT has no effect in this case. If O_EXCL is set, the open( ) will fail.

3. If the system uses virtual memory, reading the entire file with one call to read can cause excessive paging. The system will read and write each page several times to complete the copying operation.

4. The first case preserves any implementation defined flag bits.

5. The fast file copy program would copy the file and ignore any record locks. Record locks only work if all applications that access the file use them.

6. Use fseek( ) if you have a stream pointer. Use lseek( ) if you have a file descriptor.

7. You would use umask( ) before execing a program which creates files. If you don't control the source of the program you are execing, the umask( ) function is the only way you can modify the effect of open( ).

8. You would use the fileno( ) function if you need to perform a function which takes a file descriptor as an argument, for example, record locking. You would use the fdopen( ) function if you had a file descriptor and wanted a stream. The most common case occurs after calling pipe( ).

9. The data might not be written to the file in the correct order. The proper use of the fflush( ) function will eliminate the problem.

Chapter 6

1. The new process starts at the return from the fork( ) call. The fork( ) call returns a zero to the new process and non-zero (PID of new process) to the old process.

2. It never returns on success.

3. If you did not include the call to `fclose()`, the more program would never see end-of-file and would hang waiting for more input. If you did not include the call to `wait()`, the parent could exit before all of the output is displayed.

4. The `waitpid()` function allows you to specify the PID you want to wait for. If you are writing a general-purpose function which does a `fork()` and a `wait()`, it is possible that the `wait()` will collect status for one of your caller's children instead of the process you created. The `waitpid()` function solves this problem.

5. Before performing the actions of `_exit()`, the `exit()` function calls all of the functions registered by `atexit()`, flushes and closes all open streams, and deletes all files created by `tmpfile()`. You should use `_exit()` only in case of catastrophic error.

6. A signal mask is a set of signals to be blocked. It starts out as the empty set.

7. The `SIGSEGV` handler can print an error message and exit. It might also attempt to restart the program.

8. The program will be terminated when the alarm goes off.

9. No. The `printf()` function is not on the list of safe functions given on page 113.

10. The POSIX signals have several advantages over the Standard C signals: you can save and restore the full signal state, you can block other signals from being delivered, and you can pass additional flags to the system.

11. The required code is:

```
sigset_t set,oset;

    . . .

sigfillset(&set);                       /* All possible signals */
sigaddset(&set,SIGINT);                 /* Remove SIGINT */
sigaddset(&set,SIGHUP);                 /* and SIGHUP */
sigprocmask(SIG_SETMASK,&set,&oset);    /* Set the process mask */
```

12. The additional code is:

```
sigpending(&set);                       /* Get the set of pending
                                         * signals. */
if (sigismember(&set,SIGALRM) == 1)     /* See if SIGALRM is one */
    {
    /* Executed if SIGALRM is pending */
    }
```

13. The use of `sigsuspend()` avoids a possible race condition. See Figure 6-1.

Chapter 7

1. The get login() function returns the name that the user used to login to the system. The getpwuid() function returns the name associated with a given user ID. There may be several login names associated with a single user ID. The functions return different information; one is not better than the other.

2. The real user ID is the one associated with the name that the user used to login to the system. The effective user ID is the owner ID of a SETUID program that the user is running. If the S_ISUID mode bit is not set for the program file of the current program, then the effective user ID and the real user ID have the same value.

3. There is no return value to indicate an error.

4. POSIX does not require there to be a /etc/passwd file. Even if there is an /etc/passwd file, it may not be readable by your process.

5. Use the value returned by getgroups() when you want to know the actual number of groups your process can use. Use the symbol NGROUPS_MAX when you need a value at compile time, say to allocate a static array. Use the value returned by sysconf(_SC_NGROUPS_MAX) if you need to know the maximum possible value at runtime.

6. The information returned by uname() can be printed in a message. There is no other portable user for the information.

7. POSIX Section 8.1.1 requires that the timezone be known.

8. The following program works for my birthday from 1991 to 2010:

```
#define _POSIX_SOURCE 1

#include <stdio.h>
#include <stdlib.h>
#include <time.h>
#include <unistd.h>

int main(int argc,char **argv)
{
struct tm    timestr;
int          i;
char         buff[81];

/*
 * Setup the time structure
 */
    timestr.tm_sec = 0;        /* Seconds */
    timestr.tm_min = 0;        /* Minutes */
    timestr.tm_hour = 9;       /* 9:00 AM */
    timestr.tm_mday = 13;      /* 13th day of month */
    timestr.tm_mon = 3;        /* April */
    timestr.tm_isdst = 0;      /* Not daylight time */
    for (i = 91; i < 91+20; i++) /* 1991 - 2010 */
        {
        timestr.tm_year = i;      /* Put year in structure */
```

```
               (void)mktime(&timestr);  /* Update day of week */
               (void)strftime(buff,(size_t)80,"%Y %A",&timestr);
               (void)puts(buff);        /* Print year and day */
               }
          exit(EXIT_SUCCESS);
     }
```

9. The `%x` specifier formats the date correctly for the current locale.

10. If you compile your program in one place and execute it in another place, the number of clock ticks per second can change. Since `CLK_TCK` is a compile-time constant, your program will get the wrong answers when it is moved. It is better to use `sysconf(_SC_CLK_TCK)`.

11. The values can be reported to the user.

12. The biggest disadvantage to using environment variables is that the names can conflict from application to application. The number of environment variables can also get out of hand. The biggest advantage is that they are easy to code and use.

14. It returns the maximum length filename that can be created in the `/usr` directory.

Chapter 8

1. First, it depends on the `stat()` function to return the file size and terminals do not have a fixed file size. Second, the `read()` function will return when the first newline character is read even if fewer than hunk bytes have been typed. There is no easy way to fix the program.

2. Yes.

3. Having the computer echo characters instead of having the terminal print them directly allows the computer to print something different than what the user typed. The ability to control what is printed is used to suppress the printing of passwords and to allow full-screen editors such as `vi` or `emacs` to operate.

4. You would use non-canonical I/O whenever you wanted to capture every character read from the terminal port.

5. Process groups are normally only used by the shell. A normal application would only use `setpgid()` if it were trying to simulate the shell's job control functions.

6. The `setpgid()` function is used to change the process group id of a process. The `tcsetpgrp()` function is used to assign the terminal to a specific process group.

7. 30.

8. The only baud rates that can be set are the ones for the communications port on the computer. The baud rate of the terminal itself cannot be changed by the application.

9. The ISTRIP flag masks input characters to 7-bits. This is useful if an application does not want to see the parity bit. Setting (or clearing) this flag may cause other applications sharing the terminal to fail.

10. The OPOST flag has no defined functions in POSIX and should not be used by a portable application.

11. The ISIG flag prevents the INTR character from generating a signal. The sigaction() function can be used to achieve a similar effect by ignoring the SIGINT signal. The ISIG flag affects all processes sharing the terminal while the sigaction() function only affects the process calling it.

12. Use it whenever you want to wait for all characters to be transmitted before changing the terminal attribute.

13. An application uses the tcdrain() function when it wants to wait for characters to be displayed on the terminal.

14. No. Changing the c_cc array affects all processes sharing the terminal.

Chapter 9

1. They are the same thing.

2. `printf("howard=%d\nharriet=%d\n",a,b);`

3. It pastes two tokens together.

4. If you ever need to use one of the functions defined in <math.h>, you will have a name/space conflict.

5. You should include system headers before any of your headers. You can then override symbols in the system headers with your own symbols.

6. The function takes a variable number of arguments. There must be at least two arguments. The first argument has type int. The second argument has type pointer to int. The integer pointed to by the second argument is not modified by this function.

7. The first definition says nothing about the number or type of arguments. The second definition says that there are no arguments.

8. Use volatile when the variable changes in a way that it cannot be predicated by the rules of C; for example, flags set by signal catching functions or hardware device registers.

9. Multi-character constants, such as '??', do different things on different implementations.

10. The compiler may pack the structure into three bytes. The compiler may insert pad bytes. The address of seconds must be greater than the address of minutes.

Chapter 10

1. The term *internationalization* refers to making an application work independent of the locale. The term *localization* means making the application work in a specific locale.

2. "Eight bit clean" means that the application considers all eight bits of a codeset byte to be data and does not assume that text is restricted to 7-bit ASCII.

3. The C locale is the rather vanilla locale specified by Standard C where no special localization takes place. The default locale is the one specified by the environment variables.

4. The `strcoll()` function can give a different answer from `strcmp()` in locales other than the `"C"` or `"POSIX"` locale. The `strcmp()` function is usually faster.

5. The only use for the output of `strxfrm()` is as input to `strcmp()`.

6. The question is ambiguous. One argument is that every place is in the C locale and programs written to the C locale should work every place. The other point of view is that no place is in the C locale (except maybe the United States and Canada).

7. The scheme has a major good point: it is easy to use and understand. The bad points are that the function may be quite slow, and you may have difficulty with the order of format specifiers when you translate from one language to another.

Related Publications

This bibliography suggests some publications that you might find of interest.

The Standards

The following standards are legal documents which must exactly define the standards. They tend to state things exactly once. Unambiguous and precise does not mean easy to read. For legal standards, these documents are very readable. They each contain a lengthy rationale to explain why the standard says what it does. I have attempted to include the most interesting points of the rationale in this book.

POSIX standards are available from:

> Publication Sales
> IEEE Service Center
> P.O. Box 1331
> 445 Hoes Lane
> Piscataway, New Jersey 08854-1331
> (201)981-0060
> (800)678-IEEE

Europe:

> IEEE Computer Society
> Jacques Kevers
> 13, Ave de l'Aquilon
> B-1200
> Brussels, Belgium

Asia:

> IEEE Computer Society
> Ms. Kyoko Mikami
> Ooshima Building
> 2-19-1 Minami Aoyama
> Monato-Ku, Tokyo 107 Japan

The document numbers for the standards are:

> POSIX.1:
> ISO/IEC 9945-1:1990
> IEEE Std. 1003.1-1990
> List Price $75.00

POSIX.2:
ISO//IEC 9945-2:1992
IEEE Std 1003.2-1992
List Price TBD

POSIX.3:
IEEE Std. 1003.3-1991
List Price $20.00

POSIX.9:
IEEE Std 1003.9-1992
List Price $42.00

American National Standard for Information Systems—Programming Language C,
X3.159-1989; available from:

Sales Department
American National Standards Institute
1430 Broadway
New York, NY 10018
(212)642-4900

ISO 8859-1: 1987 *Information Processing—8-bit single-byte coded graphic character
sets—part 1: Latin Alphabet No. 1;* available from:

International Organization for Standards
1, rue de Varembe
Case Postale 56
CH-1211
Geneva, Switzerland

Other Documents of Interest

The X/Open industry group publishes a set of recommendations for portable systems:

X/OPEN Portability Guide III
Prentice-Hall
200 Old Tappan Road
Tappan, NJ 07675
(201)592-2498

Index

About the Author

Donald Lewine has been writing computer programs for fun and profit since 1960. He has been teaching Computer Science in the State-of-the-Art (evening) program at Northeastern University for the past eight years, including courses on Assembler, VAX/VMS, Pascal, C, and UNIX. This book was written and tested over the last two years at Northeastern University.

Mr. Lewine spent 13 years with the Digital Equipment Corporation developing operating systems and central processing units. He was Technical Director for the MicroVAX Program when he left.

For the past nine years, Mr. Lewine has been with Data General Corporation, and is currently Director of Engineering. In this role he has been developing the AViiON family of open systems. He is a founder and a member of the Board of Directors of 88open, a member of the Board of Directors of UNIX International, and Data General's representative to the Open Software Foundation.

Colophon

꘍

Edie Freedman designed this book. The text is set in the ITC Garamond family; examples are Courier and figures use Helvetica Condensed. Pages are produced with FrameMaker 2.1 on the X Windows and Macintosh platforms. Figures are produced with Aldus FreeHand 2.0 on the Macintosh. Printing is done on a Tegra Varityper 5000.

More Titles from O'Reilly

UNIX Programming

Programming Python

By Mark Lutz
1st Edition October 1996
906 pages, ISBN 1-56592-197-6

Programming Python describes how to use Python, an increasingly popular object-oriented scripting language. This book, full of running examples, is the most comprehensive user material available on Python. It's endorsed by Python creator Guido van Rossum and complements reference materials that accompany the software. Includes CD-ROM with Python software for all major UNIX platforms, as well as Windows, NT, and the Mac.

UNIX Systems Programming for SVR4

By David A. Curry
1st Edition July 1996
620 pages, ISBN 1-56592-163-1

Presents a comprehensive look at the nitty gritty details on how UNIX interacts with applications. If you're writing an application from scratch, or if you're porting an application to any System V.4 platform, you need this book. It thoroughly explains all UNIX system calls and library routines related to systems programming, working with I/O, files and directories, processing multiple input streams, file and record locking, and memory-mapped files.

Programming with curses

By John Strang
1st Edition 1986
78 pages, ISBN 0-937175-02-1

curses is a UNIX library of functions for controlling a terminal'sdisplay screen from a C program. This handbook helps you make use of the curses library. Describes the original Berkeley version of curses.

Power Programming with RPC

By John Bloomer
1st Edition February 1992
522 pages, ISBN 0-937175-77-3

RPC (Remote Procedure Calling) is the ability to distribute the execution of functions on remote computers. Written from a programmer's perspective, this book shows what you can do with RPCs, like Sun RPC, the de facto standard on UNIX systems. It covers related programming topics for Sun and other UNIX systems and teaches through examples.

POSIX.4

By Bill O. Gallmeister
1st Edition January 1995
568 pages, ISBN 1-56592-074-0

A general introduction to real-time programming and real-time issues, this book covers the POSIX.4 standard and how to use it to solve "real-world" problems. If you're at all interested in real-time applications—which include just about everything from telemetry to transaction processing—this book is for you. An essential reference.

Pthreads Programming

By Bradford Nichols, Dick Buttlar &
Jacqueline Proulx Farrell
1st Edition September 1996
284 pages, ISBN 1-56592-115-1

POSIX threads, or pthreads, allow multiple tasks to run concurrently within the same program. This book discusses when to use threads and how to make them efficient. It features realistic examples, a look behind the scenes at the implementation and performance issues, and special topics such as DCE and real-time extensions.

O'REILLY™

TO ORDER: **800-998-9938** • *order@oreilly.com* • *http://www.oreilly.com/*
OUR PRODUCTS ARE AVAILABLE AT A BOOKSTORE OR SOFTWARE STORE NEAR YOU.
FOR INFORMATION: **800-998-9938** • **707-829-0515** • *info@oreilly.com*

UNIX Basics

Learning the UNIX Operating System, 4th Edition

By Jerry Peek, Grace Todino & John Strang
4th Edition December 1997
106 pages, ISBN 1-56592-390-1

If you are new to UNIX, this concise introduction will tell you just what you need to get started and no more. The new fourth edition covers the Linux operating system and is an ideal primer for someone just starting with UNIX or Linux, as well as for Mac and PC users who encounter a UNIX system on the Internet. This classic book, still the most effective introduction to UNIX in print, now includes a quick-reference card.

Learning GNU Emacs, 2nd Edition

By Debra Cameron, Bill Rosenblatt & Eric Raymond
2nd Edition September 1996
560 pages, ISBN 1-56592-152-6

Learning GNU Emacs is an introduction to Version 19.30 of the GNU Emacs editor, one of the most widely used and powerful editors available under UNIX. It provides a solid introduction to basic editing, a look at several important "editing modes" (special Emacs features for editing specific types of documents, including email, Usenet News, and the World Wide Web), and a brief introduction to customization and Emacs LISP programming. The book is aimed at new Emacs users, whether or not they are programmers. Includes quick-reference card.

Learning the bash Shell, 2nd Edition

By Cameron Newham & Bill Rosenblatt
2nd Edition January 1998
336 pages, ISBN 1-56592-347-2

This second edition covers all of the features of bash Version 2.0, while still applying to bash Version 1.x. It includes one-dimensional arrays, parameter expansion, more pattern-matching operations, new commands, security improvements, additions to ReadLine, improved configuration and installation, and an additional programming aid, the bash shell debugger.

Learning the Korn Shell

By Bill Rosenblatt
1st Edition June 1993
360 pages, ISBN 1-56592-054-6

This Nutshell Handbook is a thorough introduction to the Korn shell, both as a user interface and as a programming language. The Korn shell is a program that interprets UNIX commands. It has many features that aren't found in other shells, including command history. This book provides a clear and concise explanation of the Korn shell's features. It explains ksh string operations, co-processes, signals and signal handling, and command-line interpretation. The book also includes real-life programming examples and a Korn shell debugger called kshdb, the only known implementation of a shell debugger anywhere.

Using csh and tcsh

By Paul DuBois
1st Edition August 1995
242 pages, ISBN 1-56592-132-1

Using csh and tcsh describes from the beginning how to use these shells interactively to get your work done faster with less typing. You'll learn how to make your prompt tell you where you are (no more pwd); use what you've typed before (history); type long command lines with few keystrokes (command and filename completion); remind yourself of filenames when in the middle of typing a command; and edit a botched command without retyping it.

Learning the vi Editor, 5th Edition

By Linda Lamb
5th Edition October 1990
192 pages, ISBN 0-937175-67-6

This book is a complete guide to text editing with vi, the editor available on nearly every UNIX system. Early chapters cover the basics; later chapters explain more advanced editing tools, such as ex commands and global search and replacement.

UNIX Basics

sed & awk, 2nd Edition

By Dale Dougherty & Arnold Robbins
2nd Edition March 1997
432 pages, ISBN 1-56592-225-5

sed & awk describes two text manipulation
programs that are mainstays of the UNIX
programmer's toolbox. This new edition
covers the sed and awk programs as they are
now mandated by the POSIX standard and
includes discussion of the GNU versions of these programs.

SCO UNIX in a Nutshell

By Ellie Cutler & the staff of O'Reilly & Associates
1st Edition February 1994
590 pages, ISBN 1-56592-037-6

The desktop reference to SCO UNIX and
Open Desktop®, this version of UNIX in a
Nutshell shows you what's under the hood
of your SCO system. It isn't a scaled-down
quick reference of common commands, but
a complete reference containing all user,
programming, administration, and networking commands.

UNIX in a Nutshell: System V Edition

By Daniel Gilly &
the staff of O'Reilly & Associates
2nd Edition June 1992
444 pages, ISBN 1-56592-001-5

You may have seen UNIX quick-reference
guides, but you've never seen anything like
UNIX in a Nutshell. Not a scaled-down quick
reference of common commands, UNIX in a
Nutshell is a complete reference containing
all commands and options, along with generous descriptions
and examples that put the commands in context. For all but the
thorniest UNIX problems, this one reference should be all the
documentation you need. Covers System V, Releases 3 and 4,
and Solaris 2.0.

What You Need to Know: When You Can't Find Your UNIX System Administrator

By Linda Mui
1st Edition April 1995
156 pages, ISBN 1-56592-104-6

This book is written for UNIX users, who are
often cast adrift in a confusing environment.
It provides the background and practical
solutions you need to solve problems you're
likely to encounter—problems with logging
in, printing, sharing files, running programs, managing space
resources, etc. It also describes the kind of info to gather when
you're asking for a diagnosis from a busy sys admin. And, it gives
you a list of site-specific information that you should know, as
well as a place to write it down.

Volume 3M: X Window System User's Guide, Motif Edition

By Valerie Quercia & Tim O'Reilly
2nd Edition January 1993
956 pages, ISBN 1-56592-015-5

The X Window System User's Guide, Motif
Edition orients the new user to window
system concepts and provides detailed
tutorials for many client programs, including the xterm terminal emulator and the
twm, uwm, and mwm window managers.
Later chapters explain how to customize the X environment.
Revised for Motif 1.2 and X11 Release 5.

UNIX in a Nutshell, Deluxe Edition

By Daniel Gilly, et al.
1st Edition August 1998 (est.)
444 pages (est.), Includes CD-ROM & book
ISBN 1-56592-406-1

This deluxe package includes the bestseller,
UNIX in a Nutshell, System V Edition, plus
a powerhouse of online UNIX books from
O'Reilly, including UNIX in a Nutshell, System
V Edition; the complete text of UNIX Power
Tools, 2nd Edition; Learning the UNIX Operating System, 4th
Edition; Learning the vi Editor, 5th Edition; sed & awk, 2nd
Edition; Learning the Korn Shell, as well as UNIX in a Nutshell.

UNIX Tools

Programming with GNU Software

By Mike Loukides & Andy Oram
1st Edition December 1996
260 pages, ISBN 1-56592-112-7

This book and CD combination is a complete package for programmers who are new to UNIX or who would like to make better use of the system. The tools come from Cygnus Support, Inc., and Cyclic Software, companies that provide support for free software. Contents include GNU Emacs, *gcc*, C and C++ libraries, *gdb*, RCS, and *make*. The book provides an introduction to all these tools for a C programmer.

Applying RCS and SCCS

By Don Bolinger & Tan Bronson
1st Edition September 1995
528 pages, ISBN 1-56592-117-8

Applying RCS and SCCS is a thorough introduction to these two systems, viewed as tools for project management. This book takes the reader from basic source control of a single file, through working with multiple releases of a software project, to coordinating multiple developers. It also presents TCCS, a representative "front-end" that addresses problems RCS and SCCS can't handle alone, such as managing groups of files, developing for multiple platforms, and linking public and private development areas.

lex & yacc , 2nd edition

By John Levine, Tony Mason & Doug Brown
2nd Edition October 1992
366 pages, ISBN 1-56592-000-7

This book shows programmers how to use two UNIX utilities, lex and yacc, in program development. The second edition contains completely revised tutorial sections for novice users and reference sections for advanced users. This edition is twice the size of the first, has an expanded index, and covers Bison and Flex.

Managing Projects with make

By Andrew Oram & Steve Talbott
2nd Edition October 1991
152 pages, ISBN 0-937175-90-0

make is one of UNIX's greatest contributions to software development, and this book is the clearest description of *make* ever written. It describes all the basic features of *make* and provides guidelines on meeting the needs of large, modern projects. Also contains a description of free products that contain major enhancements to *make*.

Software Portability with imake, 2nd Edition

By Paul DuBois
2nd Edition September 1996
410 pages, ISBN 1-56592-226-3

This Nutshell Handbook®—the only book available on *imake*—is ideal for X and UNIX programmers who want their software to be portable. The second edition covers the current version of the X Window System (X11R6.1), using *imake* for non-UNIX systems such as Windows NT, and some of the quirks about using *imake* under OpenWindows/ Solaris.

Porting UNIX Software

By Greg Lehey
1st Edition November 1995
538 pages, ISBN 1-56592-126-7

This book deals with the whole life cycle of porting, from setting up a source tree on your system to correcting platform differences and even testing the executable after it's built. It exhaustively discusses the differences between versions of UNIX and the areas where porters tend to have problems.

UNIX Tools

Exploring Expect

By Don Libes
1st Edition December 1994
602 pages, ISBN 1-56592-090-2

Written by the author of Expect, this is the first book to explain how this part of the UNIX toolbox can be used to automate Telnet, FTP, passwd, rlogin, and hundreds of other interactive applications. Based on Tcl (Tool Command Language), Expect lets you automate interactive applications that have previously been extremely difficult to handle with any scripting language.

Writing GNU Emacs Extensions

By Bob Glickstein
1st Edition April 1997
236 pages, ISBN 1-56592-261-1

This book introduces Emacs Lisp and tells you how to make the editor do whatever you want, whether it's altering the way text scrolls or inventing a whole new "major mode." Topics progress from simple to complex, from lists, symbols, and keyboard commands to syntax tables, macro templates, and error recovery.

UNIX Power Tools, 2nd Edition

By Jerry Peek, Tim O'Reilly & Mike Loukides
2nd Edition August 1997
1120 pages, Includes CD-ROM
ISBN 1-56592-260-3

Loaded with even more practical advice about almost every aspect of UNIX, this new second edition of *UNIX Power Tools* addresses the technology that UNIX users face today. You'll find increased coverage of POSIX utilities, including GNU versions, greater *bash* and *tcsh* shell coverage, more emphasis on Perl, and a CD-ROM that contains the best freeware available.

Tcl/Tk Tools

By Mark Harrison
1st Edition September 1997
678 pages, Includes CD-ROM
ISBN 1-56592-218-2

One of the greatest strengths of Tcl/Tk is the range of extensions written for it. This book clearly documents the most popular and robust extensions—by the people who created them—and contains information on configuration, debugging, and other important tasks. The CD-ROM includes Tcl/Tk, the extensions, and other tools documented in the text both in source form and as binaries for Solaris and Linux.

How to stay in touch with O'Reilly

1. Visit Our Award-Winning Web Site

http://www.oreilly.com/

★ "Top 100 Sites on the Web" —*PC Magazine*
★ "Top 5% Web sites" —*Point Communications*
★ "3-Star site" —*The McKinley Group*

Our web site contains a library of comprehensiveproduct information (including book excerpts and tables of contents), downloadable software, background articles, interviews with technology leaders, links to relevant sites, book cover art, and more. File us in your Bookmarks or Hotlist!

2. Join Our Email Mailing Lists

New Product Releases

To receive automatic email with brief descriptions of all new O'Reilly products as they are released, send email to:
listproc@online.oreilly.com
Put the following information in the first line of your message (*not* in the Subject field):
subscribe oreilly-news

O'Reilly Events

If you'd also like us to send information about trade show events, special promotions, and other O'Reilly events, send email to:
listproc@online.oreilly.com
Put the following information in the first line of your message (*not* in the Subject field):
subscribe oreilly-events

3. Get Examples from Our Books via FTP

There are two ways to access an archive of example files from our books:

Regular FTP

- ftp to:
  ftp.oreilly.com
  (login: anonymous
  password: your email address)
- Point your web browser to:
  ftp://ftp.oreilly.com/

FTPMAIL

- Send an email message to:
  ftpmail@online.oreilly.com
  (Write "help" in the message body)

4. Contact Us via Email

order@oreilly.com
To place a book or software order online. Good for North American and international customers.

subscriptions@oreilly.com
To place an order for any of our newsletters or periodicals.

books@oreilly.com
General questions about any of our books.

software@oreilly.com
For general questions and product information about our software. Check out O'Reilly Software Online at **http://software.oreilly.com/** for software and technical support information. Registered O'Reilly software users send your questions to: **website-support@oreilly.com**

cs@oreilly.com
For answers to problems regarding your order or our products.

booktech@oreilly.com
For book content technical questions or corrections.

proposals@oreilly.com
To submit new book or software proposals to our editors and product managers.

international@oreilly.com
For information about our international distributors or translation queries. For a list of our distributors outside of North America check out:
http://www.oreilly.com/www/order/country.html

O'Reilly & Associates, Inc.
101 Morris Street, Sebastopol, CA 95472 USA
TEL   707-829-0515 or 800-998-9938
          (6am to 5pm PST)
FAX   707-829-0104

Titles from O'Reilly

International Distributors

UK, Europe, Middle East and Northern Africa (except France, Germany, Switzerland, & Austria)

INQUIRIES
International Thomson Publishing Europe
Berkshire House
168-173 High Holborn
London WC1V 7AA
United Kingdom
Telephone: 44-171-497-1422
Fax: 44-171-497-1426
Email: itpint@itps.co.uk

ORDERS
International Thomson Publishing Services, Ltd.
Cheriton House, North Way
Andover, Hampshire SP10 5BE
United Kingdom
Telephone: 44-264-342-832 (UK)
Telephone: 44-264-342-806 (outside UK)
Fax: 44-264-364418 (UK)
Fax: 44-264-342761 (outside UK)
UK & Eire orders: itpuk@itps.co.uk
International orders: itpint@itps.co.uk

France

Editions Eyrolles
61 bd Saint-Germain
75240 Paris Cedex 05
France
Fax: 33-01-44-41-11-44

FRENCH LANGUAGE BOOKS
All countries except Canada
Telephone: 33-01-44-41-46-16
Email: geodif@eyrolles.com
English language books
Telephone: 33-01-44-41-11-87
Email: distribution@eyrolles.com

Germany, Switzerland, and Austria

INQUIRIES
O'Reilly Verlag
Balthasarstr. 81
D-50670 Köln
Germany
Telephone: 49-221-97-31-60-0
Fax: 49-221-97-31-60-8
Email: anfragen@oreilly.de

ORDERS
International Thomson Publishing
Königswinterer Straße 418
53227 Bonn, Germany
Telephone: 49-228-97024 0
Fax: 49-228-441342
Email: order@oreilly.de

Japan

O'Reilly Japan, Inc.
Kiyoshige Building 2F
12-Banchi, Sanei-cho
Shinjuku-ku
Tokyo 160-0008 Japan
Telephone: 81-3-3356-5227
Fax: 81-3-3356-5261
Email: kenji@oreilly.com

India

Computer Bookshop (India) PVT. Ltd.
190 Dr. D.N. Road, Fort
Bombay 400 001 India
Telephone: 91-22-207-0989
Fax: 91-22-262-3551
Email: cbsbom@giasbm01.vsnl.net.in

Hong Kong

City Discount Subscription Service Ltd.
Unit D, 3rd Floor, Yan's Tower
27 Wong Chuk Hang Road
Aberdeen, Hong Kong
Telephone: 852-2580-3539
Fax: 852-2580-6463
Email: citydis@ppn.com.hk

Korea

Hanbit Media, Inc.
Sonyoung Bldg. 202
Yeksam-dong 736-36
Kangnam-ku
Seoul, Korea
Telephone: 822-554-9610
Fax: 822-556-0363
Email: hant93@chollian.dacom.co.kr

Singapore, Malaysia, and Thailand

Addison Wesley Longman Singapore PTE Ltd.
25 First Lok Yang Road
Singapore 629734
Telephone: 65-268-2666
Fax: 65-268-7023
Email: daniel@longman.com.sg

Philippines

Mutual Books, Inc.
429-D Shaw Boulevard
Mandaluyong City, Metro
Manila, Philippines
Telephone: 632-725-7538
Fax: 632-721-3056
Email: mbikikog@mnl.sequel.net

China

Ron's DataCom Co., Ltd.
79 Dongwu Avenue
Dongxihu District
Wuhan 430040
China
Telephone: 86-27-83892568
Fax: 86-27-83222108
Email: hongfeng@public.wh.hb.cn

All Other Asian Countries

O'Reilly & Associates, Inc.
101 Morris Street
Sebastopol, CA 95472 USA
Telephone: 707-829-0515
Fax: 707-829-0104
Email: order@oreilly.com

Australia

WoodsLane Pty. Ltd.
7/5 Vuko Place, Warriewood NSW 2102
P.O. Box 935
Mona Vale NSW 2103
Australia
Telephone: 61-2-9970-5111
Fax: 61-2-9970-5002
Email: info@woodslane.com.au

New Zealand

Woodslane New Zealand Ltd.
21 Cooks Street (P.O. Box 575)
Waganui, New Zealand
Telephone: 64-6-347-6543
Fax: 64-6-345-4840
Email: info@woodslane.com.au

The Americas

McGraw-Hill Interamericana Editores, S.A. de C.V.
Cedro No. 512
Col. Atlampa 06450
Mexico, D.F.
Telephone: 52-5-541-3155
Fax: 52-5-541-4913
Email: mcgraw-hill@infosel.net.mx

South Africa

International Thomson Publishing South Africa
Building 18, Constantia Park
138 Sixteenth Road
P.O. Box 2459
Halfway House, 1685 South Africa
Telephone: 27-11-805-4819
Fax: 27-11-805-3648

O'REILLY™

To order: **800-998-9938 • order@oreilly.com • http://www.oreilly.com/**

Our products are available at a bookstore or software store near you.

For information: **800-998-9938 • 707-829-0515 • info@oreilly.com**

O'REILLY™

O'Reilly & Associates, Inc.
101 Morris Street
Sebastopol, CA 95472-9902
1-800-998-9938

Visit us online at:
http://www.ora.com/

O'REILLY WOULD LIKE TO HEAR FROM YOU

Which book did this card come from?

_____

Where did you buy this book?
- ❏ Bookstore
- ❏ Direct from O'Reilly
- ❏ Bundled with hardware/software
- ❏ Computer Store
- ❏ Class/seminar
- ❏ Other _____

What operating system do you use?
- ❏ UNIX
- ❏ Windows NT
- ❏ Other _____
- ❏ Macintosh
- ❏ PC(Windows/DOS)

What is your job description?
- ❏ System Administrator
- ❏ Network Administrator
- ❏ Web Developer
- ❏ Programmer
- ❏ Educator/Teacher
- ❏ Other _____

❏ Please send me O'Reilly's catalog, containing a complete listing of O'Reilly books and software.

Name _____   Company/Organization _____

Address _____

City _____   State _____   Zip/Postal Code _____   Country _____

Telephone _____   Internet or other email address (specify network) _____

neteenth century wood engraving
a bear from the O'Reilly &
ssociates Nutshell Handbook®
sing & Managing UUCP.

PLACE
STAMP
HERE

BUSINESS REPLY MAIL
FIRST CLASS MAIL   PERMIT NO. 80   SEBASTOPOL, CA

Postage will be paid by addressee

O'Reilly & Associates, Inc.
101 Morris Street
Sebastopol, CA 95472-9902

NO POSTAGE
NECESSARY IF
MAILED IN THE
UNITED STATES